KNOWN FROM THE THINGS THAT ARE

Fundamental Theory of the Moral Life

Martin D. O'Keefe, S.J.

CENTER FOR THOMISTIC STUDIES
University of St. Thomas
Houston, Texas 77006

Copyright © 1987 by
Center for Thomistic Studies

Nihil obstat:
Reverend Terence P. Brinkman, S.T.D.
Censor Deputatus

Imprimatur:
Most Reverend Joseph A. Fiorenza, D.D.
Bishop of Galveston-Houston
May 6, 1987

Library of Congress Cataloging in Publication Data

O'Keefe, Martin D.
    Known from the things that are: fundamental
theory of the moral life/ Martin D. O'Keefe.
       p. cm.
    Includes index.
    ISBN 0-268-01226-8 (pbk.)
    1. Ethics. I. Title
BJ1025.054   1987   87-16496
170—dc19   CIP

Manufactured in the United States of America

TO CLARE AND CHARLES WILBER

who have no need of instruction
in either the theory or the practice
of the moral life

CONTENTS

Page

PREFACE.   vii

I.   INTRODUCTORY CONSIDERATIONS.   1-10
      1. PHILOSOPHY AND ETHICS   1-10

II.   THE THEORETICAL PART OF ETHICS.   11-170
      A. What is human conduct?
          2. IMPUTABLE ACTS AND THEIR BASIS . .   11-30
          3. LIMITS TO IMPUTABLE ACTS   31-50
          4. CONSEQUENCES OF IMPUTABLE ACTS .   51-70
      B. What are "good" and "evil" acts?
          5. GOOD AND EVIL ACTS   71-90
      C. How decide whether an act is good or evil?
          6. THE ULTIMATE NORMS OF MORALITY. .   91-120
          7. THE PROXIMATE NORMS OF MORALITY . 121-142
          8. KNOWING THE NORMS: LAW. 143-170

III. THE PRACTICAL PART OF ETHICS   171-332
      A. Our relationships to ourselves:
          9. LIFE 171-194
          10. HEALTH 195-214
      B. Our relationships to others:
          11. THE FAMILY SOCIETY 215-236
          12. CIVIL SOCIETY 237-260
          13. LIVING IN CIVIL SOCIETY 261-286
          14. LOOKING TO OTHER CIVIL SOCIETIES . 287-310
      C. Our relationship to God:
          15. HUMANS AND GOD 311-332

INDEX 333-339

PREFACE

Although its title is taken from a verse found in the New Testament, this book is not a particularly religious one. If anything, it takes some deliberate pains not to be. For Saint Paul, in his Epistle to the Romans (from which the title is derived: Rm. 1:20), sharply criticizes the pagan world for not having arrived at the criteria for the moral life--with everything that that involves--independently of any religious revelation, whether Christian or some other. Paul says that, for the pagans, God should have been "known from the things that are." Consequently he finds their conduct simply inexcusable. That they did not know God is irrelevant; they should have known him. That they have lived the way they did is equally condemned; they should have known better. That is a startling series of statements. But it is quite uncompromising; Paul retreats from it not one inch.

This book is an attempt to take Paul at his word. It asks, and tries to answer, questions such as these: very well, then, what *can* the unaided human intellect know about the moral life, and about God as the basis of that life? And how does it set about doing this?

This isn't just a *tour de force,* some sort of intellectual game without much meaning for the real world. For there are some painful similarities between contemporary Western culture and the world that Paul discovered at Rome when he arrived there. To be sure, we have the advantage of having had two thousand years' worth of Christianity as a background to our culture, not to mention the considerable influence of other religions as well. But with all that, there remains in our world a massive materialism, hedonism, and an overwhelming subjectivity about what constitutes right and wrong. One might hesitate to call our contemporary culture "pagan," but it is undeniable that the spirit of paganism, anyway, roams freely around the world in which we live. Though it may do so in a somewhat different way today, nonetheless the Pauline challenge to ancient Rome has a pointed significance for and ·application to the present day, a significance which a thoughtful person ignores only at his or her peril.

Despite the fact, then, that its author is a Jesuit priest, this book makes no attempt to prosyletize or to foster a religion of any kind. Rather, it simply tries to demonstrate that, for the contemporary world as for the ancient one, the basic principles of the moral life can be discovered by an intelligent person of good will who uses only natural reason, and that those principles are the same for all human beings: past, present, and--for that matter--future.

vii

This is not a scholar's book, filled with learned references and footnotes. Certainly, the author has nothing against scholarly apparatus; it is a tool of his trade. But the purpose of this book is different. It seeks to be a thoughtful essay concerning what the moral life is and what a serious reader could come to know about that life. Not everyone is a scholar, or is comfortable with a scholar's paraphernalia. But everyone does have a legitimate concern with the gauntlet that Saint Paul has thrown down, and thus a serious book simply for the thoughtful reader seems very much in order. Nor does the book attempt to be the last word on all the subjects it treats. Many of its topics could be the subject of an entire chapter or even of separate books. Again, its purpose is merely to show, in initial fashion, the scope of what and how we can learn about the moral life.

The book draws heavily on the classical tradition of ethics, which had its roots in Plato and (especially) Aristotle, and which grew and flourished through many centuries of philosophical thought in Europe. One might, of course, object: why resurrect all that now? Shouldn't the effort rather be to establish a contemporary ethics, one suited to our own enlightened times? To that, one should probably resist the smart retort that the state of contemporary ethics does not make one terribly sanguine, if that is the direction that really ought to be pursued. Or that, for that matter, to call our own times "enlightened," in the moral sense, is (at the very least) not exactly to utter a self-evident statement. But one could give a straightforward answer to the objection. The chief reason why this book makes use of the classical theory is simply that this theory is probably the most powerful intellectual tool ever developed which one can use to answer the Pauline challenge. If the idea is to see just how much the human mind, unaided by revelation or religion, can discover for itself in the moral area, then the classical theory clearly leaves all of its competitors far behind. And so this book makes use of that theory—not out of any nostalgic love of tradition, nor indeed out of a sort of disillusionment with more contemporary efforts of another genre, but rather simply for the pragmatic reason that the classical method works. Despite some quite premature announcements of its demise (made chiefly through Kantian influence, although others have claimed the same), it survives, flourishes, and presents itself as a highly reasonable explanation of morality. It has always been said of philosophy as a whole that it regularly buries its would-be funeral directors; and this is eminently true of the classical ethical theory.

Just as this book makes no attempt to foster a religion of any kind, so neither does it attempt to make converts to its particular style of ethical reasoning. The reader who arrives at the end of the book may be convinced by its reasoning and adopt it as his or her own; he or she may not. In one sense, that is unimportant. But if that reader comes away from the book convinced that solid, logical reasoning is both a possible and a necessary foundation for a moral life, and convinced that the moral life itself is not merely one option among many for humans--interesting, perhaps, but not terribly important in the last analysis-- that is enough. Perhaps some other style of reasoning may suit a given reader better; and if it is as fruitful, as rigorous, and as comprehensive as the classical style, surely no one could object. The important thing is that the Pauline challenge be faced and come to terms with, for refusing to do so constitutes the abdication of one's own intellectual nature and therefore of one's own humanity.

Finally, a word or two of thanks is in order. Although this book makes no direct reference to their works, it none the less owes a vast amount to the influence of several individuals. To the late Rev. George P. Klubertanz, S.J., of Saint Louis University, the late Rev. Austin Fagothy, S.J., of Santa Clara University, and to Rev. John P. Jelinek, S.J., of Creighton University, is due the acknowledgement a grateful student owes to eminent teachers and recognized experts. To Emeritus Professor William J. Callaghan, of Michigan State University, the author owes a deep debt of gratitude; for many years, this scholar-administrator enabled students to share in the rich, pluralistic atmosphere that he so carefully nourished, fostered, and fought for in the department which he headed. Perhaps most importantly, to Professor Harold T. Walsh, also of Michigan State University, the author owes the profound admiration reserved for a philosopher who not only has few peers in his knowledge of Aristotle and in his appreciation of the significance of philosophical thought in general, but who also has a broad expertise in the moral life which spills over from the theoretical order into the practical--thereby enriching his own life, to be sure, but even more so the lives of his colleagues, friends, and students. Finally, grateful thanks are due to Rev. Leo B. Kaufmann, S.J., and to Brother Thomas J. Koller, S.J., for the painstaking and thoughtful comments they made on each chapter of this book as it was being written. If this book has any merit to which it can lay claim, it is largely due to all these men; but the book's faults and shortcomings can only be termed the exclusive property of the author.

Rome and Spokane, 1984-85.

1. PHILOSOPHY AND ETHICS

I. Introduction:
  A. A fantasy tour
  B. What is philosophy?
      1. The achievement of Thales
      2. A descriptive definition of philosophy
      3. The branches of philosophy: historical, systematic
  C. What is ethics?
      1. How branches of knowledge are differentiated:
          a. Generic object, proper object, method
          b. Limitations this imposes on branches of knowledge
      2. A descriptive definition of ethics
      3. Method and ethics
      4. Ethics and religion
  D. Questions and areas that the definition suggests.

A. A fantasy tour

Suppose we begin with an imaginary tour. We are in the classroom building of a certain university or college, somewhere in the United States. It doesn't make any difference which college or university, or where it's located. The object of our tour is to see just exactly what is going on in those classes which are listed in the catalogue under the heading "philosophy," and more specifically under the heading "ethics."

In one classroom, it looks very much as if a discussion of advanced mathematics is going on. The blackboard is filled with symbols, some of them familiar, some quite strange; and there is talk of formal and material implication. Symbolic logicians are plying their trade, we conclude. In another classroom, the professor is talking about someone named Kant (or Descartes, or Hegel), and is discoursing learnedly on how that particular gentleman influenced Western thought. In still another, Marxist analysis is the topic. Farther down the hall, someone is making a speech about the indefinability of the good, whatever that might mean. In yet another room, a professor is talking about what seems to be ancient history, with Greek words on the blackboard and the air filled with such improbable names as Thales, Anaximander, Socrates, Plato, and Aristotle.

1

Our tour doesn't result in very many answers. There seem to be a whole lot of things going on, and the relationships among all those things aren't overwhelmingly clear. But it does result in some questions. What is philosophy? Is it any one "thing," or is it a collective name for a lot of things? What is ethics? Do people all mean the same thing when they use these words? Or are they terms that mean pretty much what each individual professor (or student) wants them to mean at any given time?

Names, of course, are strange things. To some extent, they are arbitrary: different cultures give different names to the same thing, and occasionally even a single given culture gives different names to the same thing. That fact alone warns us not to try for too much preciseness, not to expect that absolutely everyone will mean exactly the same thing by the terms "philosophy" and "ethics."

On the other hand, we know that names are not completely haphazard, either. What I call a horse, you don't normally call a comet. You and I might differ as to exactly which individuals qualify for the name "horse": I might think that only a full-grown animal deserves the name, whereas you might think that the age factor doesn't make that much difference, and that both the colt and its parents deserve the name "horse." But, in general, we do have at least *some* agreement as to what the term means.

B. What is philosophy?

And perhaps much the same is true for the terms "philosophy" and "ethics." If we keep the definition broad enough, we can probably come up with a notion that most people (not all, perhaps) would accept, at least in a general sort of way. And that will do for a start. Later, we will come up with a very specific notion of what we mean, if not by "philosophy," at least by "ethics"; and when that is done, we will have to be resigned to the fact that not everyone will agree with that definition. Fair enough; there are good historical reasons why that is the case. But for the moment, let us simply try to understand, in a very broad sense, what the two terms mean.

1. The achievement of Thales

History is a good guide here. For philosophy, as the Western world understands it, had a fairly definite beginning in time and place: the sixth century B.C., in ancient Greece. It is commonly accepted that the first Western philosopher was Thales--about whom we know very little. We do know, however, that he posed this question: what, ultimately, are things made of? He was convinced that there is a single element which is the source of all the things of our experience: all the things in our everyday world are, at root, that one element, in one or other stage of transformation. And, while those things of our experience change constantly, they nevertheless do find some sort of stability, some sort of permanent reality, in being various transformations of that element. In other words, although all things do change, there is nevertheless some stable reality in them that is not subject to birth and death in an absolute sense, but only to a mere change in form.

We are not particularly interested in what Thales thought that permanent element in things was. Rather, the point to notice is that he was asking the radical question: what are things--all things--at their deepest, at their most fundamental? Put briefly, Thales was asking about the nature of reality. And he was doing something more than that (for others before him had asked what reality was all about). He attempted to answer his own question sheerly by dint of his own unaided reasoning powers. That is crucial, and it is distinctive of the Greeks. Thales did not look to any authority (human or divine) for an answer to his question, but rather attempted to answer it on his own. His particular answer (that all things are basically water, or, more accurately, "the moist") may well have been somewhat crude, may seem to us almost laughable. But what was not laughable was the fact that he attempted to answer that question sheerly by the power of his own unassisted mind. He was the first person in recorded history to pose such a question and to try to answer it in this fashion--and that fact constitutes him as the first philosopher in history.

Thales' successors, at least for a while, posed much the same question, and tried to answer it by the same means. Their answers differed, but the basic notion of inquiring about the nature of reality, and the attempt to answer it by unaided human reason, perdured. Somewhat later on, the focus shifted (with the Sophists and particularly with Socrates) to asking about the nature of a particular item within reality, i.e., human beings. But the method (the use of reason alone) remained constant.

It has remained constant down to our own day. The question being investigated has been specified, refined, examined in just about every way conceivable. It has been asked whether such an inquiry is even possible (Thales and his friends took it for granted that it was). It has been claimed that reason ought to be limited to only certain methods of operation in this quest. And yet, the fundamental endeavor that Thales put in motion is still with us: what is reality? What is really real about the things of our experience? What about things outside our direct experience? Can reason tell us anything about these things? Indeed, can reason tell us anything at all? Or are there perhaps things we cannot know? Are all the various things of our experience really at root homogeneous, or are they radically different from one another? And so on and on.

2. A descriptive definition of philosophy

And that is philosophy. Put briefly, philosophy is the investigation, by human reason alone, of reality, of the world around us. And that, perhaps, will do as a descriptive definition of philosophy, acceptable to most—whatever their own particular answers to the questions that philosophy poses.

(Obviously, by "unaided human reason" we don't mean that philosophers attempt to come to their conclusions all by themselves, in a sort of intellectual vacuum or in isolation from everyone else. Quite the contrary. In fact, philosophy is almost by its very nature a social enterprise, one that flourishes best in dialogue with others. Rather, what is meant is that the philosopher will not—and cannot—accept something as true merely because someone else (human or divine) says that it is. The philosopher must personally understand why something is so, and must accept the cogency of the reasoning (whether his own or someone else's) that brings about that understanding).

3. The branches of philosophy: historical, systematic

The descriptive definition given above is, of course, a very broad one. It may be useful to introduce some subdivisions, just to enable us to see, if nothing else, the sorts of things that philosophers have occupied themselves with in the 2500 years or so that have gone by since Thales started all this. The subdivisions are somewhat arbitrary; doubtless, one could divide the various branches of philosophy in other ways. But for our purposes, what follows will be useful enough.

The general term "philosophy," then, can be seen as having two main divisions: historical and systematic.

In *historical* philosophy, as the name suggests, we try to come to know what great thinkers in the past have in fact said about the important questions of life. One can conveniently divide the history of philosophy into four major periods: [a] Ancient Philosophy: from Thales (+ ca545 B.C.) to St. Augustine (+430 A.D.); [b] Medieval Philosophy: from post -Augustine to Descartes (+1650); [c] Classical Modern Philosophy: from Descartes to 1900; [d] Contemporary Philosophy: the twentieth century.

Other divisions are certainly possible, but these are common enough. Nor are they completely capricious. Each of the four periods indicated has certain characteristics that set it off from the other three. The thing to notice about historical philosophy, however, is that its aim is an understanding of what other thinkers have concluded; it does not seek, as such, a synthesis of their thought with anything else, nor does it directly seek to have the person studying it come to his or her own conclusions on the questions under study.

Then there is *systematic* philosophy. Here, the effort is not focused on knowing what answers other people have given to the great questions of life, but rather on formulating one's own personal answers to those questions--along with one's own personal reasons for those answers. Systematic philosophy has the following major branches: [a] The study of all the beings of our experience, considered as existing: this is the Philosophy of Being, or "Metaphysics"; [b] The study of all the beings of our experience as being caused, and particularly as being ultimately caused: this is the Philosophy of God, sometimes called "Natural Theology"; [c] The study of the beings of our experience as being embodied, as having bodies (and therefore as being changeable): this is Philosophy of Nature; [d] The study of some of the beings of our experience as living: the Philosophy of Human Nature; [e] The study of some of the living beings of our experience as knowing: the Philosophy of Knowledge, or "Epistemology"; [f] The study of some of the living beings of our experience as acting properly: the Philosophy of Conduct, or "Ethics." (As will become clear, the "some of the living beings of our experience" referred to here will be limited to human beings.)

C. What is ethics?

So much for a general idea of what philosophy is. We now turn to our special concern, ethics. We have seen that it is a branch of philosophy, and that it is concerned with proper human actions. But, since we will be spending a great deal of time on it, it is worth while to take a little more care in trying to say just what ethics, or the Philosophy of Conduct, is.

1. How branches of knowledge are differentiated

Let us start with this question: how do you tell any branch of human knowledge from any other branch?

a. Generic object, proper object, method

In some cases, this is a simple matter. All one has to do is consider the object which, in general, two particular branches of knowledge treat. For example, in the case of physics and English, it is obvious enough that they differ because one is interested in the phenomena of nature, and the other treats of the language and writings of a particular group of people. Thus, merely pointing to what could be called the "generic object" of these branches of learning is sufficient to tell them apart.

Sometimes, however, two branches of knowledge will be concerned with the same generic object, as in the case of psychology and the philosophy of human nature. When this happens, one needs to distinguish the branches of knowledge on the basis of what is called the "proper object." There is nothing particularly arcane about this traditional term. It means simply this: that particular aspect of the generic object which (to the exclusion of all other aspects) that branch of knowledge studies. For example, psychology studies human activity (and the activity of other living things), but precisely as *observable* (and, to some extent, as predictable). Philosophy of human nature, on the other hand, studies human activity (and the activity of other living things) precisely as *living:* seeking to know the difference between living and non-living things. Conversely, psychology has no particular interest in non-living things; neither does philosophy of human nature concern itself with trying to forecast conduct.

There are instances in which even the proper objects of two branches of knowledge will coincide. Perhaps the clearest example is ethics and moral theology, both of which are concerned with human conduct as *good or evil.* In such a case, a third factor enters in to allow discrimination between the two types of knowledge: the *method* that a branch of knowledge uses in pursuit of its goals. In ethics, the method (broadly speaking) is human reasoning, independent of authority; in moral theology, the method is human reasoning relying upon (divine) authority.

In summary, then: branches of knowledge are distinguished from one another on the basis of their proper objects and their method.

b. Limitations this imposes on branches of knowledge

As an aside, let us take note of something here. The fact that any branch of knowledge concentrates on one (and only one) aspect of its generic object has ramifications for the results it achieves. In brief, any branch of knowledge provides only a partial view of truth, of reality--since it is studying only one aspect of its generic object, and is ignoring all other aspects. That is legitimate enough, but it should warn us against the impression that any one branch of knowledge is somehow superior to any other branch. They all give partial views of reality, and only partial--by the very nature of the case. A similar caution stems from the method that a given branch of knowledge uses. For example, the physical sciences (physics, chemistry, biology, etc.), by and large, use the method of observation, measurement, and hypothesis. Fine, but we ought not forget that there are things which that particular method cannot touch: things such as beauty, freedom, etc., which are not physical and cannot be measured. That does not mean that perfectly valid knowledge about such things cannot be had; it merely means that such knowledge cannot be had by the method that, say, physics uses. That is a limitation, not on freedom and beauty (and other such things), but rather upon physics. Much the same sort of comment should be made about the social sciences (psychology, sociology, and so on), which use the statistical method: again, perfectly valid and good, but one must always remember that the method will yield only statistical knowledge, which has very definite limitations. (For example, one can say, within the context of such sciences, that 60% of the human beings put in a given situation will react in such-and-so a way. One can run experiment after experiment, and the conclusion will become quite firm: indeed, 60% of the human beings put into that situation will in fact act in such-and-so a way. BUT: for any given human being, the science relying on the statistical method will be unable to say whether he or she belongs to the 60% that will behave predictably, or to the 40% that will not.)

7

2. A descriptive definition of ethics

With all that as background, we can hazard an attempt at an operational definition of ethics--a descriptive definition, indeed, but one that will be widely (although not universally) acceptable. Ethics is the study, by the sole use of human reason, of whether any given instance of human conduct is good or evil, or whether any given human action should or should not be done. The generic object of ethics is human actions. The proper object is human actions as *good or evil,* as *to-be-done or not-to-be-done.* The method (broadly put, for now) is human reason acting without reliance on authority, divine or otherwise.

3. Method and ethics

It will be instantly obvious that, given this sort of proper object, the method to be used in ethics cannot be that of the physical sciences. Good and evil are not the sorts of things that can be measured. Nor, for that matter, can they be observed (although good actions and evil actions can). Nor will the statistical method be particularly useful; ethics strives for norms that will be valid for all cases: what people should and should not do, 100% of the time. (Note, however, the word "strives"; ethics is not an ironclad set of rules governing every conceivable action of human beings. Of this, more later.) What will the method of ethics be? We will probably learn best by observing it in action. For now, let us simply observe that ethics will have to have a method of its own.

4. Ethics and religion

A few comments on ethics and religion may be helpful as we finish this chapter. It was pointed out earlier that there is a clear distinction between ethics and moral theology, in that the former does not admit authority as a criterion, whereas the latter depends completely upon divine authority as its starting point. One might make the same comment about ethics and any religious code that governs activity, whether formally developed into a theology or not. Now, it is quite possible for someone who knows moral theology (or who has a religious moral code of whatever sophistication), and who also knows ethics, to keep the two of them apart, and not allow the one to influence the other. Thus, in a philosophy book or a philosophy class, readers or students have a right to expect that what will be discussed is ethics, not moral theology or a religious code. Consequently, in such a book or class, statements of a religious origin (whether a Church, or the Scriptures, or divine revelation, etc.), are out of place. Certainly, nothing derogatory to religion or to any religious moral code is intended by that last statement. But it would benefit neither ethics nor a religious code to confound the two; and a philosopher, whether student or professor, ought to take care not to do this.

On the other hand, one would not expect a valid ethics and a valid moral code or moral theology to contradict each other, either. It is not possible for something to be true in one branch of knowledge and false in another--that would be to say that something can be both true and false at the same time, which is a formal contradiction. One can, of course, encounter the situation in which these two branches of knowledge *seem* to arrive at different, even conflicting, conclusions. But all that means is that one of them (or both of them) ought to do more work on that particular point.

D. Questions and areas that the definition suggests

The descriptive definition of ethics that we saw above suggests some questions immediately. We could ask: [1] What is human conduct? [2] What is meant by "good" and "evil"? [3] How do you decide whether a given action is good or evil?

These three questions will form the framework for the first part of our study, which we might call the theoretical part of ethics. However, ethics is primarily a practical branch of knowledge, although it requires a theoretical base. And so, once that base is at hand, we will begin to apply our theoretical concepts so as to try to judge the morality of actions that bear on [1] our relationships to ourselves; [2] our relationships to others around us (human and otherwise); and [3] our relationships to the Creator--to the extent that the Creator can be known by natural reason.

SUMMARY OF CHAPTER ONE

Philosophy, which began in the 6th century B.C. with Thales's search for a common element underlying all change, is the investigation, by the unaided human reason, of the world around us. Its chief branches are (i) historical [telling us what others have said on the great questions of life]: ancient, medieval, classical modern, and contemporary; and (ii) systematic [our attempt to formulate our own answers to these questions]: metaphysics, philosophy of God, philosophy of nature, philosophy of human nature, epistemology, and ethics.

Branches of knowledge are differentiated from one another on the basis of their proper object and method. Each of these imposes limitations on any branch of knowledge, for a given branch of knowledge studies only one aspect of reality, and does so by means of a particular method which may necessarily omit a part of that reality.

Ethics is the study, by the sole use of human reason (method), of human conduct (generic object), and specifically of human conduct as good or evil (proper object). Since it does not rely on authority, ethics is different from a religiously based moral code and can be engaged in even in the absence of a religion. Even if they are (and should be) independent of each other, however, ethics and a religious moral code ought not be in opposition to each other, for truth cannot contradict itself.

2. IMPUTABLE ACTS AND THEIR BASIS

II. The Theoretical Part of Ethics
  A. The First Question: What is human
    conduct?
    1. Imputable and non-imputable acts
    2. The background of our choices:
       psychological stages in the act of choice
    3. Basic questions about intellect and will
      a. Intellect
        1) Knowledge of universals
        2) Language
        3) What these imply: immateriality
      b. Will
        1) Knowledge and reaction
        2) Implication: an immaterial power
    4. Freedom of the will
      a. Importance of the question
      b. Some needed distinctions
        1) End and means
        2) Necessity: internal and external
        3) Contingency and freedom
      c. Freedom of the will
        1) From external necessity
        2) From internal necessity (in
           this life).

A. The first question: what is human conduct?

The first major question we need to ask, then, is: what do we mean by "human conduct"? We have to be a little careful, here as very often in ethics, for the words don't mean exactly the same here as they do when we use them in ordinary speech. We might think, for example, that "human conduct" is simply human behavior, i.e., how humans act. But in ethics the meaning is somewhat narrower.

1. Imputable and non-imputable acts

In the course of a normal day, we perform all sorts of actions: rising in the morning, bathing, dressing, eating, going to work or to school, and so on. The variety of things we do is almost endless. Diverse as all of our actions are, however, they can be divided into two major types. Some of our actions are done with knowledge and choice on our part: things like deciding to study a particular subject on a given day, deciding to go out to a restaurant for dinner, etc. Other actions, though, we do either unknowingly, or unwillingly, or both. Examples might be tying one's shoes in the morning (with no particular advertence to what we are doing), or being physically forced by someone to do something that we do not wish to do. Actions of the first type (those done with knowledge and choice) are called "imputable actions"; these are the proper concern of ethics, for we are morally responsible for them. Actions of the other type, those done without our adverting to them, or without our willing them, or both, are not imputable actions. Ethics is not concerned with these; we aren't responsible for them, in a moral sense. For want of a better term, we will refer to actions like these as "non-imputable" actions.

(The traditional names for "imputable" and "non-imputable" acts are, respectively, "human acts" and "acts of man" [actus humani and actus hominis, *in Latin]. For students lacking a strong background in classical languages, however, the traditional names are perhaps more confusing than helpful, and so will not be used in this book.)*

One and the same action can, for a person in a given set of circumstances, be an imputable act--and, for the same person (or for a different person) in a different set of circumstances, a non-imputable one. I can, if I wish, deliberately choose to tie my shoes (as I might, for example, when trying on a new pair in a store); if I do, I am performing an imputable action. Or, I can tie them inadvertently, as most of us do each morning, sheerly out of motor habit and without in the least paying any attention to what I am doing. In that case, I am performing a non-imputable act. Another example: I can, if I wish, deliberately choose to shift the transmission lever in my car from Park to Drive (as I doubtless did do the first few times that I drove a car), in which case the action of shifting is an imputable act. Most of the time, however, I move the shift lever quite automatically, with my mind very far away from what I am doing--a non-imputable act.

Of course, there are certain actions we perform which are virtually always non-imputable ones. Our bodies circulate blood, the autonomic nervous system functions consistently, and so on; whether we are aware of such actions or not makes little difference, since we do not choose their operation. On the other hand, it is not possible to say, without further ado, that there are any actions which are virtually always imputable actions, for reasons that will become clear when we study factors that can impede freedom (and therefore our choice).

It is worth noticing that both mental and physical acts can be either imputable or non-imputable ones. I can choose to think about something (an imputable act); I can also merely daydream, without adverting to what I am doing (a non-imputable act). Or: I can choose to breathe (imputable act); or I can simply breathe without thinking about it (non-imputable act).

In summary, then: an imputable act is one that is performed with knowledge and choice on our part; it is the proper concern of ethics, and it can be characterized as good or evil. A non-imputable action, on the other hand, is one performed without choice, or without knowledge (and therefore without choice--for we do not and can not choose that which we do not know). Such an act lacks any moral character, cannot be characterized as good or evil, and is of no interest to ethics.

2. The background of our choices: psychological stages in the act of choice

Since the act of choice is of some importance in ethics, it will pay us to examine it in some detail. For a human choice is actually a complex process, involving interaction of both the intellect and the will.

Having said that, however, we have to be careful not to introduce a false emphasis. Although in the discussion of the act of choice we will speak of "intellect" and "will" as acting, it should be clearly understood that this is simply philosophic shorthand for saying that a human person acts through his or her powers of intellect and will. The act of choice is the act of a single agent, the human person; it is accomplished by means of the two powers of intellect and will (with subsidiary help from other powers that we possess).

The complex process of choice consists of a series of actions of the intellect and will, in quasi-dialogue fashion. In its full-blown form, this series is as follows:

> 1) APPREHENSION (intellect): the intellect judges that a given object, not yet possessed, is a good-for-me.

> 2) INTENTION (will): the will responds with a desire actually to possess the thing in

question; the will then causes the intellect to seek the means that will be needed to make this possession come about.

3) DELIBERATION (intellect): the intellect seeks to know the means that are necessary. This results in a listing of various means that will lead to the goal to be achieved.

4) CONSENT TO MEANS IN GENERAL (will): the will gives its acceptance to the use of one or other of these means, but in a general sort of way, i.e., without selecting one particular means as yet. It then commands the intellect to judge which means will be best, given the circumstances in which the choice is to be made.

5) CONCLUSION or JUDGMENT (intellect): the intellect judges which one means, of the various ones available, will best attain the end to be achieved.

6) CONSENT TO A PARTICULAR MEANS (will): the will gives its consent to the use of that means which the intellect has judged best, given the circumstances.

7) IMPERIUM (intellect and will): this is a complex operation, involving both intellect and will, in which (a) the intellect lines up the various activities and operations that must be undertaken if the means chosen by the will is to be used and the goal achieved; and (b) the will directs various other powers in the human organism (muscles, nerves, etc.) to take the steps that the intellect has determined.

8) COMMANDED ACT(S) (other powers: muscles, nerves, tissues, etc.): this is the activity of the other powers of the body of the human being, responding to the command of the will expressed in the imperium.

9) USE or ENJOYMENT (will): after the goal has been achieved, the will takes pleasure in the possession of the goal.

Merely as described above, the process of choice sounds like a great deal of dry theory, and perhaps overdone. It might, then, be helpful to watch the process in operation in an everyday setting: the acquisition of a hamburger on a particularly bleak study day. As I sit at my desk, then, staring at my calculus (or whatever) textbook:

1) My intellect recognizes that a hamburger would taste good. The hamburger, however, is not yet in hand. (APPREHENSION)

2) My will responds, tending toward the good that the hamburger is seen to be. It tells the intellect to seek out the various means that can lead to the goal, i.e., to possession of the hamburger. (INTENTION)

3) My intellect proceeds to line up the various ways in which a hamburger can be obtained, given my particular circumstances: I can fry one on the kitchen stove; I can telephone out and have one delivered; I can walk down to the corner and get one; I can get in my car and drive to a fast-food store, etc. (DELIBERATION)

4) My will accepts these various means as possibilities, and tells the intellect to determine, in view of all the relevant circumstances (how much money I have to spend, how much bother each possibility would involve, whether it's raining or snowing outside, etc.), which of the possible means would be the best for achieving the goal, to wit, the hamburger. (CONSENT TO MEANS IN GENERAL) My will, however, has not as yet accepted one of these means as the one it will choose; it may still, for other reasons, decide not to choose any of them.

5) My intellect considers the prospect of cleaning up the stove afterwards, the fact that it would take quite some time for a hamburger to be delivered, the fact that the hamburger down at the corner store is small and expensive, etc., etc. It finally comes to the conclusion that, all things considered, it would be better for me to get in the car and drive to the fast-food store. (CONCLUSION or JUDGMENT)

6) My will consents to the use of the means suggested to it by the intellect as most suited for obtaining the

goal--i.e., it elects to go to the fast-food store. (CONSENT TO A PARTICULAR MEANS)

7) Two things then happen: (a) My intellect lines up that series of actions which will be necessary if the chosen means is to be utilized for obtaining the goal. Thus: I must find my car keys; a jacket will be needed, since it is cold outside; I must remember to take my wallet with me, etc. (b) My will commands the various muscles, nerves, etc., whose co-operation is required to utilize the means and thus attain the end. So: the leg muscles are commanded to get me up from my chair, the eyes to look for the car keys and the wallet, etc. (These two, jointly, are the IMPERIUM.)

8) My leg muscles do what they are told to do, the eye muscles likewise, and so forth. (COMMANDED ACTS)

9) Finally, after the hamburger has been gotten and is being duly devoured, my will rejoices in the possession of the goal that has been achieved--the hamburger, now at last in my possession. (USE or ENJOYMENT)

Several observations need to be made on all this. First, it is obvious that what has been presented is a complete act of choice, in all its parts. It is possible, however, that in some situations wherein a choice is being made, one or other of the steps could be considerably abbreviated. If, for example, I have already had a good deal of experience of the best way for me to get a hamburger, then step #5 (Conclusion or Judgment) could be greatly shortened; there is no need to deliberate very long here, since I have already formed conclusions about the matter from previous experience. Then too, a situation could be encountered in which only one means will lead to the desired goal--in which case deliberation about various means will be unnecessary.

Sometimes, too, an act of choice will be truncated midway through the various steps, as for instance when the will decides that the use of any one of the means suggested by the intellect is simply too much trouble: cleaning the stove would be too much bother, calling out would take too long, the corner store's hamburgers are too expensive, and, since it's snowing outside, I don't want to risk driving in a blizzard just to get a hamburger. In such a case, the process of choice simply stops: I decide not to seek the goal.

Despite the complexity of the process of choice, it should not be inferred that the process takes a great deal of time. It doesn't. Frequently, a choice can be made very quickly.

In the process of choice, the characteristic of "imputable act" is acquired once step #6, the "Consent to a Particular Means," is gone through. It is only then that a real choice has been made. (It might seem that step #4, the "Consent to Means in General," would be a candidate for this. Not so, really, since the will still retains, at that stage, the option of rejecting all the various means that the intellect will propose, thus depriving the potential activity of any voluntary character.) This point is of some significance, for it means that moral responsibility is not in question in the earlier steps. Thus, the initial attraction that an object exercises on me ("Apprehension"), for example, is not a moral matter; neither is the simple recognition of that object as a good-for-me (whatever conclusion later steps in the process may provide as to the legitimacy of my possessing that particular good).

3. Basic questions about intellect and will

In the discussion of the process of choice which we just finished, we took several things for granted, among them the exact meaning of the words "intellect" and "will." For the purposes of that discussion, an "individual-in-the-street" understanding of these was enough. But before we go very much further, we ought to try to arrive at a deeper understanding of what we mean when we speak of the human intellect and the human will, for these are central to ethics. Two pairs of questions, then, suggest themselves: (a) What do we mean by "intellect"? by "will"? (b) How do we know that we have an intellect? a will? One further question will have to be answered once we have done this: the human will--is it free?

In one sense, we are going outside the proper field of ethics when we ask these questions. For--traditionally, at any rate--the freedom of the will (and consequently its existence, the proof for which depends in turn upon the proof for the existence of an intellect in the human being) is one of three items that ethics takes for granted. (The other two are the existence of God--to the extent that this can be demonstrated by the unaided intellect--and the immortality of the human person. Both of these will be discussed at least briefly later on in this book.) That is to say, human freedom is something that ethics presumes has been established in earlier philosophic studies, for example, in the Philosophy of Human Nature. However, circumstances in American higher education being what they are, it is no longer

17

legitimate to assume that students have addressed these questions before they come to the study of ethics. That may or may not be unfortunate. It is, none the less, factual. And so it is necessary to consider these questions, at least sketchily, within the context of a book on ethics itself.

a. Intellect

What, then, do we mean by an "intellect"? And do we have one? Let's approach this somewhat indirectly, by examining some facts of our experience.

1) Knowledge of universals

First of all, we are aware of knowing the meaning of such things as beauty, freedom, responsibility. But let's contrast these with some other things that we know. We are aware, for instance, of this dog, this house, this person. Or, we know these dogs, these houses, these persons. In these latter cases, what we know is a particular individual (or group of individuals). And in knowing John, we cannot automatically extrapolate from our knowledge and presume that we therefore know Steve. We know John, and our knowledge is limited to John. Whereas when we know something like beauty, freedom, etc., we know something that isn't limited to a particular individual. If we truly know beauty, then we know something about *every* object that can legitimately be called beautiful. In other words, we know that every beautiful object, without exception, somehow shares in the quality to which the general concept "beauty" can be assigned. In recognizing, therefore, that a particular painting possesses beauty, we can and do thereby know that any other beautiful object will, in its own way, possess the same quality that enabled us to call that painting beautiful.

Put simply, we can know things *as individual things*. And we can know things *as sharing in a quality possessed by more than one individual*. In philosophic shorthand, we can know particulars, and we can know universals—meaning by this latter term concepts that fit every member of their class.

But that raises a question. I know that I share the ability to know individual things, as individual, with other species of living beings. For example, it is perfectly clear that my dog can know his supper dish as well as I do. In fact, he (or she) may well

18

know it better than I do; after all, Rover has a vested interest in it that I lack. But: though I cannot prove this apodictically, nothing whatever suggests to me that my dog has the remotest idea of what is meant by beauty, freedom, responsibility, and the like. At least as far as external evidence is concerned, I can know the same sorts of things that an animal can, but I can also surpass that animal in knowing things (universals) of which a dog (and other animals) is--as far as any instance in history testifies--unaware.

(It isn't necessary for our present purposes, but it should--just for accuracy's sake--be stated somewhere in all this that, while we are saying that we share with lower animals the ability to know individuals, we are not saying that we know individuals in precisely the same way that animals do. The results obtained are the same; the method whereby they are obtained is not. Human knowledge of individuals is intellectual in character, rather than being mere sense-level cognition. But this is a point that pertains more to the Philosophy of Human Nature, and we need not go into it here.)

So: I can know individual things as individuals, and this is an ability that I share with other types of living things. But I can know more than this. I can know universals, i.e., concepts which are not restricted to given individuals, which fit every member of a given class. While, therefore, I have a knowledge ability which I share with animals, I also have another, distinctive knowledge ability that I do not share with them.

2) Language

Much the same point can be made by examining the fact of language, that is, the use of external (generally arbitrary) signs that carry a meaning. It is common experience for us to use words, and sometimes to use signals other than words (facial gestures, movements of the hand, etc.), in order to tell something to some other human being. Some reflection on this common experience, however, can be very instructive. The distinctively human part of the use of language lies in this: when we use a particular word or gesture, our intention is that it convey a meaning--and a meaning that may have nothing to do with the word itself. I can, of course, use a word that is suggestive of the meaning I want to convey, as, for example, when I point to a tire that is going flat and say, "Psssss." Here, I am imitating the sound of the escaping air. But I can also say something like "damaged," or "defective," when referring to that same tire. In that case, the words I use are not imitative of the meaning that I am trying to convey; none the less, they do convey to the person with whom I am speaking my idea that the tire is useless for its intended purposes.

Now, something stands out when we do this. We know of no other animal that uses sound (or its equivalent) in the same way. It is true that other animals do make sounds: dogs bark, parrots screech and imitate other sounds, monkeys chatter. But--recent experiments with dolphins and baboons notwithstanding--there is little if any clear evidence to indicate that these animals are using arbitrary sounds, i.e., that they intend to convey a meaning that is independent of the sound itself. (If they did, we would expect that a different meaning would be assigned from time to time to a given sound, or else that a different sound would be used to convey the same meaning. But, in fact, nothing of the sort takes place. Dogs said "Woof!" in the earliest days of recorded canine history, and they are still doing so. Nothing suggests that that "woof" is anything more than a simple vocal reaction to a stimulus of one sort or other; and certainly, nothing suggests that it is intended by the dog to be an arbitrary sign intended to convey an understood meaning to some other animal.)

Humans, therefore, have the ability to choose an arbitrary sign --a word, a gesture--and use it as a means to convey a meaning to someone else, who understands the intended meaning. This is an ability that they do not share with lower animals. Moreover, as we have seen, humans know universals as well as particulars; and this, too, is something that they do not share with lower animals. We conclude from all this that the human power of knowing is qualitatively different from knowledge power as found on the animal level. Traditionally, this has been expressed by saying that animals have sense knowledge, and humans have intellectual knowledge.

But a difference in abilities says something about the possessor of those abilities, too. For something *acts* in accord with what it *is*. Consequently, if I am interested in discovering what something is, the best way to do so is to look and see what it does (or can do). For instance, if I want to know what a certain object is that is directly ahead of me in the roadway, I examine its activities. I may even take some action aimed at getting it to display its activities for me--such as blowing the car horn. If that object bares its teeth at me and snarls, I conclude that it is a dog. If it moos, I conclude that it is a cow. And so on.

Similarly with the activities of knowledge. From the fact that

20

humans can do things on the knowledge level that lower animals cannot, I conclude that the human being exists on a different level from that of lower animals. Human knowledge ability dictates that, in the human make-up, there exists something that gives men and women the ability to do the distinctively human things that they do, to know the distinctively human things that they know. And this "something," traditionally, has been called an intellect.

3) What these imply: immateriality

Suppose that we push this a little further. We have an intellect, something that enables us to know universals and to use language. Can we know anything more about this power? Perhaps, particularly from the knowledge of universals.

A universal concept is one that fits an entire class, i.e., is not limited to a given individual. What is it that makes an individual be an individual? Take, for example, a group of young people: Peter, Paul, Rose, Anne, John. They all share something in common, i.e., the fact that they are all human beings. They therefore all possess something which makes each of them such: human nature, or "humanness," if you will. But each member of this group also possesses something which makes him or her unique, something not shared with the other members of the group: individuality. Now, just as we could see that human nature gave the group what they have in common, we can ask what gives each member his or her uniqueness and individuality.

To simplify our question, suppose we limit the matter to two individuals, Peter and Paul. And let us suppose that they are identical twins. Suppose, too, for the sake of argument (though this would hardly ever be verified in real life) that they are completely identical in height, weight, appearance, intellectual ability, personality, and so on. By hypothesis, then, one is a complete "carbon copy" of the other. And yet, they are two, not one. Why? Because each has a distinctive location in space and time. No matter how similar two things may be, the one thing in which they must differ (unless the two are actually to become one) is this: each occupies a different physical space. Each has a body, and no two bodies can be in exactly the same space at the same time. In technical terms, Peter and Paul both have their own "matter," their own corporeity, their own "embodiedness." And this they cannot share--no matter how many other things they might have in common--under pain of ceasing to be two and becoming one.

21

Now let's return to the notion of a universal concept. Precisely in that it is capable of being true of many things at the same time, it has to lack, or omit, that element which is unique to each individual member of its class. It must represent what is held in common, and omit what is particular. In the example of the identical twins, it can embrace "humanity," "blue-eyedness," and everything else the twins share. But it must abstract from, eliminate, what is unique to each of the twins: their particular position in time and space, their materiality, their corporeity.

Now, an intellect, as we have seen, is a power that can know universals, that can know what is common to many things, while at the same time blocking out of consideration that which is particular to each, i.e., the individual matter or corporeity of each. What does this tell us about the intellect, about the power that can do this? It tells us that the intellect is capable of an immaterial action, one that is exercised in complete independence of corporeity, of embodiedness. But, since actions are a function of (and reveal) nature--in other words, since what a thing does tells us what it is--this means that the intellect exists in an immaterial way, i.e., does not have a body. Neither, therefore, does it have those qualities that are associated with bodies: the intellect does not have length, breadth, and depth (or, technically, it is not "extended in space and time"), it cannot be seen, touched, or measured, and so on. In brief, the intellect is an immaterial power.

Another consideration can help confirm our understanding of this. When the eye sees, for example, it can take in the entire spectrum of the color chart, precisely because the organs of sight (rods and cones) themselves lack color. Indeed, if a color is introduced into the process of seeing (as, for example, when I put on colored sunglasses), that color is blocked from my perception, in whole or in part. So also, the ear can hear all ranges of sound, within certain limits, precisely because the ear's diaphragm is aperiodic, i.e., has no particular vibration of its own. On the other hand, in the operation of those senses which *do* have a particular quality of their own (for example, the temperature sense, which exists in flesh having a given temperature), we perceive only relative temperatures, not absolute ones: there are certain temperature sensations that this sense does not receive, because they match the ones which that sense already has.

The conclusion from this is that any power of knowledge receives the qualities of whatever it knows in the exact proportion in which it itself does *not* have those qualities. Consequently, if the intellect (the chief power of knowledge that we have) does in fact know what color is, it follows that the intellect itself does not have color. If it knows what heat is, it itself lacks heat. And: if the intellect knows what corporeity is, what extension in space and time is, or, in a word, knows whatever it is that makes an individual to be an individual, it follows that the intellect itself does not itself have that particular quality: the intellect itself is not corporeal, is not extended in space and time. Once again: put briefly, the intellect itself is an immaterial, non-bodily power.

(As an aside: a great deal of material has necessarily been compressed into a short space in our discussion of immateriality, and that always involves the danger that one or other point will be either misrepresented by the author or misinterpreted by the reader. The present writer is acutely aware of this fact, and hopes that the present reader will also be. In the Philosophy of Being and in the Philosophy of Human Nature, a great deal of time is devoted to questions of individuality and to the immateriality of the human intellect, and these are there explained at far greater and more satisfactory length. In ethics, we need the conclusions of these arguments, and perhaps some indication of the arguments themselves; but one cannot present those arguments fully without repeating lengthy segments of other areas of philosophy. And so, should the present explanations prove unsatisfactory to a given reader, he or she is invited to pursue the fuller treatment of these questions that can be found in other branches of systematic philosophy.)

This answers the first set of questions that we posed. We do have an intellect, i.e., that immaterial, non-corporeal power that enables us to know universal concepts and to use languages. We have also answered a corollary question which we didn't even ask: beings below the human level do not have intellects, as far as any evidence suggests (though some do have a different, less powerful knowledge ability).

b. Will

Then there is the question of the will. What is this, and how do we know that we have such a thing?

1) Knowledge and reaction

Let us go back, yet once more, to the fact that we know

23

universals: such things as patriotism, freedom, justice. And we also know such things as racial prejudice, oppression, and hatred. But notice something. We don't simply know these things, period. We don't look upon them in some dispassionate sort of way; we react to them. We cherish freedom, justice. We dislike oppression, racial hatred. But this liking or disliking of such things is different from knowing them, even though it is associated with that. It is a separate activity. This can be seen fairly clearly by taking the case of a universal to which two humans react differently, e.g., the case of patriotism. Two different people will each have the same idea of what this is. But whereas one may react with a sort of "America: love it or leave it" attitude, another may react with a type of disdain, considering the concept to be old-fashioned, outmoded.

In virtually every case of intellectual activity, then, we find a concomitant activity of liking or disliking. True, this reaction may be strong or weak, depending on what it is that we know. And it will differ from one person to another. But it is something that all of us do: not only do we know something (a universal, in the case being discussed), but we also seek to possess it or seek to shun it. And, to parallel our earlier discussion, this is something that is distinctively human: we do not find animals that are attracted to patriotism or repelled by racial prejudice.

2) Implication: an immaterial power

The principle once again applies: from the fact that we perform certain actions (here, seeking or shunning a known universal), it follows that, in our make-up as humans, there is an element or power that enables us to do so. Traditionally, this is the "will."

A moment's reflection will be helpful here. From the fact that the intellect knows universals, we concluded that it itself is immaterial: it acts in an immaterial way, and therefore it exists in an immaterial way, i.e., is immaterial--actions, again, giving a clue to nature. Can the same be said of will? Yes, and for the same reasons. For the will is a power whereby we are able to seek universals, just as the intellect is one whereby we are able to know them. But appetition and knowledge are both activities, and the general rule will hold good: that which acts immaterially, exists immaterially. In short, the will, like the intellect, is an immaterial, non-corporeal power: it has no physical body, and therefore it has none of the characteristics proper to a physical body (it cannot be seen, touched, etc.).

24

4. Freedom of the will

The final question that we need to examine in this chapter is that of the freedom of the will. The meaning of the question is easily enough stated: when we make a choice of something (when we chose to go to the fast-food store for the hamburger, earlier in this chapter, for example): could we have done otherwise? Were we really free in the choice that we made? Or were we somehow forced into doing what we did?

That isn't quite as obvious a question as it might seem. Certainly, our basic instinct is to believe in our own freedom, to conclude that we are the masters of whatever it is that we wish to do. But, for a number of reasons, over the years a number of thinkers have concluded that this instinctive conclusion of ours is an illusion, that we are, indeed, determined (i.e., forced) to do what we do. Obviously, no one forced us to get the hamburger in the sense of pointing a gun at our heads and threatening to kill us if we did not. Nor did anyone pick us up physically and carry us, willy-nilly, to the fast-food store. But: the very environment in which we live--how much of an influence does this exert on our actions? Our culture, our upbringing, the expectations that others have of us: to what extent do all of these things, in their undoubtedly real influence on us, leave us any real degree of freedom?

a. Importance of the question

Obviously, this is a question of major importance to ethics. For if there is no freedom, there is no point in formulating an ethics at all. One can ask the "should" question intelligibly only within the context of the "can": there is little point in someone's telling me that I should do something if I don't have any choice about the matter anyway. If I am, somehow or other, inevitably programmed to do X, what is the use of someone's telling me that I really ought to do, should do, Y?

b. Some needed distinctions

The answer to this question is not a very simple one. And there are some necessary definitions and distinctions that have to be seen--tools that we need for the discussion to come.

1) End and means

Let us consider first what is meant by an "end" and a "means." An "end" (or a "goal"--the two words mean the same thing, for our purposes) is an object that is sought in and for itself. It is that because of which we set in motion a chain of activities designed to ensure possession. A "means," on the other hand, is something that, although it may be good in itself, is something that none the less is not sought for its own sake, but rather is sought in order that it can lead us beyond itself to the end we have chosen. A means, then, is sought--but not for its own sake.

A means can be something quite unpleasant, something that we would not choose as an end. Its goodness, in being chosen, stems from the fact that it leads us to the end, which we do see as a good in itself. A dreaded visit to the dentist could be such an unpleasant means (the end being dental health); so could attendance at a very boring (but required) course (the end being graduation). If, indeed, a means is such that we can see absolutely no good in it, considered in itself (when, that is to say, its entire, whole goodness, as far as we can see, stems from the fact that it leads to the end), then we have a "pure means." Finally, a "unique means," as the name suggests, is the sole means that would lead to a goal that is desired.

2) Necessity: internal and external

Next we need to consider the whole question of necessity and its opposites. In general, necessity is the condition of something whereby it cannot be other than what it is. There are several varieties of this. One can speak of *internal* necessity and *external* necessity, for example. In internal necessity, we are speaking of a necessity that is based on the nature of the thing in question. For example, it is of internal necessity that a triangle have three sides--because that is the nature of a triangle. A "triangle" that had four sides would not be a triangle, whatever else it might be. The strictest type of internal necessity is called "metaphysical" necessity: a necessity based on an object's nature and admitting of no exceptions. The triangle example, cited a moment ago, is an illustration of metaphysical necessity. Another type of internal necessity, somewhat less strict, is "physical" necessity: a necessity, again stemming from the object's nature (for it is still a variety of internal necessity), and generally having to do with that object's actions, but admitting of exceptions. With this sort of necessity, an apple tree has to produce apples (and not peaches or pears)--*but* there is the possibility that it simply will not produce anything at all. *If* an apple tree produces anything, it will (by internal, physical necessity) have to produce apples. But it does not have to produce anything at all in order to remain an apple tree.

Then there is the question of external necessity, one that does not stem from an object's nature but rather is imposed upon it from the outside. If, for example, I am being physically held down, I necessarily do not move. But this does not come from my nature--I can be human in whatever physical position I happen to be. Rather, it stems from something or someone outside me.

3) Contingence and freedom

The opposite of necessity is either contingence or freedom. Contingence refers to a lack of internal necessity, whether metaphysical or physical. If I say that I exist contingently, I mean that there is nothing in my human nature that requires that I exist: I may, or I may not. Human nature, as such, does not involve necessary existence (or, putting it another way, human nature is contingent): it can exist, but it does not have to. There was, after all, a time when human nature did not exist.

Freedom, on the other hand, means the absence of both internal and external necessity. Thus, when I choose to stand up: nothing in my nature says that I have to stand up (a human can be fully a human when seated or lying down), and no one outside myself is forcing me to stand.

To summarize: there is such a thing as *internal* necessity (metaphysical or physical), and such a thing as *external* necessity. *Contingence* means the lack of internal necessity; *freedom* means the lack of *both* internal and external necessity.

c. Freedom of the will

With that as background, we can now turn to the question of whether the will is free. The obvious way to do this is to show that the will, in making its choices, is not (and cannot be)

27

subject to either external or internal necessity.

1) From external necessity

The will cannot be subject to external necessity, for such necessity (i.e., physical force) always involves the contact of one body upon another, one physical organ on another physical organ. But the will has no physical parts, as we have seen; it is a spiritual, immaterial power. Consequently physical contact with the will is impossible, and as a result external necessity is impossible.

Note, however: though the will itself has no physical parts, it does in this life make use of a material organ as an instrument (the human brain); this feature it has in common with the intellect. Briefly put, the situation is this: the intellect relies on the brain and the senses for the subject matter of its knowledge. However, though there exists this dependence for the start of the knowledge process, it can be shown that the intellect, once given the phantasms from the brain, can then go on and operate independently of the brain and the senses. The same is true, *mutatis mutandis,* of the will. And thus the argument from immaterial activity to immaterial existence remains in force.

It is, of course, perfectly possible for external necessity to be imposed on the brain. This is a physical organ, subject to contact with other physical agents. Thus, brain surgery can radically alter the structure of the brain, and can thereby radically alter the instrument that both intellect and will utilize in order to start the process of knowledge and appetition. But this is, precisely, to impose external necessity on the *instrument* used by the intellect and the will, not on those two powers themselves. Consequently, this sort of surgical intervention would not involve imposition of external necessity on the will or the intellect.

2) From internal necessity (in this life)

So much for external necessity. What of internal? In this life, the will is not subject to internal necessity either, whether this be of the metaphysical or the physical variety. Some brief reflection will make that clear. Whenever my will seeks an object, it seeks it precisely as an object that is seen as a good-for-me. (My judgment as to whether a given object is, objectively, good for me may or may not be correct, in any given instance. But that is beside the point--which is, again, that the object is *seen* as a good.) No one ever seeks evil, as such. Even something that is objectively evil is always sought under some guise of good. But--since actions flow from and reveal nature--that means that it is the will's nature to seek the good-for-me, purely and simply. Now, any created object that the will seeks is a mixture of goodness and evil--meaning by the latter either a lack of some goodness that the object in question ought to possess, or (in a looser sense of the term "evil"), a lack of some or all of the goodness or perfections that some other object has. Put briefly, no created good is a perfect good. When, therefore, there is question of the choice of some created, imperfect good, the will can direct the intellect to consider either that object's good qualities or its bad ones. For instance, a piece of chocolate cake might appear as a good to me. My will can direct my intellect to concentrate on its flavor, its sweetness, how enjoyable it would be to eat. Or, the will can direct the intellect to concentrate rather on the fact that the cake contains a fierce number of calories, none of which I particularly need. By choosing to have the intellect concentrate on the object's imperfections, the will can escape being inevitably drawn to the object's goodness. In other words, no created object can necessitate (force) the will to choose it.

It would take an object that is sheerly good, one that had absolutely no admixture of evil, to necessitate the will, to force the will to choose it. We have no experience of such an object in this life. However, we know from Philosophy of Being that there exists a first uncaused cause, which by its very nature is totally good, without evil of any kind. This, indeed, is the sort of thing that could necessitate the will. However, we have no direct knowledge of this being; our entire knowledge of it stems from our knowledge of the creatures it has produced. Knowledge through creatures, however, always implies the imperfections of those creatures; and once again, the will can choose to have the intellect concentrate on the imperfections rather than the perfections, and thus can escape being necessitated.

To sum up: the will is not subject to external necessity. Moreover, although the will is subject, by internal necessity, to choosing a perfect good perfectly known, in this life all created goods are not perfect goods; and even the one perfect good we know about is not perfectly known. The will, therefore, is free in this life.

But what of the questions of environment, upbringing, etc., which were raised earlier in our discussion? Certainly, these have an influence on the will's choices; and we will see more of them when we come to consider factors that can limit or impede our freedom. We will even see that certain of these factors can, in given cases, totally take away freedom from an individual person. For now, however, all we wish to claim is that, in principle and for human beings in general, freedom is a quality that we possess--whatever be said of a given individual in particular circumstances.

SUMMARY OF CHAPTER TWO

1. An imputable act is one that is done with both knowledge and choice; a non-imputable one, one done without one or both of these. Ethics is concerned only with the former. In full-blown form, an imputable act of choice involves some nine successive stages of activity on the part of the intellect, the will, and other powers: apprehension, intention, deliberation, consent to means in general, conclusion or judgment, consent to a particular means, imperium, commanded act(s), and use or enjoyment. In this complex act, it is the exclusive function of the intellect to know and to judge; and it is the exclusive function of will to choose and to command.

2a. We know that we have a distinctive power of knowing ("intellect") because we can know universals and can use arbitrary symbols called language to communicate meaning; animals below the human level give no sign of this ability. But a universal is that which lacks an individuating characteristic: materiality, or corporeity. Now, a power which can know an immaterial item such as a universal is therefore capable of an immaterial action. So, since actions follow upon and reveal nature, the intellect also exists in an immaterial way: it does not have a body. (To say the same thing in other words: a cause [the intellect] which can produce an immaterial effect [a concept] must itself possess any perfection which it gives to its effect, and thus the intellect must possess the perfection of immateriality.)

2b. We do not simply know something; we always react to it, positively or negatively. But in choosing (or not choosing) a universal, our power of choice (the "will") is performing an immaterial act; once again, since it acts in an immaterial way, it too exists in an immaterial way.

3. Our immaterial wills are free in this life because (i) being non-corporeal, they are not subject to external necessity (which always implies physical, bodily contact), and (ii) they are not subject to internal necessity either, since this could be effected only by a perfect good perfectly known--which we do not encounter in this life. In regard to any other good, the will can always direct the intellect to concentrate on that object's evil or imperfect aspects, and thus can escape internal necessitation.

3. LIMITS TO IMPUTABLE ACTS

II. The Theoretical Part of Ethics
  A. The First Question: what is human
    conduct?
      5. The make-up of an imputable act:
        action, motive, circumstances
      6. Some characteristics of an imputable
        act: voluntariness, attributability,
        merit
      7. Limitations on imputability:
        a. Levels of intention
        b. Factors affecting an act's voluntary
          character:
          1) Ignorance
          2) Very strong emotion
          3) Intellectual fear
          4) Force
          5) Habit
          6) Other factors.

We have seen that an imputable act is one that is performed with knowledge and choice. And we have spent some time examining the complexity involved in an act of choice, and in investigating something of the nature of the two main powers involved in such an act, i.e., the intellect and the will.

Some further study of an imputable act, though, will repay us. For it turns out to be complex from yet another point of view.

5. The make-up of an imputable act:
action, motive, circumstances

Take this situation: a hunter, out in a field, aims at an object and fires his rifle. A human act? Indeed; he is deliberately taking aim, deliberately firing the weapon. Yet, we feel instinctively that we are talking about quite different things if the target involved is a deer or (whether intentionally or unintentionally on the hunter's part) is a fellow hunter. In one case we are talking about shooting an animal. In another we are talking about shooting a fellow human being, whether accidentally or deliberately. And these, we feel, are by no means the same thing, even though the action involved (pointing a rifle and shooting it) is one and the same in each case. Or, take another example: a woman steals some food from a grocery store. In one case, she is doing so merely for the thrill of stealing. In another, she steals because she is a kleptomaniac and cannot really help herself. In a third, she takes the groceries because she has several starving children at home and has no other way to feed them. Again, an imputable act, certainly: one done with knowledge and choice. And the same external action each time. Yet we feel quite different about each case. What accounts for the difference?

Some analysis and reflection will show that any imputable action really involves at least three elements. There is the physical action involved: the pointing of the rifle and the pulling of the trigger; the theft of groceries. But there is also the matter of the motive, i.e., the reason why the action is performed. And here we have the intention of killing a deer, the intention of killing a fellow human being (or, in the case of the accidental shooting, the lack of such an intention); in the other example, we have the gaining of a thrill, the following out of a neurotic impulse (to the extent that that can be called a motive at all), and the feeding of one's starving children. Finally, we have the question of circumstances: the various factors of time and place that enter into the situation in which the physical action is performed. Put briefly, these latter are the answers to the questions "Who?" "What?" "Where?" "How?" and "When?"--the classic questions of the newspaper reporter.

To illustrate the notion of circumstances: I drive my car down a road at 65 m.p.h. That is the physical act. I do so simply for the thrill of it. That is the motive. But notice what a difference is made by *who* I am. If I am a 12-year-old who shouldn't be driving a car in the first place, that colors the action considerably. Or, if I am a professional race-car driver: that gives what I do a quite different flavor. Or: if I am intoxicated or high on drugs: that, again, gives the same action quite a different tone. Then there is the matter of the *what:* it is one thing if I am driving a new Cadillac, in perfect mechanical shape. It is quite another if I am driving an old jalopy whose brakes are questionable at best. The *how:* a great deal of difference is made to the quality of the act if I am driving with full attention to what I am doing, as opposed to driving with one hand on the wheel, one eye on the road, and most of my attention on my passenger (male or female, as appropriate) in the front seat. The *where:* it makes quite a difference if the road on which I am driving is a superhighway, or is a two-lane winding road leading through a populated area. Similarly the *when:* it is one thing to drive at that speed at 3 a.m., when most people are safely at home in bed; it is quite another to do so at the height of the rush hour.

32

When we speak of an imputable act, then, we refer to more than simply an action performed under the guidance of knowledge and choice (though we certainly assume those two factors). By a conscious, chosen, imputable act, we mean the totality of (1) the physical action itself, (2) the motive, and (3) the circumstances. Thus, to refer once again to the examples cited above (the firing of the rifle and the stealing of groceries): we are speaking of three quite different imputable actions in each of the two examples: the killing of a deer, the accidental killing of a fellow human being, the deliberate killing of a fellow human being; and, theft simply for "kicks," neurotic theft, and theft made necessary by a higher need. The moral quality differs in each of these six.

For reasons which we will see in greater detail later on, if an action is to be morally good, *all three* elements (physical action, motive, and circumstances) have to be morally good (or at least morally indifferent, i.e., neither good nor evil). If any one of the three is evil, the entire action is vitiated, is evil (for, as we shall see, there is deliberate choice of evil involved). And so, suppose that:

(a) In order to salvage my reputation from a blackmailer's threats (motive), and in view of the fact that I am a respected member of the community, with a wife and several children, employing several hundred employees whose welfare depends on my continued well-being, etc., etc. (circumstances), I murder the blackmailer (physical action). The motive is good, the circumstances are all good, but the physical action, murder, is evil; result, the entire action is morally evil.

(b) I give a large amount of money (physical action) to a group of starving people in desperate circumstances who need some assistance if they are not otherwise to engage in robbing and looting a group of stores near me (circumstances), but I do so precisely in order that I will win their votes for a certain politician to whom I owe a political debt but whom I know to be about as honest and upright as Gengis Khan (motive). Physical action and circumstances are fine, but the motive is vitiated, and hence so is the entire action.

(c) I am a commercial pilot, flying a 747 from New York to San Francisco (physical action), since this is part of my job which I need to support my family (motive), but I am doing so in defiance of a red light on the flight panel that tells me that something is wrong with the oil pressure in one or more of the engines (circumstances). Here, the action and motive are fine, but one circumstance renders the whole action at least questionable from a moral point of view.

To summarize, then: the imputable act, which must be an action performed with knowledge and choice, is itself a complex one, consisting of the physical action itself, the motive, and the circumstances. For an action to be morally good, all three of these latter factors have to be good (or at least morally indifferent); if any one of them is evil, then the entire action is vitiated in its moral character and becomes evil.

(To be even a little bit more accurate: an imputable act can be even more complex than the examples indicate, since we often perform actions out of more than one motive. For our present purposes, however, we need not enter into this--apart from noting it.)

6. Some characteristics of an imputable act: voluntariness, attributability, merit

There is yet another way of looking at a morally imputable act which will shed some further light on it for us. Traditionally, an imputable act has been looked upon as one that is voluntary, is attributable, and is meritorious. We have already seen some of these characteristics, particularly the first one, in part; none the less, a few words about each will not hurt.

We can dispose of the first such traditional characteristic, for now, fairly rapidly. To say that an imputable act is voluntary merely means that it is one that is deliberately willed. We have seen this already, and it is included here only by way of a warning that the term "deliberately" is going to need some qualification, as we shall see later in this chapter.

To say that an imputable act is attributable means that such an act can properly be referred to the person who performed it as his or her own, as belonging to him or her, for good or ill. However, though again not a great deal needs to be said on this point here, it is worth noting that an imputable act is attributable to its author exactly insofar as that author had knowledge (whether correct or incorrect) of the act that he or she was about to perform. For example: in anger I lash out and strike the person next to me, unaware that he happens to be my father. I am guilty of assault, but not of irreverence toward my parent. Or, I steal what I believe to be a sack full of money--which

34

is actually full of old newspapers. I am guilty of grand theft, not petty larceny (from a moral point of view, if not from a legal one).

Finally, an imputable act is said to be meritorious. This means that a relationship exists between such an act and the approval or disapproval, expressed tangibly, by the society in which the author of that act lives. The act itself may be quite transitory--over and done with in an instant; but the relationship between it and the reward or punishment that it is seen to deserve is a lasting one. For example, we put murderers in jail even long years after the foul deed is done, if that's how long it takes to catch them. Or, we award medals for bravery, sometimes many years after the particular act of heroism was performed--and we feel that, somehow or other, justice has not been served until we do so.

Voluntariness, attributability (or "responsibility"), and merit: these, then, are three characteristics that we feel properly attach themselves to an imputable act in the moral order. By contrast, we ordinarily do *not* feel that these attach to a non-imputable act--though the legal order and the moral order may diverge somewhat here. (From a legal standpoint, for instance, we might not punish the theft of a suitcase filled with old newspapers in exactly the same way as we would have punished the actual theft of a considerable amount of money. Or, the legal statute of limitations may have run out on a particular crime committed years ago, and consequently legal punishment may not in fact be administered for it. We still, however, consider the perpetrator of such a crime as *worthy* of such punishment, even if, for other reasons, society does not in fact see fit to impose it.)

7. Limitations on imputability

Let us return for a moment to the statement that an imputable act is voluntary, since this, too, needs to be made a little more exact.

a. Levels of intention

Take the situation in which I plan to rob a bank. After getting all the preliminary "casing" done, I carefully plan just how I will set about separating the bank from its hoard of money. Few, if any, other thoughts intrude upon my attention while I am doing this. Then, on the day that I have set for the hold-up, I leave my home and go to the bank. En route, I am thinking of little else than what I will do when I get there: I go over in my mind just what door I will go in and how, what I will say to the bank teller, what I will do about the guards, how I plan to escape after the money is safely in my possession. My entire attention is focused on what I am about to do, in all its details.

Contrast this, now, with another case. I decide to take a walk downtown, say, to see a movie at a theatre in the center of the city. I set out from my home, intending to go to the movie. En route, however, all sorts of things intrude on my attention: what a perfect day it is, the fact that people seem very cheerful today, the street sweeper that is busily at work at the corner, other plans that I have for the day. In short, I pretty much forget, for the moment, the idea of the movie--though that notion still governs my action (for I do, after all, eventually arrive at the theatre). For all intents and purposes, I have completely put the thought of the movie out of my mind, and have mentally reviewed a thousand and one other things as I walked along. I may even be somewhat surprised when I arrive at the theatre, and be a little startled when I remember that this, after all, was the original motive I had when I set out.

Both of these acts--robbing the bank and walking to the theatre--are voluntary. Yet they are quite different. Let us examine that difference in some detail.

Certain quite distinct "levels of intention" can be distinguished. That is to say, I can be more or less aware of my decision to perform a certain act when the time actually comes for me to perform it. There is, first, an *actual* intention: a decision that I make to do something, which I never revoke, and which consciously influences my performance of that act. I am quite aware of what I am doing, and of my decision to do it, at the very time that I am performing the action. The example of the bank robbery, cited above, is an instance of an actual intention.

I can also, however, have a *virtual* intention: one which I made, never revoked, and which influences the act I perform, although I am not explicitly aware of it when I perform the act. The walk to the movie theatre illustrates this type of intention: a good part of my walk was made by means of it, even though I started out with an actual intention.

There is also such a thing as an *habitual* intention. This is one which I make, never revoke, but which never actually influences an action which I perform (usually because I never get around to a deliberate performance of that action). Suppose, for example, I resolve to run a red light, just to see how it feels. I never change that intention, i.e., never explicitly decide not to do so. However, neither do I ever manage to run a red light--because, for example, I decide to sell my car, and thus find myself a confirmed pedestrian. That would be an habitual intention. Or, suppose that I make such a resolve (the red light, again), never revoke it, never actually follow through on it deliberately. Then, one day, forgetting completely my resolve, I do in fact by sheer negligence run a red light. Again, this would be an instance of an habitual intention. An intention of this type, though certainly conceivable and real enough, is of relatively little importance in ethics, apart from certain applications that it can have in the areas of rights and law.

For completeness' sake, we should perhaps also mention what is traditionally called an *interpretative* intention. This is one that was in fact never made, but which someone else judges I would have made had I been aware of a given set of circumstances. Once again, this, like the habitual intention, is not of great importance in ethics, except in the matter of interpretation of law. (In that particular area, it can be significant, as, for example, when I judge that the City Council would have made the speed limit on a particular street 25 m.p.h. rather than 35 had the Council members been aware of what poor shape the street was in--or, conversely, when I judge that the Council members would not intend that a speed law apply in certain emergency situations, such as a hasty drive to the emergency room of a hospital.)

In brief, for an act to be voluntary, in the sense in which ethics is truly interested in it, it must be one that is performed with either an actual intention or at least a virtual intention.

b. Factors affecting an act's voluntary character

Even actions performed with an actual or a virtual intention, however, can have their degree of voluntariness influenced by several other factors. It will pay us to spend some time on these.

1) Ignorance

The first such factor is *ignorance*. Again, however, the word has a special meaning in ethics that is different from the ordinary use of the term: we are talking, not about a simple lack of knowledge, but rather about a lack of some knowledge which a person *ought* to possess. For a sea captain to have no knowledge of astrophysics does not constitute ignorance in this sense; a sea captain has no need to know astrophysics in order to ply his trade responsibly. For him to have no knowledge of navigation, however, *does* constitute ignorance in the ethical sense, for that is knowledge which, given his trade, he ought to have.

There are several different kinds of ignorance that we should note. *Invincible* ignorance, as the name suggests, is ignorance which a person cannot reasonably overcome, given the amount of time, opportunity, and talent available to him or her, and given the degree of need which he or she has for that knowledge. One can be invincibly ignorant of something for one of two reasons: either the person simply does not know that he or she ought to know something, or else, although aware of that fact, the person cannot reasonably overcome the obstacles that stand in the way of having that knowledge. Suppose, for example, I am taking a trip through Europe, and on one occasion I find myself in the position of having to drive a car somewhere, even though I had no intention of doing so when I started out. Suppose further that it is late at night, on a country road. I am simply unaware of the fact that certain insurance formalities are required in this particular country (certain documents have to be in my possession). I am invincibly ignorant of this requirement, for, though (if I am to drive) I should know this, it doesn't even dawn on me that there could be such a requirement, and thus there is no way in which I could learn about it in those circumstances. Or, let us suppose that I am a hunter, and am in the wilderness somewhere near the Idaho-Washington border. It is early in the morning, and I have no notion of exactly where I am--i.e., whether I am in Idaho or in Washington. I *should* know this, absolutely speaking, since I know that the two states have somewhat different laws on hunting certain types of game. Moreover, I know that I should know it. However, though I could (again speaking absolutely) go back to a town somewhere and find out just where I am, there is a great disproportion between the effort needed to acquire the knowledge in question and the importance of my having it. In both of these cases (Europe or Washington-Idaho) I could be said to be invincibly ignorant: in the one case, I simply do not know that I should have knowledge of a certain item; in the other, I do know that fact, but the effort required to possess the knowledge is disproportionate to the importance of possessing it.

If one thinks about it, it becomes obvious that invincible ignorance is a relative term, one that varies with given individuals and circumstances. What is invincible ignorance for one person (a very unintelligent one), say, might not be so for another one (a very bright one); what is invincible ignorance for one and the same person in one set of circumstances may not be so in another set (e.g., what is invincible ignorance in the wilderness may not be so inside a town).

Then there is *vincible* ignorance. This is ignorance that can reasonably be overcome, taking into account a person's talent, the opportunity he or she has to acquire the needed knowledge, the urgency of the matter to be known, and so on. In vincible ignorance, in other words, a person who can reasonably be expected to know something has failed to acquire the knowledge that he or she could have and should have. If I am a citizen of a particular state, and have lived there for some time, I can reasonably be expected to be aware of the tax laws of that state, at least as they pertain to me. If I am none the less unaware of them, we have an instance of vincible ignorance: one that I could and should reasonably have overcome.

Finally, there is such a thing as *affected* ignorance. This is deliberately sought ignorance: I take means to ensure that I do not know something because of an obligation that would devolve on me if I did know it. This is ignorance of the "Don't tell me; I don't want to know" sort. For example: suppose I know that I have an unpleasant duty to perform on the 28th of this month. Suppose, too, that on a given day late in that month, I honestly forget just what date it is. I take some pains *not* to discover whether today is the 28th or not; I don't want to know. This is affected ignorance.

These are the different types of ignorance that we can encounter. How does each of them, in turn, affect the voluntariness of an imputable act?

First, *invincible* ignorance destroys the voluntary character of an action, and consequently destroys responsibility. Again, an action can be attributed to its author only to the degree that he or she has knowledge of it--which, by the nature of the case, is impossible here. I may, indeed, drive without the appropriate insurance forms on my European country road; but I am not morally responsible for doing so, for the knowledge required to make me guilty of that is simply lacking, by invincible ignorance. (This, of course, may not be very impressive to a police officer who stops me. But then, there do exist occasional differences between the moral order and the legal order!)

Vincible ignorance, on the other hand, does not destroy responsibility for a given action, though it does lessen it. And so a doctor who, through vincible ignorance, prescribes a drug whose dangerous side effects he does not (but should) know is, indeed, responsible for the harm that comes to his patient; but he is less responsible than another doctor who, fully knowing those side effects, nevertheless deliberately and heedlessly prescribes the drug anyway.

Finally, *affected* ignorance does not destroy responsibility, and does not decrease it. In fact, it may increase responsibility, at least to the degree that it adds malice to the act. We will see the reason for this later on, when we consider the question of deliberately choosing an evil, known or unknown.

2) Very strong emotion

The next factor which is capable of modifying the degree of voluntariness of an act is very strong emotion. This term refers to any powerful emotion, e.g., fear, hatred, anger, greed, and so on. These emotions, though quite different in themselves, can be grouped together for our purposes since, while they may actually make the performance of an act more forceful, they also render the agent less controlled, less in charge of his or her act. Thus they all have the same effect on the moral character of the actions we perform under their influence.

We can distinguish such emotions on the basis of whether they precede or follow our conscious awareness that we are under their influence. *Antecedent* emotion, then, is that initial appetitive response that arises in us immediately after we become aware of certain things, and before there is an opportunity for the will to act. For example, suppose that I am a very reserved person, not given to expressions of hearty effusiveness. Someone comes up behind me, and slaps me on the back in token of a cordial greeting. My initial reaction to this may well be anger and resentment--not as a reasoned response at all, but rather simply as an immediate, non-reflective reaction to such a "greeting." Or: suppose that I am walking along the street, and suddenly meet a large, unfriendly-looking German shepherd--I who, let us say, do not particularly like dogs in general, even friendly ones. My immediate reaction is fearfulness, even before I have a chance to determine whether that is an appropriate response to this particular beast or not.

There is also such a thing as a *consequent* emotion. This is an emotion that I experience, recognize as such, and deliberately foster. For instance, I can deliberately allow myself to brood over a real or supposed injury, making myself angrier and angrier, either for the satisfaction that I get from doing so or, in some cases, for purposes of working up sufficient courage to take some particular action in response to the injury. Or, I can become conscious of the desire for something, and can deliberately foster that desire, on the premise that if I want something badly enough, I may take the extraordinary means needed to get it.

The two types of emotion affect the moral character of an act in quite different ways. In some cases (usually rather rare ones), antecedent emotion can be so powerful as to take away reason entirely. In that case, it would also take away the voluntary character of my action, and therefore my moral responsibility for it. Imagine a person who, being extremely afraid of dogs in general and encountering our unfriendly German shepherd, becomes so terrified that he or she "loses his/her head," as the expression goes, and flees in sheer panic. Such an act of flight would not be an imputable act. Similarly, it is conceivable (at least as a limiting case) that a person could be so overcome with anger that he or she literally would not be responsible for an action taken in response to that anger.

Such cases, however, are unusual. More commonly, antecedent emotion does not destroy an act's voluntary character; and the act remains an imputable one. But an antecedent emotion does lessen the degree of responsibility that a person has for that act, since it makes any sort of calm deliberation about options, choices, and consequences much more difficult. We all know from experience, for instance, that it is much harder to make a reasoned choice about something if we are ragingly angry. It *can* be done--but it's harder. So also, when we want something very badly, that is ordinarily not the best time to make a calm, reasoned decision about that thing: someone who is on a diet, but who is also very hungry, will have considerable difficulty in acting in accord with cool rationality when he or she comes upon a piece of chocolate cake.

On the other hand, *consequent* emotion does not lessen the voluntary character of an act, nor the responsibility that I have for that act. In fact, such emotion may even increase my responsibility, since there is here question of an emotional reaction that is itself deliberately chosen and fostered. The earlier example of harboring anger at some injury can serve to illustrate the point. Suppose that I am your classic "97-pound weakling," into whose face the proverbial bully has just kicked sand. I may well become angry right on the spot, but prudence suggests that I do not take on someone who is three times my size, so I do nothing about it. But I allow myself to brood over this, and I become angrier and angrier. It then occurs to me that, while I am no match for my sand-kicking enemy on a physical level, a Colt .45 is a great equalizer of physiques. I continue to brood, and get myself so worked up and angry that I actually do acquire a gun, go looking for my adversary, and proceed to do him in. Had I, on the other hand, not allowed myself to brood over the insult I received, I might very likely have felt some resentment, but this would have passed and I would not have become homicidal.

Consequent emotions are sometimes said to be "voluntary in themselves," and the actions which stem from them are said to be "voluntary in cause." When properly understood, these two terms provide a useful way of stating the case; and understanding them is relatively simple. "Voluntary in itself" means simply something which I directly will. As for the term "voluntary in cause": if A causes B, and B causes C, then A can in some sense at least be said to have caused C: if A hadn't caused B, then C would never have taken place. In the consequent emotions, A is I myself, B is the consequent emotion, and C is the action that I take because of that emotion: I cause the emotion, and the emotion (in some senses at least) causes the action; therefore I can be said to cause the action. The action is then said to be "voluntary in cause."

3) Intellectual fear

The third factor that can influence the voluntary character of an action is intellectual fear. Here, though, we should be careful of our terminology. We are not speaking of an emotional reaction to a threatening situation (that would be a "very strong emotion," in the sense which we have just examined in the preceding paragraphs), but rather of an intellectual realization of some impending evil, with the choice of rational means to avert it. This may be quite devoid of any emotional reaction of any kind. Someone may, for instance, have intellectual fear of economic poverty, and consequently take a variety of means to avoid it--without experiencing a bit of emotion. Or, someone may have an intellectual fear that a blackmailer will reveal unpleasant things about his or her past, and decide to take effective means to ensure that the blackmailer is unable to do so. Again, there may be no emotional content to this at all.

Also, we need to be aware that we are speaking of actions that are done *from* fear, *out of* fear, i.e., with fear as a motive. It is quite possible for someone to have great intellectual fear, and yet

42

carry on exactly as before, ignoring the fear and taking no means to ward off its dire consequences—the classic instance being the soldier who, although knowing full well that his life is in danger, nevertheless stands his ground: a situation known as acting *with* (as opposed to *from* or *out of*) fear.

Intellectual fear does not destroy the voluntary character of my action or my responsibility for that action. The choice that is made from intellectual fear is still a rational and knowledgeable one. But such fear does diminish the voluntary character of my act and therefore my responsibility: I end up making a choice that I wish I did not have to. Perfect liberty is not present, and therefore, since my freedom is somewhat diminished, so is my responsibility. Someone piloting his own jet airplane, faced with the necessity of making an emergency landing, decides to dump his extra fuel, since it could explode in such a situation. Of course, this means the loss of a considerable amount of money; jet fuel is not inexpensive. He would of course rather not incur that loss, and so, if things were otherwise, would not decide to empty the fuel tanks. But things are not otherwise, and he dumps the fuel—a free and reasoned action, but one that he would rather not have had to do, one in which his freedom was less than complete. In general, most actions done under duress and intimidation ("an offer one can't refuse," in popular terminology) fall under the heading of actions done out of intellectual fear.

4) Force

The term "force" refers to the use of actual physical power so as to make someone do something against his or her will. Notice, however, that threats do not fall into this category (rather, they would come under the heading of either strong emotion or of intellectual fear). There must be, not the mere threat of, but rather the actual use of physical power, if there is to be question of this particular impediment to an action's voluntary character.

Estimating the effect that force has on voluntariness can be a little complicated. For, though someone can, through the use of physical force, make us do something against our wills, he or she cannot force us to will whatever it is that is being demanded. As long as we refuse to will it (even though we are physically forced to do whatever it is), there is no question of responsibility, for there is no voluntariness at all and therefore no imputable action on our part. In such a case, force completely destroys voluntariness and responsibility. Thus, an individual who is tied up and carried to, say, the gate of a factory is not morally responsible for blocking the gate--even though he or she is, as a matter of fact, blocking it.

The question comes up, however: what happens if we are overcome by physical force, but also yield our consent to whatever is being demanded? The answer to that depends on what is being demanded. In the case of kidnapping, for instance: one could be morally justified in yielding consent to being kidnapped, for there is nothing particularly immoral about being in one place rather than another. When, however, what is being demanded is itself immoral (rape is the classic instance of this), then we are required to withhold assent and co-operation, to the extent that this is possible; otherwise, the act becomes voluntary on our part (subject, however, to the comments made earlier about intellectual fear and strong emotion).

5) Habit

For our purposes, we can define a habit as a constant way of acting, acquired by constant repetition of the same act. If we think about it, we realize that very many of the things we do in the course of a normal day are done out of habit: brushing our teeth in the morning, having two (or however many) cups of coffee for breakfast, smoking (if we do), and so on. Habits are a very useful part of human life, for they enable us to accomplish routine things easily and therefore free our minds to concentrate on other things. Precisely because they do take our minds off some actions, however, they also influence the moral character of those actions, to some degree.

To count the number of habits that each of us has would be virtually impossible, and not particularly fruitful. None the less, we can group them by types, and that is enough to allow us to see their ethical implications.

Some habits, first, are deliberately acquired, as for instance the motor habits that athletes develop, or that pianists do. The old saying that "practice makes perfect" often means nothing more than "practice develops habits." One sets out to acquire a particular skill, has every intention of acquiring that skill, and, given enough repetition of the same action (and, in some cases at least, a modicum of natural talent), does acquire the skill--which is to say, does acquire a habit.

Then there are habits which one acquires, not by deliberately intending to do so and taking means toward that end, but rather by deliberately performing certain actions that are known to be habit-forming: the actions themselves are intended, the habit is not. An example would be narcotic addiction: one intends the use of drugs, and knows that they are habit-forming, but certainly does not intend to become an addict (even though, of course, that is what does eventually happen).

Finally, there are habits which are acquired quite unconsciously, merely by repetition of some action, or its repetition in some particular way. For example: a youngster has the habit of walking with his toes pointed inwards. He certainly did not intend the habit, and probably did not specifically choose that particular way to walk, either. He just did walk that way for quite some time, and eventually had the habit of doing so.

The moral character of an action done under the influence of a habit will depend on which of the three types of habit is in question. Deliberately acquired habits are voluntary in themselves (to use the terminology developed a few paragraphs ago): they are the direct object of the will's free choice. The actions that stem from these habits, then, are either also voluntary in themselves or, perhaps more often, voluntary in cause. Which of the latter two they are, makes little difference from the moral standpoint.

Habits that are not deliberately acquired as such, but that stem from deliberately chosen acts that are known to be habit-forming, are voluntary in cause. That is to say, in deliberately choosing the acts, I have also accepted their known consequences or effects. And so, the narcotics user is, indeed, morally responsible for contracting an addiction (and for the acts that stem from that addiction), even though he or she did not choose the addiction as such.

Unconscious habits are somewhat more complicated. As long as I am unaware of them, they (and the more or less unperceived actions that spring from them) are completely non-voluntary and consequently non-imputable. When, however, they do come to our attention, then one of two things will occur. Either (a) I decide, for good or bad reasons, to retain the habit. In that case the habit then becomes voluntary in itself, since I have deliberately chosen it, and actions stemming from it become either voluntary in themselves or voluntary in cause, as the case may be. Or (b) I choose to try to rid myself of the habit. In such a case, the morality of actions stemming from the habit, while I am in the process of trying to break it, will have to be judged individually in each case, with consideration being given to such factors as the degree of difficulty and effort required to overcome the habit in any given situation, the amount of urgency in my doing so, and so on.

6) Other factors

If necessary, one could point to several other factors that would modify the voluntary character of an action done with an actual or virtual intention: such things as sickness, sleepiness, pain, alcohol, drugs, abnormal mental states such as neuroses or psychoses, and the like. In all these cases, however, there is question either of something that can be judged on the same basis as one or more of the five modifying factors that we have seen thus far (ignorance, strong emotion, intellectual fear, force, or habit), or else of something that bears on the degree of knowledge of which we are capable in a particular situation. In the latter case, we have already seen the general rule: we can be responsible for something only to the degree to which we know it. Most cases, then, can be judged on those grounds.

This is perhaps the right time to return to a question that was raised (but not answered) earlier. What are we to say of the effect of environment on us? of past training? of our cultural milieu?--and so on and on. Do all of these things determine our actions, take away our freedom? In the last analysis, are we really conditioned, by a variety of factors, to do the things we do?

These are not frivolous questions. They have been seriously advanced as theories by some quite thoughtful people down through the ages. Nor are they the sorts of things that can be disposed of in a line or two--they are not straw men, vulnerable to the swift parry and thrust of a deft distinction or a slashing syllogism. The full answer to questions like these lies in a knowledge of where they came from, why they arose: in short, in the history of philosophy. And we are not pretending to do history of philosophy here. Nevertheless, some observations can and should be made about such questions, even at this point in our study of ethics.

First of all, there is no question but that our environment, our cultural milieu, and so on, *do* influence our thinking, do influence how we look upon things. Someone raised on a farm in Oregon will often have a quite different (not necessarily inferior, merely different) view of moral questions than will someone raised in the considerably more liberal atmosphere of a large city such as New York. Or, someone raised in a ghetto, struggling with poverty for most of his or her young life, will very likely have a quite different conception of the rights and wrongs of private property than will someone, say, raised in a wealthy family somewhere. We do tend to absorb into our thinking the values that we learn from people around us, whether these be parents, peers, religious figures, or what have you.

All of this, however, bears chiefly on where we find ourselves when we come to the study of ethics. It says very little about our ability to change our minds, to come to appreciate other points of view. It does say a number of things about the need for education, for exposure to the thinking of others who differ from us. It says a very great deal about the necessity of coming to form our own personal, reasoned point of view, based on our own thinking and effort and quite independent of whatever others (whoever they be) may say about these questions. It may be (because of our past training and associations) quite difficult for us to do this. But it is not impossible.

This, however, does not touch the basic assertion of someone who claims that we are fundamentally determined in our moral choices, for such a person thinks that, whatever we may *think* of our own situation, we are in fact morally determined long before we come to a study of ethics. This determination is a matrix, within which our very reasoning takes place: put in extreme form, we are, as it were, determined to believe that we are not determined.

That, of course, is a "no-win" assertion. And if it be true, then anyone attempting to do ethics is simply wasting time. But one can challenge such a claim, radically and pointedly. Does it square with our experience? For philosophy (of which ethics is a part) is--if it is anything--a reasoned explanation of our own experience. For someone to make the assertion (as the conclusion of a particular reasoning process) that I do not in fact have some experience which I know perfectly well that I do have: this is to get things backwards, to misconstrue completely the nature and function of philosophy (and, for that matter, of human thought in general).

(There have been philosophers, particularly during the classical modern period, who have concluded that human beings do not know a number of things which they believe themselves to know. For example, it has been claimed (for very erudite reasons) that human knowledge is limited to material things, and that anything which cannot be seen, heard, measured, etc., cannot be known. In working through the history of philosophy,

one can certainly come to understand how such a conclusion might have been drawn. But that does not alter the fact that the conclusion flies in the face of our everyday experience. And one is justified in being highly suspicious of someone who asserts that, for reasons complicated and diverse, one simply cannot do some particular thing. The temptation is very strong simply to go right ahead and do that thing anyway, even in the face of the assertion that it cannot be done.

So also with ethics. There are philosophers who claim that ethics is an exercise in futility: there is no freedom, no "can"; therefore there is no "ought." Fair enough--but, as noted above, there are also philosophers in other areas who claim that there is no knowledge of non-material things, or at least no valid knowledge. Neither position squares with experience. For it is a fact that I experience myself as free--just as it is a fact that I experience myself as capable of knowing things that lie beyond the range of sensible particulars. If one wants to claim, for other reasons, that such experience is chimerical, one can of course certainly do so. But this is to run the risk of irrelevancy. I engage in philosophy because I want to explain the facts of my experience, not deny them.

It would be foolish, on the other hand, to claim that our experience is the touchstone of all truth. It isn't. Very often, we discover that our experience is partial, slanted, in need of interpretation and precision. If it were otherwise, there would be no need for education. But with all that being said, one would still be thoroughly justified in being very slow to accept the assertion that one's experience is totally wrong, chimerical. If, in the course of an investigation that I undertake to determine what some object of my experience, say, "X," is all about, I come to the conclusion that X doesn't even exist, I had better go slowly. For it was with the existence of X that I started the investigation in the first place. The suspicion becomes quite strong that there is something wrong with the investigation, rather than with X, in such a case. It is conceivable that there is no X, to be sure. But the proof for that had better be overwhelmingly convincing. And--to return to our present case--when X turns out to be human freedom, about all that one can honestly say is that the proof for X's non-existence has, thus far in history at any rate, been rather underwhelmingly demonstrated.)

SUMMARY OF CHAPTER THREE

From a moral point of view, an imputable act includes the physical action, the motive (the "why"), and the circumstances (the "who," "what," "where," "how," and "when"); all three elements must be good if the imputable act is to be good. Such an act also includes the characteristics of voluntariness (= it is deliberately willed), attributability (= it can be referred to the agent as properly his/her own, for good or ill--but only as that agent knew the act), and meritoriousness (= there exists a relationship between the act and the [dis]approval of the agent's community, expressed tangibly). Some imputable actions are performed under an actual intention (my intention consciously influences my performance of the act while I am performing it), others under a virtual intention (my intention was made and not revoked, but I am not conscious of it while performing the act--which act, however, is completed). One can also speak of an habitual and an interpretative intention, though these are rarely of interest to ethics.

The level of voluntariness of an act (and therefore also its attributability and meritoriousness) can be influenced by several factors: (i) Ignorance is the lack of knowledge which I should have. Invincible (= morally insuperable) ignorance destroys voluntariness and hence moral responsibility. Vincible ignorance (= ignorance that can reasonably be overcome) lessens responsibility; and affected (= deliberately chosen) ignorance may even increase responsibility by adding malice to the act. (ii) Very strong emotion, when it is antecedent (i.e., preceding any act of choice on our part in its regard) can, in rare cases, completely take away responsibility; usually, it simply lessens it. When consequent (i.e., deliberately chosen), it does not lessen and may even increase responsibility. (iii) When an action is done out of (as opposed to with) intellectual fear, liberty is lessened and hence so is responsibility. (iv) Force, or the use of physical power to make someone do something against his/her will, destroys responsibility, unless consent is yielded. (v) Habit, or the constant way of acting acquired by the repetition of some act, can be something deliberately acquired; if so, an action done out of the habit is voluntary in cause. If the habit is not deliberately acquired, but the act leading to the habit is knowingly and willingly performed, then an action stemming from that habit is voluntary in cause. Unconscious habits, as long as they are unconscious, result in non-imputable acts; when they become known, they generate actions that are either voluntary in themselves or must be judged individually, depending on whether I do or do not choose to retain the habit of which I have become aware. (vi) Other factors can usually be reduced to one of the preceding five or else bear on the degree of knowledge available in a particular situation. Our environment and cultural milieu do influence how we look upon things; but they do not prevent us from being able to alter the views we have acquired from them. And moral determinism, though sometimes asserted, does not square with experience and has yet to be convincingly demonstrated.

4. CONSEQUENCES OF IMPUTABLE ACTS

II. The Theoretical Part of Ethics
  A. The First Question: what is human conduct?
    8. Imputable actions with more than one effect
      a. The four conditions of the Principle of
         the Double Effect
      b. Meaning and scope of these conditions
      c. Examples of the use of the Principle
    9. Imputable acts causing others' actions:
       the question of "scandal"
      a. Meaning of
        1) Consciously causing others' acts
          a) And willing to do so (as end, as means)
          b) Without willing to do so
        2) Non-consciously causing others' acts
      b. The morality of each of these
    10. Joining others in performing imputable acts: the
        question of co-operation in evil
      a. Meaning of formal and material co-operation
      b. Morality of formal and material co-operation

Imputable actions, as we have seen, can be quite complicated items, by the time that we get through looking at the interplay of intellect and will; at physical action, motivation, circumstances; at voluntareity, attributability, merit; at various factors that can affect the degree of voluntariness that an imputable action can have. Alas, that is not the end of the story of such actions' complicatedness.

8. Imputable actions with more than one effect

Many of our actions are further complicated in that they result in more than one thing, i.e., they have more than one effect. For example, I may seek recreation by driving my dune buggy over very rough terrain. One effect of my doing so is that I do, indeed, get the recreation I seek. Another effect is that my tires get battered by the rough ground, and it costs me a considerable sum of money to replace them. Or, I may seek a break by taking a walk. I take my walk, and I do get my recreation. I am also consequently away from my desk, and I miss an important phone call.

Now, this feature of human action poses no ethical problem as long as both of the effects are morally good or at least neutral. I may legitimately drive my dune buggy, provided that I am willing to put up with the damage to my tires; I may take my walk, provided that I am willing to risk missing the phone call. The situation gets much thornier, however, when one or more of the consequences of an action that I am planning would be harmful to me or to someone else. For example, a doctor seeks to restore his patient's health through surgery; but he also causes pain in the process. Two effects, one good (the restoration of health), one evil (pain). Or, another somewhat classic example, again from the world of medicine: the excision of a diseased uterus results in the halt of a cancer and the restoration of the patient's health; it also results in the death of the fetus that happens to be in that uterus.

(For purposes of shorthand, in this discussion we will be referring to the "good effect" and the "evil effect" of an action. We need to be aware that we have not yet discussed the meaning of the term "evil." We shall, at a later point. For this discussion, however, our intuitive idea of what "evil" means--something that is bad, for me or others, in some sense--will be adequate, provided that we recognize that the notion needs [and will receive] a more precise meaning.)

Illustrations could be multiplied. The point, however, is that very, very many of our actions have multiple effects, some of them evil. Our question will be: under what circumstances can we legitimately allow these evil effects to take place?

The basis of our answer will be this: while (for reasons that will become clearer later on) we may never intend evil, either as an end or as a means, we are not therefore bound to *prevent* evil from happening in all cases. The reason for this is obvious enough: to be thus obligated would create a far worse evil than all the evils we're trying to avoid, since it would for all intents and purposes make human life impossible.

With all that as prelude, we come to the Principle of the Double Effect. This principle states that, given the fulfillment of four conditions--*all four*--an action with at least one good effect and with one or more evil effects may legitimately be performed.

Let us first just list the four conditions. Then we shall examine them briefly, and finally will make use of some examples so as to see the Principle of Double Effect in action.

a. The four conditions of the Principle of Double Effect

The four conditions, then, are:

> (1) The action itself must be morally good or at least morally indifferent (neither good nor evil);

> (2) The good effect must not be obtained *through* the evil effect, i.e., *by means of* the evil effect;

> (3) The evil effect must not be intended, but rather only tolerated;

> (4) There must be a sufficiently serious reason to justify allowing the evil effect.

Some comments, now, may be useful about each of these four conditions. What, exactly, do they mean? And what justifies us in laying them down?

b. Meaning and scope of these conditions

In the first condition, when we speak of the "action," we are referring, not merely to the physical action, but to the complete, imputable human act: physical action, motive, and circumstances, but without specific consideration of its consequences (which are the proper scope of all four of the conditions). Thus, to refer back to an earlier example, when the hunter aims his rifle at a deer and fires, the action in question is "shooting a deer." If there is question of the same hunter, but performing the same action outside of the hunting season, then the action is "poaching a deer." If, in the same example, a fellow hunter is accidentally the target, the action is "accidentally shooting a fellow human being." In no one of these cases is it sufficient to say, simply, that the action is "aiming a rifle and pulling the trigger"--because, again, three quite different imputable actions can be represented by that one physical act, and the morality of those actions (as also the morality of their consequences) may well differ in each case.

On the other hand, it should be noted that very few imputable actions are, in and of themselves, morally evil: blasphemy and voluntary suicide are such, but there are not many others.

53

(Murder is also usually viewed as an intrinsically evil act, and, indeed, it is. But this is a slightly different matter, for it is a case of definition: murder is *defined* as the deliberate and unjustified killing of an innocent human being. The addition of the adjectives "deliberate" and "unjustified" to the definition is what gives murder its specific moral character.) If an action is morally evil in itself, it may never be performed, under any circumstances; by the nature of the case, to perform it is to embrace evil, for whatever reason or in whatever circumstances one may choose to do so. Generally speaking, however, the presumption will be that the action in question will be morally good or at least neutral--that is to say, there will be at least some limiting circumstances in which that action could legitimately be taken.

Secondly: in asserting that the good effect may not be obtained *by means of* the evil effect, we are simply saying that one may not use an evil means to achieve a good effect--no matter how much good may thereby be achieved. For it makes little difference whether we choose evil as a means or as an end: we are still choosing evil, and that is the essence of immorality. The point is worth insisting on, for it goes completely against the sort of pragmatist thinking that pervades our own culture. We are liable to feel, for example, that telling just a little lie is all right, provided that great good can come of it. But that is to misconstrue the nature of evil, which is not a matter of weights and measures. Of this, we shall see more in the chapters to come.

Next, in saying that the evil effect may not be intended but rather only tolerated, we are repeating the same moral principle: we may not intend evil, as a means or as a consequence or effect. We do not, indeed, necessarily have to take means to prevent its occurrence; but we may not positively will its happening.

Finally, in stating that there must be sufficient reason for allowing the evil effect, we are merely maintaining that there must be some proportion between the good that we expect to get out of our action and the evil that will follow in the wake of that action. This is but a specific instance of the general ethical principle that we must always act reasonably, rationally. Of this, again, a great deal more will be said later on; but for the moment, our "individual-in-the-street" approach will be enough: it is not reasonable, in general, to allow a great evil to occur simply so that we can derive some minor good. Conversely, a minor (and in some cases not so minor) evil may be tolerated if the good that is the positive effect of an action is strong enough.

In the examples that follow, we will see some illustrations of sufficient and insufficient reason. Even at this point, however, an observation could be made that bears, not simply on the Principle of Double Effect, but upon many aspects of ethics. Very frequently, the judgment as to whether an action is morally justified or not is precisely that: a human judgment, and a potentially fallible one. It is possible that a person, making an ethical judgment, and using both solid principles and all the reasoning power at his or her command, will nevertheless come up with a judgment that is objectively wrong. That is inevitable, for we are dealing with human judgments, and human beings are prone to making mistakes, even with the best of will. The remark was made earlier in this book (P. 8) that ethics strives to come up with principles that will govern 100% of the morality of human actions. That remains perfectly true. But it also needs at least two qualifications. First, as stated, this aim of ethics is an ideal, and one that is not always achieved in practice. Secondly, even the ideal concerns *principles,* not the application of those principles to individual, concrete cases. When the question of the application of those principles comes up, then the possibility of error enters in strongly, for the person doing the application is a very fallible human being. Whatever else it is, ethics is not some sort of calculus that will infallibly enable every human being to make an objectively correct ethical judgment about the morality of every conceivable imputable act.

Moreover, it is very possible for two quite intelligent human beings, judging the same ethical situation on the same principles, to come up with quite disparate judgments on that situation's morality. Objectively speaking, one will be right and the other wrong (or else both will be wrong); but both cannot be right, if their conclusions are contradictory. There is, after all, such a thing as objective truth. None the less, whatever their disagreement in the theoretical order, it still remains possible for both of our disagreeing ethicians to act morally in that situation--as we shall see when we discuss the matter of conscience, later in this book.

c. Examples of the use of the Principle

Now let us turn to some examples of the Double Effect Principle at work. As a prelude to this, though, we should realize that it is very necessary to determine, clearly and in advance, the answers to the following questions, prior to seeing whether the four conditions of the Principle are or are not verified: (1) What is the action in question? (2) What is (are) the good effect(s)? (3) What is (are) the evil effect(s)? (When first working with the Principle of Double Effect, it is good to force oneself to make these preliminary distinctions explicitly; later on, given some practice, we will find that we do so automatically.)

EXAMPLE #1: A man rushes into a burning house, having seen that there is a child stranded near a third-floor window. He succeeds in saving the child, but loses his own life in the process. Is he justified in doing this?

(1) Preliminary: This example is an old chestnut, showing up in nearly every ethics book ever written. None the less, it is useful, for it is clear. The action in question is: running into a burning building to save a child. The good effect: saving the child's life. The evil effect: the man's losing his own life.

(2) Analysis:

(a) The action itself is morally good or at least indifferent. (There certainly are some circumstances in which it is legitimate to run into a burning building. Firemen do so, for instance, not only legitimately but laudably.)

(b) The good effect is not achieved by means of the evil effect: the child is saved, not by the man's death, but by being thrown out the window to the firemen below.

(c) The evil effect is not intended: the man does not intend to commit suicide; in fact, he will do everything possible to avoid this, while still saving the child.

(d) There is sufficient reason for allowing the evil consequence: a life for a life.

(3) Conclusion: since all four conditions are met, the action in question is morally licit.

EXAMPLE #2: I am a military commander, in charge of field operations in a given area in time of war. There is an enemy ammunition dump located in my sector. I know that if I order it bombed, a great source of danger to my men will be removed; on the other hand, a number of people in the area (enemy soldiers, but also some civilians) will be killed. May I order the bombing?

(1) Preliminary: the action is: ordering a bombing. The good effect is: the destruction of a major threat. The evil effect: the loss of numerous lives, including civilian ones.

(2) Analysis:

(a) The action itself is at least morally indifferent. (It may be repugnant to some, but that is another question altogether. Again, if an action itself is morally evil, it may never be done, for whatever reason; and certainly there can be times when ordering a bombing is legitimate.)

(b) The good effect is not achieved through the evil effect. (The threat is eliminated by the destruction of the ammunition dump, not by the death of the bystanders.)

(c) The evil effect is not intended, but merely permitted.

(d) There is sufficient reason for permitting the evil: the commander can reasonably assume that the ammunition dump will ultimately cost his side at least as many lives as its destruction will cost the enemy.)

(3) Conclusion: again, since all four conditions are verified, the action is licit.

EXAMPLE #3: I am a physician, specializing in OB-GYN. One of my patients has a cancerous uterus, and is pregnant. She also has eight other children and no husband, and the last thing she needs is one more mouth to feed. I can certainly take care of this latter problem for her; in surgery, I remove the uterus and child, destroying both. Am I justified?

(1) Preliminary: This case is a variant on another old classic. The action in question: surgical removal of a diseased organ. The good effect:

restoration of health, i.e., the halt of a potentially spreading cancer. The evil effect: the death of the fetus within the uterus.

(2) Analysis:

(a) The action is morally good or at least indifferent.

(b) The good effect (restoration of health, stopping the cancer) is not achieved by means of the evil effect (the death of the fetus), but rather by the removal of the uterus.

(c) The evil effect, however, is intended by the surgeon.

(d) There is sufficient reason for the action (ultimately, the preservation of the mother's life).

(3) Conclusion: since condition #3 is not met, the action is not morally justified. (Notice that condition #3 failed, in this case, simply because the physician did in fact intend to kill the fetus. It would be quite possible to have a case--indeed, the classic statement of this particular case is usually phrased to illustrate just this--in which the physician had no such intention, but rather intended only the halt of the cancer. In that case, the action would be justified. One and the same physical act--but intending the evil effect or not intending it makes a large difference in the moral quality of the two instances.)

For some, it may not be immediately clear why step (b) is true. The following may help. Suppose that, despite all odds, the fetus managed to live (via respirators and other medical means) after the uterus was excised--something that is conceivable even if not particularly likely. The good effect, however (the restoration of the mother's health) would still occur--which means that the good effect was not caused by the evil effect (the death of the fetus), since, in this case, the fetus didn't die.

EXAMPLE #4: I am a political activist, of a quite radical bent. I am profoundly disturbed by certain activities of my government, which I feel are seriously injuring people in other lands. But no one seems to be paying any attention to this. To dramatize my cause, having first alerted the local TV and radio stations, I go to the Capitol Building, pour gasoline all over my clothes, and set myself on fire in protest. I know that I will be gravely injured or possibly killed. My protest--and therefore my cause--certainly do receive all sorts of publicity. But I end up in the emergency room of the local hospital with third-degree burns over 60% of my body. Was I justified in doing this?

(1) Preliminary: The action is: setting myself on fire for political reasons. The good effect is: dramatization of what I feel to be a just and worthy cause. The evil effect: serious injury to my own health.

(2) Analysis:

(a) The action (setting myself on fire) is certainly morally questionable. But there could, perhaps, be certain circumstances that might render it at least morally indifferent.

(b) The good effect (dramatization of my cause) is indeed achieved by the evil effect (my own serious injury)

(c) The evil effect is intended, at least implicitly: if I deliberately take an action that will inevitably have a given effect, then I do intend that effect (it is, in other words, at least voluntary in cause).

(d) Sufficient reason is lacking: there are far less violent (and probably more effective) means available to achieve the end that I have in mind.

(3) Conclusion: since conditions #2, #3, and #4 are not met, the action is not morally justified. (In passing, we might note that, once condition #2 failed, I could have halted my analysis, since *all four* conditions have to be met. In this example, then, whether conditions #3 and #4 are or are not met is really a moot point.)

EXAMPLE #5: Miss LaTour, a famous movie star, is actually Mamie McNally, a former call girl from Boston's Back Bay area. No one in Hollywood knows this, however--no one, that is to say, save Spike O'Malley. Mr. O'Malley has threatened to reveal all unless his silence is handsomely recompensed. Miss LaTour has worked hard to achieve her new status and feels that this situation is most unfair. She contracts with Mr. L. Diamond to do a small chore for her in Mr. O'Malley's regard. Mr. Diamond sees to it that Mr. O'Malley's tongue is cut out and both of his hands amputated, thus ensuring his silence in both speech and writing. Miss LaTour's reputation is thus safe. "A little rough," thinks Miss LaTour, "but he had no right to blackmail me, so it serves him right." Is Mr. Diamond's action (for which Miss LaTour contracted, and for which she is therefore responsible) justified?

(1) Preliminary: The action is: amputation of tongue and hands. The good effect: preservation of Miss LaTour's reputation. The evil effect: the deprivation of the power of speech and writing on Mr. O'Malley's part.

(2) Analysis:

(a) The action of cutting out Mr. O'Malley's tongue and amputating his hands is at least not immediately evil in itself; there could be (in other circumstances, at least) good surgical reasons for performing these actions. (Remember that if an action is evil in itself, then there are no reasons for which it can be justifiably done.)

(b) The good effect, however, is precisely realized by means of the evil effect: the reason why Miss LaTour's reputation is safe is that Mr. O'Malley has suffered the ill effects of Mr. Diamond's ministrations.

(c) Whether the evil effect is intended or not is moot, since the second condition has not been met. (In fact, however, the evil effect is indeed intended, and so the third condition would fail also.)

(d) Whether or not there is sufficient reason

is also moot, since condition #2 (and condition #3, for that matter) have not been met. In point of fact, condition #4 would not be met either; surely there has to be some less drastic way of handling the situation than this!

(3) Conclusion: Mr. Diamond's action (and therefore Miss LaTour's, in contracting for it) is immoral, since conditions #2, #3, and #4 are not met.

We have seen that our actions can have more than one effect, one of which can be evil. And we have looked at the moral principle that governs actions like this. This has been one way of viewing the consequences of our actions.

9. Imputable acts causing others' actions: the question of "scandal"

But, while we are on the subject, it may pay us to look at the consequences of our own actions in a different light. For some things we do or say cause other human beings, in their turn, to act. In fact, in many cases others' actions are contingent upon ours, in the sense that if we had not done what we did, they in turn would not have done what they did. And so it may be appropriate for us to look briefly at the responsibility that we might have for the actions of other people, when those actions are caused by our own.

An example may help. I walk down the street, wearing the latest fashion in, say, hats. Another person sees me, admires the hat, determines to get one too, and proceeds to do so. That person might never have gotten that hat if it hadn't been for my wearing what I did on that particular day. In a sense, I have "caused" that person to buy a particular style of hat.

The example is innocent enough. But there can be cases that are anything but innocent. For example: suppose that I am an eighteen-year-old, and am walking down the street with my thirteen-year-old sister. I take out a marijuana cigarette, light it, and proceed to get pleasantly "high." My sister watches me, and decides that she should do the same thing, when she can, since I, whom she admires very much, evidently think that it is a "smart," an "in" thing to do. She might well never have made

61

that decision had she not seen me light up the marijuana. Or: suppose that I am the father of a family, and it is income-tax time. I discuss with my wife--in the hearing of our two teen-age children--what ways (legal and illegal) there might be to beat the Internal Revenue Service; and we decide on an illegal way. Our children hear us, of course; and in the backs of their minds is implanted the notion to do the same, once they are in our situation--a decision, again, that they might well never have made had they not heard us doing so.

What we do or say, then, can influence the actions of other people. To use the time-honored term, this is the question (when our actions lead others to do evil, at any rate) of "scandal."

Let us first distinguish between two general types of our actions that influence others. (a) First, there are acts that we do which we *know* will influence others. (b) And then, of course, there are actions whose effects on others we do not know, and which we might or might not reasonably guess.

a. Meaning of: 1) consciously causing others' acts

To examine briefly the first type: one of two things will have to be true. Either (i) I know that my action will influence another person's action and I will that that should be the case; or (ii) I know that this will happen, but I do not intend that it should--rather, I merely allow it.

a) And willing to do so (as end, as means)

(i) Suppose, then, I know that my action will influence someone else's action, and I intend that that should be the case. For example, I am the author of a liquor advertisement in a commercial magazine, and I write good ads. I know that someone, somewhere, is going to read my ad, and then go out and buy a bottle of the particular brand of Scotch that I am advocating. Moreover, I intend that this should happen--else why write the ad?

Again, this is innocent enough; there is nothing particularly wrong in influencing someone to go out and buy a particular brand of Scotch. But the matter gets more serious, from a moral point of view, when my action leads someone to do something immoral, and I intend that it should have just that effect. For example, let us suppose that I am running a brothel. By my "advertising," I certainly do intend that people should commit immoral acts.

We can get more precise. Suppose that I know my actions will lead others to evil, and suppose that I want that to happen. One of two things has to be going on in my mind. First, maybe I simply want these others to become bad people: I just want to corrupt them, for one reason or other (say, because their level of moral goodness offends me). Obviously, this isn't something that I would do very often, for it would be truly diabolical; nevertheless, this sort of thing can (and does) happen. It is an instance of willingly causing another's evil action *as an end:* I have no further purpose in mind. Secondly, maybe I don't particularly want these other people to become corrupt, but I do want something else I'll get if they perform certain evil actions. The example of the brothel, cited above, is an instance of this: the madam running the place certainly intends that her customers perform evil acts (adultery or fornication), not specifically so that they will become morally corrupt, but rather so that they will pay her money for her services in providing the opportunity for their escapades. Another instance might be a rabble-rousing political orator who fires up his or her audience so that they will rush out and start a destructive riot. The orator knows (and intends) what will happen. But he or she isn't particularly interested in simply corrupting the audience; rather, the idea is that certain political aims will be furthered by means of the riot. The madam and the orator are examples of willingly causing another's evil action *as a means* to some further goal, rather than as an end in itself.

b) Without willing to do so

(ii) Then there is the other type of action which I perform, knowing--but *not* intending--that it may well cause evil actions on the part of other people. A graphic (if somewhat outrageous) example of this is the bishop who attends an X-rated movie, knowing well that some of his flock could see and recognize him. His intention--whatever else it may be--is certainly not to influence the members of his flock to see the movie. But he is aware that, if some of them see him doing so, they could be led to do likewise.

Some of my actions, then, cause other people to do things, and this with my knowing it. Sometimes I will my actions to have that effect; sometimes I merely recognize that they are likely to do so, but I do not positively intend that they should.

2) Non-consciously causing others' acts

Then there is the situation in which I do some particular thing, and I do not know (or else, perhaps, at most merely guess) that other people will be influenced by it to do something evil on their part. For example, a business executive takes his secretary out to lunch. Someone who sees them at lunch is led--for reasons quite peculiar to the viewer--to take malicious delight in the executive's cheating on his wife (which, in fact, he is not doing), and to spread all sorts of gossip about the impending breakup of his marriage. The executive, of course, is completely unaware of all this; he is merely hungry, or he wants to get some additional office work done over the lunch table, or he wants to honor his secretary on her birthday, or some such. At all events, he has no idea that his innocent action is having the results that it is.

These, then, are the types of cases in which our actions can influence others to perform evil acts. Let us summarize them and put names on them; then we shall consider their morality.

The entire process whereby an action of mine leads someone else to perform an evil act, we shall call an "occasion of evil." There are two main types, depending on whether I do or do not *know* that my action will have this particular effect:

a) I know that my action will cause someone else to perform an evil act:

(i) and I intend that it should have that effect, either as an end in itself (i.e., solely in order to corrupt some other person morally), or else as a means to some other goal that I wish to achieve. Let us call this a *direct, conscious* occasion of evil;

(ii) and I do not intend that it should have that effect, though I foresee that it will probably do so even though I may not wish it to. This we shall call an *indirect, conscious* occasion of evil.

b) I do not know, and do not necessarily even guess (although I might) that my action will have such an effect. This we shall call a *non-conscious* occasion of evil.

b. The morality of each of these

What, then, should be said about the morality of actions such as these?

First, as regards the two types of conscious occasion of evil: (i) in the case of a *direct, conscious* occasion, I am completely responsible for this. I do, in fact, intend the evil action on the other person's part, whether as an end or as a means. My action is immoral, for intending evil is precisely what is meant by immorality. Thus, the brothel madam's advertising is immoral; so is the rabble-rousing orator's speech. (ii) In the case of an *indirect, conscious* occasion, I may or may not be responsible for the other person's action (and so I may or may not be morally guilty). This is exactly the sort of situation that is envisioned in the Principle of Double Effect, and its morality must be judged in accord with that principle.

In the case of the *non-conscious* occasion of evil, a distinction will have to be drawn. If the other person is led to do evil in such a case sheerly because of his or her own malice, then I have no responsibility for the subsequent evil action; the person could and should know better. In the case of the executive's taking his secretary to lunch, for example: the person observing them has no legitimate cause to draw the inference which he or she does, and makes the rash judgment merely because of malice--i.e., he or she is simply a gossip who is usually prone to suspect the worst. Morally speaking, that is the gossip's problem, not the executive's. However, when the other person is led by my action to do evil because of his or her inexperience, weakness, youthfulness, or something of that order, then something else enters the picture and must be considered. For charity toward our fellow human beings requires (even if justice does not) that, when possible, we refrain from words or actions (even quite innocent ones) that would be a source of damage to the weak. Once again, the Principle of Double Effect would be the instrument for judging the morality of any such situation.

10. Joining others in performing imputable acts: the question of co-operation in evil

The influence of our actions on others brings to mind another question. What happens when we not merely cause the actions of others by our own acts, but actually join with them (willingly or otherwise) in the performance of some act (an evil act, for our purposes)?

To illustrate: suppose there are two bank robbers, one of whom actually sticks up the teller and the other of whom drives the get-away car. Now, in one sense, the driver of the car limits his or her activity to driving: he or she does not actually hold up the bank. Is the driver guilty of the robbery? Or, to take another case: two people kidnap a child. I am not one of the two, and, in fact, am many miles away when the kidnapping takes place. However, I lend my car to the kidnappers, knowing full well what use they plan to make of it. Am I guilty of kidnapping? For, after all, I certainly had no part in the kidnapping itself. Or, yet a third example: a bank manager, under the threat of a robber's gun, opens the safe and enables the robber to have access to the money--which the thief could not get without the manager's help. Is the bank manager guilty of robbery, in any sense?

This whole question is one that is usually called "co-operation in evil." But, as can readily be seen from the examples we have considered, we instinctively feel that there are quite different sorts of co-operation, with quite different sorts of moral responsibility in each case. And that instinctive feeling is correct.

a. Meaning of formal and material co-operation

In general, we can distinguish two quite different kinds of co-operation in evil. (a) First, there is the sort of co-operation in which I intend to take part (directly or indirectly) in another person's evil action, and I do so. To use the traditional terminology, let us call this *formal* co-operation in evil. The illustration of the driver of the get-away car, and of the lender of the kidnappers' vehicle, cited above, are instances of this: in each case, the person involved intends to take part in the evil action of someone else. (b) Then there is what is traditionally called *material* co-operation in evil: a situation in which I do not intend to take part in someone else's evil act, and I do not approve of that act, but yet I knowingly aid that evil action by some action of my own which is not itself evil. The bank manager, opening the safe under threat of a gun, is an illustration of this: he obviously does not intend to rob his own bank, nor does he approve of the robbery; but he does aid the theft by his own action--in itself innocent--of opening the safe. (He is, of course, under some duress to perform that innocent action.) Another example of material co-operation might be this: I am an assistant manager of a food-processing plant, part of whose sales are to a third-world country. I know that a certain product which my company sells is bad for the health of the people in that country. Specifically, I know that if I approve a certain shipment, a number of pregnant women are going to suffer some very dire consequences during their pregnancies. I also know, of course, that if I do not approve the shipment, I will be fired and someone else, with a less delicate conscience, perhaps, will soon be in my place and will indeed approve the shipment. I don't intend the suffering of these women, nor do I approve of it--but, at the moment at least, without my signature that shipment isn't going to leave the plant that produced it.

b. Morality of formal and material co-operation

What of the morality of actions such as these? Again, we will need to keep in mind the distinction between formal and material co-operation: between co-operation directly intended and co-operation not intended but supplied anyway, for some reason (usually fear).

First, as regards formal co-operation: if I intend an evil act, whether I am the principal agent or merely a subsidiary means, I am still in the position of willing evil, which, as has been said, is the essence of immorality. In such cases, my actions are immoral, and cannot be justified under any pretense whatever. The driver of the get-away car is as guilty of robbery as is the actual stick-up man himself; the willing lender of the kidnap car is as guilty of the crime as are the individuals who perform the actual kidnapping. In each case, everyone involved intended evil, and therefore everyone involved has committed an evil act.

Things get much less simple, however, when there is question of material co-operation in evil. Again, the general moral principle governing the morality of the action is the Principle of Double Effect; and the particular emphasis that such a case gives to the Principle bears on the strength required in the sufficient reason (condition #4). Some considerations can be offered that will be helpful in determining whether a sufficient reason is truly present that would justify material co-operation. One needs to consider, for example, the amount of evil that my co-operation enables to take place--less reason would be needed to justify a robbery of a grocery store than would be required in the case of a break-in at Ft. Knox. Then, one should consider the amount of evil that will come to me if I *don't* co-operate. It is one thing if the consequence of my non-cooperation is a knock on the head; it is

67

another if it means that I will be shot, leaving behind destitute my wife and ten children. Finally, consideration has to be given to the degree of proximity between my act and the other person's evil act. In the writing and publication of a pornographic article in a magazine, for instance: (a) the author is, of course, the *doer* of the evil deed; (b) the publisher is a *formal co-operator:* he or she intends that the pornographic article should be published; (c) the typesetters, proof-readers, and so on, are *material, proximate co-operators* (without their co-operation, even unwilled, the article will not see the light of day, or else will do so in unacceptable fashion); and (d) the pressmen, binders, delivery truck drivers, etc., are *material, remote co-operators*--their degree of involvement is much less knowledgeable, much less deliberate.

Some norms will be useful. However, even given these, it will be instantly obvious that a goodly scope is left for a prudential judgment on the part of anyone trying to judge the morality of material co-operation. And so, disagreement, if found, will not be particularly surprising. Such, after all, is the human condition.

In general, the more proximate the material co-operation, the greater or stronger the sufficient reason must be in order to satisfy condition #4 of the Double Effect Principle. The proofreader needs more of a sufficient reason than does the delivery truck driver, to continue our example. Also, the more indispensable to the potential evil that I am, the greater the sufficient reason required: if I am the only one with the combination to the safe, I need greater reason to justify opening it for the thief than would be the case if, say, four or five other people in the office also knew that combination. Finally, the more I have an explicit duty to prevent the evil, the greater the reason needed to justify my material co-operation: a policeman needs greater justification than an average citizen would when there is question of material co-operation with criminals; customs inspectors need greater justification for co-operating with smugglers than would ordinary travelers; and so on.

A backward glance may be useful here, for we have now answered the first of the three major questions that occupy us in the theoretical part of ethics: what do we mean by human conduct? We have seen that human conduct, as ethics is interested in it, means imputable activity, actions done with knowledge and will. We looked at the complex internal structure of an imputable act, i.e., an act of choice. We examined what we mean by an "intellect" and a "will," and some of the evidence for their existence as distinctively human powers. We looked at the question of the freedom of the will. Then we examined an imputable act in some detail, looking at its total make-up (physical action, motive[s], circumstances), and its chief characteristics (voluntareity, attributability, merit). We investigated factors that can influence the level of voluntareity (types of intention, ignorance, strong emotion, fear, force, habit). Then we looked at the consequences of some imputable acts, i.e., the possibility that some of them can have more than one effect, that some of our acts can influence the actions of others, that our actions can be conjoined, morally, with others' acts in various ways.

Two other major questions remain to be treated in theoretical ethics. What do we mean by "good" and "evil"? (Thus far, we have simply taken these meanings for granted.) And: how do you tell whether any given action is good or evil? To these questions we must now turn.

SUMMARY OF CHAPTER FOUR

Some actions have more than one effect, one of which is evil. This evil effect can sometimes be morally permissible, since, while we may never intend evil, we are not always bound to prevent it from happening. When this is permissible is a matter governed by the Principle of Double Effect, which states that when all four of the following conditions are fulfilled, an action with both one (or more) good effects and one (or more) evil effects may be performed: (i) the imputable action must itself be morally good or at least morally indifferent; (ii) the good effect must not be obtained by means of the evil effect; (iii) the evil effect must not be intended but rather only tolerated; (iv) there must be a sufficient reason for permitting the evil effect(s). A judgment made on the basis of this principle is a human--and therefore fallible--one. Prior to using the principle, one should clearly determine three things: (a) what is the action in question? (b) what is the good effect? (c) what is the evil effect?

Sometimes our actions can cause other people to do immoral things that they would not have done otherwise. This (called "occasion of evil" or "scandal") can happen in several ways: (a) I know that my action will cause this, and I intend that it should happen, either as an end in itself or as a means to some further end; in this case, I am morally responsible for causing the other person to act immorally. (b) I know that my action will cause this, but I don't intend to cause the other person to act immorally. I may or may not be responsible for the other's evil; this is a Double Effect situation. (c) I don't know that my action will have this effect, or I merely suspect it. In this case, I ordinarily have no responsibility for the other's action, unless charity imposes an obligation on me to refrain from acting (e.g., when the other person is young, inexperienced, etc.).

On other occasions, I sometimes (willingly or otherwise) join with others in the performance of an evil act. This "co-operation in evil" can take different forms: (a) I intend to take part in the other's evil act ("formal co-operation"); here, since I intend evil, my action is evil. (b) I don't intend to take part in another's evil act, but I knowingly aid that evil act by some act of my own which is not itself evil ("material co-operation"). The morality of this situation is decided by the Double Effect principle, with special attention being given to the question of sufficient reason; the more proximate my material co-operation, or the more indispensable to the potential evil I am, or the more I have an explicit duty to prevent the evil: the greater the sufficient reason required.

5. GOOD AND EVIL ACTS

II. The Theoretical Part of Ethics
   B. The Second Question: what is meant by "good"
     and "evil," i.e., "good acts" and "evil acts"?
     1. Extrinsic theories of morality
       a. Authoritarianism: informal and formal
       b. Pleasure-pain: formal and informal
       c. Others
       d. Questions that these raise
     2. An intrinsic theory of morality
       a. Preliminary tools needed
         1) Principle of final causality
           a) Ultimate and proximate goals
           b) Goal of the work and goal of the
             worker
           c) Establishing the principle
             (1) Some agents act for a goal
                (cognitive, non-cognitive)
             (2) All agents act for a goal
         2) Imputable actions always aimed at a
           goal that is not also a means
         3) Intrinsic relationship between act
           and end
         4) Subjective and objective orders
         5) The experiential fact of "oughtness"
       b. Stating the theory.

B. Second Question: what are "good" and "evil" acts?

In our discussion of human conduct so far, we have often used the words "good" and "evil." Reflecting on that, we notice that we have been operating on a non-defined, instinctive awareness of just what these words meant--which, for the purposes that we had in mind at the time, was all right. After all, one cannot do everything at one and the same time; some notions have to be studied after other ones, and very often the order in which these happen to be taken up is a matter of arbitrary choice.

Now, however, we do need to turn our attention explicitly to the meaning of "good" and "evil," and see in detail just what these mean. Let us ask the question specifically, however. It would, of course, be possible to speculate about "good in itself," or "evil in itself"; and Philosophy of Being does do just that, among other things. Ethics, however, is concerned with actions; and so our question will be: what is a good *act,* an evil *act?*

We can start this way. One of two things has to be true: either (a) an act is called "good" or "evil" because of something stemming from the very nature of the act, or (b) it is called "good" or "evil" because of something quite extrinsic to that act, something having nothing to do with that act's nature. For instance, either stealing is wrong because there is something disordered about the very nature of stealing, or else it is wrong simply and sheerly because, say, the society in which I live says that it is so. Depending on which of these two we choose, an action will be judged either on the basis of intrinsic morality or extrinsic morality.

It will be the contention of this book that an action's goodness or evil is something intrinsic, something stemming from the act itself. However, before we get into that, it will pay us to look at the opposite theory, at least briefly.

1. Extrinsic theories of morality

At the very first, a disclaimer. The paragraphs that follow will give only a thumbnail sketch of a few extrinsic theories, and they will make no pretense at all to completeness. The full treatment of extrinsic theories of morality belongs to the history of philosophy, for only there can their genesis be appreciated and their worth evaluated. Those who have advanced them are serious thinkers, and deserve to have their work taken seriously. The present writer does not happen to be convinced by those theories, but neither is he naive enough to think that they can be adequately explained (let alone refuted) in the few paragraphs available for the purpose in this book. Our purpose in even mentioning extrinsic theories is simply to point to their existence, and to contrast their nature with that of the intrinsic theory which will be advanced later in this chapter. Which type of theory the reader of this book will eventually adopt as his or her own, is the business of that reader; ethics is, again, one's own reasoned position on the morality of human actions, not a position that one merely acquires from someone else--whether that "someone else" be the writer of a textbook or a major figure in the history of philosophy.

a. Authoritarianism: informal and formal

The first type of theory that we might want to examine could be termed an "authoritarian" one, initially on an informal sort of level. In the very beginnings of serious thought on the matter, an external criterion of morality was very much operative. An act was right or wrong because the gods said so. Thus, for someone to become too prosperous, too good, too wealthy, etc., was seen (by the early Greeks) as an act of *hubris*: an action whereby one tried to be like the gods--who were notoriously unsympathetic toward humans that had aspirations to divine status. It made little difference whether the act in question seemed good or evil to the human performing it; it was forbidden by the gods, and therefore it was evil. Moreover, its evil character was backed up: the gods punished it, sometimes rather spectacularly.

The authoritarian theory is not merely an antiquarian view, something confined to the ancient Greeks. Each of us, in his or her own way, started our moral lives in the same fashion (albeit, perhaps, without the Greek gods). Something was right or wrong because our parents said that it was. Again, it made little difference whether we saw anything wrong with a particular forbidden act; it was *verboten,* and a trip to the woodshed lay in store for the unlucky child who chose to violate that prohibition.

Some people retain this view throughout their entire life. They look upon actions as being right or wrong because someone else tells them that they are. Obviously, parental authority passes out of the picture after some years' growth; but all too often, it is replaced by other, equally authoritarian, voices: peer pressure, the mores of the society in which we live, religious authorities, and so on. There is nothing particularly wrong with this, in and of itself; such authorities, of whatever nature, may well give us adequate guidance on moral questions. The problem with it, of course, is that it is the mode of operation proper to children--of whatever physical age those children happen to be.

The same general sort of theory can be found on a more formal philosophic level. Serious thinkers have maintained that an action is good or evil because others (whether the state or some less formalized entity) have so declared it. For example, there is the Social Contract theory: a notion, popularized chiefly by Thomas Hobbes (+1679), which held that, prior to the formation of the state, human beings lived in a state of nature that was also virtually a state of chaos. Every human being had the right to do whatever was to his or her advantage. Now, in such a situation, maintaining even a minimum quality of life--to say nothing of maintaining even life itself--proved to be difficult or even impossible; and so human beings invented the state, an entity to which each person surrendered some of his or her rights so as to be able to enjoy other rights. The state, however, existed not for the common good, but rather for providing a situation wherein each person could achieve the most for him/herself, within the limits imposed by the state. It is, then, the state that declares some actions obligatory and good (others prohibited and evil), chiefly on the basis of what is necessary to make human life possible at all. Prior to the organization of the state, however, there was no such thing as right and wrong.

The state is not the only thing that, in the history of thought, has been seen as having the power to declare what is right and what is wrong. In what could be called the Social Pressure theory, some other group apart from the state determines morality in accord with its own self-interest. The group, of course, varies according to what particular thinker happens to be in question: for Nietzsche (+1900), for example, morality is merely the means whereby the weaker keep the stronger (but less numerous) in check. Variants of this theory can be seen even in our own day, in the religious sphere, the political, the ideological, etc. (How often, for example, is something judged to be right or wrong because it fosters or hinders, say, the liberal point of view, or the conservative one.)

b. Pleasure-pain: formal and informal

Let us suppose, however, that one rejects the authoritarian approach (whether the authority be the state, parents, or some other). Another possibility then comes to mind: the pleasure-pain theory, wherein an action is good if it causes its author pleasure, and it is evil if it causes its author pain.

Depending on just whose pleasure or pain is in question, this theory takes two main historical forms. There is first hedonism: the pleasure or pain is only that of the individual performing the action, without regard to any impact the action may have on others. The first real reference in history to an hedonistic theory is in the work of Aristippus, an ancient Greek. He held that happiness consists in pleasure, simply: anything I do is good, if it produces pleasure for me; and anything I do is bad, if it produces pain for me. Moreover, the more pleasure an act produces, the better it is; conversely, the more pain it produces, the worse it is.

On the face of it, this is a little bit crass, and the theory was soon refined somewhat by another ancient Greek, Epicurus. In Epicureanism, the goal of life is not simply intense pleasure (in a crude, quantified sense), but a sort of abiding peace, a cheerful tranquillity of mind. It is true that the wise man regulates his life so as to get the greatest amount of pleasure and the least amount of pain; however, one must also take account of the fact that there are different *kinds* of pleasure, some of which are better than others. For Epicurus, intellectual pleasures were qualitatively better than sense pleasures, though one also needed sense pleasures for happiness. However, despite the distinction between quantified and qualified pleasures, an action was still deemed good or evil to the degree that it did or did not provide the best type of pleasure; and that life as a whole was good (as were the aggregate of actions leading thereto) that provided the maximum amount of the best quantitative and qualitative mix of pleasures.

Hedonism has been persistent throughout history, and we are not interested in trying to trace its entire course. But we should notice that it exists very strongly in our own culture, and in a sense that shows little advance over where it was when Epicurus finished with it. On an informal level, it takes only a superficial reading of the advertisements in the daily newspapers to show that, as a popular philosophy at any rate, the possession of the "good life" is the goal, and whatever leads to it is good, whatever leads away from it is evil. People actually do live their lives this way--that is good which enables them to "get ahead"; conversely, whatever hinders that advancement is evil. Nor is this confined to popular, unreflective thinking. There are contemporary philosophers too who consider the possession (or non-possession) of such things as health, friendship, contentment, etc., to be the criteria of good and evil. Some pleasures are to be sought more than others, some pains to be avoided more than others (Epicurus would have been very much at ease with this), but pleasure and pain are still the criteria of human action in much of our current culture.

There is also a somewhat more sophisticated sort of pleasure-pain theory. Supposing that the pleasure or pain in question is not limited to the individual, but is also seen to embrace the group in which one lives (and thus, the criterion of good or evil is the collective well-being [or ill-being] of the group): we are then dealing with Utilitarianism. Jeremy Bentham (+1832) and John Stuart Mill (+1873) are the classic names associated with this line of thought, though it--like hedonism--is by no means merely an historical curiosity. For Bentham, a sort of socially minded Aristippus, pleasure and pain are the sole motives that govern human beings, and personal pleasure and pain are dependent on the general happiness and prosperity of the group. An action is therefore good if it promotes the common welfare (and therefore also the personal advantage of the person performing the action); it is evil if it promotes the opposite. Mill, like Epicurus before him, recognized a qualitative difference in the various pleasures and pains. Given the hierarchy of pleasures, it is better to choose a smaller amount of a better pleasure than a greater amount of a lesser one--and the reverse in the case of pain. For Mill, the goal of human life is an existence as free from pain and as rich in pleasures (taken both quantitatively and qualitatively) as possible.

Utilitarianism is around today, too, at least in informal fashion. Commonly, that is seen to be good which fosters the well-being of the human race as a whole: the elimination of poverty, ignorance, and hunger, for example. That is evil which hinders or threatens that well-being (such as--in the view of some, anyway--excessive capitalism, exploitation, and, in an extreme sense, the nuclear arms race).

(Obviously, eliminating hunger and poverty, etc., is a good, and exploitation of other people and similar actions are evil. But it is one thing to say that something is a good (or an evil), and quite another to say that it is a criterion of good or evil, a touchstone determining the morality of actions fostering or hindering it. Utilitarianism, in its contemporary, popular guise, often makes the latter assertion, not merely the former.)

c. Others

So: authoritarianism (formal and informal) and pleasure/pain, with its two sub-headings of hedonism and utilitarianism (again, on both the philosophic and the informal level of thought): these are some of the theories of extrinsic morality that the history of human thought has produced. There are others. One might, for example, call an action "good" or "evil" to the extent that it is or is not in conformity with some ideal external model--to the extent, that is to say, that it is a good imitation of something else. Plato seems to have thought something like this, as have (in one way or other) the legion of Platonists who have succeeded him. Or, something is good because it somehow actually participates in the divine, evil because it does not: the number of people (quite serious thinkers and otherwise) who have opted for this possibility is beyond counting. Or, something is good if it furthers the advent of something else (say, a new social order), evil if it hinders it: Marxism in its various guises. And so on and on.

d. Questions that these raise

None the less, all of the extrinsic theories we have seen raise questions in our minds. An authoritarian theory, for example (whether the authority be parents, the state, or some other group): something like this may perhaps be very convenient for someone else, but what does it really say to me about the goodness or badness of my own actions? It is at least unsatisfying to say that the criterion for my actions ought to be the interests of someone else, whoever he or she may be. Granted, it is good to be aware of the interests, desires, and needs of others. But does it follow from this that I should regulate my whole life on that basis? Perhaps it does--but that is not immediately self-evident, to say the least.

Or, take the claim that pleasure is the end of life, the criterion of good and evil. Now, it is certainly true that people very often do act out of motives of gaining pleasure and avoiding pain. But do they always do so? A soldier remains at his post, despite considerable danger; does he do so out of motives of pleasure? A man sacrifices his life to save another person: does this give him pleasure? Surely not--for the good reason that, being dead, he is not around to enjoy the pleasure. Moreover, there remains the sneaking suspicion that there is more to human life than pleasure and pain. Of course, these two are large elements in human life. But do they control all our actions? It is difficult to think so. As Plato once hinted, human life is a good deal more than the life of an oyster.

If we wanted to, we could go through the various extrinsic theories and examine them at some length. We could, for instance, spend some time considering the nature of pleasure. In doing so, we would see that pleasure is always associated with activity: if no activity on our part, then no pleasure. But pleasure is never the goal toward which our activities themselves are aimed; rather, it is a feature that accompanies the normal use of one or other of our powers (intellect, will, one of the senses, or what have you). True, pleasure may be the goal that *we* intend by our activities. But it is never the goal that those activities, in and of themselves, seek. For instance: the goal of our using our power of sight is to see something; the pleasure that we experience in doing so is merely a concomitant of the act, something that goes along with it. Or: the goal of the act of eating is the nourishment of our bodies. The pleasure involved is simply something that may or may not accompany that act; it is not the goal of the act itself--as witness the fact that nourishment will take place even when we eat some food that we happen to find quite unpleasant.

There simply is no act whose goal is sheerly and solely pleasure (though, again, pleasure may be *my* goal in performing some act). Furthermore, the purpose of pleasure is to draw us on to perform some activity with which that pleasure is associated. We eat to stay alive, though eating is also pleasurable; and the whole point of its being pleasurable is to entice us to perform an act that we might not otherwise do, or at least do very often or very well. But: if pleasure is simply an enticement to activity, a phenomenon that accompanies our activities, and if those activities all have further goals that are independent of pleasure, then we might wonder what sense it makes to say that pleasure is the goal of human life, or that pleasure is the criterion of good and evil.

We could do all this. That is to say, we could take the various extrinsic theories that have been proposed down through the ages, and pick holes in them. But when we finished that process, the same conclusion would come to mind that also suggested itself at the very beginning of the process: these extrinsic theories present themselves as being either somewhat alien to oneself, or as being unworthy of oneself as a human being. In brief, they are unsatisfactory, given the sort of creature that the human being is.

2. An intrinsic theory of morality

Is there anything better? Perhaps. It does, however, take some work to establish it.

a. Preliminary tools needed

We need several tools to establish an intrinsic theory, the first of which is the Principle of Final Causality.

1) Principle of final causality

This principle states that every agent acts for a goal, an end. But we need to define what we mean. An agent, first, is any being which acts, which exercises an activity of its own. A dog, chewing a bone, is an agent in this sense. So is a sub-atomic particle, radiating ions (or whatever sub-atomic particles radiate). So is a human being, walking down the street. A goal, on the other hand (as we saw in Chapter 2), is that which is

78

known and sought after--known, that is to say, by someone (not necessarily the agent, though it is sought after by the activity of the agent). Finally, the name of the Principle ("Final Causality") derives from the Latin word *finis,* meaning an end or a goal; "final," then, in this sense, has nothing to do with "last," "terminal," or anything of that sort.

a) Ultimate and proximate goals

Some distinctions will be useful. An *ultimate* goal is one that is sought for its own sake; a *proximate* goal is one sought, not merely for its own sake, but for the sake of some further goal which it helps the agent to achieve. I may, for example, seek money as my goal--a proximate goal, however, since (unless I am a confirmed miser) I do not particularly want the money in and for itself; I want it for what it enables me to buy (which latter is the ultimate goal in this situation). We might note, in passing, the closeness in meaning between "proximate goal" and "means," which we saw earlier. The two terms are quite close, although not absolutely identical. One could have a means (i.e., a pure means) which was not a proximate goal. But, for the most part, unless there is indeed question of a pure means, the two terms are nearly identical.

b) Goal of the work and goal of the worker

Also helpful is the distinction between the goal of the work and the goal of the worker. Suppose that I am driving somewhere, and I press the gas pedal to the floor. That action has two goals: the goal of the work--that toward which the action inevitably and of its nature tends--is the positioning of the gas pedal parallel to the floor; the goal of the worker--that which the agent has in mind in performing his or her act--is, let us say, to beat the traffic light that is immediately ahead of me. Or, suppose that I am a worker in a factory, and my job is making shoes, which I do by pressing a series of levers on a large machine before me. When I press those levers, the goal of the work is to place those levers in a certain position (and thereby to make shoes). The goal of the worker is to earn my salary, to make money so as to support my family, and so forth.

c) Establishing the principle

So much for the definition of the terms involved in the Principle of Final Causality, and for some preliminary distinctions. How do we establish (i.e., prove) the principle itself? Let us take this in two steps.

(1) Some agents (cognitive and non-cognitive) act for a goal

(a) There are different kinds of agents, and instances of goal-directedness can be found among each kind. (i) First, there are cognitive agents, i.e., agents which act through knowledge. Among the cognitive agents, some act through intellect and will, e.g., a man building a house in order to shelter his family, or the individual running the shoe-making machine referred to earlier. Such an agent may be perfectly conscious of his or her goal, or may be only minimally conscious of it: goals can exist at different levels of awareness. Then there are other agents which are cognitive, i.e., acting through knowledge, but non-intellectual knowledge: a dog digging to locate a buried bone, a wolf raiding a flock of sheep in order to find food, etc. Here, again, the agent is aware of its goal--though it is perhaps worth our while to notice that the goal is known in this instance only concretely: the bone, the sheep, etc., are not known by the dog or the wolf *as a goal*, under the universal formality of being a goal, but rather only as individual concrete goods to be attained. In sum, then, among all kinds of cognitive agents (human and sub-human), we can point to instances where goals are known (whether precisely as goals or not) and are sought.

(ii) Then there are non-cognitive agents, i.e., beings which truly are agents, truly act, truly do have an activity of their own, but which do not act through knowledge. Among these, one could distinguish living (but non-cognitive) agents and non-living ones. As examples of living but non-cognitive agents, we could point to such things as a tree, acting to seek water and thus sending its roots deeply or shallowly, depending on where the water table happens to be in that tree's neighborhood. Similarly, we could point to a heliotrope, seeking more sunlight through its flower's following the sun around during the day; finally, a plant pushing through various obstacles (hard-baked earth, for instance), to get to sunlight. Among non-living, non-cognitive agents, examples might be hydrogen, which, when combined with oxygen in appropriate proportions, acts in a certain way (a quite predictable and spectacular way, for that matter); crystals, which form in certain predictable ways, might be another illustration; yet another would be sub-atomic particles, engaging in their own mysterious sorts of radiative activities. Goal-directedness, in these latter instances, is indicated clearly by the fact that the action of these agents (1) does reach results, and (2) reaches results that are constant and consistent--in some cases always so, in other cases at least within certain definite ranges.

Our first step, then, in establishing the Principle of Final Causality has been to observe that there are different kinds of agents, some cognitive (whether on the intellectual or simply the sense level) and some non-cognitive (whether living or non-living). What we have claimed thus far is that, on all of these levels, goal-directedness can be found, at least in some instances. However, we should bear in mind something that has been remarked before: "goal" is defined as that which is known and sought after--but not necessarily known by the agent itself (though, obviously, in some cases that will be true as well). In some cases--practically, in the case of any agents below the human level--the goal is known, not by the agent itself (at least *as an end*), but by whoever or whatever made the particular agent such that it always acts with the degree of constancy and consistency which its actions manifest.

(2) All agents act for a goal

(b) The next step in demonstrating the Principle of Final Causality is to show that *in every instance of agency (action) there is goal-directedness*. This is a much broader assertion than we made in the previous step, in which we merely claimed that *some* agents display goal-directedness.

This second step is established in one of two ways, depending on whether we are talking about human agents (i.e., human beings performing imputable acts) or some other type of agents. Let us look at human agents first.

(i) To establish that all imputable activity is goal-directed, we might use what is called a "reverse proof": we will assume the opposite of what we want to prove, and see what consequences that assumption leads to. Suppose, then, that there is some imputable act (i.e., one done through knowledge and will) which seeks no goal, is random, is totally purposeless. Now, of course, the will is the power whereby we choose one thing rather than another, or choose to act rather than not act. That is the very nature of the will; it is the faculty of choice, of choosing. Now,

81

this totally purposeless act which we have assumed (1) is one whereby a human chooses one thing rather than another (for it is an imputable act, one done through the will), *and simultaneously* (2) it is one whereby a human does not choose one thing rather than another (for it is purposeless, and hence there is no question of choice). This, of course, is a contradiction, and so the supposition leading to it, that there could be a purposeless imputable act, is false. But either that supposition or its opposite has to be true; there is no third possibility: an act either is or is not purposeless. Consequently, the opposite of the supposition that we made has to be true. And the opposite of that supposition is that no imputable act is purposeless, i.e., that all imputable acts are purposeful, are goal-directed.

(ii) So, all imputable acts are goal-directed. Though for purposes of ethics, we do not absolutely need to complete the proof for the Principle of Final Causality (i.e., to show that it applies to non-imputable acts as well), still, for completeness' sake, it will be useful to do so. And so, as a short digression if for no other purpose, we might ask: what of all other acts, those that are not done with intellect and will (for whatever reason, i.e., either because the agent does not possess an intellect and will, or because he or she does not happen to be using them at the time of the action)? We notice first a universal fact: in every instance of action like this, we find that constant and consistent results are obtained: the same action, left to itself and not interfered with, *always* gives the same result. Conversely, if a specific goal must be reached, then a specific action proportionate to that goal must be performed. And this is true every time. To illustrate: a tree, in a particular location, will always send its roots down to where they can have access to the water table in that place. So will any other similar tree, put in the same location. On the other hand, if there is question of, say, getting sunlight rather than water, as in the case of certain plants, we don't find those plants sending down deep roots; we find them pushing through hard ground, etc., trying, as we would say, to get to the sunlight. It is, therefore, the result to be obtained, the goal, that determines the type of activity that the agent performs: the activity is determined by the end, is proportioned to the end. If this were not the case, then the constancy and consistency of results--the fact, that is to say, that a given activity always achieves a certain result, and conversely, the fact that if a given result is to be achieved, an action proportioned to that result must be performed every time--would be unintelligible. To put it another way: if the goal to be achieved did not dictate the type of action to be undertaken, then there would be no reason why two quite different (indeed, contrary) actions would not achieve the same result, at least sometimes. For instance, there would be no reason why our tree, in its quest for water, would not in some cases succeed in reaching that water by sending its roots down to the water table, and in other cases succeed in doing so by sending them straight up into the air. But nothing of this sort happens, ever. To put all this briefly, an agent always acts for an end, for the end determines the type of activity that the agent performs--in all cases.

In summary, then: the consistency with which a given action achieves a given result (and, on the other hand, the absolute necessity that, for a given result to be obtained, a particular action proportioned to that result--and not some other--must always be performed), it follows that there is a close relationship between activity and end. This relationship is one of governance: the result determines the type of action to be performed. This, in turn, is merely another way of saying that, for every action on the sub-human level, the agent always acts for an end. Such an agent does not, of course, recognize that it is doing so: an end must indeed be known, but not necessarily by the agent itself.

We have said that the Principle of Final Causality, at least as applied to imputable acts, is the first tool that we need in establishing an intrinsic theory of morality. After wading through the somewhat heavy material of the last several paragraphs, however, we might be tempted to wonder just what importance that principle has: it is of some interest as metaphysical speculation, perhaps, but what good is it going to do us?

2) Imputable actions always aimed at a goal that is not also a means

And so we turn to the application of the Principle of Finality (i.e., of Final Causality) to ethics. Once again, let us state at the outset what we hope to demonstrate, and then set about doing so. The statement to be proven, then, is this: every imputable act at least implicitly aims at an end that is solely a goal and is not also a means to some further goal.

Suppose we begin our proof of this assertion by noting a curious fact. No matter what I do, I can almost always ask the question "Why?": Why do I stand up? (to get my coat.) Why get the coat? (to be able to go outdoors.) Why go outdoors? (to get a sandwich.) Why get the sandwich? (to satisfy my hunger.) Why satisfy my hunger? (to maintain my health.) And so on and on. Now, one of the many conclusions that we might draw from this state of affairs is that my actions are generally part of a series.

I am usually aiming at some intermediate goal, which itself is a means to some further goal, which in its turn is a means to some yet further goal. But the question can be asked: is this always the case? Is the "Why?" question always applicable?

To try to answer that, we need to consider the difference between what is traditionally called the "order of execution" and the "order of intention." The technical names should not be a source of concern. Consider a series of actions, say, ABCDE. In order to get B, I have to do A; in order to get C, I have to do B; to get D, I have to do C; to get E, I have to do D. This is simply a description of the chronological order in which I have to perform the acts if I eventually want to arrive at E. That is one perfectly legitimate way of looking at such a series, and it is called the "order of execution": the chronological order in which I must perform, or "execute," a series of actions leading to some goal at the end of the series.

There's another way I could look at the same series (ABCDE). I want to get E--that's my ultimate goal in the series. To do that, I have to do D. To achieve D, I have to do C. To do that, I have to do B. And to do that, I have to do A. In looking at the same series, I can, if I wish, start at the end rather than at the beginning, i.e., start with what I ultimately want to achieve, at the thing which I "intend" as a goal, and work backwards in order to line up the means I have to take to achieve it. This is called the "order of intention."

But look carefully at the relationship between these two orders, these two types of series. If there is no goal in the order of intention, the order of execution doesn't even take place: if there's no sandwich to be gotten, I don't bother getting up from my chair--or, in the terminology of the series, if there's no E that I want to achieve, I don't bother doing A (let alone B, C, or D). What follows from this is just an extension of the Principle of Final Causality: just as it is true that there is no imputable act without a goal, so also is it true that there is no series of imputable actions without a governing goal for the whole series, a final goal toward which all intermediate goals are aimed.

Let's take this a step further. Suppose now that you have a series of series: series ABCDE, wherein E turns out to be a means to some further goal, J, itself achieved by means of another series of actions FGHI. Yet J is a means to some other goal, O, to be achieved by actions KLMN. And so on and on. Even so, we can see that our earlier rule holds: no matter how many actions or series of actions you may have in the order of execution, there still has to be an over-all goal for the entire series of series   in the order of intention; otherwise the order of execution simply does not take place.

But consider the nature of the members of those series of series.   They consist in a group of intermediate goals: goals which are sought for the sake of something further. The precise reason why you have a series in the first place is that each goal is an intermediate one. But ultimately there has to be something further, something sought only for itself and not for the sake of something else. For again, no matter how many actions you have in the order of execution (and it is precisely the characteristic of being an intermediate, rather than a final, goal that results in the multiplication of those numbers), if you have nothing other than an intermediate goal in the order of intention to start the series off in the first place, the order of execution simply will not get off the ground.

And the conclusion follows: no matter how many actions there may be in a series, and no matter how many series   of series   I may have, if there is no final goal in the order of intention--no goal, that is to say, which lacks the characteristic of an intermediate goal that would generate yet others in the series--there is no order of execution at all. And so: in every human act that I perform, I am at least implicitly (i.e., with, perhaps, only a very dim level of awareness) aiming at something which is only a goal and not also a means to something else.

3) Intrinsic relationship between act and end

Why did we want to establish this, i.e., that human activity is always at least implicitly aimed at a goal that is not also a means? Consider: we can ask what it is that makes an act *good* in the physical sense, i.e., what makes that act possess everything that it should in order to be a complete act. Now, we have said, thus far, that all action is goal-directed, and all specifically imputable action is directed ultimately at a goal that is not a means to some further goal. But to say all this, i.e., to say that all actions are goal-directed, is merely another way of saying that act and end (or goal) are correlative terms: you cannot have an act that does not aim toward a goal, and you cannot (realistically, at any rate) have a goal that is not achievable by, proportioned to, some act. This, in turn, means that an act is essentially ordered to a goal, and that its quality *as an act* is precisely measurable insofar as it does or does not attain that goal toward which it is ordered. If it does so, it is a (physically) good act, i.e., it possesses everything that it should possess in order to be a complete act;

if it does not attain its goal, it is a (physically) evil one, not possessing everything that it should have in order to be a complete act. This is a question of physical, rather than moral, goodness at this point, true. But even on this level, we should be very aware of the intrinsic, essential relationship that exists between act and goal.

4) Subjective and objective orders

The next tool that we need, in preparing to state an intrinsic theory of morality, is the distinction between the subjective and the objective orders. Once again, we should not be put off by the technical terms. The distinction refers simply to how we perceive something to be (subjective order), and how in fact it exists, independently of our knowledge of it and our opinion of it (objective order). Put another way: how something exists *for us,* i.e., in our estimation, is the subjective order; how it exists *in itself*, independently of our estimation of it, is the objective order. Take the example where, as a child, I have been frightened by, say, a large dog, and this experience has left a deep psychological impact on me. On some occasion years afterwards, I meet up with a large, gregarious St. Bernard, who jumps up and puts his huge paws on my shoulders. Now, subjectively speaking, this overgrown pooch is an object of considerable terror to me, and I may well react accordingly. Objectively, however, the St. Bernard doesn't particularly dislike me, isn't interested in terrorizing me, is in fact simply a very friendly animal that likes people and is used to being petted and roughhoused with when he jumps up on someone. A terrorizing object? A friendly one (even if somewhat overpoweringly so)? Both. It depends on whether you are speaking of the subjective or the objective order.

5) The experiential fact of "oughtness"

Finally, one further item. We notice that some actions present themselves to us as having a sort of obligatory character to them. We call that a good action which we "ought" to do; that is an evil action which we "ought not" do; and that is an indifferent action which we may either do or not do, as we wish. Thus far, this is merely a statement of our experience. But the question can be pushed: what is the source of this "oughtness"?

Remember that act and end are essentially related to each

other. Thus, the source of this "oughtness" will have to be found either in the act itself, or in the end (the goal); there is no third possibility (at least if one properly understands what is meant by "act," as we should by now). To be sure, there are schools of thought that come very close to placing the source of "oughtness" in the act itself, i.e., to saying that "oughtness" is a constitutive part of the act. But this is largely unsatisfactory. It is nothing more than merely asserting that, for some unexplained (and unexplainable) reason, an intrinsic part of a given act is its "oughtness."

b. Stating the theory

A much more satisfying explanation is the teleological one, in which the source of the obligation, the "oughtness," is situated in the end, the goal, the *telos*--since it cannot be satisfactorily located in the act itself.

With all this in mind, we should now be ready to state our version of the intrinsic theory of morality. Relying on the essential relatedness of every imputable action (and, indeed, every action without qualification) to its goal, its end--a relationship so close that one can judge an act by its end and an end by its act--the teleological (or intrinsic) theory states that, in the objective order, that is a good action which leads us to the possession of a goal which we should achieve; that is an evil action which leads us to the possession of a goal which we should not achieve (or--which comes to much the same thing--leads us away from a goal that we should achieve); and that is an indifferent action whose performance or non-performance is irrelevant to the acquisition of a goal that we should achieve.

(Note that the theory speaks of an objectively good and an objectively evil action. The implication--and it is intended--is that actions are good or evil independently of whether we are pleased by that fact or not, whether we accept it or not. Subject to what will be said in a later chapter on conscience, the point is being made here that morality is an objective matter: it is the case that an action can be objectively evil, no matter how good we might [for whatever reason] think it to be, or might prefer that it be. Or the reverse: it is the case that an action can be objectively good [or indifferent], however distasteful it might seem to us and however much--for quite subjective reasons--we might wish to condemn it.)

The teleological theory, as proposed here, is neither more nor

87

less than what it presents itself to be: it is a theory, in the technical sense of that word. It is not an apodictic demonstration that will convince all comers; neither, however, is it merely a casual piece of guesswork. As a theory, it is a reasoned explanation of a fact that we experience in our daily lives (the fact of moral obligation), an explanation that relies heavily on an analysis of the relationship between act and end. It is an explanation that seems to fit the facts of the case far better than do extrinsic theories, and it seems to avoid many of the difficulties that those extrinsic theories bring in their train. Not everyone has accepted it (else why would there be such a thing as rival theories?); and not everyone has understood it (whether in accepting it or in rejecting it)--for reasons that may now be clear enough to the reader of this chapter. However, if it is not the only explanation of moral obligation available, it is in this writer's judgment the best and the most powerful. And that, on some topics at any rate, is as much as philosophy can hope to achieve.

So, by means of a lengthy path, we have come to the answer to the second of the three questions of theoretical ethics, i.e., "What do you mean by a good or an evil act?" A good act is one that leads us to the possession of a goal that we should achieve; an evil act is one that leads away from the possession of such a goal.

But (as is so often the case in systematic philosophy), answering one question merely serves to unleash a whole host of others. What is this ultimate goal which is only an end and not a means to some further goal? How can you tell whether any given action leads toward that goal or leads away from it? And, once those two items are satisfactorily answered, there remains the question of why I *should* aim at that goal: what is there about human beings that makes it incumbent upon them to seek this goal? The answers to these questions (and similar ones) comes in our discussion of the third theoretical question, "How do you decide whether a given action is good or evil?" And so we turn now to the question of the norms of morality.

SUMMARY OF CHAPTER FIVE

An act is "good" or "evil" either because of something stemming from what that act is, i.e., from its very nature ("intrinsic morality") or because of something completely outside it, having nothing to do with its nature ("extrinsic morality").

Extrinsic morality can be something like authoritarianism, informal or formal: something is right or wrong because someone else says that it is. In informal authoritarianism, an act is good or evil because parents, unquestioned religion, or peers decree it so. Examples of formal authoritarianism are the Social Contract Theory (the state declares certain actions good, others evil: Hobbes) and the Social Pressure Theory (some other entity does so). Another version of extrinsic morality is the pleasure/pain theory: a good act is one that causes us pleasure, and an evil act is one that causes us pain. This can take the form of hedonism (the pleasure/pain is that of the individual: Aristippus, Epicurus, our own culture) or utilitarianism: the pleasure/pain is that of the group: Bentham, Mill, some contemporary thought. Extrinsic theories do have some problems, both internally and in the fact that they present themselves to us as somewhat alien to (or unworthy of) us as human persons.

An intrinsic theory of morality demands a special application of the Principle of Final Causality. In general, this principle states that every agent acts for an end, a goal. Some cases of goal-directedness can be found among all types of agents, cognitive and non-cognitive; moreover, all agents act for a goal: all human agents performing imputable acts do so (since will--and therefore knowledge--are involved), and all other agents do so as well (for the observed consistency with which a particular action always achieves a particular result implies a relationship of governance between act and end: the end determines the type of action to be performed). Imputable acts (which are ethics' concern) always aim at least implicitly at a goal which is not also a means to some further goal; an intermediate goal in the order of intention (one sought for the sake of something further), precisely as intermediate, could not ultimately initiate an action in the order of execution. Finally, any action is "good" (in the physical sense) if it is complete, if it reaches its goal; act and end are, therefore, correlative terms.

Now, some actions present themselves as having a certain obligatory character. Given the fact that act and end are essentially related, the source of this obligatoriness will need to be either in the act itself or in the relationship that the act has to an end. The intrinsic theory of morality states that, objectively, a good action is one that leads us to a goal that we should achieve, and an evil action is one that leads us to a goal that we should not achieve (or leads us away from one that we should achieve).

6. THE ULTIMATE NORMS OF MORALITY

II. The Theoretical Part of Ethics
  C. The Third Question: how does one tell whether a
    given act is good or evil?--the norms of morality
    1. Meaning of a norm of morality
    2. Types of norms: subjective and
      objective, ultimate and proximate
    3. The four norms of morality
      a. Ultimate norms
        1) Ultimate subjective norm
          a) A characteristic common
            to all imputable acts
          b) Unlimited happiness
        2) Ultimate objective norm
          a) Preliminary observations
          b) What such a norm would
            have to be (if it exists)
            (1) Argument from exclusion
            (2) Positive argument: required
              and sufficient
          c) But does it exist? Philosophical
            proof for the existence of God
            (1) What we are trying to prove
            (2) The phenomenon of change
              (a) Types of change, and what is
                shown in each type: "meta-
                physical parts" on three levels
              (b) Meaning of "parts" here
              (c) How the "parts" relate to one
                another: act and potency
            (3) The Principle of Efficient Causality
            (4) The adequate cause of a changing
              being: proof for God's existence
              as uncaused cause
            (5) Significance of all this for ethics.

1. Meaning of a norm of morality

What does it mean to speak of "norms of morality"? In English, a "norm" can mean several things. For instance, it can be a pattern of behavior that represents what most people in a given group do; and in this sense we speak of an action's being "normal," and of one opposed to it as being "abnormal." In other words, "norm" can simply mean what is average; and this is commonly what we do mean when we use it. In its earlier days, however, it had another meaning. It was derived from the Latin *norma,* which meant a carpenter's square, or, in general, any rule or standard. A line that was drawn, for instance, was either a good line or a poor one, depending on the degree to which it approximated the accuracy dictated by the carpenter's square. We still use this meaning for "norm," though perhaps less frequently than was once the case. At all events, it is in this older sense that we use the term in ethics. A norm of morality is a standard, against which our actions are judged. To the extent that they conform to that standard, they are good actions: they lead us to a goal that we should achieve. To the extent that they deviate from that standard, they are evil, leading us away from a goal that we ought to achieve.

2. Types of norms: subjective and objective, ultimate and proximate

In the last chapter, we noticed the distinction between the subjective and the objective orders: how something appears to us, and how it exists in itself independently of our knowledge or opinion of it. The distinction can be applied to the norm of morality, too. There can be such a thing as an objective norm--that standard according to which an action is right or wrong, good or evil, independently of whether we agree with it, care for it, or even know about it. There can also be such a thing as a subjective norm: that standard of conduct which we do in fact consciously use in judging an actions's rightness or wrongness. Obviously, there should not be a vast disparity between the two, in the ideal order; on the contrary, the relationship between the subjective and the objective norms should be very close indeed. None the less, the distinction remains valid between the norm of morality as it exists in itself and the norm as we conceive of it, know it. And so it is perfectly correct to speak of the norms of morality (plural), subjective and objective.

There is more to it than simply that. The ultimate norm for telling the time of day, for example, is a highly sophisticated piece of equipment, an atomic clock, say, kept under government supervision somewhere. If I want to be exactly sure (for scientific purposes, say) just what time it is, down to the last fraction of a second, then that is the norm to which I must refer. However, it is rarely necessary (and even more rarely practical) to go to such lengths. If I want to know what time it is, I look at my wrist watch--a practical enough norm for most purposes of daily life. However, the point remains: there is such a thing as an ultimate norm of time and a proximate one: the atomic clock and my watch, respectively. The same will be true for the norms of morality: there will be an ultimate one, and one that is nearer to me which I use for practical purposes in my daily moral life.

3. The four norms of morality

Putting the last two paragraphs together, then, we find that we can really speak of four norms of morality: a subjective ultimate one, an objective ultimate one, a subjective proximate one, and an objective proximate one. In a perfect world, these four norms would coincide perfectly. In the world in which we live, their coincidence is considerably less perfect, often enough--which, however, does not affect the truth of the statement that they *should* mesh as well as possible.

What are these four norms? We will take each of them in turn, and at some length, in this and the following chapter. In the present chapter, we will be concerned with the ultimate norms, subjective and objective.

a. Ultimate norms

We said at the conclusion of the last chapter that an action is good if it leads us to a goal that we should achieve, evil if it leads us away from it. We also said that every imputable act implicitly aims at a good which is only a goal and not also a means to some further goal. Our question now, then, is this: in any action that we perform, just what is it that we are implicitly aiming at--at least in our own minds? What is it that I want, in anything I do--whatever that may be?

1) Ultimate subjective norm

At first, that might sound like an unanswerable question. For, surely, there are as many human motives as there are human imputable actions; and there are countless human imputable actions performed every day. What are we supposed to do--take a survey? It would have to be quite a survey, and its results probably wouldn't be very satisfactory anyway.

93

a) A characteristic common to all imputable acts

On the other hand, there are some common characteristics that can be found in human motives. I may seek money, for instance, and you may seek power; someone down the street may seek peace and quiet. But I don't seek money just for the sake of being rich; neither do you seek power for power's sake, and the individual down the street is really after something more than just peace and quiet. I seek money, you seek power, and our neightbor seeks peace and quiet precisely because of what each one of us thinks that the object of our quest can *do* for us. When I get through asking all the "Why?" questions about the money I'm seeking (the process that we saw earlier), eventually I come down to the fact that, in one way or other, I'm seeking the money because ultimately I think that it will make me happy. You seek power for the same reason. And the same for the person seeking his or her peace and quiet. The common denominator in all of our strivings is, then, happiness.

Now, obviously, you, I, and the person down the street may have wildly different ideas about what happiness is, and about what means will bring us happiness. Were it otherwise, why am I seeking money (and not power or peace and quiet), you power (and not money or peace and quiet), and the other person peace and quiet (and not money or power)? But, whatever happiness is and however we are to come by it, we are all seeking it; that is the common characteristic of all our strivings. Nor is that true of just the three of us in the example. It is true of every human action.

All this, so far, is nothing terribly erudite or controversial; it's just a matter of observation. Thus far in human history, at any rate, we have no recorded instance of someone who deliberately set out to achieve his or her own *un*happiness by means of imputable activity. This is true even in the extreme case of the masochist, who ·seeks the happiness of being unhappy! Once again, people's ideas of what happiness consists in can vary quite widely. Seriously, however, even on those rare occasions when a form of unhappiness is deliberately sought, we notice that this is never an ultimate goal but only a proximate one, a means. The ultimate aim is always satisfaction, happiness.

(What of psychic states wherein a person does indeed operate with subconscious and self-destructive motives? An example would be the case where a person believes himself or herself unworthy of happiness, and deserving only of, say, punishment. There are, certainly, such cases. But they would hardly constitute

94

*instances of imputable actions, and therefore they are not
pertinent to a discussion of ethical norms.)*

b) Unlimited happiness

We can push our observations a step further. Once we have
achieved some limited form of happiness, an interesting
phenomenon takes place: we seek more and more of it. For
example, if I achieve my goal of acquiring $1000, I am
happy--until I realize that there is another $10,000 out there
somewhere that I could get. You are elected mayor, and are
happy--until you realize that the governor's post has a lot more
power, and you stand a good chance of being elected to it if you
wish. The man down the street is happy with his peace and
quiet, until he sees that travel brochure showing the far greater
peace and quiet that he could have in a condominium in Florida.

We aren't, then, seeking just any sort of happiness, it seems.
We are after as much happiness as we feel that we can get. And
we aren't interested in limits on it, either quantitative or
qualitative. For, suppose that I acquire all the money I could
ever want. I am very shortly looking for something else--power,
for example. You, on the other hand, become the most powerful
person in history; and you find yourself seeking something else,
say, money. And whatever our peace-loving friend in his
condominium in Florida wants, we can be reasonably sure that he
won't be content very long with just sea and sun.

We could generalize from all this. Just from observing human
nature in action, we can conclude that, as an ultimate aim of all
of their conscious, imputable actions, people are seeking complete
and perfect happiness: the permanent and total satisfaction of all
their desires, all their powers. On this, they all agree--however
much that agreement ceases when each person starts to specify
just what he or she thinks will achieve that goal. This desire for
perfect happines, we can note, (a) is universal: all human beings
without exception have it--at least thus far in recorded human
history; (b) it is unavoidable: it is life-long, and one can neither
outgrow it nor get rid of it; and (c) it is irresistible: it demands
satisfaction, and refuses to be ignored.

We might also note, in passing, that the "Why?" series of
questions pretty much comes to an end when we get to happiness
as a goal. If someone asks me why I seek happiness, I am hard
put to it to give the sort of answer I would give if, say, someone
asked me why I seek money or power. To someone asking why I

seek happiness, about all I can answer is, "Well, I just do!" True enough--I just do. As we shall see, that's simply the way that I am made. For now, however, we might notice that the inapplicability of the "Why?" question to happiness is, at least, an indication or a clue to the fact that happiness is an ultimate goal, rather than a proximate one, in the subjective order. As such, it is the ultimate subjective norm of morality.

2) Ultimate objective norm

The next question is immediate and obvious: what is it which, by being possessed, will lead to happiness, to this permanent and perfect satisfaction of all of our faculties? That is to say, what is this object in itself, apart from how you, I, or anyone else may view it?

a) Preliminary observations

Two preliminary comments need to be made before we try to answer that question. First, at this point the discussion leaves the merely observational level, and becomes a good deal more controversial in nature. Up to this point, everyone could agree with what we have said about the ultimate subjective norm. That will not be the case from here on. For there are implications involved when we try to identify what it is that will provide us with the sort of happiness we have described. Specifically, if it turns out (and it will) that only one thing can do that, in the objective order, then the consequence is that everything else cannot. The further consequence is that anyone who thinks that anything else can provide happiness will be wrong. He or she might be a person of immense good will, a lovely soul through and through. He or she will also be wrong. Not evil, necessarily (as we shall see later when we discuss conscience), but wrong. Or, to use the terminology that we have been developing in this chapter, in the case of such a person the objective and subjective orders have seriously diverged. However much this state of affairs may offend our egalitarian sense, one person's notion of the objective ultimate moral norm is not, unhappily, as good as anyone else's.

Secondly, our identification of the objective ultimate norm will be a two-stage process. We will first try to see just what sort of object would be required, in order to give us the sort of happiness we have described. But then we must go further. For, logically at any rate, there would be no contradiction in stating what sort of object would be required, and then turning around and saying that, of course, there is no such thing, or at least one cannot show that there is. Naturally, that would make hash out of the norms of ethics, and hence of ethics itself. And so, since we cannot reasonably presume that everyone reading this book has had the opportunity to become familiar with the matter, we must go on and engage in the quite lengthy process of proving the existence of that ultimate objective norm.

b) What such a norm would have to be (if it exists)

Having said all that by way of preface, let us begin. Our question is: what is it (considered in itself, without reference to how we or anyone else may view it) which will lead to happiness, i.e., to the perfect and permanent satisfaction of all of our faculties? There are two sorts of argumentation that can be used here.

(1) Argument from exclusion

First, there is the argument from exclusion--i.e., we try to show what sorts of things will *not* provide that happiness. What is left will then be the sort of thing that will. In this type of argument, the object whose possession would bring us perfect happiness would have to be (a) something below the human level, (b) something on the human level, or (c) something above the human level. This is exhaustive; there are no other possibilities.

Let us, then, first consider things below the human level, and ask whether they can provide us with perfect happiness. We are here referring to such things as wealth, family, fame, honor, power, position, etc.--in general, the sorts of things that are usually called "goods of this world." Now, although these are certainly goods in themselves, they cannot constitute the perfect good we are looking for, since no one of them is permanent: their possession is always marked with care and concern over keeping and possessing them. A little reflection shows us that goods of this sort will not measure up to what we are looking for, however good they may be in themselves. I may acquire money, perhaps a great deal of money--more, say, than any other person in history. Is that, in itself, sufficient to bring me happiness? No. For, if I am not seeking ways to increase its amount, I am at least seeking means to safeguard it, i.e., to ensure that I continue to possess it. That is to say, its possession is always attended by a certain amount of care, of unease--enough so that my happiness is at least tinged with a cloud of uneasiness. In other words, I am not perfectly happy, becasue my happiness's permanency is not guaranteed. The same is true of other goods of this type: at the very least, I am always concerned with making sure that they last, and that means that their very possession carries with it some sort of unease, some sort of unhappiness. From another point of view, too, there are some desires that I have which no goods of this sort can satisfy: I desire, for example, knowledge, love, beauty: but certainly wealth, honor, power, etc., will not--at least necessarily--bring them to me in such a way that I never have to worry about retaining them.

Chiefly because of their transient nature, then--the fact that I *could* lose them--goods of this world, whatever they may be, will not form the object of perfect happiness. The happiness that they can being me is of the same nature as they themselves--transient; and very often they do not even bring me that. Moreover, there are things I want which are not included in the class of "goods of this world."

Very well, then. What of goods on the human level? There are various sorts of these. I could, for example, seek my ultimate happiness in goods of the body: things like health, strength, beauty, physical skills, and the like. But these won't do either, for they have the same problem as do "goods of this world": they are transitory. I may enjoy health and strength now; can I guarantee that I will also have them fifty years from now? I cannot. And the same for every other good of this sort.

Then there are goods of the spirit: such things as knowledge and virtue. There certainly have been thinkers throughout the history of philosophy who have located human happiness in these. Will they serve? No, not really. Knowledge will not do, for our knowledge is always partial: there is always more to be learned than there is time or talent to learn it. Virtue has the same problem: it, too, is always partial, however much we may strive for total perfection. Moreover, virtue is by its very nature a means to something else, and cannot be an end in itself. And so, goods of the spirit will not answer our quest.

What of the possibility of goods of the body and goods of the spirit taken together? Our very inability to give a good example of these makes us hesitate. And the conclusion is lurking in the background: if neither goods of the body nor goods of the spirit taken separately will suffice, it is unlikely that a combination of the two will be very much better: an increase in quantity (which we might get by adding goods of the body together with goods of the spirit) will not automatically result in an increase in quality. And it is on the level of quality that both goods of the body and goods of the spirit have failed the test thus far.

So far, then, neither goods below the human level nor goods on the human level will work. What about goods above the human level? This would have to be either angels or God; we know of nothing else above the human level, and certainly something we do not know will not be a likely candidate for making us happy.

Fine, then, let us revert to our catechism days and ask whether something on the level of the angels would suffice to give us perfect happiness. The answer, of course, is a swift no. At least on the level of philosophy, we know absolutely nothing about angels, however much we may or may not know about them from other sources. And, again, an unknown goal is no goal at all, let alone a final one.

We are then left with the only remaining possibility, the possession of God. The possession of God--however one wants to conceive that, for the moment--would certainly satisfy the human yearning for the possession of a permanent, complete good, one that would satisfy all our desires and would do so in such a fashion that would leave no room for care or concern about a future loss thereof. For God (and again, we are for the moment operating only on an intuitive, unreflective level of awareness of what God might be) would certainly be able to satisfy all our desires, and to do so permanently: that is to say, the possession of God would give us happiness. IF, that is to say, there is a God.

So much for the argument from exclusion. Perhaps it will be useful to see exactly where we are at the moment, before we press on. We have said that an act is good if it leads us to a goal that we ought to possess; and, ultimately, every imputable act that we perform aims at a goal that is not also a means to some further goal. We have asked what this ultimate goal is. We have seen that its possession will bring us happiness; and happiness is, in fact, the ultimate subjective norm of morality. But then we asked what object would, by being possessed, bring us happiness. The answer has turned out, in the argument from exclusion, to be God. If all this is correct, and if indeed there is a God (which is to say, if the entire endeavor of human ethics makes any sense at all), then an action will be good if it leads us, somehow, to the possession of God; it will be evil if it leads us away from possessing God.

(2) Positive argument: required and sufficient

Now let us look at another argument, a more positive one than the argument from exclusion, and one which leads to the same conclusion. We have seen that that alone can make humans perfectly and permanently happy which can perfectly (and therefore permanently) satisfy all their desires. But, this argument will maintain, only God can do this. For (1) God is required: no lesser being will do, since humans are rational beings by nature, and their rationality has two main tendencies: of the intellect, to know all truth; and of the will, to possess all good. Only God, however, (again, operating as we are for the moment on a non-reflective, somewhat intuitive level) appears to us to be perfect truth and goodness. For any other truth is by its very nature only partial: no single thing that we know about the world or anything else gives us complete insight into the entire cosmos; no good of our experience is a complete good, completely satisfying every desire. Moreover, (2) God is sufficient: the possession of God would render all other objects of possession superfluous, for there is no truth not found in God, who is Truth itself, and no good not found in God, who is Goodness itself.

c) But does it exist? Philosophical proof for the existence of God

What we have said about the ultimate objective norm of morality thus far has been provisional. But eventually the question has to be faced: is there a God who can in fact serve as this ultimate norm? More pointedly, can we show that there is such a God?

The answer is yes, one can show philosophically (i.e., by natural reason alone) that there is a God. It is by no means an easy thing to do, and it requires a great deal of background knowledge. But it can be done. And, since the point is obviously of such crucial importance for ethics, and since, as has been noted previously, in American higher education it can no longer be presumed that this investigation has been gone through at an earlier point, that effort has to be undertaken within ethics itself. We will now try to do that.

(1) What we are trying to prove

It will help, however, if we have clearly in mind, right from the start, just what it is that we are trying to do. The "God" of whom we will speak is not the God of revelation or religion. Philosophy can, indeed, establish the existence of a supreme being; but it cannot even come close to demonstrating the sort of supreme being that dominates the Judaeo-Christian tradition of thought. Philosophy will certainly not controvert that tradition, to be sure. The being whose existence we will establish is a pale reflection of the God of Christianity and Judaism. But it is in accord with that God, however dim the image. And that is sufficient for our purposes.

The "God" to which we will be referring is simply the first cause of all being, discovered and established in Philosophy of Being and Philosophy of God. There is no connection with, nor dependence on, anything like religious revelation (of whatever variety) in the philosophical reasoning that establishes the existence of this supreme being. Rather, this type of reasoning simply argues, on the basis of observed evidence, to the existence of an uncaused cause, which is pure act without potency (the terms will be explained later), and which therefore is perfect truth and perfect good. The conclusion (the existence of a God) is therefore established solely by natural reason--which is only what we would expect, if the definition of philosophy given in the first chapter of this book has any validity at all.

(Obviously, the present writer has nothing against divine revelation. But, as has been remarked earlier, it does no service either to revelation or to philosophy to confound the two. And even though the God whose existence can be established by natural reason is only a pale reflection of the God whose existence is given in divine revelation, none the less it is significant--and quite crucial, if one is interested in doing an ethics that is not a moral theology--that unaided reason can discover the existence of God, even in that "pale reflection" form.)

So much for preliminary remarks. Now let us begin to assemble the background that we will need for this investigation.

(2) The phenomenon of change

Let us start with the common fact of change in our everyday world. As we look around, we notice that grass grows, trees leaf out, people grow old, our possessions wear out and we have to replace them. All of these are instances of change--a process wherein something goes from one state to another. Obviously, there are all sorts of changes, and to attempt to catalogue all of them would be futile; change is a universal characteristic of absolutely everything of our experience. Precisely because it is so common and so universal, however, change affords us with a starting point for investigating everything that exists: since everything of our experience does change, perhaps the fact of change (and what it implies) will tell us something about everything in the world. Perhaps also what it tells us will have significance for our knowledge of God, considered as the cause of all the beings in the world--if, again, there is a God.

In general, change (of whatever sort) reveals that the changing being is composed of more than one "part." For the evidence of change tells us that the being in question in one sense changes, and yet in another remains the same. For example, take the case of someone who has suffered a severe sunburn: he or she remains the same person as before, but he or she is also changed, and that in a rather painful sense. But this means that there is more than one part to him or her, since the reverse hypothesis, i.e., that that person is *not* composed of parts, involves the contradiction that one and the same thing both changes and remains the same at the same time. These "parts" are called such analogously--they aren't "parts" in precisely the same sense as wood, metal, nails, bolts, etc., are parts of a table. Nor are they parts in the same sense that blood, bone, muscle, etc., are parts of a human. Of this, more later; for the moment, let us simply say that they are parts in a special sense.

(a) Types of change, and what is shown in each type: "metaphysical parts" on three levels

If we consider the phenomenon of change a little more closely, however, we notice that there are various kinds of changes. In some cases, the changing being remains the same *kind* of being that it was, though it does undergo some further modification within that type. The sunburn instance, once again: there was a human being at both ends of the change process, though he or she was somewhat altered within that type (from being a white person to being a red one). Nevertheless, that person still remains the same kind of being that he or she was (a human). However, there are other sorts of changes wherein the being in question does *not* remain the same kind of being. The most graphic instance of this latter is the change that we call death: a living being is a quite different sort of thing from a non-living one. We recognize this instinctively in the different ways that we treat a living being and a corpse: we bury corpses, something that that we do not normally do to living beings.

Technically, we determine a being's type by the activities of which it is capable. For instance, the reason that we say that a living being is of a different type from a non-living one is that a living being can do things that a non-living one cannot (e.g., can nourish itself, can grow, can reproduce, etc.). Similarly, we say that a dog is a different type of being from a human because a human can do things that a dog cannot (e.g., think).

It is not always possible to tell which of the above two types of change we are dealing with in any given situation, nor is it necessary for our purposes. It is enough that at least in some cases there are clear instances of each type.

Granted, then, that there are two different kinds of change. What does each of these show us?

In the first type of change (the one wherein the changing being does not change its type--the sunburn patient), the evidence shows that the person in one respect changes, but in another stays the same. That, of course, means that he or she must be composed of more than one part, as we have already seen. It also means that these parts must be real rather than imaginary; imaginary parts cannot account for a real change, which this all too evidently is. Our sunburn patient is therefore composed of one real part whereby he or she is human; and this part does not change, in this example. He or she is also composed of one part whereby he or she is white. The change consists precisely in the loss of this latter part and the gaining of another part, this time one whereby he or she is red. Moreover, that part whereby this person is white cannot be the same as that part whereby he or she is red, for otherwise there would be no change. And neither of these two latter parts can be the same as that whereby the changing individual remains the same kind of being, for otherwise he or she would not be the same kind of being (i.e., human) *at both ends* of the change.

Although the exact nature of these various "parts" is something that we can let go for the moment, it will be useful to give them some technical names. Traditionally, then, that component part of a changing being whereby it remains the same kind of being throughout a change of this type is called "substance." Those component parts of a changing being whereby it receives further specification (white, red) within its unchanging type are traditionally called "accidents." Finally, a change of this sort (wherein the being remains the same type after as before) is called an "accidental change." (A caution: we should beware of pirating in other meanings of "accidental" or "accident" [e.g., fortuitous, unplanned] in this context.)

Now let us turn to the other type of change, the one in which the changing being *does* turn into a different kind of being after the change. The example we used earlier was the death of a living being. We find two things to be true in such a change: (a) the being undergoing the change has, indeed, become a different type of being; and (b) it has not simply been annihilated, but rather (by the fact that it does remain in some fashion or other) it manifests the characteristic of being able to be more than one type of being (at different times, of course, i.e., before and after the change). This type of change, then, shows that a changing being is, whether before or after the change, a given type of being, and it is *capable of being more than one type.* Now, the former factor is precisely what has changed: it was one type, now it is another. But the latter factor has remained constant throughout the change: the being *was* able to be different types before the change, *and it still is.* Therefore we have a factor of change and a factor of stability in this type of change, once more, just as we had in accidental change--a different set of factors, of course, but the same sort of thing nevertheless. Conclusions can be drawn here analogous to those we drew from the sunburn illustration. Thus: a being undergoing a change of this sort must be made up of one real part whereby it *is* of a given type, and another real part whereby it *is able* to be of different types at different times. These two parts must be distinct, for one changes and the other does not. The change consists of the loss of that part whereby the being was of one type (e.g., living) and the gaining of a quite different part whereby it is now of a different type (e.g., non-living). Moreover, the two sorts of constituent parts must be real, i.e., must actually exist within the being--for the change is real, as is the living person before the change and the corpse afterwards; and only something real can explain the real.

The traditional names for these constitutive parts of a changing (and therefore composed) being are as follows: that part whereby a being is of one or other type of being at either end of such a change is called that being's "substantial form"; that part whereby before, during, and after the change it is able to be more than one type at different times is called its "prime matter." A change of the sort discussed here is called a "substantial change."

Now let us run a slightly different sort of analysis, again on changeable beings, but only somewhat (not perfectly) akin to the two analyses we have just completed. In those two analyses, we saw that on least two different levels a changing being manifests a factor of stability (or sameness) and a factor of instability (or difference). Take, now, a situation in which you have standing before you an elephant, a camel, a horse, and a dog. Now, all of these are quite different beasts, obviously enough. Yet they do share one common characteristic: they all exist. We have, then, a situation of (a) difference, and yet of (b) sameness or stability (in that, despite their differences, they all exist). Diagrammatically, where x stands for their common existence, we get:

$$\frac{e}{x} \quad \frac{c}{x} \quad \frac{h}{x} \quad \frac{d}{x}$$

We know several things about these beasts immediately. For instance, we know that e, c, h, and d (that by means of which the elephant is an elephant, that by means of which the camel is a camel, etc.) are all different; otherwise elephants would be camels, camels would be horses, horses would be dogs, and dogs in turn would be elephants. But x, that by means of which each exists, is the same throughout: each of these four beasts shares that characteristic with the other three, i.e., they all exist. Consequently, x cannot be identical with e, c, h, or d, for these latter are all different from one another. Neither can x be identical with any one of the four--say e--taken singly, for, again, that would mean that the principle of difference in this situation is the same as the principle of sameness, and that is a contradiction. (It would also mean that everything which exists is an elephant, which, fortunately, is not true.)

We have, then, a third level of composition here: one part whereby a given being is what it is, and another whereby it exists, simply. These parts are real, for these are real animals: elephants, camels, horses, and dogs; imaginary parts would not account for such. And, to add on the technical names: that part of a composed being (i.e., one which has parts) whereby it is what it is is called its "essence"; that part of a composed being whereby it exists, simply, is called its "act of existence" (or, perhaps more commonly, its "esse").

We now need to summarize the discussion of the preceding few paragraphs, for we have packed a great deal of metaphysics into a very short space in our discussion thus far. So:

(1) The analysis of accidental change shows, in any being undergoing such a change, the presence of at least two constituent "parts" (in a special sense, to be

explained later): one whereby the being remains a
certain type of being (SUBSTANCE), and another
whereby that being undergoes certain modifications
within that type (ACCIDENT). (There are many kinds
of accidents; different kinds of accidental changes
reveal that fact.)

(2) The analysis of substantial change, on the other
hand, reveals, in any being that undergoes such a
change, the presence of two other constituent factors
or parts: one whereby a being *is* a given type
(SUBSTANTIAL FORM), and one whereby the being *is*
capable of being different types at different times
(PRIME MATTER).

(3) An analysis of the fact that there are many
different kinds of changing beings in the world, all of
whom despite their disparity nevertheless share the
common characteristic that they all exist, shows within
each such being the presence of two further factors or
constituent parts: one whereby the being is what it is
(ESSENCE), the other whereby the being exists, simply
(ACT OF EXISTENCE, or ESSE).

One final thought in all this. We might wonder about the
relationship of these different constituent parts to one
another--for instance, many of them seem to have something to do
with the fact of being a given type. Though what follows would
need a good bit of explanation, the relationship among the "parts"
could be summarized as follows:

Prime Matter + Substantial Form = Substance;
   Substance + Accident(s) = Essence
      Essence + Esse = the existing, changing (or
                        at least changeable) being.

(b) Meaning of "parts" here

We have seen that a changing being is composed of various
"parts." The next thing is to look briefly at the nature of those
"parts." We know already that they are "parts" in a slightly
different sense from our normal meaning of the word; but they
are real parts, for the real changes that they explain cannot be
rendered intelligible in any other way. But we do not see, touch,
taste, hear, or smell prime matter, substantial form, etc. The
reason for this is contained in the essential relationship that
matter bears to form, substance to accident, and essence to esse:

106

it is not possible for one to exist without the other. Accidents cannot exist without a substance in which to inhere (we don't just have "white" floating around; what we encounter are white *things*), nor can substance exist without at least some accidents: it may be white, red, or green, but it must have *some* color, it must have *some* quantity (though no particular one in itself is indispensable), and so forth. Similarly, prime matter as such does not exist by itself; everything around us *is* some kind of being, even though it has the ability to be different kinds of things at different times. On the other hand, we do not find substantial forms roaming around by themselves: man-ness, horse-ness, and so forth, do not exist in the real world: what exist are men and horses, i.e., concrete instantiations or particularizations of that substantial form. And the same sort of thing could be said of essence and esse.

This, then, is the situation that we have: these various "parts" of a changing being are real, i.e., they truly exist, for the reason given; but they are not complete in themselves, i.e., cannot exist independently: they must have their correlative in order to exist. Thus: prime matter does not exist without substantial form and vice-versa; matter and form, however, together constitute substance, which in its turn cannot exist without at least some accidents (and vice-versa); substance and accidents together constitute essence, and that in turn cannot exist without esse and vice-versa. In other words, of the six component "parts" of a changing being, no one of them can exist in the real world unless its correlative does too. Now, this state of affairs is designated by calling these parts "incomplete beings," or better, "principles of being."

Note, by contrast, "parts" in another sense: blood, bone, muscle, etc., as parts of human beings. Each of these is capable of existing as a real being in itself (which would mean, incidentally, that each of them is itself capable of being analyzed in terms of *its* matter and form, substance and accidents, essence and esse). When blood, bone, muscle, etc., are actually forming part of the human body, they are subsumed into the higher unity that is the human, and cease to be independent beings; nevertheless, they could revert to that status. Herein lies the difference between them and the metaphysical "parts," which latter are never capable of independent existence. Note, however: the fact that the metaphysical "parts" are incapable of independent existence does not prove that they are not real or could not be parts of a changing being; it merely warns us not to limit our definition of the word "part" too narrowly. The fact that some types of parts are capable of independent existence is no warrant for saying that all types of parts must be so capable.

107

(c) How the "parts" relate to one another: act and potency

We have seen one feature of the metaphysical "parts" (their inability to exist separately). Now let us observe another: the effect that each of them has on its correlative. A useful way to do this is to look at each of the six parts in two ways: first, seeing what it is considered in isolation from its correlative (even though it never actually exists that way), and then seeing what it is when in conjunction with its correlative.

Let us group the six parts into two sets. We will first look at the set composed of substantial form, accident(s), and esse; as we will discover, they have something in common.

(1) First group: substantial form, accident(s), and esse:

(a) Substantial form, taken by itself, is that part whereby *any* member of a given type has that type. The substantial form of humanity, for example, is that whereby you, I, and every other member of the human race are members of a given type, namely the human type. Considered in conjunction with its correlative prime matter, though, substantial form is that whereby *this particular member* of the type has that type. Prime matter has, therefore, individualized substantial form once the two are joined together. It has brought down the substantial form, if you will, from the universal to the particular; in traditional terms, it has *limited* substantial form, limited the scope of what substantial form can do.

(b) Next, take accident. Again, considered simply in itself, accident is that part whereby *any* being is a particular color, size, etc., (depending on which accident you are talking about). But considered in conjunction with its correlative substance, accident is that part whereby *this particular being* is of a given color, size, shape, quality, etc. Substance, therefore, has individualized accident once the two are conjoined--it has brought accident down from the universal to the particular, or, again, it has limited it, restricted the scope of what it can do.

(c) The same is true with esse. Taken by itself,

esse is that part whereby *any* being exists. When joined with essence, however, it is that whereby *this particular being* exists. The same phenomenon: essence has individualized esse, limited the scope of what esse can do.

And thus we get:
  —prime matter limits the scope of what substantial form can do;
  —substance limits the scope of what accidents can do;
  —essence limits the scope of what esse can do.

(2) Second group: prime matter, substance, and essence:

(a) To begin with prime matter: considered in itself, this is that real part whereby a being *can* have *any* substantial form, though none is actually possessed. When conjoined with its correlative substantial form, however, prime matter is that real part by means of which a thing does actually have one definite substantial form, while also retaining its capacity to have other substantial forms at other times. But substantial form has limited the scope of what prime matter can undergo, can have done to it: it is no longer capable of receiving *any* substantial form, but rather can now receive only any substantial form *except the one that it has*--for it is not possible to receive something that you already have.

(b) Then there is substance. In itself, this is that real part whereby a being *can* receive *any* appropriate accident, though none is actually possessed. When conjoined with its correlative accident, though, substance becomes that real part whereby a being does have certain accidents, though retaining the capacity to receive others at other times. But once again: it is no longer capable of receiving *any* accidents, but rather only any accidents *except the ones that it already has*. And so accidents have limited the scope of what substance can undergo, can have done to it.

(c) Finally, essence. In itself, this is that real part whereby a being *can* have an act of existence (esse), though no such act is in fact possessed. Conjoined with its correlative esse, however, it is that real part whereby a being *does* have an act of existence. It is therefore no longer capable of receiving an esse, for the good reason that it already has one. Thus, esse has limited the scope of what essence can undergo, can have done to it.

Again, in summary fashion:
  -substantial form limits the scope of what prime matter can undergo, can have done to it;
  -accident(s) limit(s) the scope of what substance can undergo, can have done to it;
  -esse limits the scope of what essence can undergo, can have done to it.

(Another way of looking at these last three parts [prime matter, substance, and essence] might be helpful. Prime matter is that whereby a being can have any substantial form; substantial form specifies which one prime matter will, in fact, have. Substance is that whereby a being can have any appropriate accidents; accident specifies which ones it will in fact have. Essence is that whereby a being can have an act of existence [or not have one]; esse specifies that it shall, in fact, have an act of existence. One could therefore say, in summary: substantial form specifies (= makes specific) prime matter; accidents specify substance; esse specifies essence.)

As we have just seen, on each of the three levels of the component parts of a changing being, we find two reciprocal actions going on: limitation of what a correlative can do, and limitation of what a correlative can have done to it (*or, if one prefers, two reciprocal actions of limitation and specification*). Different parts are being limited in the various ways, of course; but an analogous, two-fold action is taking place in each of the three sets of component parts. It would be useful if a single terminology could be employed that would fit all three levels, on the basis of this analogous terminology. Such a terminology is ready at hand.

(a) Let us give the name "potency" to any part of a changing being which limits the scope of what its correlative can *do*. Thus, prime matter, substance, and essence can all be called "potency."

(b) Let us give the name "act" to any part of a changing

being which limits the scope of what its correlative can *undergo,* can have done to it *(or: which specifies its correlative).* And therefore, substantial form, accident, and esse will be termed "act."

Our lengthy examination of the metaphysical parts of a changing being has been geared to strictly one end, i.e., the intuitive realization of what is meant by "potency" and "act." To summarize this:

(1) Seen from the viewpoint of the action that any of the six parts exercises on its correlative, potency is that which limits what its correlative can do, and act is that which limits what its correlative can undergo *(or: act is that which specifies its correlative);*

(2) Seen from the viewpoint of what it is in itself, potency is the ability to receive some perfection, in one or other order (i.e., the order of prime matter/substantial form, substance/accident, essence/esse); act is the perfection that is conferred on that potency.

One final item. We can also use "potency" and "act" in a larger sense, speaking now not of the principles of being (the six "parts") but rather of the complete and entire being that is made up of those principles. For instance, we can say that a human is in potency to becoming a corpse (in the sense that he or she can, by virtue of prime matter, lose one substantial form and take on another); a white person is in potency to becoming a red one, and so forth. On the other hand, the human is actually a human (or "is a human in act") by virtue of the fact that he or she truly does have one particular substantial form rather than some other one; a white person is white in act (since he or she does in fact have the accident of whiteness). What is going on here is that, by virtue of philosophic shorthand, we are speaking of a complete composite being itself as being in act or potency with regard to some perfection because of the activity of some one of that composite being's constitutive metaphysical parts.

(3) The principle of efficient causality

So much, then, for the analysis of change, terminating as it does in a realization of just what is meant by "potency" and "act." But we also need one further tool if we are to examine the philosophical proof for the existence of God; that tool is the principle of efficient causality. An efficient cause--and once again, we are using a word ("efficient") in a technical sense, rather than in its everyday meaning--is one that contributes to the existence of its result (its effect) by means of some action which that cause performs. This general notion is one that is already quite familiar to us; in normal speech, when we speak of the "cause" of something, it is usually the efficient cause that we mean. So, for example, a builder is the efficient cause of a house, an author the efficient cause of a book, and so on. Now: the principle of efficient causality states (in broad form) that whatever advances from a state of potency to a state of act in regard to any perfection, does so not all by itself but rather under the agency of some being that is already in act. (This merely states that every effect has a cause, but it does so in terms of potency and act, for reasons that will appear shortly.) A little reflection on the nature of potency and act will show why this principle has to be true. Remember first, however, that change--whether substantial or accidental--can be defined as the transition from potency to act. After all, change is merely the loss of one act and the gaining of some other act to which the changing being was in potency.

Now, then: suppose that the *reverse* of the principle of efficient causality were true. Suppose that some being, itself strictly in potency, puts itself into act. That means that it gives itself the act for which it is in potency. But if it has the act to give itself, then it cannot be said to be in potency in the first place. Either it does not have the act in question (which is what is meant by saying that it is in potency) and thus cannot give that act to itself (for nothing gives--whether to itself or to anyone else--what it itself does not have); or else it does have that act to give itself, but then it cannot be said to be in potency. And so, if the act cannot be self-conferred, but is as a matter of fact conferred, then the only viable conclusion is that it is conferred by another, which other does have that act to confer, i.e., is in act.

Some interesting consequences, for our purposes, follow from this principle of efficient causality. Everything that goes from potency to act requires a cause, itself in act, for this. But everything that changes does, in fact, go from potency to act; again, change is merely the transition from potency to act in regard to some accidental or substantial perfection. Therefore everything that changes requires a cause for its change. This does not, as yet, show the necessity for God's existence (for there is nothing, so far, to say that the cause of a changing being cannot be simply some other changing being); but it lays most of the groundwork we need.

112

(4) The adequate cause of a changing being: proof for God's existence as uncaused cause

Now let us pose the chief question that we have had in mind all along. What is the *adequate* cause of a changing being—that cause which does not need to be explained in terms of other causes? Is there one? And how do we show it?

Suppose that we put the matter even more exactly than that. Some changes are fairly trivial (the sunburn, for example); others are quite radical (conception, death). But all changes, whether trivial or radical, require some cause for that change, external to the changing being. That changing being itself cannot come into being or go out of being, either completely or in part, all by itself. And so we can ask our question in one of two ways. What is required in order to explain, with full adequacy, the phenomenon of change? Or, perhaps more pointedly: can the fact of change be completely explained merely by the activity of other beings, themselves changeable? Or is something else required?

Two explanatory points first. (a) Any being that changes is a contingent being, i.e., there is no absolute requirement that it exist. For any changing being is a compound being, as we have seen, composed of at least an essence and an esse which are distinct from each other. Such a being can, therefore, not-exist; its essence is not identical with its esse, its essence is not to-exist. If existence is not of the essence of a being, then that being can either exist or not exist; and that is what is meant by a contingent being. (Conversely, if a being's essence *is* identical with, not distinct from, its esse, this means that its essence is, precisely, to exist—in other words, it cannot not-exist.) Put in these terms, our question becomes: what is required as the adequate, sufficient-unto-itself cause of a contingent being?

It is obvious that changing (and hence contingent) beings are often caused by other contingent beings. For example, we see the accidental change of an increase in temperature in a piece of wood being caused by fire—itself a contingent being. We see the death of a deer being caused by a hunter—himself a contingent being. But: is the causality exercised by one contingent being on another contingent being sufficient to explain *completely* the change that is brought about?

(b) We also need to know the difference between what is called an essential series of causes and an accidental series of causes. For instance, let us examine a change situation, one in which a match is lighted. What causes the fire? Friction, combined

113

with its action on sulphur (and whatever else goes into a match). What caused the friction? My hand. What caused the movement of my hand? My arm. What caused the movement of my arm? The nerves, muscles, etc., involved. What moved these latter?--and so on and on. As is obvious, a single action can have quite a number of causes.

However, quite a different sort of series could occur. Take the case of a row of dominoes, wherein domino #1 causes #2 to fall, #2 causes #3, and so forth, until the last domino in the row falls. In this sort of series, domino #1 exercises no direct causality on, let us say, domino #10 (for I can remove #1 from the row while #5 is falling, and still eventually get #10 to fall). In a series like this, the causal activity of any one member of the series is limited to its immediate neighbor in the causal chain.

Suppose that we call the domino-type series an "accidentally ordered" series of causes, as the traditional terminology would have it. In such a series, (i) the causal activity of any member is limited to its next-door neighbor in the causal chain, as has been said, and (ii) it is not necessary for all the causes to operate simultaneously in order for the effect to be produced. Let us call the other type of series (lighting the match, for example) an "essentially ordered" series: in this, (i) the causal activity of each member in the series is not restricted to its immediate next-door neighbor in the causal chain, and (ii) it is absolutely necessary that all the causes operate simultaneously if the effect is to be produced: take away any one of them, at any time during the causal action, and no effect results.

In both types of series, we have true causality at work. They are simply different types of series, and they operate differently. But: *when we are considering a series of causes in our discussion of the existence of God, we are thinking of an essentially ordered series, not an accidentally ordered one.*

Now to turn to the actual argument for the existence of God. We can ask: even when a series of causes is required (as opposed to a single cause), is even (an essentially ordered) series of merely contingent causes sufficient to explain change? Or must there be, at the back of the series, a non-contingent, necessary cause? The argument can be set out in several stages.

   (a) Nothing goes from potency to act except through some other being already in act, as we have seen.

   (b) Suppose you have some being, a combination of potency and act (i.e., an existing being, but one whose essence isn't to-exist, or, in other words, a contingent being).Let us call this being #5. And suppose that #5 was caused by #4.

(c) What of #4? One of two things has to be true: either it is not a composed being, or else it is a composed being. In the former case, you have a necessary being, one which is pure act without composition of act and potency. In the latter case, then #4, too, being composed, is a mixture of act and potency (in other words, it is a being which does exist, but whose essence is distinct from its esse, and therefore whose essence stands to its esse in the relationship of potency to act). In this latter case, we can then ask what gave act to #4's potency, i.e., what its cause was. And suppose that the answer is some other being, #3, maybe but not necessarily pure act without potency, i.e., a non-composed being.

(d) Repeat the same questions for #3 that were asked for #4.

(e) Thus we get a series: #1--- #2--- #3--- #4--- #5. Note that it makes no difference how many members the series has. The series in this particular example has five, but that is arbitrary; there could be as many as you like.

(f) Now, of this series, one of two things has to be true: either it is started by some being concerning whom the act/potency question cannot be raised (i.e., one that is pure act without potency), or else it is not. Let us examine the consequences of those two possibilities.

(i) If it is, then we have arrived at a being which is pure act, and there is no need to look further.

(ii) If it is not, then:

(1) For one thing, what we are really saying is that the series has no beginning, i.e., that there is no #1. For #1, as the *first* member of the series, would not be caused by anything outside of itself (otherwise it would not be first). However, it itself is a mixture of act and potency: it exists, but does not necessarily exist--i.e., it is (by hypothesis) contingent. However, it could not have actualized its own potency, for reasons that we have already seen in the principle of efficient

115

causality. Consequently that potency would not in fact be actualized. Therefore #1 would not exist.

In that case, look at #2, which is also act/potency, joined in fact together, i.e., caused. But, since there is no #1, there is nothing to actualize #2's potency; and #2 cannot do this for itself. Thus there is no #2, either. And so, if there is no #2, there is no #3, #4, or #5, for the same reasons.

BUT: there is, in fact, a #5--the entire discussion began, after all, with its existence. Therefore there must also be a #4, a #3, a #2, and a #1. Therefore the hypothesis that led to the conclusion that there is no #1 is wrong. Therefore also the hypothesis that this in turn depends on, i.e., that there is no being that is pure act without potency at the start of the series, is also wrong.

(2) Furthermore, under this hypothesis, we would be saying that the beings in the series simultaneously are and are not causes. For they would have to be in act in order to be causes--something is a cause only insofar as it is in act, not insofar as it is in potency. But the beings in the series cannot put themselves into act, for reasons already seen; and there is nothing else, by hypothesis, to put them into act. Therefore they are not in act. Therefore they are incapable of being causes. BUT: the discussion started out with the fact that they *are* causes.

(g) Therefore: since the hypothesis that the series is not begun by a being which is pure act has led to contradictory conclusions, and since there is here question of a complete dichotomy (the series either is or is not started by a being which is pure act--there is no third alternative), the conclusion must be that the series is, indeed, begun by a being concerning whom the act/potency question cannot be raised, i.e., one that is pure act without potency.

(5) Significance of all this for ethics

Such, then, is the argument that establishes the existence of a first cause of all change, a being that is pure act without potency. But the question comes up: once we have done all this, exactly what do we have?--that is to say, what good is it for ethics?

First, we have a necessary being, one which cannot not-exist. For since there is no potency in this being's make-up, its essence must be identical with its existence (its *esse*); we cannot, therefore, be talking about a composed being. And so we have a being which cannot go out of existence--and which could not have come into existence: in other words, a being which always was and always will be.

Next, let us reflect a bit upon the nature of act. In and of itself, act implies nothing but perfection; any imperfection that an act may have, in the beings of our experience, stems precisely from the limitations imposed on that act by the potency that receives it. The perfection of intelligence, for example, in and of itself implies no limitation; conceptually at any rate, there could be an intelligence which knew all things. Intelligence as we experience it, however, is limited intelligence--but its limitation comes from the particular human beings who happen to possess that perfection, not from the perfection itself. That is why we can have different levels of one and the same perfection in two different humans: one person can be more intelligent than another.

Moreover, the reason that something can be in potency to an act in the first place is that, at present, it doesn't have it. I cannot be in potency to some act that I already have; I can only be in potency to an act which I do *not* have. The reason that our necessary being, our uncaused cause, isn't in potency to any further act is that it already *has* all possible act. In other words, it has all possible perfections, without any of the sorts of limitations that potency--which this being doesn't have--would impose on those perfections.

If, however, this being has all possible perfections, in unlimited degree--if there exists no perfection that it doesn't have--then we can readily see that it possesses all good (or rather, since there is no composition in this being and hence no distinction between what it has and what it is, we should say that it *is* all good, *is* perfect good). Such a good would, if perfectly known, be a necessitating object for the human will, which seeks

117

goodness, simply, without taint of evil.

And--the point from which the very lengthy discussion of this present chapter started--such a being is both required and sufficient to constitute the ultimate objective norm of morality. The difference between our viewpoint now and the one we had when we first began the discussion, however, is: such a being would be required, would suffice, if it exists: which it does, a fact which we now see can be shown to be true.

SUMMARY OF CHAPTER SIX

A <u>norm</u> of morality is a standard, against which our actions are judged; actions conforming with the norm are termed "good," those at variance with it, "evil." Four norms of morality can be distinguished: ultimate subjective, ultimate objective, proximate subjective, and proximate objective; ideally, these should be in accord with one another. Chapter Six deals with the ultimate norms of morality.

<u>Ultimate Subjective Norm</u>: In whatever action we perform, we are seeking happiness, and, indeed, unlimited happiness. The proof for this is merely observational; the assertion is non-controversial. "Happiness" can be defined here as the permanent and total satisfaction of all one's desires, all one's powers. This desire for happiness is universal (possessed by all humans), unavoidable (life-long), and irresistible (relentlessly demanding satisfaction).

<u>Ultimate Objective Norm</u>: The argument identifying the object whose possession will result in perfect happiness is twofold: (i) from exclusion: that object cannot be something on the sub-human level ("goods of the world"); all such goods are partial and lack assured permanence--they are essentially transient. Neither can it be something on the human level (goods of the body or of the mind or of both taken together); these, too, are always either partial or impermanent. Finally, on the supra-human level: this could refer only to angels or God. The former are unknown philosophically and thus cannot serve; therefore, if such an object exists, it must be God. (ii) A positive argument: that alone can make humans perfectly and permanently happy which can totally satisfy their desires. But this requires such a being as God, for only He is perfect truth and goodness; moreover, God would be sufficient since He contains within himself all truth and goodness: there would be no need to possess anything else. However, one then needs to show that there is a God, if He is to function as ultimate objective norm. Philosophy can demonstrate the existence of "God" in the sense of a first cause of all being. While this "God" may be a pale shadow of the God of religious revelation, nevertheless the demonstration of his existence is not dependent upon authority.

The analysis of change is necessary background for this. Change always implies composition in the changing being; different sorts of changes indicate different levels of composition: accidental change (wherein the being's type does not change) indicates the presence of substance and accidents; substantial change (wherein that type does change), that of prime matter and substantial form. Moreover, an analysis of the fact that beings differ in their kind but are alike in that they truly exist reveals the presence of essence and Esse. These six are "imperfect beings," or "principles of being"; none of them can exist without the simultaneous presence of its correlative. Prime matter, substance, and essence resemble one another in that each limits what its correlative can do; substantial form, accident(s), and Esse resemble one

118

another in that each limits what its correlative can have done to it (or in that each specifies its correlative). Of these, the first three are traditionally called "potency," the second three "act"; this use of the two terms is based on the action that each principle of being exercises on its correlative. Seen from the standpoint of what it is in itself, potency is the ability to acquire some perfection, act is that perfection itself.

Also required for the proof is the principle of efficient causality, which states that nothing goes from a state of potency to a state of act (i.e., nothing changes) except under the influence of some being already in act. This statement is proved by the contradictions inherent in assuming its opposite.

The nub of the proof for the existence of a first uncaused cause is this: in an essentially ordered series of causes (not an accidentally ordered one), it is impossible to have an ultimate result that is a contingent being unless at the head of the causal series there is a necessary being; the very nature of a contingent being precludes its being the first cause of such a series. Such a necessary being, however, would have to be pure act, i.e., possess all possible perfections in permanent fashion; and that is what is required by our criteria for an ultimate objective norm of morality.

119

7. THE PROXIMATE NORMS OF MORALITY

II. The Theoretical Part of Ethics
   C. The Third Question: how do you tell whether a
      given action is good or evil?--the Norms of Morality
      2. The four norms of morality
         b. Proximate norms
            1) Need for proximate norms
            2) Proximate subjective norm: conscience
               a) What conscience is
               b) How it expresses itself
               c) Types of conscience
               d) Degrees of certitude, and the cer-
                  titude required for the moral life
               e) Norms governing the
                  operation of conscience
                  (1) a certain conscience: certain
                      and correct; certain and erroneous
                  (2) A doubtful conscience
                      (a) Direct means of solving a doubt
                      (b) Indirect means: safer
                          course, "lex dubia"
            3) Proximate objective norm: human
               nature completely considered
               a) Need for and characteristics of such a norm
               b) A problem, and the basis for a solution
               c) The proximate objective norm
               d) What "human nature" means
         c. A backward look: relationships among the norms.

b. Proximate norms

In the last chapter, we examined at some length the ultimate norms of morality, subjective and objective. We asked first what it is that we are ultimately aiming at in any imputable act we perform; and we saw that the answer to this is happiness: we are aiming at the complete and perfect satisfaction of all our desires. Then we asked what it is which, if we succeed in possessing it, will lead to happiness. We then saw that there is only one such thing, God. And we spent a good amount of time seeing that the unaided human reason can show that there is a supreme being, a first cause of all change. We did not (and did not attempt to) demonstrate the existence of God, in the full, rich sense that the Judaeo-Christian tradition asserts that existence. But we did show the existence of a being which, while admittedly a pale reflection of the Judaeo-Christian God, none the less makes the quite further step of accepting the existence of that Judaeo-Christian God a reasonable thing to do. And even the sort of "God" that we did succeed in establishing is sufficient to ground what we have said is the ultimate objective norm of morality--for that being can be shown to be pure act, pure perfection: in brief, that being which is capable of completely and permanently satisfying all our desires.

Now we face another question. We have already seen that people have wildly different notions about what will bring them happiness; and so, while this is a true ultimate (subjective) norm, it is not all that useful for judging the morality of actions in our everyday lives. For just about any action at all can (rightly or wrongly) be seen by someone as contributing to his or her happiness. Doubtless Adolf Hitler felt that the establishment of a master race through the extinction of entire nations and classes of people would bring him happiness; but few of us would regard the sort of genocide that occurred during World War II as being particularly moral. Hitler was, indeed, aiming at happiness; and to that extent, he was following the ultimate subjective norm of morality. But the very extravagance of the illustration show us that, while this is a true norm, it is not terribly helpful, by itself, in determining *accurately* whether a given action is good or evil. You need to be sure that the subjective and objective norms are in conformity before you can rely with much confidence on "happiness" as an adequate, day-to-day norm. Obviously, in Hitler's case, that conformity was not there. But even for the rest of us, the matter isn't a great deal easier. For exactly how do you know that your subjective and objective norms conform? That is to say, how *do* you know that an action which you feel will bring you happiness will, in fact, do that--i.e., will lead to the possession of God, wherein alone true happiness is to be found? Certainly, just assuming that something will make you happy, without further ado, will not do the job.

1) Need for proximate norms

Both of these ultimate norms need to be brought down closer to home if they are to be helpful moral guides for us. Are there other norms--auxiliary ones, if you like--that will be somewhat more practical? There are, as it turns out. And so we now turn our attention to the *proximate* norms of morality, both subjective and objective. We'll start with the subjective order.

2) Proximate subjective norm: conscience

The example of genocide, cited a paragraph or two ago, is perhaps too graphic, for this is something which--fortunately--does not come up all that often in human history. And so we might be tempted to see it as an aberration: something terribly tragic, of course, but not something to be considered very much when we are trying to formulate general norms that apply to normal people. And so let us take another example, one perhaps a bit distant from ourselves, but a good illustration of a point nevertheless. What does one make of a cannibal, who is truly convinced that it is perfectly acceptable (morally), right, good, and tasty to boil and eat missionaries? He is objectively wrong, of course. But let us suppose that he is also invincibly ignorant of that fact; as far as he knows, what he is doing is right. Is it legitimate to say that someone is blameworthy because he or she does something which that person believes to be right, even though it is in fact wrong?

Nor do we have to go that far away from home for examples. What do we make of a student, for example, who is quite convinced that it is morally acceptable to cheat on examinations and papers (provided only that one doesn't get caught)? For the sake of argument, let us assume that this is the student's honest conviction. Is he or she blameworthy for doing what he or she believes to be a good act--even though it is objectively wrong? Or: what of the person who sincerely believes that racial prejudice is perfectly all right--even sanctioned and encouraged by the Bible (as certain people in our own country actually do believe)? We would probably want to say that they are wrong. But are they blameworthy? Are they evil people because they perform actions that are objectively evil--even though they don't believe that that is the case?

This, then, leads us into the whole area of conscience, which will be the proximate subjective norm of morality. We can ask several questions about conscience.

a) What conscience is

First, what is conscience? Maybe a good way to start is to say what conscience is *not*. It is not a "little voice" inside us, telling us what is right and wrong. This may be an interesting metaphor; it may be a certain species of poetry. But it is nothing more than that. It certainly is not a description of conscience.

Conscience is a person's reason, making a practical, concrete judgment about the morality of an action that that person is about to perform (or has already performed).

b) How it expresses itself

It is worth noting just how the reasoning process involved in a judgment of conscience works. First, any particular dictate of conscience is, without fail, the conclusion of a deductive mode of reasoning called a syllogism--though it may not always be expressed in that full-blown a fashion. And so, when I make the judgment, "I should not tell this lie," the following premises lie back of it: "I should not tell lies; but this is a lie; therefore I should not tell it." We can ask where the major premise of this syllogism, in turn ("I should not tell lies") came from. This, too, is the conclusion of a further, antecedent syllogism, something like, "I should not do things that destroy society; but telling lies destroys society; therefore I should not tell lies." The major premise of *that* syllogism, in turn ("I should not do things that destroy society"), can be traced back to yet a further premise--something like, "I should not destroy things necessary for human life; but society is necessary for human life; therefore I should not destroy society." And so on and on. However, eventually one arrives at a fundamental principle that, in itself, is not the conclusion of some anterior reasoning process. That principle is: "Do good and avoid evil." This is a principle that is known by immediate intellective induction, or "intuition"; it does not rely on anything more general than itself for the good reason that there is nothing in the moral order more general than it.

(By way of a brief tangent, it might be worth our while to note here a fact--disconcerting to some, perhaps--about human reasoning. When one is still fairly new at the enterprise that is philosophy, the temptation is strong to insist that everything must be "proved." If this merely means that everything must be shown to be reasonable, that it not rely on sources outside of the unaided human reason, etc., it is laudable enough [and by no means confined to beginners]. If, on the other hand, it is intended to mean [as it often is] that every conclusion must be capable of being "proved" in the sense of being put into the form of a deductive syllogism, wherein the conclusion is shown to be simply the implication of a wider truth that forms the major premise of that syllogism, then this is to place impossible restrictions on philosophic thought. For not everything can be thus derived from a wider truth--there comes a point in

human reasoning where there is no wider truth from which to deduce conclusions. To demand otherwise is to insist on an infinite regress. As Aristotle [Metaphysics, *IV, 1011a 11-15]* once snapped about people who insist on such a thing: "They are after a reason for things for which no reason can be given--the starting point of demonstration is not demonstration." There are two ultimate truths, not deducible from some further premise, in human reasoning: one in the speculative order [the principle of contradiction], and one in the moral order [do good and avoid evil]. These truths must be known in some other way [for, again, from what would one deduce them?], which other way is, not deduction, but rather intellective induction, or intuition.)*

c) Types of conscience

What sorts of conscience are there? We can look at the idea of "conscience" in various ways. The following types are merely the most common designations, and they are not mutually exclusive. First, there is a *correct* and an *incorrect* conscience. As the names would indicate, a correct conscience judges something to be good (or evil), which something *is,* objectively, good (or evil). An incorrect conscience does the reverse. Thus, the cannibal who feels justified in feasting on missionaries possesses an incorrect conscience. So does the sincerely cheating student.

Then, one can look on conscience as *antecedent* or *consequent.* An antecedent conscience judges the morality of an act that a person is about to perform, and a consequent conscience is concerned with the morality of an action that has already taken place. And so, when we speak of "examining our conscience," we are normally referring to consequent conscience. On the other hand, that familiar "Should I do this or shouldn't I?" question is usually the operation of antecedent conscience.

There can also be question of a *scrupulous* conscience or a *lax* one. A scrupulous conscience (which can be either antecedent or consequent) tends to exaggerate obligations; and a lax one--also either antecedent or consequent--tends to minimize them.

Finally, there is the distinction between a *certain* and a *doubtful* conscience; and the distinction is of some importance for us. Telling the two types apart is easy enough: a certain conscience makes its judgment about the morality of an action without fear of error, whereas a doubtful conscience either refrains from making a judgment at all, or else makes one with considerable fear of being wrong. One area of importance the distinction has for our purposes lies in this question: how certain does a conscience have to be, if an action is to be moral? For we are all acquainted with some situations in which we have no doubt that an action we are about to do (or have done) is good, others in which we have no doubt (though we may regret) that our action is or was evil. But there are a fair number of situations about which we simply are not certain. The question is worth some investigation.

**d) Degrees of certitude, and the
certitude required for the moral life**

First, there are various degrees of certitude which I can have in different situations. (i) There is such a thing, for example, as *metaphysical* certitude. In this, the opposite of what I judge to be true is a formal contradiction in terms. To take a time-honored illustration, I judge it to be metaphysically certain that every triangle has three sides. The opposite of that judgment would be a contradiction: a triangle, which is *defined* as a three-sided figure, would--granted the opposite of my judgment--also be able to have a different number of sides, i.e., would both be and not be a three-sided figure. That is a contradiction. (ii) Secondly, there is *physical* certitude: the opposite of what I judge to be true is not a formal contradiction in terms, but it would take a miracle to bring it about. For instance: I judge that an unsupported object, in certain circumstances, will fall. I have physical certitude of this. For, while that object *could* stay suspended in the air (there is nothing intrinsically contradictory about the idea), it would none the less take a miracle to bring it about. (iii) Finally, there is *moral* (or *"prudential"*) certitude. This is the certitude that someone has who excludes all *prudent* fear that the opposite of his or her judgment may be true. It doesn't exclude *all* possibility of error; but the reasons in favor of the judgment are strong enough to satisfy a normally prudent person in an important matter, even though there may still be a theoretical possibility that he or she could be wrong. Prudential certitude, then, excludes all *reasonable* fear of error. It isn't a 100% assurance; on the other hand, neither is it merely a high probability that I am not in error.

In ordinary human life, metaphysical certitude is rarely come by. We encounter it, on those infrequent occasions when it is present at all, largely in the area of the speculative sciences--and certainly, we almost never find it in ethics.

Physical certitude is equally rare, when there is question of human actions (or at least of imputable ones). And so, in ethical judgments, moral or prudential certitude will turn out to be all that is required, for the good reason that it is often (usually, in fact) all that is available.

That, however, points to something worth noticing. While ethics, in general, seeks to establish norms of conduct that have a high degree of certitude (different degrees, perhaps, in the case of different norms), none the less the *application* of those norms to individual, concrete cases will not have that same degree of certitude. For while the norms themselves may be quite certain, their degree of applicability to a given case may be quite another matter, and in any event, is going to be something accomplished by a quite fallible human intellect, making the best possible judgment in the circumstances--which judgment may be wrong. And so, again, moral or prudential certitude will be about the best that we can achieve, when judging the morality of at least some particular cases.

What we have seen thus far, then, are the types of conscience, and the varieties of certitude available to a conscience on different occasions. Now, conscience is a judgment; and as such, it properly belongs to the intellect. It tells us when an action is evil, when it is good, and when it is doubtful. But we can ask: so what? That is to say, what obligations do I have in regard to the judgments of conscience, and why? That is a long and complicated question, but for now it can at least serve to introduce us to the moral rules that govern our response to the dictates of conscience. The full justification of those rules is something that we will be able to see only at the end of this chapter.

e) Norms governing the operation of conscience

There are two rules governing our response to conscience, both of them much more easily stated than applied: (a) Always obey a certain conscience; (b) Never act with a doubtful conscience. Let us consider each of these in turn and at some length.

(1) A certain conscience: certain and correct; certain and erroneous

First, then, we should always obey a certain conscience, i.e., a judgment about the morality of a given action that is made without fear of error. This rule causes little problem when there is question of a conscience that is both certain and correct; all that is then being said is, "Follow the proximate subjective norm of morality"—and, if one seeks the ultimate justification for that, all we are doing is following the fundamental precept of all morality, "Do good and avoid evil." And so, for instance, when my conscience tells me that a given action I'm planning is morally good, it tells me that I may perform that action, if I wish, and if I do so, I will be doing good and avoiding evil. I plan, for example, to give a certain amount of money to a favorite charity of mine. Conscience, having reviewed my motives for doing so, the circumstances of the act (e.g., whether the money is mine to give, whether I can give it without harming myself and others, etc., etc.), concludes that such an act would be good, and that I may perform it morally. Here, my conscience is certain (my judgment is without reasonable fear of error), and it is correct: it *is,* objectively, good for me to donate the money, in the particular circumstances in which I find myself. Much the same sort of process would have been followed in an instance wherein conscience judged that some act which I am planning is evil.

The problem, of course, comes when my conscience is both certain and erroneous: I judge an action to be good (or evil), and I do so without any fear of being wrong. The only problem is that I am in fact wrong: from an objective moral standpoint, the action is the reverse of what I judge it to be. The case of the cannibal who has a taste for missionaries, cited earlier, is an instance of this. What obligations do I have in such a case, and why?

First, if the error is vincible, then obviously I must correct it. Otherwise I am freely embracing the possibility of doing evil, and that is the same thing as intending evil—the essence of immorality, as has been said. What I am really saying in such a case is, "This may be good and it may be evil, and I don't care: I'm going to do it, whichever it is." However, this is more theoretical than practical, since it is open to question just how a vincibly ignorant conscience could be a certain conscience in the first place (though there could perhaps be a limiting case or two in which that might be true).

However, if the error is invincible—and we should recall to mind the various ways in which we can find ourselves in invincible ignorance, which we have seen earlier (pages 38–39)—then we must follow our conscience, even though the action is objectively wrong. The reason for this is that, practically speaking, in such a case the erroneous conscience is the only guide that a person has; and that person's obligation is to *choose* (for, again, human nature is a rational one) the action that he or she judges will be good. The person is wrong, obviously, but not blameworthy, since he or she is not *choosing evil voluntarily.*

The point is worth stressing, for it is the explanation of the cannibal, the cheating student, and other such. No one ever said that conscience would protect against all error; in fact, fallibility is itself a part of human nature. It is possible to have an action that is objectively wrong and subjectively right--and vice versa. Moreover, an invincibly ignorant and erroneous conscience cannot really be distinguished, operationally, from a correct one: the obligation to follow the one entails the obligation to follow the other. For by its nature, the will chooses the good *as presented to it* by the intellect--even if the latter happens to be dead wrong.

In summary, then: we must always follow a certain conscience, whether it is correct or whether it is invincibly erroneous. Why? The reason is not hard to see. The fundamental human operation involved is choice, and the basic ethical principle is that in our choices we must always opt for the good--but the good as humanly known. That latter factor always admits the possibility of error.

(2) A doubtful conscience

There remains, now, the question of what we are obligated to do when our conscience is doubtful. The principle that was cited earlier read, "Never act with a doubtful conscience." That does not mean that, in such circumstances, we cannot act at all. It means that we must solve the doubt, by one or other means, before acting. There are various ways to do this--which, incidentally, have to be used in the order in which they will be given below.

(a) Direct means of solving a doubt

There is first the direct means of resolving a doubt. We can sometimes clear up a doubt by asking questions of someone else, by reading, by reasoning, etc. Generally, this is an attempt to answer the question, "What are the facts of this case? Is this action, in itself, good or evil?" Frequently, given the added information that our searching provides, we can resolve our

129

doubt. For example: I discover that my checking account's balance, according to my bank statement, is $20 more than I had figured it was. My question is whether I can go ahead and spend that $20. Of course, I am not sure whether it is mine or not--and, obviously, I cannot spend someone else's money, i.e., money that was put into my account, say, by error. One obvious direct means is to go over my check stubs and see whether my own arithmetic is correct. I may thereby solve the doubt. I can also call the bank and have the accounted reviewed. That, also, may solve the doubt. Those are instances of direct means.

(b) Indirect means: safer course, "lex dubia"

If I can resolve a doubt my a reasonable use of a direct means, then I must do so. However, there are times when I cannot do so--at least reasonably, i.e., by means of an amount of effort proportionate to the seriousness of the matter in question. Suppose that I am the leader of a safari in Africa, and a member of my party is bitten by a certain variety of snake. My native guides tell me that the roots of a certain tree are a good cure for this particular bite. They may be; they may also be quite deadly poison in themselves. May I morally administer the medicine? Certainly, I am in no position to take direct means to resolve my doubt: the nearest doctor, or medical book, is miles away--and the patient needs treatment now. Or, to revert to the example of my checking account once more: if the sum in question had been twenty cents instead of twenty dollars, then the amount of checking on my arithmetic that I would reasonably be required to do decreases considerably, given the triviality of the matter; certainly, I would have no obligation to call the bank! The *reasonable* use of direct means has become impossible in both of these examples--even though, strictly speaking, I could (if ornery and persistent enough) probably resolve the matter of the twenty cents if I kept after it long enough.

Even though I cannot, in such cases, answer the question that the direct means seeks to answer ("What are the facts of this case? Is this, in itself, a morally good action or not?"), I can and must always resolve this question: "Granted that the facts of the case are and will remain unclear, what obligation do I have in this case? What must I do about this matter here and now?" When--*and only when*--we find ourselves in a doubtful conscience situation, and when the direct means cannot reasonably be used, then there are two principles that can be employed: (a) "The safer course should be followed"; and (b) "A doubtful law does not bind." These two are *not* alternatives; there are definite

130

instances when one or other can, and when one or other must, be used.

(a) "The safer course should be followed": I *may* always use this principle, and by means of it I will certainly solve the doubt I have about my present obligation. I *must* use this principle when there is question of some goal that I am obligated to achieve, a duty that I am obligated to perform--and when my doubt is merely about the means that have to be used in order to achieve that goal or perform that duty. To borrow the classic example: a doctor is obligated to achieve the goal of saving his or her patient, if possible; if there is a choice between two medicines, one of which will certainly cure the patient and the other of which, though of personal interest to the doctor, is more or less experimental and may or may not work, then the doctor is obligated to use the surer one. So also, a lawyer is obligated to defend his or her client; the use of weaker (but perhaps more flashy and clever) arguments is impermissible if there are stronger ones available. And so on. We will see other instances of this principle at work later on in this book.

(b) "A doubtful law does not bind": sometimes, following the safer course can impose a serious burden that I may not wish needlessly to undertake. In such cases, and unless there *is* question of a goal or duty to which I am obligated, I can use this principle, known traditionally as the "lex dubia" principle. Suppose, for example, I am driving along the street in a strange city late one night. I do not know what the speed limit is. There are no reasonable direct means of finding out: filling stations are closed, I have no map in the car that would give me the information, there are no posted signs, etc. I *could*, of course, take the safer course: I could stop driving and wait until the morning, and in that way I would certainly not violate any speed law. But this is far more than I can reasonably be expected to do. For one thing, the hotels are closed too, and spending the night sleeping in my car is a pretty stiff price to pay for assuring conformity with a minor law! I therefore use the "lex dubia" principle and, while (for other reasons) driving sanely enough, yet do not worry about the obligation imposed by that particular law.

Notice, however, which "doubt" this principle is resolving and which one it isn't. It is answering the question of whether I am obligated to do something or obligated to refrain from it. It is not answering the question of whether the action in question (e.g., driving at 35 m.p.h. rather than 25) is objectively in conformity with the law, is objectively moral or not. The principle merely asserts that an uncertain law--whatever it is in itself--cannot

131

impose a certain obligation. And so, in circumstances where this principle is legitimately applied, I may go ahead and perform the action, or not perform it, as I choose.

3) Proximate objective norm: human nature completely considered

Let's consider for a moment just where we are in our investigation of the norms of morality. We have seen the ultimate subjective norm, happiness; and we know what that means. We also know that, while a valid norm, it is not particularly useful in our daily lives, because people have such a disparity of ideas as to what will bring them happiness. And so we investigated a norm that is closer to home, in the subjective order: the norm of conscience. Now, we know that the ultimate and the proximate norms should coincide, at least ideally: if we follow our consciences, we should arrive at happiness. (That last sentence is fairly carefully stated: the ultimate and proximate norms *should* coincide. We have not yet established that in fact they *do* coincide. We will discuss this point near the end of this present chapter.)

We have also looked at the ultimate objective norm of morality, God. And we have seen that God is the sole object whose possession can provide us with true happiness. If, then, following the norm of conscience should mean that we are thereby following the norm of happiness, it should also mean that we are following the norm that is God: as far as a correct conscience, at least, is concerned, that should be termed a good act which leads us to the possession of God, and that should be termed an evil act which leads us away from God.

a) Need for and characteristics of such a norm

Fine. But how do we know what sorts of acts will lead us to the possession of God? Or--the same question, really--conscience is supposed to make judgments concerning the morality of our actions. On what basis? What is the criterion that it will use? God? Certainly, God (and the possession of God) would be a true criterion for the judgments that conscience must make. But that criterion, while true, wouldn't be very helpful, for God is a difficult sort of thing to know--to say nothing of the difficulty in knowing what sorts of actions will lead to the possession of God, and what sorts won't. We are in a parallel position to where we were when we considered the ultimate subjective norm, happiness: our ultimate norm is true, but it is not all that useful. Once again--this time in the objective order--we need a norm that is closer to us, one that we can know readily and thus can make use of in our everyday lives. Obviously, if it is to serve its purpose, it will have to be a norm that is in conformity with that ultimate objective norm: that is, in seeking to abide by it, we must also be able to have confidence that we are thereby also abiding by the ultimate norm, God.

However, since we are seeking a proximate norm in the objective order rather than the subjective one, there are several other characteristics that will have to be true of this norm, if it is to be of any help to us. For example, it will need to be *uniform,* in the sense that it will apply to all men and women. For we are all human, with the same objective goal of the moral life. Furthermore, such a norm will have to be *universal:* it must be capable of telling whether *any* human act, without exception, does in fact lead us or not lead us to our ultimate goal. It must also be *accessible* to us, readily available in all times and places--for, after all, the reason that we are seeking it in the first place is that the ultimate objective norm is *not* readily accessible. And finally, such a proximate norm will need to be a *fixed* one, one that is equally valid for one age as it is for another. For, just as the ultimate norm does not change from one age to another, so also neither must the proximate one--for humans don't change very much, either, at least substantially. On the other hand, it will need to be flexible enough to take account of varying circumstances in different ages, for there are *some* changes in human life that have to be taken into account, anyway. Our proximate objective norm, then, ought to have all these characteristics, if it is to be both true and useful--which is, after all, why we are seeking it.

b) A problem, and the basis for a solution

We have seen the sort of norm we need. But is there such a thing? For, obviously, we have a problem here. We have two things: action, and a goal (God). We are trying to judge the morality of the actions. On what basis? The goal won't work for us, for it is not well enough known. Obviously, the actions themselves cannot function as a criterion--they're *what* we are trying to judge, and so they cannot be the criterion of that judgment.

Where do we go from here? Truth be told, we have more than

133

just actions and goals to work with. If we think back on what we saw while laying the groundwork for the proof of the existence of God, we will remember that one of the constituent metaphysical "parts" that make up human beings is substance. This is that constituent part which makes a being to be, fundamentally, the sort of thing which it is. Now, our explanation of substance was necessarily brief when we saw it earlier. But a moment or two of further reflection on it will be helpful now. If I am concerned with what a being *is,* in the main (i.e., without worrying about its accidental qualifications), I am concerned with its substance. This we have seen. What, however, if I am concerned with what a being *does* (again, in the main, and without accidental qualifications)? With what am I dealing in that case? I am once again dealing with that being's substance, for something acts only in accord with what it is. That isn't particularly esoteric. A human being acts humanly only if it exists humanly; a dog, for example, does not act in a human fashion, for the good reason that it does not exist as a human. So also, a tree produces apples only if it exists as an apple tree: something which exists as, say, a pig does not produce apples. Actions, then, follow upon and are a function of the type of being that is in question; and a being's type, as we have seen, is a function of its substance. However, we can notice some traditional terminology that will be useful to us. If I am concerned simply with what something *is,* with no further qualifications, I am concerned with its substance. If, on the other hand, I am concerned not only with what that something is but also with what it *does,* then I am concerned with its nature. The two terms "substance" and "nature" do not differ very much: nature is nothing more than substance, except that it is substance viewed with reference to the activity that is proper to that substance. Nature, then, *is* substance, but under a particular aspect, that of activity.

Using that terminology, then, we can say that a being always acts in accord with its nature. Again, this is saying nothing more or less than that a being always acts in accord with its substance--according to that principle that makes it be the sort of being that it is (and therefore which makes it act in the particular way that it does).

All this is more than idle speculation, for our purposes. For it means that we are *not* limited just to acts and goal when we are looking for a proximate objective norm of morality. Actions always involve something else: they involve a nature. For that matter, actions are always dictated by a nature: as a being is, so does it act. And so, if (as we have seen) we cannot use the goal or the actions in trying to discover our proximate norm, then perhaps we can use the nature back of those actions for that purpose.

Let's look at an example from the animal kingdom to see how this might work. Consider the activity of an animal in, say, nourishing itself. What is the goal of this animal's activity (i.e., the goal of the work, not the goal of the worker)? That goal--not, obviously, known by the animal itself, at least as a goal--is to be the best possible animal of its species, given its particular circumstances. In particular, the goal of the action of nutrition is the growth of the animal to full maturation, and then the preservation of that animal's well being. But notice something. Take two animals, say, a Saint Bernard and a parrot. Both exercise the same activity of nourishment. But in the case of the Saint Bernard, the activity is directed toward the growth of a bushy tail, healthy (and huge) paws, etc. In the case of the parrot, it is directed toward the development of feathers, wings, etc. Nourishment is *not* directed toward the development of large paws in the case of the parrot; neither--fortunately--is it directed toward the development of wings on the Saint Bernard. Rather, activity like this is always directed toward the perfection of the specific nature of the individual being that performs it. That is to say, the Saint Bernard's activity is directed toward the production of the best Saint Bernard possible, the activity of the parrot toward the best parrot possible in these circumstances, and so on. The same thing will be true of all other activities (generation, organization, irritability, adaptation, etc.), wherever these are found: each is directed toward the perfection of the nature of the being performing it--and not some other nature. To put all this briefly, the activity of a particular being is always directed, in accord with that being's nature, toward that being's ultimate perfection, its last end.

Can the same thing be said of human activity? Is human activity always directed toward the perfection of human nature? For here, too, we are dealing with a given nature, just as we were in the case of the animals. The answer is a qualified yes; some care needs to be taken. For human beings are rational animals, and an essential part of their rationality is their freedom of choice, as we have seen. And so all of their imputable acts are free acts. It follows, then, that while the Saint Bernard's actions will always be aimed at the true good (and final end) of the Saint Bernard, a human's actions may in fact not be--though they will always be aimed at what that human *thinks* is for his or her perfection (whether or not it actually is so in the objective order).

None the less, in the case of humans too, the relationship among nature, act, and goal will hold. Any action done in accord with nature will lead to the end of that nature, and that end is the ultimate good of the being in question. Any action done not in harmony with nature will lead away from that end, will hinder the gaining of that end. Of course, it is only on the human level that you have an agent capable of choosing acts that do, objectively, lead away from the true end of its nature.

c) The proximate objective norm

And so we have our proximate objective norm: any action that is done in accord with human rational nature will lead to that nature's ultimate end, its ultimate good, and so that action will be itself good. Any action done in disharmony with that nature will lead away from that end, and so will be evil.

d) What "human nature" means

Isn't all this, though, a matter of defining something that isn't too clear by means of something that is even less clear? To say that an act is good if it is in accord with human nature is fine, provided that one knows what is meant by "human nature."

The matter really isn't all that complicated. A satisfactory working notion, at least, of what human nature is can be gotten by some fairly easy reflection. What is it to be human? It is at least the following: (1) It is to be made up of certain parts, which stand to one another in a certain ranked order of importance, as we have seen in the analysis of change. At the very least, it is to be made up of rationality and animality, with the former enjoying the more important place. Each of these two, in turn, can be subdivided further, again in an ordered series of importance: intellect and will, as powers of the soul, in the case of the rational part of humans; sense powers, physical parts (arms, legs, muscle, bone, etc.) in the case of the animal part of human nature. (2) Moreover, to be human is to possess a certain number of relationships. First, there is a relationship to God, for as contingent beings, humans have a relationship of dependence on their ultimate first cause. (Remember that every change a human being undergoes, no matter how trivial, has as its ultimate cause, in the essentially related series of causes, the necessary being: the uncaused cause.) Then, a human being has a relationship to other human beings. Humans are by their nature social beings (a fact that we will see in more detail later on), and they must live and work with others of their species. Finally, humans have relationships to things on the sub-human level—i.e., they have need for the use of certain material things (food, drink, clothing, etc.); about all this, again, more later.

Seen in this light, the proximate objective norm of morality could be stated this way: that is a good act which fosters and develops human nature (in all of its ordered parts and ordered relationships); that is an evil act which hampers and tends toward the destruction of human nature (again, in all its ordered parts and ordered relationships). This obviously needs some fleshing out and application. But at least we now have our basic norm in place.

In passing, we might note that it is sometimes said that the proximate objective norm of morality is "right reason." We have said, instead, that it is "human nature," or, to be more exact, "human nature taken completely" (i.e., in all of its parts and relationships). But the difference between these two statements is much more verbal than real, and the two can be combined satisfactorily. For it is reason that judges when an action is or is not in conformity with human nature taken completely; and when it does so properly, it is called "right reason." The question is simply whether one wants to stress the power (reason) that makes the judgment --and the quality of that judgment--or wishes to stress the item on which that judgment is passed (human nature taken completely). Perhaps one could accommodate both sides of this minor dispute by saying simply that the proximate objective norm of morality is human reason judging correctly (= "right reason") about the conformity or disconformity of a given action with human nature taken in all its parts and all its relationships.

c. A backward look: relationships among the norms

Now we need to go back and answer a question which--quite deliberately--we slighted earlier. We said that the ultimate and the proximate norms that we have identified *should* coincide: by following the proximate, we should be following the ultimate. But do they? Are we? Moreover, we said that the subjective and the objective norms *should* coincide, so that by following the subjective--truly following them--we are also following the objective. Do they? Are we? This, then, is the question of the relationships among the four norms of morality. As we examine these relationships, we will hope to answer our earlier, slighted question. We may also find that our knowledge of the norms themselves gets sharpened a bit in the process.

The visual sketch on the next page may help.

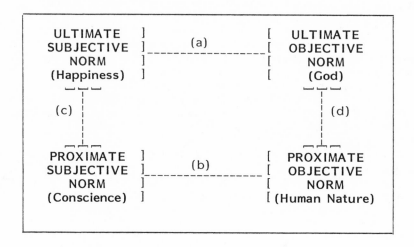

Let us first look at the relationship suggested by the two horizontal broken lines, (a) and (b), the relationship between the subjective and the objective. In each case (ultimate and proximate), this is a relationship between (i) something expressing a need, and (ii) the adequate object needed to satisfy that need. This is easy to see in the case of the ultimate norms. Happiness is the expression of a need: for an object, namely, that can perfectly fulfill all our desires; and God is the sole object that can fulfill that need. In sum: the subjective norm expresses a need, and the objective one satisfies it. Much the same thing can be said on the proximate level. For conscience is also the expression of a need. Conscience is to make judgments on an action's morality, but on what basis? There is a need of something whereby it can make those judgments; and human nature turns out to be the object that will exclusively provide the fulfillment of that need: it is the only criterion that will meet the need that conscience expresses.

That last statement, however, needs some proof, since it is anything but immediately obvious. First, let us recall some things that we already know. God, as first uncaused cause, is pure act, without potency. God therefore has all perfections, and in the highest degree. God is therefore truthful. Also, as first uncaused cause, God is ultimately responsible for the make-up of human nature: he made humans to be what they are. Having given them a certain type of nature, however, he *therefore* also gave them a certain type of activity that is proper to them (for nature, remember, is simply essence viewed in terms of activity). That activity, however, always has as its goal (the goal of the work, not the goal of the worker) the perfection of the nature in question. All this we have seen before.

Now, we can go on and also say that it is therefore the intention of God that humans should act in accord with their nature and thereby perfect that nature. For if it were otherwise (i.e., if God intended humans to perform some sort of action that was not in conformity with their nature), then he would be involved in a contradiction: by giving them a certain nature, he automatically wills them to perform acts of one type (i.e., the action suited to the perfection of their natures), *and simultaneously* (by hypothesis) he really wills them to perform some other, contrary type of act. That, of course, is an impossibility, for it has God both willing and not willing something at the same time--a contradiction, something not possible in the case of an all-perfect (and therefore all-truthful) being.

Result: human nature taken completely turns out to be exactly what conscience is looking for as a criterion for its judgments, for the perfection of that human nature, through its own activities, is precisely an expression of the commandments of God, the ultimate norm.

The relationship between subjective and objective norms which we sketched, then (expression of need, adequate object to satisfy that need), is established. Now let us look at the vertical broken lines in the diagram, (c) and (d), the relationship between the ultimate and the proximate. If we recall why we needed a proximate norm in the first place (the ultimate norm was either too ill-defined or too difficult to know), then the following relationship suggests itself: precisely in and through following the proximate norm, we thereby follow the ultimate one. By following conscience's judgments, we are following the norm of happiness. By performing actions in conformity with human nature taken completely, we are following the ultimate norm, God.

The relationship suggests itself, yes. But is it correct? We have already seen that in the case of the objective norms it is indeed correct: that is exactly what we had to show in order to prove the point that human nature taken completely is the adequate criterion for the judgments of conscience. By following the criterion of human nature, then, we are following the criterion of God. Is the same thing true of the subjective order? That is to say, when we follow the dictates of conscience, are we also following the criterion of happiness? Yes. A little reasoning will show that it has to be so. For happiness consists in the complete and total fulfillment of our desires. But that fulfillment is possible only if human nature attains its fulfillment in the possession of God--and it is toward that fulfillment of human nature that the judgments of conscience are directed. In other words, by following (a correct) conscience, we arrive at the perfecting of human nature, which in turn leads to the possession of God, which in turn leads to happiness. And thus--to skip the middle steps in this particular sorites--by following conscience we do arrive at happiness.

Two final observations need to be made on all this. First, exactly what do we mean when we say that God is the ultimate objective norm? For we seem to be using the term "God" in different senses--in one case, we refer to God's commandments as a norm, in another we speak of the possession of God by us as a norm. True enough. Indeed, in human terms, we have to do this. But: since in God there is no composition, no division into parts, there is equally no division between God's essence and his activity. Thus, there is no difference between saying "God is the ultimate norm" and saying "God's activity in giving commandments [or those commandments themselves, for that matter] is the norm." Equally, there is no difference between saying "God is the ultimate norm" and saying "God's activity in bestowing happiness in our possession of him is the ultimate norm." And so, though it does *seem* that we use the term "God" in different senses (and, as has been remarked, we have to speak that way in human terms), in reality this is not the case.

Secondly, what does all this mean, in practical terms? It means simply this: if we follow the dictates of conscience--a conscience which is "correctly formed" (i.e., bases its judgments properly on human nature)--then our actions will be moral and will lead to happiness in the possession of God, our uncaused first cause. If on the other hand we do not follow the dictates of such a conscience, then our actions will not be moral and they will not lead to happiness; indeed, they will lead to complete unhappiness, ultimately. That, in brief, is the whole burden of this chapter and the preceding one.

SUMMARY OF CHAPTER SEVEN

Chapter Seven deals with the proximate norms of morality. Though the existence of the ultimate norms of morality has been established, they remain somewhat impractical: people vary widely in what they think will provide happiness, and God is rather far removed from us--what actions will lead us to the possession of him? Other, more useful, norms are needed.

The <u>Proximate Subjective Norm</u> is conscience, i.e., the judgment of reason on the morality of some action which we contemplate performing or have performed. Conscience always expresses itself in the form of a judgment, which is in turn the conclusion of a practical syllogism; the ancestry of that syllogism can be traced back to a single moral principle ("Do good and avoid evil") which is known by intellective induction ("intuition"). Conscience can be characterized in various ways: antecedent or consequent (to the action to be performed); correct or incorrect (depending on its conformity to objective morality); scrupulous or lax (if it tends either to exaggerate or to minimize obligations); and certain or doubtful (depending on the degree of certainty that underlies its judgment). Certitude, in general, is either metaphysical (the reverse involves a contradiction), physical (the reverse would require a miracle to come about), or moral (excluding all reasonable fear of error); moral judgments ordinarily attain only moral certitude, since this is all that is usually available.

Two chief norms govern the operation of conscience: (i) Always obey a certain conscience (even when it is objectively wrong--since it is the only guide available in some cases to help us fulfill the obligation of not choosing evil); and (ii) Never act with a doubtful conscience. The latter imposes on us the obligation of solving a doubt, whether by direct means (asking others, reading, etc.), or, failing that, by means of one of the two reflex principles of (a) safer course (which must always be used when there is question of a clear obligation that we have and when the doubt centers merely about the means of fulfilling that obligation) and (b) lex dubia (which may be used when there is no such obligation).

The Proximate Objective Norm, if it is to be helpful, must be uniform (applying to all human beings), universal (governing all imputable acts without exception), and accessible (readily available to us when needed). Such a norm can be neither the action itself (which is what we are trying to judge) nor the (ultimate) goal, God (who is too distant from us to be a useful norm). However, actions are always a function of substance (whose other name, when considered with reference to activity, is nature). We notice in the sub-human world that agents always act in accord with their nature, and thereby attain their end, which is the perfection of that nature. The same is true for humans, though with reservations necessitated by human free will: human activity is always aimed at what humans think will be for the perfection of their nature, whether it actually be so or not. None the less, on the human level as well as the sub-human, the relationship among nature, action, and end will hold true: an action which is in fact done in accord with human nature will lead to the perfection of that nature, and one done out of accord with that nature will lead to the detriment of that nature. An action's accordance with human nature, then, or "rational action," is the proximate objective norm of morality. "Human nature" here means to be made up of certain parts (particularly rationality and animality) in ranked order of importance, and to have certain ranked relations (to God, to other human beings, to other beings on the sub-human level). And so that is a good act which fosters and develops human nature in all its ordered parts and ordered relationships; that is an evil act which does the reverse of this.

The conformity of the various norms of morality with one another can be shown. (i) Subjective norms conform to objective: The subjective norms, whether ultimate or proximate, are the expression of a need (for an object that can fulfill all our desires [ultimate], for a criterion whereby moral judgments can be accurately made [proximate]). In each case, the objective norms form the sole object that can satisfy that need (God [ultimate], human nature [proximate]). (ii) Proximate norms conform to ultimate: Moreover, by following proximate norms (conscience, human nature), we are thereby following ultimate norms: by following the norm of human nature we are following the criterion of God himself who gave that nature; and by following the norm of conscience we are thereby following the norm of happiness, since the latter can be achieved only through the fulfillment of human nature in the possession of God--toward which possession the judgments of a correctly formed conscience are directed.

141

8. KNOWING THE NORMS: LAW

II. The Theoretical Part of Ethics
  C. The Third Question: how do you tell whether a
  given action is good or evil?--the norms of morality
    4. Coming to know what the norms say:
    the question of law
    a. Definition of law
    b. Characteristics that the definition implies
    c. Purpose of law
    d. Law and freedom
    e. Types of law
      1) The question of eternal law
      2) Natural law
        a) What it is
        b) That it is
        c) Its scope
        d) Its immutability
      3) Positive law
        a) What it is
        b) Its types: declarative and determinative
        c) Need for it
        d) Its binding force
        e) The question of popular acceptance
        f) Authority to interpret it
        g) Obeying unjust laws
        h) The question of purely penal law
    f. Sanction and law
      1) Meaning of sanction
      2) Types: natural and arbitrary,
      perfect and imperfect
      3) Need for it
      4) Purpose of it
      5) How it functions
        a) With natural law
          (1) in this life
          (2) in the afterlife: the
            question of immortality
        b) With positive law.

4. Coming to know what the norms say: the question of law

We have examined the norms of morality at some length: what they are, how many there are, what their interrelationships are. But there remains one important area about those norms (or at least some of them) which has to be investigated further, and that is the question of how we come to know just what those norms concretely specify. We don't need to do this with the ultimate norms, whether subjective or objective; after all, the reason that we needed proximate norms in the first place was that it is too difficult to know what the ultimate norms require us to do. So, we can concentrate here on the proximate norms; if we can learn what they have to say, we can be confident of knowing what the ultimate ones require too. Nor, really, do we need to ask this question concerning the proximate subjective norm, conscience; generally speaking, we *know* what it tells us to do in a concrete case, and to the extent that anything further might need to be said about it, what we have already seen will probably be adequate.

The proximate objective norm, however, is quite another matter. We have seen a sort of working definition of what is meant by "human nature completely considered": human nature taken in all its ordered parts, all its ordered relationships, etc. For purposes of understanding the nature of the norm, that was good enough. But it still remains somewhat theoretical, when there is question of judging a specific, concrete case; and it would be helpful if we knew a little more specifically just what it implies. Furthermore, as we know, there are all sorts of people in the world who, though they are wonderful, great-hearted folk, yet would not have the faintest idea of what we were saying if we confronted them with "human nature completely considered" as a norm for their actions. That, of course, merely says that not everyone in the world is a philosopher, a fact that is neither unexpected nor startling. How, then, is the proximate objective norm of morality (human nature), on which we recall that the proximate subjective one of conscience depends, going to become known by the vast majority of the human race?

With that as preface, then, we turn to the whole area of law, which is the great means whereby this norm of morality becomes known to people at large. We will consider several things about law, in general: its definition, its characteristics, its purpose, its relationship with freedom, its types, and its concomitant, sanction.

a. Definition of law

First, then, what is a law? The definition is a classic, well-established one, in which, as we will see, each word counts. Law is an ordinance of reason, for the common good, promulgated by the one who has the care of the community.

b. Characteristics that the definition implies

The definition is the basis for the characteristics of law that we will discuss. (i) First, a law is an *ordinance*. This means that it is not a mere wish, a piece of advice, or a suggestion. It is an order, a command; it is binding, and it imposes moral obligation on the person whom it binds. However nicely it may be phrased, it is always expressed in the imperative mood: thou shalt, or thou shalt not. (ii) Next, law is an ordinance *of reason,* i.e., a reasonable command. It cannot be some sort of arbitrary whim, but rather has to be a reasoned ordering of means to an end. Some other things follow from that characteristic. A law must be *consistent,* both with itself and with other laws; one cannot impose contradictory obligations without thereby becoming unreasonable. A law must also be *just,* respecting rights guaranteed by other laws, and distributing burdens and privileges equitably; a truly unjust law (as is commonly recognized) is no law at all. A law has to be *capable of being observed,* for no one can be obligated to do the impossible. It must be *enforceable,* for otherwise only the good obey it, and the wicked--who are the ones that really need the law--don't. Finally, a law has to be *useful:* it is, after all, a means to an end, and a needless obligation or restriction of liberty serves no purpose. (iii) The next characteristic is that law must be for the *common* good. In this, it differs from a command imposed on a single individual and aimed solely at his or her own good; law looks to the benefit of the community as a whole, rather than to private or personal good. (Thus, when a stern father tells his teen-age son or daughter that the curfew hour is 11 p.m., we might say, in popular language, that he is "laying down the law"; but, in fact, he is laying down a precept or a command, not a law.) Laws are generally territorial, binding the people within a given territory for as long as they are in that territory; and they are ordinarily relatively permanent, since they are rules for general action, something that extends, normally speaking, over a period of time.

(iv) Next, laws must be *promulgated,* i.e., made known. This can be done in a variety of ways; TV, radio, newspapers, etc., are common ways of promulgating laws in civil society. In general, a law has to be promulgated in such a way that the people who are expected to obey it can come to know it without undue difficulty. It is not necessary, however, that each and every person subject to a law actually do know it. Once it is promulgated, it binds objectively, even though certain individuals remain unaware of it--as has been said, ignorance of the law is no excuse. (Ignorance of the existence of a law may indeed excuse one on the subjective level, of course: if through invincible ignorance I do not know of a given law, my violation of it may well be free of moral guilt. However, I will still have to pay the traffic ticket, for instance, that my ignorance of the law earns for me....) (v) Finally, law stems from the person who has the care of the community, i.e., from the person who has jurisdiction. Law is, therefore, *authoritative*. The person having that jurisdiction might be an individual human being (a king, for instance, in some cultures), or it might be a moral person (a city council, a national legislature): in general, someone who, for one reason or other, has authority.

c. Purpose of law

We have already said something about the purpose of law, i.e., to serve as a means whereby people can come to know concretely what "human nature completely considered" requires us to do. This is usually stated by calling law a "provocative means." It is a means, in that it has the function of telling human beings what actions do in fact lead to their final end and of commanding that those actions be done (or, conversely, of telling them which actions detract from their final end, and of commanding that those actions not be done). In this sense, law is a means, a help. But it is also a provocative means: not only does it say, "You should do such-and-such," but it also adds an incentive: "And if you don't...." In that sense, even the sanction attached to a law has the function of helping us determine what is moral and what is not, and of seeing that this is done or not done.

d. Law and freedom

What is the relationship between law and freedom? By being subject to law, do humans lose their freedom? No. For I can always disobey any given law. Although law may show me what actions I should freely choose if I am to attain the end of my nature (and thus may show me how I should properly use my freedom), I am still free to decline to do those actions, even though I do so at the conscious risk of doing something that will hinder the gaining of my final goal. The so-called opposition of law and freedom turns out to be a myth, when one looks closely

146

at the nature and purpose of law.

The first four things that we have considered about law (its nature, its characteristics, its purpose, and its relationship with freedom) have been relatively brief, uncomplicated, and straightforward. We probably should note in passing, though, that this uncomplicatedness is the fruit of centuries' worth of painstaking legal thought in Western culture, starting even before the time of the ancient Romans and continuing throughout European culture's middle ages and modern period, not to mention the two centuries of legal practice and theory in the United States.

e. Types of law

The aspect of law which we will now undertake to discuss, however, is not brief, and it is complicated. It *is* straightforward, but it is complex for all that. This is the whole area of the types of law.

In general, we can distinguish different kinds of law, even within the confines of the strict definition of law which we saw at the beginning of this chapter (i.e., even if we do distinguish out such things as Murphy's Law, the Law of Diminishing Returns, the laws of the physical sciences, and the like). On the basis of duration, for instance, we can speak of either eternal or temporal laws. Or, on the basis of laws' mode of promulgation, we can have laws that are either natural (promulgated through the very nature of the being that a given law governs) or positive (really, posit-ed, i.e., laid down): promulgated through some external sign of enactment such as TV, radio, newspapers, and the like. Or, according to their origin, laws are either divine (given by God) or human (given by human beings). Two types of law--natural and positive--interest us in ethics, though a word first needs to be said about eternal law, since the word does come up in ethical discussions from time to time and since it has relevance for our understanding of natural law.

1) The question of eternal law

The term "eternal law" means simply that the Creator--the first uncaused cause, in the sense that we have seen--has given all beings a particular type of nature, and commands that those beings live in accord with that nature. In the last chapter, we saw that the Creator, under pain of contradiction, could not give a being a particular nature, and then command that that being perform some type of activity other than the activity proper to that nature. The present discussion is akin to that, but asks whether the Creator necessarily insists that the being perform any activities at all. The argumentation is similar to what we have already seen. Once the Creator has given a being a certain type of essence or nature, then it is not possible that he be indifferent as to whether the being fulfill the goal of that nature (by its activities, of course) or not. That would put the Creator, once again, in the position of both willing the fulfillment of that nature (since the Creator did give it, and since it does, just by the fact of its existence, have a certain finality or fulfillment toward which it tends), and not willing it (as being, by hypothesis, indifferent to its fulfillment, insofar as the Creator is indifferent as to whether the creature does or does not perform any actions--the means by which the creature's nature would be fulfilled). That, of course, is once again a contradiction.

On that understanding of "eternal law," it is not hard to see that it does fulfill the definition of true law. It is an ordinance (a command, not a wish or a piece of advice), of reason (the divine intellect), promulgated (generally through the nature of the being in question), for the good of the community (it is aimed at the acquisition of the final goal by *all* of the beings who possess that nature), by the one who has the care of the community (i.e., by the Creator, who has the care over all beings of the universe, irrespective of any given community, city, state, etc., in which they may live).

Apart from noting that there is such a thing as divine law (discoverable by natural reason--as opposed to, say, divine law as made known by religious revelation, e.g., the Ten Commandments), and apart from noting that it is true law, however, we will spend no further time in this area, since whatever else we might need to know of divine law will come back into our thinking when we consider the question of natural law, to which we turn next.

2) Natural law

An historical comment on natural law can serve to start us off. Two things seem to be true of natural law. First, it is a perfectly valid concept, one well established in the history of philosophic thought, and one that can be very valuable to us in ethics. Second, it is also a concept that has been badly overworked in some treatments of ethics. Without getting into specific examples, this present writer can remember numerous instances in the not-too-distant past where, in writings on ethics, natural law was used almost as a club to ward off any and all adversaries--a phenomenon which did not particularly endear the concept to the minds of readers. But, here as elsewhere, it is true that from the fact of something's being abused, it does not follow that it should not be used at all. It follows only that it should not be abused, and that is all. In our treatment of natural law, we will try to make valid use of it, without at the same time managing to drive it into the ground.

a) What it is

Let us first work toward a clear understanding of what natural law is. As a start, we can consider that all creatures are governed by divine law, whether they like it or not. We, of course, are particularly concerned with the special variety of creatures called humans; but they, no differently from other creatures of whatever stripe, do not create themselves: what they are, and the fact *that* they are (i.e., the fact that they exist at all), is not something that they choose or are responsible for. Rather, both their nature and their existence are given them by another, by their first uncaused cause. Now, we remember that there is an intrinsic relation between nature and goal, such that one cannot have a nature that does not have a specific goal, nor can one have a goal that is not attainable by at least some nature. The two terms "nature" and "goal," then, mutually imply each other. Consequently, if the Creator gives a creature a nature, he is also thereby giving it a goal, and is, furthermore, willing the fulfillment, the achievement, of that goal. For, once more, the Creator cannot both give a goal, something to be achieved, and simultaneously be indifferent as to whether that goal is to be attained: it either is or it is not a goal. Thus, to give a nature is to give a goal; the two are inseparable. To be indifferent as to whether the goal is achieved is, precisely, *not* to give a goal. And no one, not even the Creator, can both give and not give a goal at the same time, any more than he can both give and not give a nature.

The Creator, therefore, is in effect saying to the creature: you are given such-and-such a nature; now, achieve the goal of that nature. Now, this fits the definition of law quite nicely: it is an ordinance, a command, of reason (the divine reason); it is promulgated (through the nature itself), for the common good (the good of every being that has that nature), by him who has the care of the community (the Creator, who has the care of every creature he creates). And so, to repeat: all creatures, independently of whether they might wish it, like it, or even know it, are in fact governed by divine law, a law expressed in their very natures. This is true of every creature without exception: sub-human, human, and supra-human (if there are any supra-human beings--again, insofar as these might be knowable by unaided reason).

The fact that human beings are governed by divine law, however, presents something of a special case. For human nature involves the possession of intellect and free will. Furthermore, the fulfillment of human nature involves the use of that intellect and free will, for these are the distinctively human actions. But knowledge and volition--the use of intellect and will--embrace as part of their scope the understanding and acceptance/rejection of human nature and of the law which governs it. In other words: human knowledge of divine law (as it applies to the fulfillment of human nature), and human freedom in respect to that divine law are part and parcel of how humans are to achieve their final end, for they are part of the activity proper to human nature by which the final end of that nature is to be achieved. This, obviously, involves knowledge of what human nature is, what the final end is, and what actions will either lead to that final end or will lead away from it.

The term "natural law," then, means simply this: the humanly understood obligation that human beings have to live according to their nature, i.e., rationally. The term is applied only to human beings, since only a human being, i.e., a rational being, can understand what is meant by a goal considered precisely as a goal; only a rational being can understand what a means, *as means,* is; only a rational being, for that matter, can understand what a nature is. Now, this humanly understood obligation to live according to nature also fulfills the definition of law: it is an ordinance (a command, not something optional, advisory, etc.) of reason (the reason of the Creator), promulgated (through the human's understanding of his or her nature itself), for the common good (the good, that is to say, of attaining the final end of every creature that has this particular nature), by him who has the care of the community (the Creator of all).

In summary: the Creator's command, given to the human creature, to live according to human nature, i.e., to live rationally, so as to attain the end of human nature: (a) *as given,* is the divine law; (b) *as received and understood,* is the natural law. Or, to put it another way: if we look at the divine command from the standpoint of God who gives it, we are speaking of

150

divine law. If we look at it from the standpoint of us who receive and understand it, we are talking of natural law.

b) That it is

We have seen what natural law is. And implicitly, at least, we have already demonstrated its existence--for there does exist such a thing as human nature, and there does exist such a thing as a Creator who is the author of that particular nature, a nature which is rational and free. One can argue to the existence of a natural law from another perspective, too. It could be stated, for instance, that there is such a thing as natural law for the very good reason that there has to be. For: (i) Humans have an obligation to attain their end, their final goal. (ii) Therefore the means that are necessary to achieve that goal must be available to them. Otherwise, the Creator is, in effect, both willing and not willing, simultaneously, the attainment of that goal--an impossible contradiction. (iii) Such means would need to be both efficacious (otherwise they wouldn't be means) and suited to human nature as rational and free (otherwise they would be such as to force humans to attain their end, thus violating human nature *as free*). (iv) But only a law can be such a means. For anything less than a law (e.g., a wish, some advice, etc.) would lack binding force and therefore would not be efficacious; on the other hand, anything stronger than a law would force compliance, and thus would violate human nature *as free*.

c) Its scope

That, then, is what natural law is; and these are the arguments that lead us to say that there is such a thing. Next, we might ask something about the scope of natural law: what sorts of things can we know which it commands? Briefly, it tells us things on four difference levels of clarity. (i) First, there is the basic moral principle: do good and avoid evil. Other formulations of this same thing might be: live a life in accord with your rational nature; or, seek your last end. This most general truth of the moral life, in one of these or some similar formulation, is known to everyone who has the use of reason. (ii) Then there are some common or general principles that follow virtually immediately from the first principle, with very little reasoning required: things like, preserve your own being, care for your offspring, revere the Creator, etc. Since the reasoning process needed to get to these conclusions from the first moral

151

principle is quite easy, it is generally said that these conclusions are known to every morally mature adult. (The wording of that last sentence, however, is deliberate. We must remember that there can be such a thing as a person who is physically and mentally mature, but morally an infant--someone who, for one reason or other, has had little or no moral education whatever. This may or may not be that person's fault.)

(iii) Then there is another group of moral principles, equally certain in themselves, but arrived at only after a fairly complex, sophisticated process of reasoning. Some people may be unable to follow this sort of reasoning, for reasons good and bad, and hence may not know about these principles. Examples are the principles governing suicide, euthanasia, divorce, abortion, and so on. Thus, though the principles of the natural law governing such things are quite certain in themselves, they may for various reasons be unknown to certain people, even morally mature ones. (iv) Finally, there is the situation where a known principle of the natural law needs to be applied to a particular case. Here, too, people can make mistakes: they mis-apply, for one reason or other, a principle which they know perfectly well. For example, someone may know quite clearly that murder is wrong. But this present case that he or she is trying to judge: is this murder or not? One thinks, by way of illustration, of the case of taking the life of a particularly tyrannical and cruel dictator. Murder or not? In this area, people can make mistakes, even with the best of intentions.

To summarize the scope of what we know from natural law, then: the first principle is known to all who have the use of reason. The immediate principles that follow from it are known to all except persons who are, for whatever reason, moral infants. The more remote principles may not be known to some people, because they cannot follow the reasoning process necessary to get from the first principle to these principles. And finally, people can and do make mistakes when trying to apply even a very well known principle of natural law to a particular case.

d) Its immutability

Even when not seriously overworked, then, natural law does have some very definite things to say about the moral life. We might wonder, however, whether natural law could ever change. Certainly, the sort of law with which we are more familiar (positive law) can and does change from one age to the next. Can natural law? Could it ever be the case that, say, murder might *not* be forbidden by natural law, in some far-distant age of the human race?

Consider: if a law is to change, there are only two ways in which this can happen. (a) Law--any law--can change *internally*, i.e., one or more of the five elements that go to make it a law (an ordinance of reason, for the common good, etc.), cease to be verified in the case of a particular law--at which point that law ceases to be a law. A case in point might be that ancient law on a town's books somewhere in the western United States, prohibiting the presence of horses in saloons. Whatever may have been the merits of such a law in its day, one could hardly contend that it is still reasonable or for the common good in an age and place where there are no more horses. And so, whether still on the books or not, it is no longer a law. Or (b) a law can change *externally*, i.e., it is repealed by the lawmaker or that lawmaker's legitimate successor. The obvious example in U.S. history is prohibition (the Volstead Act) and its subsequent repeal. (A variant on an external change of a law is the instance of dispensation or exception: the lawmaker declares that, for a particular reason, the law does not bind a given individual in certain circumstances. For practical purposes, this could be considered a temporary repeal of a law.)

None of these situations, however, can occur in the case of natural law. An internal change would mean that the natural law had ceased to be an ordinance, or reasonable, or for the common good, or promulgated by him who had the care of the community. But that would mean that the Creator would have to change, and we have already seen that that is impossible: pure act is, precisely, that which is not in potency to any change whatever. An external change, on the other hand, would mean that the Creator would now will that humans *not* live in accord with their nature. Unless the Creator also changed the nature involved into some other nature, this would again mean that the Creator is both willing the fulfillment of that nature (since he gave it in the first place) and not willing it (as changing natural law): again, a contradiction. Finally, a dispensation from natural law would in effect be a declaration that the law does not bind a given individual here and now. But the only reason that would justify such a dispensation from natural law would be a person's no longer being human. In other words, the dispensation would have to be, not from natural law, but from being human. The Creator could do such a thing, of course, but only on condition that he changed the nature itself--in which case the creature would then be bound by the laws of its new nature.

153

2) Positive law

So much, then, for the first type of law with which ethics is concerned, natural law (with a brief preface on the question of divine law). We have seen what it is, that it is, its scope, and its immutability. Of course, we have not yet tried to spell out each and every one of the principles that natural law dictates (after all, we do have to leave *something* for subsequent chapters of this book to do!), but we have gotten a reasonable introduction to it. We need now to turn our attention to the other type of law that concerns us, positive law.

a) What it is

By positive law is meant, simply, law that is promulgated not through a being's nature, but in some other way: publication in a newspaper, a magazine, in a posted public notice, by TV, and so forth.

When we began to discuss natural law, we spent a few minutes at the beginning in discussing divine law. In theory, we could do the same here, for there is such a thing as divine positive law, and we should perhaps at least know the meaning of the term, even though it lies completely outside the scope of ethics. Divine positive law, then, is law promulgated by the Creator in some way other than through human nature. One clear example that we have in religious history is the giving of the Ten Commandments: a definite law, and promulgated by the Creator through Moses and by means of written tablets.

But, while there is such a thing as divine positive law, we know of it only through religious revelation, not through natural reason. In ethics, then, we are not concerned with it. Rather, we are concerned only with human positive law. And our first question could be about the types of positive law.

b) Its types: declarative and determinative

First, there is *declarative* law. This sort of law merely states explicitly what is already a conclusion of natural law. Thus, a human law against murder in a given society would be a declarative law—it merely states, once again and perhaps more clearly, a prohibition that is already contained in natural law. Not all positive laws, however, are merely declarative. For occasionally the natural law allows for alternative means that could be used to achieve a given end, and it is the function of *determinative* law to choose one such means over other possible ones. The standard example of this is the traffic law that directs that cars move on the right side of the street rather than the left. Another would be tax laws, specifying just how the state is to be supported. For the state could be supported in a number of ways, and the function of this sort of law is to specify which one will in fact be used in a given state. So also the right-hand law: natural law might well dictate that we drive rationally, but there are a number of ways in which this could be done, and it is the function of determinative law here to specify which one of these will in fact be used.

c) Need for it

Our next question centers around the need for positive law. After all, we are rational and free beings. Why do we need laws, which, in the last analysis, will have the effect of curtailing our liberty? But, as it turns out, we do have such a need. In the first place, although natural law is perfect and adequate in itself (it is, after all, the product of a perfect Creator), none the less *our knowledge* of natural law is not perfect, and we need civil law to supplement natural law as a guide in the moral life. There are two reasons for this. (a) First, as we have already seen, there are principles of the natural law which are arrived at only after a complex process of reasoning--a process of which not everyone is capable or for which not everyone is trained (or inclined). And, as we know, error can occur in the attempt to apply a known principle of natural law to a particular instance. Then too, there are individuals who, for one reason or other, are moral infants: they do not know even the fundamental principles that follow from the basic principle of moral law. People such as we find in all three of these cases require further guidance in the moral realm. And, of course, that further guidance has to take the form of law, for only law has the necessary characteristics of (i) imposing an obligation through a command (mere advice or exhortation would not be strong enough to motivate people like this to do good and avoid evil), and yet (ii) respecting human nature as rational and free: for anything that would impose an external or internal necessity on people like this would take away their freedom, whereas law, on the other hand, imposes only a *moral* necessity on them, leaving their freedom intact. (b) The second reason why we need civil law as a supplement to natural law is that (as we will see later in this chapter) sanction is necessary for maintaining law. But the sanction attached to natural law, while (again, as we will see) perfect in itself, is not known perfectly in this life and hence cannot by itself serve to motivate obedience to natural law. Moreover, there are people who do not believe in immortality, and for whom therefore the idea of a sanction that is found in its perfect form only in an afterlife will not serve as adequate motivation. There is, therefore, a need for positive (i.e., civil) laws, and for the positive sanction that these laws carry with them.

The first reason, then, why we need positive law is that natural law is not a perfect enough guide, as far as we are concerned--however excellent it may be in itself: our knowledge of it is too imperfect. A second reason, however, is that human beings are by their nature social beings: not only *do* they in fact live together, but, as we will see later, they *must* do so. But that fact carries some consequences with it. For natural law, on occasion, allows for alternative means in order to reach a necessary end, as we have seen. When there is question of individual actions done by one person, this poses no problem. But sometimes there is a need for teamwork, for concerted action, in order to reach a necessary goal of society. In that case, there is need for determinative laws, so as to select one means out of many possible ones to achieve the end in question. Moreover, when we are talking about those individuals who for one reason or other cannot (or at least do not) know the natural law: not only do they themselves need assistance in coming to know the moral law (as we have seen), but society itself needs to be protected from their actions on occasion. Thus, again, the need for civil laws. Finally, human social life changes from time to time, e.g., when a people changes from being industrial to being technological. When this happens, a whole new set of applications of natural law is required. But the application of natural law to individual cases is, as we have seen, an area where error is frequently found. And so the further aid of positive law is required.

d) Its binding force

So, we have seen what positive law is, what types of it there are (declarative and determinative), and why we need it. Next, we might consider just what force it has. In the traditional terminology, can it be said to "bind in conscience"? And immediately we need to define our terms. For when we speak of "binding in conscience," the reference is not to sin, which is a religious concept and therefore outside the scope of ethics. Rather, what we mean in asking whether a law can bind in conscience is this: if I obey a law, am I thereby performing an act that will lead me to my ultimate end? And if I disobey it, am I thereby performing an act that will lead me away from my ultimate end? Or--on the other hand--is law simply something that I can take or leave, as I choose (provided, say, that I do not get caught)?

Can positive law bind in conscience, in the sense that we have defined that term? Yes, it can. For obedience to civil law is always grounded in natural law, and the latter always binds in conscience. For humans are, by nature, social beings. Natural law therefore requires that they live in society. Whatever is required for humans to live in society is, consequently, also required by natural law. But obedience to civil law is required if humans are to live successfully in civil society; the alternative is chaos. And thus obedience to civil law is required by natural law.

Civil law, however, can involve different levels of binding in conscience: the more serious the good to be achieved, or the evil to be avoided, the more serious the obligation in conscience (and therefore, the greater the degree to which my action leads me toward or away from my final end). Along that line, we might ask just what are the levels of obligation that civil law can impose on us. If I decide to run a red light, is this going to make me lose my final end, for heaven's sake? Or if I don't pay my taxes some year, am I therefore going to forfeit my ultimate goal of complete happiness?

We need to remember the distinction between declarative and determinative laws, if we are to see the degree of "binding in conscience" that civil law can impose on us. A declarative law, in the first place, imposes the same obligation as the natural law does; all that a declarative law does is make explicit the natural law precept. If that natural law precept carries with it a serious obligation, then so does the declarative civil law. And so, when we have a civil law prohibiting murder: this is merely an explicitation of the natural law precept that forbids the same thing; since this is a serious question in natural law, it will also be a serious one in civil law. A determinative law, on the other hand, works somewhat differently. For there is here question of alternative means, any one of which would work equally well in achieving the goal, and the purpose of the law is merely to select one of those means for a given society. If the law concerns a serious matter, and the lawgiver intends the obligation to be serious, then, of course, the obligation the law imposes on us is

157

a serious one. If, on the other hand, the law concerns a non-serious matter, then the lawgiver cannot impose a serious obligation. A law must be just, i.e., there must be a proportionality between the matter and the obligation. Thus, the running of a red light (in ordinary circumstances, anyway),is a trivial matter, and could not be the subject of a serious obligation: ordinarily speaking, one will not lose complete and total happiness because of running a traffic signal! Finally, if the matter a law treats is serious, but the lawgiver intends to impose only a non-serious obligation (feeling that the law will be sufficiently observed in that way), then the obligation is non-serious. This latter case, however, is largely theoretical; few if any lawgivers act this way. If anything, they tend toward the other extreme.

A law, then, can impose a serious obligation on us, and by this we mean that the violation of a law, in a serious matter, can significantly jeopardize our success in reaching our final goal. Not all laws do this, as has been seen; but the point to be noted is that certain laws *can* do so, and we violate them only at our own great moral peril.

e) The question of popular acceptance

The next question we could ask about civil law concerns whether or not popular acceptance of any given law is required before that law can properly be considered obligatory. That is to say: if I don't like a certain law (and, indeed, if a lot of people don't like that law), does it bind me? Or can I simply refuse to accept it? I can do this only if the nature of the civil society in which I live, or if the nature of the law in question, requires popular acceptance for validity. Otherwise, such acceptance is not required. In the case of a pure democracy, for example, where laws are passed by an assembly of all the people, we would have a case where the nature of the state itself required popular acceptance. (Such democracies, however, have been rare in human history. Certainly, the United States is not one.) Cases where the nature of the law itself required popular acceptance are more difficult to exemplify. A law that became effective only upon an affirmative referendum might be such a case--though it is difficult to imagine a legislature that would pass such a law.

It is of course possible that popular dissatisfaction with a law may in fact signal that one of the five essential elements of a law is missing, and that the law has therefore ceased to be a law internally. That this is the case, however, is not to be assumed automatically any time that there is popular dissatisfaction with a law. As a generalized rule of thumb, then, the fact that I do not like a certain law may or may not say something about me; it ordinarily says nothing about the law, its validity, or my obligation to obey it.

f) Authority to interpret it

Who has the authority to interpret civil law, i.e., to tell its authentic meaning? There are really three different possible interpreters. In the first place, a legislator himself (whether this be one person, or an elected body such as a legislature) could be asked for an interpretation; so could that person's successor. Another possibility would be lawyers and judges who possess the stature to provide interpretations in a given country--which varies, of course, from nation to nation. Finally, a very interesting possibility as an interpreter is custom: a way of looking at a law that has grown up in the minds of a large number of people over a lengthy period (forty years, in the case of some types of laws), without protest from the legislator. For example: suppose there were a law in, say, Kansas which barred sales on Sundays. Over the course of many years, the people subject to the law had understood it as not applying to the sale of groceries or gasoline. And suppose that the Kansas state legislature had never expressed a contrary view. After a certain amount of time, the authentic meaning of the law becomes exactly that: sales are banned on Sundays, except for groceries or gasoline. Whether that was the law's original intent is beside the point.

g) Obeying unjust laws

We spoke earlier of the obligation that can arise to observe laws that we do not particularly like. An allied question, however--with a quite different answer--comes up when there is question of the obligation to observe unjust laws. Is there such an obligation? First, in the case of a "law" that is genuinely unjust (not, therefore, one which I merely happen to dislike), a distinction has to be made. Some laws merely command (or prohibit, as the case may be) something unjustly. Others command something that is truly immoral (e.g., a law mandating euthanasia). In the case of the former, it may be disobeyed (it doesn't have to be: though I can never *do* unjustice, there is nothing immoral on my part about *suffering* injustice); in the case

159

of the latter, i.e., a law commanding something immoral, it *must* be disobeyed. The reason for both of these is obvious. Neither is a case of true law, since a law must be just in order to be a law at all. As for a "law" commanding something immoral: no lower law can cancel a higher law, and the immorality of something like euthanasia would stem from natural law—a higher law than civil law.

A much more difficult question, however, is the case when I judge a law to be not merely unwise, but truly unjust, and other people disagree with me—i.e., I might be wrong. A fairly prominent example in recent American history has been the draft law: certainly, many saw this as an unjust law, though its unjustness was not something that was immediately obvious to many others, although a number may have questioned its wisdom. What do I do in such a case? I must, of course, follow my conscience—but forming that conscience correctly is not a simple matter. The circumstances would have to be weighed and a prudential judgment made on a case-by-case basis. Examples of such circumstances might be: what effect would my civil disobedience have on others? (If, for instance, the situation is such that my act will, because of some office or position that I hold, lead others to conclude that laws in general can be obeyed or not, according to one's preference, I might well have the obligation to obey the law, since such a conclusion on the part of others would be disastrous.) What will be the good effects of my act? (If great benefit will come of it, that is one thing; if the good results will be negligible, that is quite another—for inevitably there will be some harm caused by it.) What harm will come to me, or to those who depend on me, or to others, because of my actions?—and so on. Put briefly, even in making the sincere judgment that a law in such a case is unjust, I must also be aware of the consequences of my decision, and must take these into account in determining whether my civil disobedience is morally permissible or not.

h) The question of purely penal law

The next question is an extension of the one we have just seen, i.e., the obligatory character of law. Granting for the moment that, in general, laws do bind in conscience: do *all* laws do so? Or are there laws which bind in some other fashion? Historically, this has been a disputed question, with competent experts opting for both sides. Some say that obligation is intrinsic to the nature of law: there cannot be a law that does not have obligation, i.e., that does not bind in conscience.

160

Others say that a legislator may intend either one of two things: obedience to the law, *or else* payment of a penalty by a violator who gets caught--the reasoning being that the legislator feels that this is sufficient motivation to ensure compliance with the law. Laws such as this latter, commonly referred to as "penal laws" (Latin: *poena,* penalty) are traffic laws, tax laws in some cases, and the like. Those who opt for the existence of purely penal laws do have some problems in determing which are purely penal and which are not. However, since the experts disagree on the question, we can in good conscience adopt either view.

f. Sanction and law

Our final question in our study of law concerns sanction. First, what do we mean by the term?

1) Meaning of sanction

In general, a sanction is what happens to someone when he or she either does or does not obey a law. A sanction is basically a motive for keeping the law; and the word can refer to a reward that one gets for keeping a law, or to the penalty one suffers for violating it. More commonly, however, the term is used to refer to the penalty that one suffers for violating a law.

2) Types: natural and arbitrary, perfect and imperfect

What sorts of sanction are there? We can distinguish them on the basis of either (i) where they come from, or (ii) whether they are sufficient or not. As regards (i), the source of sanction: first, there is such a thing as a *natural* sanction, one that follows from the very nature of a given act. For example, my action of jumping from a very tall building has the natural sanction of my falling to the ground. A natural sanction *always* takes place. And it makes little difference whether my action of jumping from the building is morally good or morally evil, whether it is blameworthy or innocent: I will still end up on the ground in any case. A *positive* sanction, on the other hand, is an arbitrary one, one that does not follow from the nature of the act but rather is imposed by the will of a legislator. It does not always take place--rather, only when and if the lawbreaker is caught. A

161

prison sentence is an instance of a positive sanction; there is nothing about, say, the nature of robbing a bank that, in and of itself, implies the spending of a certain amount of time behind bars. This sanction, rather, is something arbitrarily imposed by civil authority. A positive sanction admits of exceptions, excuses, etc.; a natural sanction does not.

(ii) To look, now, at the question of the adequacy of a sanction: it can be either perfect or imperfect. It is perfect if it is both *adequate* and *proportioned*: if it both provides a sufficient motive for keeping a law (adequacy), and if it establishes an equality, a parity, between the gravity of the offense and the gravity of the penalty (proportionality). An imperfect sanction, as the name implies, is one that is either inadequate, disproportioned, or both.

3) Need for it

These, then, are the chief sorts of sanctions, at least those of which mention is commonly made. But why should there be such a thing? What need is there of sanction when we are talking about a law that governs rational and free beings?

Practically speaking, sanction is necessary if the law is not to be a dead letter. Rational and free beings we may indeed be; weak beings, however, we also are, and there is need of some incentive if a law (particularly one that we do not find especially pleasant) is to be kept. If there is no sanction to a law, then generally only the good will obey that law--and they are, ordinarily speaking, the very beings who do not need the law in the first place. The wicked, who on the other hand do need the law, will not obey it if it lacks sanction. If, then, a law is not to be useless, there must be sanction. And if there is to be a society, then there must be law--and, indeed, effective law; otherwise society is simply impossible. And, of course, you must have a society if you are to live according to natural law. Or--running it the other way around--if we are to live as humans we must have society; if we are to have society, we must have law; if we are to have law, then we must have sanction.

4) Purposes of it

That leads us to a consideration of the purposes of sanction. We have already seen one of its purposes, i.e., to persuade people to keep the law and to dissuade them from breaking it. But sanction has at least one other purpose, one that is less obvious to us until we think about it for a while. Technically put, that purpose is to restore the objective order of justice after a law has been broken. To illustrate just what that means: suppose that a thief breaks into a grocery store late at night, and robs it of $500. Let us further suppose that he is later caught, and is forced to restore the $500. Is this sufficient? Not really. The owner of the store does recover his $500, true. But: that store owner, along with everyone else in the community, *also* has the quite separate right not to have his or her property stolen in the first place: the right to possess his or her goods in peace. And so, when the robbery took place, *two* rights of the storekeeper were violated: the right to ownership over the $500, *and also* the more general right not to have *any* of his or her property (not just this or that particular piece) stolen. Now, if the thief is caught and forced to make restitution, then the injury that has been done to the first of these two rights is corrected. But the damage done to the second is not. Something further needs to be done to rectify the violation of that right--a right which the storeowner holds in common with everyone else in the community. That "something further" needed here is what is meant by sanction.

To put all this another way: the thief, in robbing the store, did indeed commit an injustice against the store owner. But he also committed an injustice against *everyone* in the community--for each and every one of the members of that community has the common right to possess his or her goods in peace, and the thief violates that common right as well as the individual right of the storeowner. Restitution may take care of the violated individual right of the storeowner; it does not take care of the violated right of everyone else in the community. To do this, there is need for sanction.

Sanction has two other purposes, as well: to correct the offender, and to deter others from imitating his or her offense. We will say more about these at the close of the present chapter.

5) How it functions

So much, then, for the nature of sanction, its types, its necessity, and its purpose. Let us now try to see how sanction functions, first as regards natural law, and then as regards positive law.

a) With natural law

In regard to natural law, then. First, there is a natural sanction to natural law: if one violates the natural law, then the automatic consequence is that that person moves further away from his or her final end. That is simply because of the nature of the act involved; it is not an arbitrary penalty imposed by a lawgiver.

(The following point may be worth mentioning, since it involves not only all of us who consider a natural law sanction from a philosophic viewpoint, but also those who bring a religious point of view to the study of ethics: one sometimes hears puzzlement about a vengeful Creator who would, say, damn a human to hell for some particular offense (or, in philosophic terms, who would condemn a human to the non-acquisition of his or her final end for that offense): what are we to make of such a Creator or God? Nothing. For such a conception misses the point entirely. The Creator is not vengeful, and, for that matter, cannot with perfect propriety be said to damn the creature at all. What happens is that the creature condemns itself, by the very nature of his or her own act: that is precisely what a natural sanction means.)

One could also ask, however, whether in addition to the natural sanction, natural law could also carry with it a positive sanction, i.e., one attached to it by the will of the lawgiver. The answer to the question is yes. It is at least possible that there could be such a thing as a divine positive sanction, although we know nothing of such by natural reason (we do know instances of it from non-philosophic sources, e.g., the Old Testament). And it is also possible that there can be human positive sanctions attached to violations of natural law. Certainly, whenever there is question of a declarative positive law, there are such sanctions; a declarative law, we recall, is merely the re-statement of natural law, although that re-statement may add sanctions of its own. Thus, natural law says: do not steal. The natural law sanction for this would be: and if you do, you will move further away from your final end. The declarative law says: do not steal. And it adds the sanction: and if you do, you will spend 20 years in prison.

So, there is a natural sanction attached to natural law, and there can also be positive sanctions attached to it as well, whether (at least possibly) from a divine source or (quite certainly) from a human source. Now, this divine sanction: is it perfect or imperfect?

That raises a very good question. On the one hand, natural law must have a perfect sanction, i.e., one that is both adequate and proportioned. For if the Creator assigned only an inadequate sanction, the consequence should be familiar to us by this time: he would both be willing that the creature achieve its end (since he gave the creature the nature that seeks that end), and at the same time not willing it (since he gave insufficient motivating force for the observance of that law). That, of course, is impossible. So, we know that there must be an adequate sanction for natural law. Moreover, that sanction must be proportioned as well as adequate: there must exist a sanction wherein there is equality or parity between the badness of an action and its punishment. Otherwise, the Creator is being unjust, either to the guilty party himself or herself or else to the objective order of law. But, again, this is not possible: a being which is pure act possesses all perfections in the highest degree--and justice is, precisely, such a perfection. Thus, the Creator could not be unjust. And so, the sanction attached to natural law must be perfect: adequate and proportioned.

(1) in this life

However, that adequate, proportioned sanction is apparently not located in this present life, at least according to any reasonable conclusion from observable evidence. For, according to such a sanction, living in accord with human reason ought to produce a perfect proportioning of all of the human's various constituent parts and relationships, and thus result in happiness, harmony, peace, joy, etc., in this life. Sometimes, indeed, it does do so. But sometimes also, as common experience tells us, it does not. Conversely, living in disobedience to the natural law should produce disharmony among human parts and relationships, resulting in unhappiness, disharmony, war, sorrow, and so on. Again, once in a while it does. More often, however, it does not; we all know cases where the wicked seem to prosper very well indeed. And so we have two apparently opposed conclusions: there must be an adequate and proportioned sanction for natural law; otherwise God would not be God. But there isn't such a sanction, as everyday experience tells us: the good do not always prosper, nor do the evil always suffer--at least in this life.

165

(2) in the afterlife: the
question of immortality

The conclusion suggests itself, tentatively: if there must be an adequate and proportioned sanction for the natural law, and if it is not had in this life, then it must come in an afterlife. Such a sanction would consist, of course, in the possession of the supreme good (and consequent joy), or in the loss of that good (and consequent endless frustration). *If,* that is to say, there is such a thing as an afterlife.

The question is a nagging one, and it will pay us to investigate it, even at the price of engaging in a tangent (for the question does not really belong to ethics proper). Is there any way that we can show that human beings somehow do survive the phenomenon of death, do have a life after death? That is to say, can this be shown by natural reason? Yes, it can. In fact, a good deal more than that can be shown by natural reason. It can be shown that, not only do humans have life after death, but that that life is an endless one. From the reasoning that we have done in considering the existence of God, and from that involved in showing the freedom of the will, we already have the background that is needed to do this.

(First, a note. Usually, arguments for immortality are couched in terms of the immortality of the soul, not the intellect. Granted; it is the soul, rather than simply the intellect or the will, whose immortal status should be argued. For our purposes, however, that isn't necessary. For the intellect is a power of the soul: technically, it is an operative principle or cause of an activity which inheres in the soul and is immediately responsible for a given immanent or transient activity. For what we need here, then, in regard to immortality: what is true of the intellect will also be true of the soul, since the intellect is, as noted, a power of the soul. Thus, if the immortality of the intellect can be established, that is enough: since the intellect is a feature, a property, of the soul, then if the one is naturally immortal, the other also is. Furthermore, doing it this way also absolves us from the necessity of explaining in some detail the exact relationship of soul and intellect--which, again, is quite far outside the scope of ethics.)

Let us go back, then, to the fact that humans can know universals, i.e., can have universal concepts. That is the fundamental fact of experience from which the proof of immortality

166

proceeds. What is a universal? We recall that it is a concept that fits all members of a given class and, therefore, is not limited to any one member of that class. But what is it that would limit something--whatever it may be--to one member of a class? Again, we remember that it is the presence in that being of prime matter. A universal concept, therefore, is one *not* limited to a single member of a class, and therefore is one which, in its essence, does not contain prime matter. To use the technical term, it is *im*material.

Immateriality, however, is not simply a negative concept. It is a positive perfection, denoting the ability to exist without dependence on matter: the ability, that is to say, to exist in a higher, less restricted mode of being than the merely singular. Let us remember, too, that such immaterial concepts are the products of the intellect; universals, as such, do not exist in the real world (i.e., there is no such thing as whiteness, goodness, etc., roaming around the world in which we live--there are only singular white things, singular good things, etc.). The universal concept, therefore, stands to the intellect in the relationship of effect to cause: a universal concept is the product, the effect, of the intellect. We need not bother wondering here just *how* all this occurs (that is a very lengthy story that is examined in the Philosophy of Human Nature); the mere fact *that* it occurs is enough for us here. Now, an effect cannot contain more perfection than its cause; as we have seen, nothing can give what it itself does not have. Consequently, if the effect (the universal concept) is immaterial, it follows that its cause, the intellect, is also immaterial, i.e., does not contain prime matter as a constituent part of its make-up. (Remember, however, that we are speaking of the make-up of the intellect itself; we are not speaking of the relationship of the intellect to the body--which latter most certainly does contain prime matter as a constituent part of *its* make-up.)

The intellect, therefore, is immaterial in its action (the action of forming universal concepts), and therefore also in its being. What does this say about its immortality? A good bit. For something can go out of existence in one of three ways--there is no other alternative. Either it is broken down into its physical component parts, or else something upon which it depends for existence is broken down into its physical component parts, or else it is simply annihilated (i.e., put out of existence by a higher power). But: (i) the intellect cannot be broken down into its component parts, for the good reason that it doesn't have any. Only things with bodies can be broken down into physical component parts--and, not having prime matter, the intellect does not have a body. (ii) Nor does the intellect essentially depend for

167

its existence on something else that could be broken down into *its* component parts, i.e., the body. For although the intellect (and the will, for that matter) are dependent upon the body for *some* of their activities (e.g., perception), none the less they are not dependent upon it for others (such as the formation of immaterial concepts)--and that is sufficient to demonstrate an independence in action and therefore in being. (iii) The intellect could, of course, in principle be annihilated by its Creator: having brought it into existence, he could also extinguish that existence. But we have no reason to suspect that this is likely to happen, and numerous reasons to conclude that it will not. For if the intellect's Creator makes it such as by its very nature to be internally indestructible, by that very fact he shows his intention of retaining it within that nature--i.e., his intention of making it permanent, of not annihilating it.

Perhaps a short summary of all this may help. The human intellect is capable of forming universal concepts. But these are immaterial, precisely because they are universal. Therefore their cause (the intellect) is also immaterial, since any effect cannot contain more perfection than its cause, and immateriality is a perfection. Now, that being is immaterial which is not essentially dependent upon matter (in this case, upon body). Our intellects are, therefore, not essentially dependent upon our bodies for their existence (although they are accidentally dependent upon them for some of their activities); they therefore can perdure after the destruction of those bodies. The intellect could, of course, be externally annihilated (by God), but there is no reason for believing that this will occur, and good reasons for believing that it will not. At all events, the intellect is not internally corruptible, and the fact of the physical death of the body says nothing about the perdurance of the intellect before, during, or after that death.

b) With positive law

So much for our excursus into immortality. One final section on sanction remains to be seen, and that is the relationship of sanction with positive law. We have seen what sanction means when there is question of natural law, but what of those laws with which we are more immediately familiar? We are, then, talking here about the question of civil penalties or punishments.

Penalty or punishment has three aspects: (i) the vindicative (N.B.: *not* "vindictive"), which looks to the interests of the person who has been wronged--again, both the individual who has been wronged (the storeowner whose money was stolen) and the class of people who share a common right with that individual (e.g., the right to live in peaceful possession of their goods); (ii) the corrective, which looks to the interests of the criminal; and (iii) the deterrent, which looks to the interests of society in general, in terms of protecting it from future criminals.

Ideally, all three of these aspects should be present in any penalty. But sometimes this cannot be done. Sometimes the individual person who has been wronged cannot be repaid (e.g., if he or she has been murdered). Sometimes the corrective aspect of a penalty is impossible--there are, after all, such things as incorrigible criminals. Sometimes, too, the deterrent aspect is absent: no matter how many people get caught cheating on their income tax, there are always others who think it can't happen to them.

The one aspect of sanction, however, that is always present, in whatever punishment, is the vindicative one, at least as regards the class of persons who share a right that is violated by a crime against some individual member of that class. Punishment--the sanction of positive law--is always, and by its very nature, vindicative, at least of the objective moral order.

(As a final note to this chapter, we should advert to the inadequacy of the claim--often made in the American popular press--that certain penalties [e.g., the death penalty] lack any deterrent value and should therefore be abolished. This is not the proper place to discuss the death penalty as such; but the point can be made here that, in this claim, the premise may be quite correct, but the conclusion does not follow. For the deterrent aspect of a sanction, as we have seen, is only one of several, and its presence or absence says nothing, in and of itself, about the nature or validity of the penalty in question.)

SUMMARY OF CHAPTER EIGHT

A. Law in General: Most people come to know the proximate objective norm (human nature) by means of law. Law is an ordinance of reason, for the common good, promulgated by the one who has the care of the community. As an ordinance, law expresses a command. As reasonable, it must be consistent, just, observable, enforceable, and useful. As looking to the common good, it governs the actions of a group, usually within a given territory and for a stable period of time. As promulgated, it must be capable of being known by a majority of those subject to it without undue difficulty. As coming from the one who has the care of the community, it is authoritative. The purpose of law is to act as a "provocative means": it tells what actions are (and what are not) in accord with human nature, and it adds an incentive for the performance (or non-performance) of those actions. Law and freedom are not antithetical, for one can always disobey a law (albeit at a price). Laws can be eternal or temporal, natural or positive, divine or human. "Eternal law" refers simply to the fact that God has given all beings a particular type of nature, and commands that those beings act in accord with that nature.

B. Natural Law: "Natural law," a notion restricted to human beings, refers to humans' recognition of the fact that they have been given a particular type of nature (a rational one), and therefore must act in accord with that nature so as to achieve that nature's goal. Natural law is necessary for humans, for nothing else would be both efficacious and respectful of human rationality and freedom. By natural law, everyone with the use of reason knows the basic principle of the moral life; every morally mature person knows the general principles immediately following from that basic principle; morally educated people know principles that follow from the basic one through argumentation; applications of these principles, however, can vary in their certainty in individual cases. As incapable of change (whether internal or external) or excusation, natural law is immutable.

C. Positive Law: "Positive law," or civil law, is law promulgated, not through a being's nature, but in some other way (TV, publications, etc.). Declarative law merely restates explicitly something that is already a precept of natural law. Determinative law, however, makes a choice among means to end when natural law allows for alternative means to reach a necessary end. Humans need positive law because, although natural law in itself is perfectly adequate as a moral guide, our knowledge of it is imperfect; moreover, the social nature of humans and the periodic need to apply natural law to new situations demand it. Civil law can "bind in conscience" (i.e., obedience or disobedience to it can result in our moving closer to or farther away from our final end), since it is grounded in natural law; there can, of course, be differing degrees of binding force in question, depending on whether we are dealing with declarative or determinative law. Popular acceptance of civil law is not required for its validity (unless the nature of the law or of the civil society makes it so--a rare occurrence). Civil law is appropriately interpreted by the legislator himself (or his legitimate successor), lawyers and judges having the requisite stature, or (in some specific cases) custom. A truly unjust law (one commanding an immoral action) must be disobeyed; a merely unjust law (one that commands or prohibits something legitimate, but does so unjustly) may be disobeyed or obeyed. In doubtful cases, a prudential judgment must be made, taking applicable circumstances into account. Whether or not there exist "purely penal" laws is disputed; one may legitimately presume that there are.

D. Sanction: Sanction is the reward or penalty one receives from keeping or not keeping law. A natural sanction follows from the very nature of a given act, and always takes place; a positive sanction is an arbitrary one, imposed by the legislator, and does not always take place. A perfect sanction is one that is adequate (it provides a sufficient motivation for keeping the law) and proportioned (a parity exists between the gravity of the offense and the gravity of the sanction). Practically speaking, sanction is needed if law is not to be a dead letter. Sanction has four purposes: restitution to the individual, restitution to the community, correction, and deterrence. In an ideal sanction, all four aspects are addressed; practically speaking, this is rarely possible, though restitution to the community must always be present. Natural law has the automatic (natural) sanction that obedience to it leads a person towards the ultimate goal and disobedience leads away from that goal; it can also have positive sanctions in given cases. The perfect (i.e., adequate and proportioned) natural sanction that Natural Law must have is factually not found in this life and thus must be located in the afterlife. Human immortality is established by showing that the intellect (and hence the soul or substantial form in which that intellect inheres) is immaterial in its actions (it causes immaterial products [concepts] and hence itself must possess the perfection of immateriality) and hence is neither capable of being destroyed by being resolved into constituent parts, nor essentially dependent for its actions (and therefore for its being) on something that can be destroyed by resolution into constituent parts (the body); the soul could be annihilated, but we have no reason to expect this and considerable reason to expect the contrary.

9. LIFE

III. The Practical Part of Ethics
   A. Introductory comments
   B. Our relationships to ourselves
     1. Life
       a. Suicide
         1) Its meaning
         2) Its morality
       b. Murder
         1) Its meaning
         2) Its morality
       c. Euthanasia
         1) What it means
         2) Its morality
         3) What it does not mean
       d. Abortion
         1) What it means, and doesn't mean
         2) Arguments in favor of abortion
         3) Examination of the arguments
         4) Morality of abortion
         5) Legalization of abortion
       e. Self-defense
         1) The right to self-defense
         2) How far it extends:
           the four conditions
         3) Is self-defense a duty?
         4) What things does it include?

A. Introductory comments

At the very beginning of this book, the comment was made that ethics is primarily a practical study, designed to help us determine the morality of the actions of our everyday lives. Practical assistance like that, however, depends on a fairly healthy spate of theory, if it is not to be the sort of "top-of-the-head" counsel that might depend as well on the feelings of the moment as on the reason. And so, we have spent a great deal of time laying the theoretical basis for ethical judgments.

That theoretical work is now largely done, and the time has come to begin applying what we have seen to some concrete situations of our lives. Obviously, those situations are quite numerous and quite different in kind. In the chapters of this book that remain, we will try to show the application of our ethical theory to some of the major areas that concern us. We won't succeed in covering every question that could be asked; to do that would take far more than the space available for this book or the time available for a standard ethics course. However, we can show *how* those ethical theories of ours are applied to some situations, and in so doing we can give a clue as to how they might be applied to some others that are not specifically treated. That, in fact, would be consonant with what we have implied that ethics is, i.e., the personal judgment of a reasonable adult concerning the morality of his or her actions. For while there are moral standards which are quite objective, none the less the application of those standards to concrete cases can be done only by the person who finds himself or herself in the particular circumstances wherein that judgment has to be made. No textbook can substitute for a personal judgment in those circumstances, for they are too diverse; nor should a textbook try to do so, even if it were possible. For, again, ethics is a matter of each individual person's making a judgment (founded, indeed, on ethical principles) about his or her unique action--an action whose circumstances are probably unreduplicated anywhere in human history, at least in some of their particulars. The gaining of one's final end is the personal responsibility of each moral adult. A book can help--but can do no more than that. Ultimately, the decision to judge something as moral or immoral, and to act morally or immorally, belongs to each individual human being. Of course, so do the consequences that come in the train of such a decision.

At an earlier point in this book, when we were speaking of human nature completely considered, we referred to all of human nature's ordered relationships. We could arrange those relationships in a variety of ways, of course. But one possibility is to speak of a person's relationships (i) to himself or herself, (ii) to other beings (persons or things) that surround that person on earth, and (iii) to God. We shall adopt that particular frame of reference in the chapters that follow. But first we might note two items. First, one can quibble about whether it is even possible, properly speaking, for there to be a relationship with one's own self; a relationship is ordinarily a two-termed thing, in which the two related items are quite different from each other. Granted. But by this time, surely we are aware that, at least mentally, I can distinguish my own total being, taken as a whole, from one or other aspect of that being, and so can regard these as two things at least for methodological purposes. Second, it will become obvious as we proceed that, while these three relationships form the basis of division for the chapters to come, they are not perfectly separated or walled off from one another. And it will be equally obvious that the succeeding chapters will make no attempt to treat them as if they were. The divisions are useful tools. But there will be overlappings. For example, while (in the first division) we are speaking of the relationship that we have to ourselves and to our own lives (while treating of such questions as suicide), it is convenient and natural to treat also of the relationships that we have to someone else's life (and thus to consider such things as murder, euthanasia, and the like). In other words, the division we will make into relationships with ourselves, with others, and with God is only a rubric; it should not be pressed too far, and, when appropriate, it will be overridden.

B. Our relationships to ourselves

With all that as a starter, let us turn to the general topic of the relationships that we have to ourselves. Two major topics will engage us, one in this chapter and one in the next: life, and health.

1. Life

In our day and age, it is almost axiomatic to say that human life is the greatest value that we possess. And so we find people saying that nothing can ever justify the taking of a human life, that life must be sustained for as long as possible (whatever the cost), and so forth. However, the fact that something is axiomatic does not thereby make it true. Human life is, indeed, of very great value. But there are things of greater value, things which can (and sometimes must) be chosen in preference to biological life. Examples might be freedom, fidelity to the Creator, love of one's own fellow human beings--all of which can, in certain circumstances, present themselves as mutually incompatible alternatives to life when a choice must be made. Though he was uttering an aphorism, Patrick Henry's famous statement of "Give me liberty or give me death" does make a valid ethical point. So does the mute testimony of people who have given their lives in order to serve other human beings: one thinks, for example, of a Damien in his leper colony. One thinks of the martyrs in early Christian history, for whom fidelity to their God was a greater value than was the continuation of life. Or one thinks of numerous other individuals who have sacrificed their lives rather than violate their consciences, in one or other way. Again: human life *is* of very great value. But it is not *the* supreme value of our experience.

173

We need, then, to consider the whole question of the morality of the taking of a human life. We will talk about suicide, murder, euthanasia, abortion, and self-defense. However, we will defer until a little later the question of capital punishment, since we need more background for its consideration than we presently have.

a. Suicide

The first question is that of suicide. This means the direct taking of one's own life, on one's own authority. Both elements of that sentence, clearly, need some explanation.

1) Its meaning

When we speak of the *direct* taking of one's own life, we mean that one's own death is intended, either as an end in itself or as a means to some further end (e.g., as a means to being rid of pain, of depression, etc.). A suicidal act can be a positive one (i.e., I perform some action with the intention of ending my life: I shoot myself, I jump out of a window, etc.); or it can be a negative one (I do *not* do some action which I should perform to maintain my life: I fail to eat, to drink, etc.). On the other hand, when we speak of taking one's own life *on one's own authority*, we have to be aware that it is at least conceivable that God, as the author of life, could order someone to kill himself or herself--though we know of no instances where this has in fact occurred (nor could we know of such apart from a special revelation, which fact in itself would put the matter outside the realm of ethics). Or (granting for the moment the legitimacy of the state's inflicting capital punishment) it is conceivable that civil society could order a condemned criminal to kill himself--as seems to have been the case with Socrates and the hemlock. Whatever be made of these two sorts of cases, historically speaking, this much is clear: in neither situation would we be dealing with suicide.

2) Its morality

That is what suicide is. What of its morality? First, we need to distinguish carefully between the subjective morality of suicide (i.e., the guilt incurred by the person who commits it) and the

174

objective morality of the act itself (i.e., whether suicide, in itself, is moral or immoral, independently of the circumstances of any given case). Ethics makes no attempt to judge the subjective morality of such an action. In the first place, it is not its business to do so; in the second, only the suicide himself or herself is in a position to know all the factors necessary to make a valid judgment on the matter--and, indeed, even that person may not be in such a position in every case. There seems to be good evidence that most if not all acts of suicide are attended with a certain amount of pathology, permanent or temporary, which would mitigate the subjective responsibility of the person involved if it does not entirely take away that responsibility.

The morality of suicide in and of itself (the objective morality), however, is another matter, and is by no means unclear. Objectively speaking, suicide is always immoral. Some brief reflection will show why that is the case. Human beings do not give themselves life; neither do they give themselves their own natures or the goal of those natures. They do not establish the number and types of good actions that will perfect those natures, nor the amount of time that will be required for those good actions to be accomplished. All of these are assigned to them by the Creator, the author of their natures. Now, suicide is precisely the denial of all this. It is the assertion that a human being (the suicide) does have full dominion over his or her life (since the suicide, not the Creator, makes the decision as to when that life will end), over his or her nature and its goals (since the suicide, not the Creator, decides the final degree to which that nature can be perfected), and over the number and types of actions whereby human nature can be perfected (since the suicide, not the Creator, determines when those actions shall cease). All of these, of course, are fundamental untruths.

Viewed in one way, the entire moral life is simply an acceptance of one's created (and therefore dependent and subordinate) status, and an attempt to live out the implications of that status. From that perspective, suicide represents a total rejection of the whole moral life. That is why it is always an evil act; it is, in fact, one of the few examples of an intrinsically evil action (one that is always and under all circumstances wrong) to which one can point.

(What does one make of such things as civil protests made by means of starvation fasts, political self-immolations [setting oneself on fire], and the like? Are these morally justifiable, and even--as some have opined--noble? Prescinding from the subjective morality of such acts, and assuming that we are speaking of true suicide, i.e., an act done with the intent of taking one's life [in other words, assuming that we are not dealing with a mere threat or a

175

bluff], then in such cases we have an act that is evil in itself and thus morally impermissible--no matter what the motive: one may not do evil that good will come of it, however great and noble that good might be. Very often, however, in such cases the person's death is more accidental than truly intended: the real intent was in fact a bluff. In that case, we are dealing with another set of moral considerations, those governing the care of one's health. We will consider these shortly.)

b. Murder
1) Its meaning

A topic allied to suicide is that of murder, by which is meant the unjustified taking of someone's life, the direct killing of an innocent person. Once again, the killing is direct: it is intended, either as an end in itself or as a means to some further end. It is not merely something permitted, as the unfortunate but necessary result of some legitimate action (justifiable on the Principle of Double Effect).

As in suicide, there is question of a killing done on one's own authority. Once again, the Creator or the state could conceivably order someone to kill someone else; and, whatever be said of this for the moment, it is not murder in the sense that we use the term here. (The questions of capital punishment and the sort of killing of human beings that goes on in time of war will be considered later on.) Moreover, there is question of killing an *innocent* human being, not one who could be said (as might be the case, as we shall see, in self-defense) to have forfeited his or her right to life.

2) Its morality

With that as a definition, the morality of murder is simple enough. While, once again, the question of subjective moral responsibility may be another matter altogether (because of such factors as ignorance, strong emotion, intellectual fear, etc.), in the objective order murder is always immoral, for reasons analogous to those forbidding suicide: the murderer falsely arrogates to himself or herself complete dominion, not over his or her own life, nature, goals, etc. (as in suicide), but rather over someone else's.

We should notice that this is not an argument against all homicide, but rather only against murder. Homicide is a wider term than murder, and refers to all instances of the killing of a human being, for whatever reason; we will see instances of justifiable homicide later on. But for now, it is perhaps enough to remark that only in the cases of murder and suicide is there question of an arrogation of *complete* authority over human life.

c) Euthanasia
1) What it means

A polite version of murder, in our society, is euthanasia. By this term is means some direct action (either positive or negative) that a person takes to terminate the life of another, generally someone who is suffering some sort of severe physical or mental pain. Once again, the killing is direct: it is intended, either as a means or as an end. It may be through some positive action (e.g., lethal injection of a drug), or it may be by the omission of some action which is obligatory on the person performing the act of euthanasia (feeding a patient, giving him or her water, etc., in the case of a doctor or a nurse).

2) Its morality

The morality of euthanasia is not difficult to determine. Stripped of its fancy title *(eu + thanatos,* Greek for "dying well"), euthanasia is (if done with the victim's knowledge and consent) both suicide and murder; if it is done without the patient's knowledge and consent, it is murder. Its morality can be judged accordingly. Again, one may not do evil that good will come of it.

In effect, what we have in euthanasia is a person arrogating the right to determine when some other person has done enough good to reach his or her final end--an extraordinary instance of minding someone else's business, to put the matter rather baldly. That the patient may be suffering all manner of pain, distress, etc., is indeed heart-wrenching, regrettable, and so on. It is also beside the point. It is quite possible, for example, that the patient's acceptance and tolerance of the pain is the very final act of good required for him or her to achieve the final goal, which action the perpetrator of euthanasia "kindly" renders impossible--thereby placing the sufferer in the far worse condition of losing his or her final end. A euthanasia situation is, obviously, one that is frequently very emotion-laden. But care must be taken not to allow one's well-intentioned heart to interfere with one's head, lest one's "kind" actions put him or her in the position wherein the patient, from the perspective of attainment or non-attainment of life's ultimate goal, might truly say, "With friends like you, who needs enemies?"

3) What it does not mean

Notice, however: it is *not* euthanasia simply to let a person die naturally, i.e., to refrain from going to extraordinary means to save his or her life. In such a case, I am not taking any positive steps (or omitting any steps to which I am obligated) to end the patient's life; I am merely allowing it to come to its natural end. We will consider just what is meant by "extraordinary means" a little later on; for the moment, let us simply say that when there is question of "mercy killing" (in, say, the popular press), we need to look carefully at whether we are speaking of true euthanasia or simply the lack of use of extraordinary means.

d. Abortion

If the debate about euthanasia can sometimes be a lively, emotion-laden one, it nonetheless pales into insignificance when compared with the emotional overtones of the debate on abortion, at least in the present-day culture of the United States. That is unfortunate, from an ethical standpoint. The morality of abortion is not a particularly complicated matter, in itself; but the issues--and thus the resolution of those issues--have become clouded in thick masses of rhetoric. As it turns out, only a very small part of that rhetoric is really pertinent to the moral issue in question.

Let us do several things with this question. We will first define exactly what abortion is. Then we will look at some of the issues raised in the heated debate on abortion. We will then look briefly at those arguments, attempting to see what is valid in them and what is not. Finally, we will try to establish the morality of abortion, independently--to the extent necessary for coherence--of peripheral issues: issues that are truly important, indeed, but beside the point, for all that.

1) What it means, and doesn't mean

First, then, what is abortion? The term refers to the direct expulsion of a fetus from a mother's body into an environment in which it cannot survive; alternatively, it refers to the destruction of that fetus within the mother's body. There are various means available to bring about abortions, ranging from the quite primitive to the highly sophisticated: from a do-it-yourself enterprise in a private home to a hygienically sterile operating room in a modern hospital. But the over-all effect is the same, whatever the degree of sophistication of the means.

However, there are several things that are *not* meant by "abortion." For in abortion the destruction of the fetus is intended, as a means or as an end. Thus, there is no question here of the situation wherein the fetus's death is not intended but rather merely permitted, and justified by the Principle of Double Effect, as in the cancerous uterus case that we saw earlier. Nor is there question here of such things as miscarriages (which are not imputable acts, and consequently are not proper subject matter for ethics). Nor, finally, are we talking about the medical procedure known as hastening of birth--something which, for good reasons, can be justified by the double-effect principle. No. Put briefly, what we mean by the term "abortion" is the direct (i.e., intended) killing of a non-viable fetus, one that cannot yet survive outside its mother's womb.

As an aside, we might note first that, since the killing of the fetus is intended, it is obvious that the Principle of Double Effect cannot be used to justify the morality of abortion. As we recall, one of the conditions of double effect is that the evil effect cannot be intended, but rather only permitted; thus, the principle is inapplicable in this case. Moreover, the good effect of the act of abortion (freedom from responsibility of parenthood, freedom from fear, etc.) would in fact be achieved precisely in and through the evil effect, namely the death of the fetus, thus violating another of the double-effect principle's requirements. And so the moral justification for abortion, if there be such, will have to be sought from some other source, rather than from this traditional moral principle.

2) Arguments in favor of abortion

That, then, is what abortion is. What are the arguments that are brought forth in its favor? There are a great number of them, argued with considerable persuasiveness in some cases. But perhaps we can reduce them down, in essence, to the following:

(1) The fetus is not a human being, or at least cannot be shown to be such. True, if left alone, it will develop into one. But it has not done so as yet; at present, it is merely a part of the mother's body, and therefore can be removed like any other physical organ that becomes problematic.

(2) Even if it be granted that the fetus is a human being, it is none the less not yet a human person, as the courts on occasion have held; thus it cannot be the subject of rights, even the right to life.

(3) In some cases, the fetus can be regarded as an aggressor against the life of the mother, whether this aggression be against her physical well-being (in the case where the mother cannot carry the fetus to term without significant danger to her own physical health), or against her psychological health (for any number of good reasons).

(4) Even if the fetus not be viewed as an aggressor, there can be cases where there is a collision of rights: the right of the mother to life vs. the right of the fetus to life, the right of the mother to psychological health vs. the right of the fetus to biological health. Surely, the mother's right to life, or to sanity, prevails in such a case. Or--taken a step further--others (e.g., the mother's husband, other children, etc.) have rights which can, in certain cases, be set at naught by the fetus, e.g., if the mother were to die.

(5) The right to life, as such, is not particularly helpful unless it also embraces the right to a meaningful life, i.e., a life which involves being wanted, being loved, etc.; but there are many cases wherein a fetus, unless aborted, will be deprived of such a right. Such a child, deprived of love, care, etc., may well grow into a social misfit anyhow.

(6) There is also the case where a fetus is known to have serious medical problems: Down's Syndrome, and so on. Such a fetus can develop only into a defective child, with consequent heartache and expense as the inevitable prognosis of its entire life.

(7) A woman has an inalienable right to say what will or will not happen with her own body; no one may legitimately

deprive her of that right.

(8) A woman has an absolute right to privacy: what she does with her physical body is strictly between herself and her doctor, and any state or federal laws that attempt to regulate this are simply an infringement on that right to privacy.

(9) Conception is not an activity accomplished by a woman all by herself; there must be a male in the process somewhere. But in many situations, in our society, that male can disappear, thus getting off scot-free and leaving the woman in the unjust position of having the total responsibility to care for an unwanted child. This, in turn, is an implicit affirmation of sexism, i.e., the view that males are somehow superior to females, a view that must be firmly rejected in practice as well as in theory. Indeed, anti-abortion laws (and traditional ethical principles) were made by men, and foster men's interests at the expense of women. They should be rejected by women as being mere examples of sexist prejudice.

(10) Finally, there is the case of rape, wherein a woman's body has been seriously violated. To force her to carry the rapist's child is to inflict yet another injustice on her.

3) Examination of the arguments

Perhaps there are other arguments, but these seem to be the most common ones, at any rate. And they are impressive, particularly in the aggregate. Some commentary on each of them in turn, however, may help us appreciate just what their true probative force is.

(1) It is much too apodictic to say that the fetus is not a human being; that is anything but clear. However, it is quite correct to say that it cannot be definitively shown to be such. For no evidence is available through, say, scientific experimentation, that would tell us when the soul (the substantial form of the human being) is received. History has held a variety of views on this subject, with some thinkers even saying that the soul is received by the embryo several weeks after conception. Moreover, not only *is* there no scientific evidence on this question available, but none *is ever likely to be.* This sort of question—the time of the reception of a substantial form—is not

181

the sort of thing that is amenable to scientific experimentation or hypothesis. About all that one can legitimately say about this argument is, yes, it cannot be shown that the fetus is a human being. *And:* neither can it be shown that it is not.

In passing, one can (and should, for honesty's sake) note the inborn tendency that a fetus admittedly has to develop into a human being. Certainly, it will not develop into anything else! For our purposes, however, we will confine ourselves merely to noting this fact. It would take considerable effort and ingenuity to develop it into anything more at this point, although a rather convincing argument can in fact be made on the subject if one is willing to spend the time to do so.

(2) The distinction between a human person and a human being is, truthfully, a distinction without a difference in this case. Indeed, if civil courts hold that there is such a thing as a human being who lacks the rights of a human person, this can only be based on a highly questionable theory about the source of rights--a matter which we will investigate in some detail later on. For the present, let us only say that the idea seems to smack of the assumption that whatever rights a human person has are civilly conferred, i.e., that there is no source of rights other than the state (which the civil courts represent). That has been a view popular with totalitarian civil regimes, but it should not be particularly welcome in an ordinary American context.

(3) To call a fetus an aggressor is to misuse the latter term. For an aggressor, in any sensible meaning of the word, is an *unjust* attacker. It is difficult to see in what sense an unborn child could be an aggressor against its parents, who by their own voluntary act caused it to be in the mother's womb. Aggression does not consist in merely being present, but in actually doing something harmful. If the case is such that the pregnancy is not proceeding normally and there are medical problems present, that is certainly unfortunate; but it is not the child's fault. And if the "aggression" in question is against the mother's mental health, rather than her physical well-being, it is difficult to see just how killing the fetus is going to remedy a psychological problem (whatever it may do to the immediate symptoms of the problem, i.e., the fetus). Therapy may indeed be indicated; but it would take a wild stretch of the imagination to count killing as appropriate therapy. One might as well say that the appropriate therapy indicated for paranoia is the wholesale slaughter of all of one's putative enemies.

(4) As we will see later on, all human beings are equal in their possession of the right to life. Age, and other such

circumstances (possession of a husband, a family, etc.), give no particular priority when there is question of this most fundamental of rights. Granted that there can be such a thing as a collision of rights, it is not easy to see how such a collision can morally be settled by killing an innocent person who has done nothing to forfeit his or her right to life. That is merely an instance of claiming that a stronger person's rights prevail over a weaker one's simply because the stronger is bigger and therefore able to enforce his or her rights. However, the question can be seen in another light. Take this parallel example: suppose that a parent encountered a collision of rights between, say, his or her right to freedom, happiness, etc., and the right of an already born, ten-year old to nourishment, care, and the like. Obviously, such a collision of rights could not morally be settled by killing the ten-year old. It could be asked: why, then, is the matter any different merely because of the age of the child in question? Of course, this assumes that a child in the womb is a human being--a presumption, however, that is not without weight, as we will shortly see.

(5) It is certainly true that love, care, being wanted, etc., are very necessary to the proper physical and psychological development of a child. There are clinical studies that show the devastating effect of the lack of these things, at least in a large number of cases (although not all). It could also be true that such a child might indeed grow up to be a social misfit, a drain on society, and so forth. But: even if it were true that such children always turn out that way (and it isn't: one might profitably examine the childhood of Beethoven for an instance of quite the opposite), does it follow from the fact that a child is not loved that it should be killed? The fault, if any, lies not with the child but with the parents: it may be a harsh thing to say, but it is none the less true for all that, that in having sexual intercourse, the parents took the chance of conception and *they*--not the child--are responsible for the result.

That, in turn, brings to mind a "hard saying" that ought to be uttered somewhere. No human being has an unqualified right to sexual intercourse. In this act, as in every other action whatever that a human performs, I may legitimately do something only if I am both willing and able to accept the consequences that follow inevitably from that act. If *A* in and of itself involves *B*, and if I decide to do *A*, I cannot reasonably decline to accept *B*, for that is to assert that *A* both does and does not involve *B* simultaneously: it involves it of its very nature, but it does not involve it as far as I am concerned. Such a contention is contradictory and unreasonable.

(6) This is a case where especially there is danger of the heart's badly outdistancing the head, for the emotional pull here is strong indeed. If such a deformed fetus is not a human being, then presumably it may be treated like any other pathological organ, and excised without further ado. If it *is* human, however, then there is no more right to kill it--despite its deficiencies, deformities, etc.--than there would be to kill a ten-year-old Mongoloid child: an act that might euphemistically be called euthanasia, but which (less sympathetically perhaps) would more accurately be termed murder. Physical or mental deformity is no warrant for assassination, if there is question of a human being.

(7) Although this statement is quite current in the popular press, it is very difficult to see what sense it makes when it is subjected to close examination. For what is the source of such an inalienable right? The human body was not given to either man or woman as some sort of unconditioned gift by the author of our nature, to be disposed of in whatever fashion we might choose. The human body (in perfect parallelism with the human soul) was given to human beings--men and women alike--with an intrinsic finality attached to it: as a constituent part of human nature, it is intended to be a means that we use in coming to achieve our final goal. It is given to us, therefore, not absolutely but conditionally--the condition being that we use it rationally in the pursuit of our final end. To assert an unconditioned right to its disposition is tantamount to asserting that *we*, not the author of our nature, decide what its purpose (along with the purpose of everything else we possess as humans) is, that *we* set our own final goals. And that is simply not true. Consequently, a statement like this, while perhaps impressive from a rhetorical point of view, can flatly be denied, in accord with the old philosophic dictum of "quod gratis asseritur gratis negatur" (that which is asserted without proof can be denied without proof).

(8) Is it really true to say that a woman (or a man, for that matter) has an absolute right to privacy? We will see later that a right is something that is always conditioned upon a duty: the reason that we have a right is that we have some prior duty to perform. So also, if we have an absolute duty, one which must be done irrespective of all else, and if, say, there is only one means that will allow us to fulfill that duty, then we could be said to have an absolute right to that means. But that is about the only sensible meaning that can be assigned to the term "absolute right." A woman--or a man--in whatever circumstances, has precisely that right (and that degree of right) to privacy which is necessary for performing some relative or absolute duty that he or she has; apart from this, there is no such right. Is it, then, strictly true to say that what a woman does with her physical

body is solely between her and her doctor? No, it isn't. What she does with her body is a matter among her, her doctor (perhaps), and whoever else--if, indeed, there be anybody else (such as a fetus)--in given circumstances requires her body as a means to that other person's final end. For that third party also has duties and therefore rights that have to be considered as well. Once again, we are dealing with something that has become a part of popular rhetoric--which is understandable, perhaps, except that popularity does not necessarily guarantee truthfulness or accuracy.

(9) Certainly, it is true that a women is not solely responsible for conception; there must be a man somewhere in the picture. It is also true that, in our society, the responsible male can sometimes simply disappear, leaving the woman to handle all the consequences of the act that has taken place between them. Equally, it is correct to say that this places the woman in the unjust position of having to do the duty of both parents, to whatever extent this is possible. Finally, it is quite true that the male partner is clearly at fault. But is all this justification for abortion? The act of aborting the fetus does not seem to achieve much by way of rectifying the male partner's injustice. It rather seems to be an instance of taking out on an innocent third party (the fetus) the anger and frustration that the wronged woman feels toward the male who wronged her. Grant for the sake of argument the legitimacy of the woman's desire for vengeance; it would still seem necessary that the target of that vengeance be the proper one, i.e., the guilty male, not the fetus.

As for the allegation that laws, ethical principles, etc., are made by men to protect their own interests, and consequently ought to be rejected lock, stock, and barrel by females: bluntly, this is sheer demagoguery. Men did not invent the fact that women are responsible for what they do, any more than women invented the fact that men are responsible for what *they* do. Rather, there is question here of the responsibility of human nature as such, irrespective of gender; who precisely came up with the idea is merely an accident of history and not a determinant of validity. Ideas should be judged on their own merits, rather than on the gender of their source.

(10) The case of rape is a very difficult one, since there are emotional overtones to the situation that exist hardly anywhere else in the entire area of sexuality. For, very obviously, a grave injustice has been done to the woman in this case. And it is not a transitory injustice, one that is over and done with. Even apart from the lasting psychological trauma that it inflicts, rape is a form of conception, and the woman could end up having to carry

185

to term the child whose life is the result of that rape. This seems to be asking a very great deal of the victim, to put it mildly.

But, while there is a natural tendency to seek vengeance or justice in a case like this, once again we need to be careful to make sure that the object of that vengeance is the correct one. The guilty party in rape is the rapist. It is not the child who is conceived as a result of that rape. That child has done nothing to deserve the wrath of the rape's victim, however much the child might symbolize in the mind of the victim the injustice that she has suffered. Whatever be the level and intensity of our feelings in the matter, an innocent child may not legitimately be made the victim of our vengeance. Let it be granted that it is an injustice for the victim of rape to be placed in the position of bearing a child conceived by rape. That injustice, however, is a continuation of the rapist's original injustice, rather than a new one inflicted by society, laws, etc. And aborting--that is to say killing--the child will only make for yet one more injustice. Sad to say, one injustice does not rectify or cancel another.

These, then, are observations that we could make on some of the more common arguments in favor of abortion. Now, what are we to make of the morality of the act of abortion in itself?

4) Morality of abortion

To get a clear idea of this, we must first separate out all of the side issues: things like women's rights, questions of equality, questions of (putative or real) massive violations of rights, and so forth. These issues are valid and worthy in themselves, to be sure. But they are not the central issue in our question. At most, they form part of the web of circumstances that are part of the imputable act we are considering. Recall that, for an act to be morally good, the act, the motive, and the circumstances must all be good; and on that basis, let us try to form some conclusions about the moral issue at hand.

The nub of the abortion debate comes down to one single question: is the fetus a human being or not? If it is, then to kill it is murder, an intrinsically evil act, and one which may never be done, no matter how much real or imagined good will come of it. We may never do evil for the sake of some good that that evil will accomplish, as we know. If, on the other hand, the fetus is not a human being, then one may legitimately treat it as one would any other living being on the sub-human level--which includes killing it, in some circumstances.

186

Two lines of argumentation can be used. First, we have already seen that a good way to tell what something is, is to observe what it does. As we know, a being always acts in accord with its nature, and consequently its actions can be used to discover that nature. Now, what does a fetus do? What actions does it perform? From the very first moment of its conception, the fetus engages in a process of internal self-development that will terminate in its being a fully formed human being. That, clearly, is a distinctively human action, one that only a human can perform. Moreover, this is an action which all human fetuses, without exception, perform: never in recorded history has there been a case where a human fetus engaged in a process that led to its ultimate development as a dog, a plant, or a chimpanzee. Universally, and immediately upon conception, the human fetus begins developing as a human; and on the basis of that activity, it must be concluded that the fetus is human right from its earliest beginnings.

Yes, but isn't the fetus's humanity really its mother's humanity--that is to say, isn't the fetus (at least in its early stages) simply a part of its mother's body? No. All humans are biochemically unique (apart from the special case of identical twins); the fetus has a different chromosome structure from the mother. The reason is obvious: the fetus receives only half of its chromosomes from its mother, and the other half comes from its father. Simply on the basis of chromosomatic structure, it is clear that the fetus is a distinct being from its mother.

We ought to be careful not to be deceived by appearances. To be sure, the fetus does not look like a human being (at least in its very early stages); it looks like a thing, a bit of tissue. But very little follows from that fact. Consider a parallel: a two-year-old infant does not look like the mature adult that he or she will eventually become; neither does a teenager look like the fully developed physician (or lawyer, or whatever) that he or she will later be. Human life is a matter of development, involving stages on a continuum; how something looks at any given stage is not necessarily indicative of what it will look like later.

The second line of argumentation that can be used is this: let us suppose, simply for the sake of discussion, that it is not possible to determine at what point a fetus becomes a human being (i.e., receives its human substantial form or soul). Suppose that some people claim that this occurs immediately upon conception, while others say that it happens 48 hours later, and still others say it happens at some still later time. Abortion would still be immoral. For we would be dealing with a doubtful situation--but a doubt of fact, not a doubt of obligation. There exists a clear and negative duty not to commit murder (of that, there is no doubt whatever); and the only question is, is this murder? Now, in a situation wherein abortion is being contemplated, there are two ways in which I can set about fulfilling my obligation not to commit murder. Either I can not abort (in which case I will be sure to fulfill my obligation not to murder others), or I can abort, on the premise that the fetus is only probably human (and thus probably non-human)--in which case I may or may not fulfill my obligation of not committing murder. But: since I have a clear duty to achieve the goal, *the safer course must be followed,* i.e., the fetus must be treated as a human being.

5) Legalization of abortion

So much for the morality of abortion itself. A separate (though allied) question is that of the legal status of abortion in a given country. This is somewhat complicated, since it involves both a moral consideration and a legal one. Now, it is true that the moral and the legal orders do not always coincide in our world (there are, after all, many things that are immoral, against which there is no civil law--though, obviously, there certainly is a natural law); but the two are not unrelated to each other, either. And so the question occurs: should civil society ban abortions, given the fact that they are immoral? That might seem easy. One could argue, for instance, that it is a prime duty of the state to protect the lives of its citizens, and one of the chief means that it uses to accomplish that end is law. But abortion, surely, is a grave threat to a significant number of people in the state (the babies who would be aborted). Therefore the state should ban abortions.

Sometimes, however, the matter isn't that simple; much depends on how laws are formed in a given country. In a dictatorship, for example, where the monarch's will formulates the laws, banning abortion would be readily possible. But in a country like the United States, with its quite pluralistic views on the question, the story is very different. For laws in the U.S. are ultimately the result of a consensus of the governed; and if that consensus is seriously lacking on a given point, an effective law on that point simply will not get passed. Widespread abortion became legal in the U.S., not by any legislative action, but rather by judicial fiat of the Supreme Court in the Roe vs. Wade case; but it seems likely that only legislative action will be able to change this, and such action would presuppose that a consensus of a majority of Americans had been achieved on the subject--something clearly not true at present. The current situation of the U.S., then, could well be that it *should* ban abortion but is as yet *unable* to do so. From this, two things would seem to follow. First, given the fact that literally millions of human lives are at stake, legislators and civic leaders have a serious obligation to work ultimately for anti-abortion legislation and proximately for the establishment of the required consensus, using the power of their office, their access to the media, etc., to do so. Secondly, each citizen has the duty--tempered perhaps by the limits of possibility but very real for all that--to do anything possible to achieve the same ends. It is worth noting that each citizen's ability to vote is a powerful force in the matter, and one to which legislators do pay heed.

(One common argument in this matter should perhaps be glanced at in passing, if for no other reason than that its popularity far outstrips its validity. Some say that abortion should not be banned but rather kept entirely legal, since the "procedure" can at least be done by a professional in hygienic circumstances, with far less risk of infection, complications, etc., to the mother. This is not terribly convincing. On that same basis, it could equally well be argued that, by law, bank vaults ought to be left open at night, since otherwise burglars are put at considerable risk by being forced to resort to the dangerous use of dynamite. "Those who prove too much, prove nothing at all," as the ancient philosophers used to say.)

e. Self-defense

The final question we will look at in this chapter is that of self-defense. Here, too, human life can be at risk; and so we need to ask to what extent it is legitimate for a person to use physical violence to ward off the attack of an unjust aggressor. Can one morally even go to the extreme of killing such an aggressor? We might organize our treatment of this around several questions: whether there is a right to self-defense; how far it extends, if there is one; whether it is a duty as well as a right; and what things can be defended even in the extreme degree of taking someone else's life.

1) The right to self-defense

First, there is such a thing as the right to self-defense. Each person, having the natural obligation to seek his or her last end, therefore has the right to whatever is necessary for that purpose. And one thing that is clearly necessary for it is life itself; after all, it is only through life, and the free actions that we perform during life, that we arrive at that end. But, in certain circumstances, the right to life could be rendered meaningless unless a person also had the right to defend it, and to do so personally. For there can be times when recourse to public authority is not possible, and the only available defense is self-defense.

Having said that much, however, we had better add some qualifications, so that the meaning of what we have said so far will be quite clear. The right in question is to self-defense only, i.e., to defense against actual aggression. The right is *not* concerned with the mere threat of aggression, nor is it concerned with seeking justice after an aggression has been completed, or with seeking revenge. On the other hand, the aggression of which we are speaking need not be malicious aggression. An aggressor may be a madman, not responsible for his or her actions; the danger that he or she poses to my life is no less for that fact, nor is my right to defend my life thereby diminished. Even if the aggression is unintended (as it could be in some cases), the right to self-defense remains. Put briefly, my attacker need not be guilty of a moral fault for me to have the right to self-defense.

2) How far it extends:
the four conditions

How far does this right extend? Can I, for example, legitimately kill someone else in self-defense? The plain answer to this is yes, if that is the only way I can preserve my own life. Otherwise my right to my own life becomes meaningless and, since my life is an indispensable means to my absolute goal (the gaining of my final end), that right to my own life is of the same degree of absoluteness as the goal for which it is a means. That plain answer, however, can be readily abused; and, since it involves such a serious matter (depriving someone else of the unique means that he or she needs to attain the final goal), serious thinkers have, over the years, laid down a series of conditions which must be fulfilled if the use of self-defense is to be justifiable. These conditions are simply codifications of common sense; none the less, they are useful. And so, we turn to the four conditions of a legitimate self-defense:

(1) The motive must be self-defense only. Thus, my motive in defending myself may not legitimately be hatred, revenge, etc. (This is merely saying that I may not intend evil, but doing so within the context of self-defense.)

(2) Self-defense   may   be   used   only   while   the

190

aggression is actually in progress, i.e., while I am actually being attacked. Thus, the mere threat of aggressive action against me does not justify the use of physical violence in the name of self-defense: merely receiving a threatening letter from John Jones does not warrant my going after Mr. Jones with my trusty .44 in hand! Nor can self-defense be employed after the aggression has ceased, i.e., it cannot be used to justify retaliation.

This, however, brings up a point that should be noted. Judging when an aggression actually begins can be a tricky business, and a sufficient guide is the ordinary judgment that reasonable people would make about a given situation. For example, I need not wait until the mugger actually hits me over the head; most reasonable people would judge that, if the mugger is running toward me with a club in his hand, the aggression has begun--even though the physical attack itself has not yet actually started.

(3) Physical violence may legitimately be used in self-defense *only if there is no other way* of repelling the aggression. If soft words will do the job, then hard blows are not justified. The reason for this is obvious: I may not morally do a *needless* injury to someone else.

(4) Violence may be used in self-defense *only to the extent that* it is necessary to protect my right to life. Excessive force may not legitimately be used (for the same reason as above: I may not do someone else needless harm). Thus, if knocking someone out will stop the aggression, I may not legitimately go beyond that point and kill the aggressor as well.

However, there are situations in which the only effective means of defending myself will result in the aggressor's death. In that situation, such means are legitimate. It is morally acceptable (even if perhaps repugnant to some people) to kill another person in self-defense, if that is the only way I can preserve my life.

In practice, of course, it is not always possible to make a careful judgment about the amount of physical violence required (and therefore legitimate)--at least, not while I am actually being attacked. One is therefore put in the position of having to make a very quick prudential judgment about the matter, and then of acting. Fair enough; if that is all one can do, then that is all one can do. The point to be remembered, however, is that maximum force is not always

191

allowable in every situation.

3) Is self-defense a duty?

Is there such a thing as a duty of self-defense? That is to say, granted that I *may* defend my own life, even to the extent of taking an aggressor's life in the process, *must* I do so? In general, no. It has been remarked before that, while I may never do an injustice, I may legitimately suffer one. I could therefore ordinarily choose to forego my right to self-defense if I wish. However, certain circumstances could alter this. If I am, say, uniquely necessary to the welfare of my country, or my family, or something of the sort, it is quite possible that my right to self-defense could also become a duty--this, however, because of the rights of other people who depend on me.

4) What things does it include?

We have seen that I may legitimately defend my own life, even to the point of thereby taking an aggressor's life. Are there any other things that I can defend with the same amount of vigor? Or is only life equivalent to life?

To give at least part of the conclusion first: a person has the right to certain things that make life worth living, things without which the sheer right to live would be of small value. Examples of such things are liberty, sanity, chastity, bodily completeness. These items are ordinarily considered equal in value to life itself, and may be defended accordingly.

But are there other such things? What about one's material possessions, and the force that may legitimately be used to defend them? This involves a further consideration. For there are few material things which, in themselves, could be said to be so essential to human living that they would qualify for membership in the class of "goods equivalent to life," in the sense discussed in the preceding paragraph. None the less, it is true that one's home and possessions may legitimately be defended by force (even to the point of killing the aggressor, if circumstances warrant this), not because of the intrinsic value that those material possessions have in themselves, but because of the right that all persons in a society have to possess their property in peace. It is not, then, a matter of simply weighing some material thing (a TV set, one's furniture, etc.) against an aggressor's life, but rather of weighing both that material thing *and a right essential to society* against the aggressor's life. But that same right is, indeed, a "good equivalent to life," for without it society (and therefore human life) would be impossible. On that basis, then, one's property may be defended by force, in accord with the four conditions of legitimate self-defense that we have already discussed.

In passing, we could note that one's honor and reputation, though certainly goods in themselves, are not the sorts of things that can be defended by violence. If someone sullies my reputation, using violence against him or her will not safeguard or restore that reputation. It may prove that I am stronger than he or she is, but that is not the question at issue. Violence in a situation like this, then, will ordinarily not be a matter of self-defense but rather a matter of revenge; and that is not justified by the concept of legitimate self-defense.

SUMMARY OF CHAPTER NINE

The first part of the practical section of ethics deals with our relationships to ourselves; in this, the first question concerns life—a great value in itself, but not necessarily the supreme moral value.

Suicide: This is the direct (i.e., intended, either as a means or as an end) taking of one's own life, on one's own authority, whether by positive or negative means. Objectively, suicide is immoral. The achievement of our final end via the performance of good acts is something that takes place in time, and we are never in a position to know when we have performed a sufficient number of such acts over a sufficient period of time to assure the perfection of our nature and hence the gaining of our final end. Hence suicide freely embraces the possibility of losing our final end and is thus immoral.

Murder: This is the direct (i.e., intended) killing of an innocent person, done on one's own authority. Objectively, murder is immoral for reasons analogous to those forbidding suicide (except that we are here dealing with possibly preventing someone else, rather than ourselves, from achieving the final end).

Euthanasia: This is a direct (intended) action, positive or negative, to terminate another's life (generally someone suffering great pain, terminal illness, etc.). If done with the patient's consent, euthanasia is both suicide and murder; if done without that consent, it is murder. Its morality is judged accordingly. (Euthanasia should be distinguished carefully from the refusal to employ—or to continue to employ—extraordinary means.)

Abortion: This is the direct (intended) expulsion of a fetus from the womb into an environment in which it cannot survive, or the direct destruction of the fetus within the womb itself. Though the contemporary debate over abortion is a heated one, involving many issues that are themselves worthy of consideration, these issues tend to be somewhat extraneous to the central point, which is simply whether or not the fetus is a human person. If it is, its destruction is murder and therefore immoral, for whatever reason it is performed. If it is not, then its destruction can be morally allowable under certain circumstances. That basic question, however, cannot be answered now and is unlikely to be answerable in the future. Thus a doubt of fact arises. However, there exists a clear obligation not to commit murder; and hence, in accord with the rules for a doubtful conscience, the safer course must be followed. Abortion is, accordingly, immoral. Legalization of abortion is a separate question, one pertaining to law; it must be answered in terms of the proper balance of a particular state's duties to safeguard the lives of its citizens and to preserve the value of freedom of opinion for its citizens who may disagree with one another.

Self-defense: This is the use of physical violence to ward off the attack of an unjust aggressor. Having an obligation to achieve his/her last end, each person has the right to such things as are clearly necessary for that end, one of which is life itself; thus a right to self-defense exists, which in certain circumstances may legitimately be exercised personally rather than through the state. Rules governing the legitimate use of force in self-defense are: (i) The motive must be self-defense only; (ii) Force may be used only while the aggression is actually in progress; (iii) Force may be used only if no other means will be effective; (iv) Force may be used only to the degree necessary to ward off the aggression. The right to the use of violence in self-defense extends to one's life and to certain "goods equivalent to life": chastity, bodily integrity, liberty; it can also extend to one's material possessions, since these are covered by a "good equivalent to life," i.e., the right--necessary for society--to possess one's property in peace.

10. HEALTH

III. The Practical Part of Ethics
  A. Our relationships to ourselves
    2. Health
      a. Ordinary care of health
      b. Extraordinary care of health
        1) Health vs. sickness
        2) Health vs. death
      c. Some common risks to health
        1) Narcotics
          a) Chemical substances in general
          b) Medical use of drugs
          c) Recreational use of drugs
        2) Alcohol
        3) Smoking
      d. The question of mutilation
        1) In general
        2) Sterilization and similar procedures.

We have examined at some length the obligation which I have to preserve human life: my own, and that of others. An allied question, however, is that of health, or the obligation to preserve a certain *quality* of life. For, ordinarily speaking, I need to be more than barely alive in order to perform the sorts of free acts that will lead to my final end. I need to be living with at least a certain minimal level of vibrancy, at least in most instances.

2. Health

Let us first consider the obligation that I have to maintain my health, in both ordinary and extraordinary circumstances. Then we will discuss the use of chemical substances: drugs in general, and then specifically that sort of drugs that are commonly called narcotics. Finally, we need to say something about the sacrifice of one part of the body for the good of the whole--the question of mutilation.

a. Ordinary care of health

What sort of obligation, then, do I have to take care of my health? In one sense, the question almost answers itself. For any such obligation depends on the obligation that I have to achieve my final goal. If (as is indeed the case) I have an absolute obligation to achieve that goal, then I also have the obligation to care for my health to the precise degree that my health is necessary for me to be able to use the means necessary to achieve my goal. Which is to say: I am obligated to care for my health to the extent that my health is required for me to perform the sort and number of good acts that I must do if I am to achieve that final goal.

That sounds fine in theory. But when we try to apply it to individual cases we run into slippery ground. For the achievement of *my* final goal depends on the fulfillment of *my* human nature--which, though alike in kind with the nature of every other human being, nevertheless also has individual characteristics that are unique to myself. In one sense, it is true to say that we all share in human nature, that we are all alike. In another, it is equally true to say that no two human beings are *completely* alike. For essence, of which nature is a part, includes accidents, as we have seen; and those are quite individualized.

And so, while it is quite true to say that I need that degree of health necessary for me to achieve my final goal, it is also quite uninformative. For, absolutely speaking, there seems to be no minimum degree of health necessary for *any* human being to achieve his or her goal; after all, it is perfectly possible for some very seriously ill human beings to fulfill the goal of their own individual natures. Rather, the question is one that must be answered on a completely individual basis. And if that is the case, then it is also true to say that the obligation to maintain whatever degree of health each of us requires is equally an individual matter: you, for example, may possibly have the obligation to maintain a level of health commensurate with a top-flight athlete, whereas I might have the obligation only to achieve the degree of health necessary to be an armchair spectator at Monday night football. We both *do* have an obligation, and both of us have it for the same reason. But the specifics of that obligation differ from case to case, and must be judged accordingly.

Admittedly, that is not particular satisfactory. But it is probably about as far as human reason can go, in terms of formulating a general principle applicable to everybody. For, again, only each individual person can make the judgment of precisely how much nourishment he or she is obligated to take, how much exercise, etc. The point to remember, however, is that each of us does have an obligation in this matter, whatever exactly it may be. We are not talking here of mere options, or choices, but of true obligations. Even if unspecifiable in general terms, they still must be brought to specifics by each one of us.

b. Extraordinary care of health

So much for what we might call ordinary care of health. What happens, however, when some sort of extraordinary intervention is needed? What obligations pertain then? For example: in order to maintain my health, I need open-heart surgery--a risky and costly procedure. Am I obligated to undergo the surgery? Or: suppose that I have a non-functioning kidney, and can live decently (if at all) only by means of being regularly attached to a dialysis machine. Must I spend my life depending on that sort of mechanical contrivance? And so on and on.

1) Health vs. sickness

The general principle that applies here is that we are not obligated to take extraordinary means to preserve our health; no one, after all, is bound to do the physically or morally impossible. The obligation is to take reasonable care to assure the level of health that we require. But all of this needs to be very carefully understood.

What do we mean by the term "extraordinary means"? Perhaps it is simpler to state what we mean by "ordinary means"; anything that then is not an ordinary means can be classified as an extraordinary one. By "ordinary means," then, or the "ordinary care of one's health," are meant such things as the use of proper food, shelter, appropriate moderation in work, the avoidance of foolish risks and dangers, and so forth. In brief, by "ordinary means" we mean the use of common-sense measures to ensure health: measures such as a normally prudent person, taking account of all the circumstances, would judge to be means that we would be required to use, measures that maintain some sort of reasonable proportion to the goal to be achieved.

The distinction between ordinary and extraordinary means, however, is something that is quite relative: what might be extraordinary means for one person can be very ordinary for another. For such things as cost, ability to pay, subjective dispositions, individual circumstances, etc., all enter in here. And once again, each person winds up having to make a prudential judgment as to what constitutes ordinary, and what constitutes extraordinary, means in his own her own case.

Some examples may help. Let us suppose that I am an average American, with an income in the middle-class bracket. I am in need of, say, a minor operation for hernia repair. I have insurance. The operation should be done now, for delay involves the definite possibility of strangulation of the hernia, a much more complicated surgical situation. Am I obligated to have the operation? Under ordinary circumstances, yes, I am. A means such as this operation is, in our day and age, a relatively routine procedure, one that can be accomplished without undue difficulty or expense. Much the same thing could be said for other surgical procedures of a similarly routine nature.

Suppose, on the other hand, that I do not have insurance. Such an operation might well cost me something in the neighborhood of $5000--an amount that, for the moment, I am unable to afford without inflicting considerable hardship on those who depend on me (my wife, my children). In such a case, am I similarly obligated? No, or probably not. For here I am at least getting very close to the area of the morally impossible, something to which I am not obligated. Or, suppose that I am, again, a middle-class American, this time with health insurance: I am faced with the prospect of complex pancreatic surgery, a very serious operation which, say, in my case has a 50-50 chance of a successful outcome. Am I obligated to undergo it? Ordinarily, no. That would clearly be something that would be an extraordinary means to preserve health--something that, though I might be able to afford it, is nonetheless risky enough that the common run of prudent human beings would not judge it to be something they would expect as a matter of course. I *may* choose to undergo it, of course; but our question is whether I *must* do so, as a matter of ethical obligation.

Take another example. Suppose that I am a wealthy New Yorker, whose pulmonary condition is such that my choice is either to live in the dry, hot desert of Arizona, or run the serious risk of death. For me, however, to live in Arizona is an intolerable prospect: I feel that life would simply be a matter of exile among sage, sand, cactus, and gila monsters; and such a life would not be worth living. Even the thought of having to make such a move is enough to put me in bed for a week. Am I nonetheless obligated to move to Arizona? No, or, again, probably not. It is possible to have subjective dispositions that can cause moral impossibility, however uninformed and incorrect those dispositions may be. (Again, we must keep in mind that our questions concern what is *obligatory*, not what might or might not be advisable, or what might turn out later to be quite other than we presently view it.)

The examples could be multiplied. But the point is perhaps apparent: what is ordinary for one person can be extraordinary for another; and each individual has to form a reasoned judgment as to his or her own case--a judgment which, admittedly, could be objectively wrong. But if, according to that quite fallible judgment, a given means is for me an ordinary one, then the obligation to use it exists; if it is extraordinary, then there is no such obligation. General principles can carry us no further, and it is the province of each individual to judge his or her own case.

2) Health vs. death

Suppose we up the ante somewhat. We have so far been talking about means required to preserve health. Does what we have said also hold true when the alternative to those means is not simply illness or less robust health, but death itself? What do we say about risks to one's own life, about risking death? Can it ever be deliberately--and legitimately--risked, i.e., viewed as a possibility that under certain conditions could be accepted?

In one sense, of course, merely living one's daily life involves a degree of risk to life and health. The number of hazards that exist in the average household is legion, as is well known. Even something as routine as driving a car can be very hazardous. It is impossible to avoid all risk to life and health, for to do so we would virtually have to stop living, or at least stop living any sort of life that is worthwhile.

Most risks of this sort are justifiable on the Principle of Double Effect. The risk of being injured or killed in a car accident (under ordinary circumstances), for example, is outweighed by the good effect of getting to work and thus being able to provide for one's family.

In general, however, such a risk becomes unjustifiable when the fourth step of the double-effect principle, the presence or absence of a sufficient reason, is violated. In estimating this, it will pay us to keep in mind whether the danger in question is (i) ordinary or extraordinary, (ii) merely possible, probable, or certain, and (iii) remote or proximate. Obviously, a danger that is certain, proximate, and extraordinary requires a greater justifying reason than does one that is merely possible, ordinary, and remote (or whatever other combination of these types of dangers one wishes to imagine: certain, remote, and ordinary; probable, extraordinary, and remote; etc.). Once again, each given case will require a prudential judgment as to whether a sufficient reason is or is not present. Moreover, a danger that is extraordinary for me might, because of a particular skill that another person has, be quite ordinary for him or her: the tight-rope walker faces only ordinary peril in walking a wire between two buildings, whereas I would certainly be looking at an extraordinary danger. A professional wrestler faces only ordinary danger from his opponent when he climbs into the ring; I on the other hand would be in considerably greater peril. A trained soldier faces less risk than does a raw recruit. And so on. The categories of ordinary-extraordinary, possible-probable-certain, and remote-proximate always have to be estimated with reference to individual people, taking into account their particular talents, skills, and so on.

Sometimes mere entertainment (of oneself or others) can be a sufficient reason for an ordinary risk. Here belong such things as the risk of possible injuries in sports, in acrobatics, etc. A given person may have skills that, in his or her case, render the risk of injury reasonably remote. In general, however, the greater the risk (once it is finally determined), the greater the reason required to justify it.

So much for the question of risking life and health in what might be termed ordinary circumstances. One other area remains, however, which we have not yet fully explored, although we have touched on it in passing. That is the very sticky question of the "right to die": that is to say, what my obligations are if the time comes wherein I either make use of extraordinary means, or else I decline to do so and surrender myself to death. Or, to make the question even more pointed: does there come a time when someone else may legitimately decide that a non-compos patient in his or her care will be accorded no further treatment, but rather will simply be allowed to live out his or her normal life span and then die?

The question is a very difficult one, since it is loaded with emotional content. Yet it is a question that has to be asked. The aim of medical science is to preserve life, to do all that is possible to ensure the continued life and health of the patient. While that is a commendable goal (and, surely, we would have questions about any doctor or nurse who did not subscribe to it!), none the less we can rightly wonder: particularly in modern times, given technological advances in medicine, can this be carried too far on occasion?

We already know the fundamental principle governing such cases: there is an obligation to use ordinary means to prolong one's life, or the life of someone for whom one is responsible. There is no obligation to use extraordinary means for that purpose--or to continue the use of extraordinary means, if these have already been started. For, again, we have entered the realm of the morally impossible, to which no one--either an individual in his or her own regard, or a person responsible for another individual--may legitimately be bound.

Granting that we always realize that the words "extraordinary means" constitute a relative term, one whose precise meaning must be determined in any given situation, and realizing too that one may never use some positive act to terminate someone's life (one's own or someone else's), it is nevertheless legitimate to decline to perform acts that constitute extraordinary means, even though one foresees that death will inevitably result from that choice. It is also legitimate to take positive action to terminate extraordinary means that have been employed (for, if there is no obligation to use them in the first place, there is no obligation to continue their use). So: one may not deliberately suffocate or administer a lethal injection to a terminally ill patient; that would be a positive act to terminate his or her life. One may, however, refuse to authorize the use of life-support systems in a hopeless case. One may also decide to terminate the use of such systems ("pull the plug," in the less-than-elegant terminology ordinarily used) if they have already started to be used. On the other hand, it is immoral to decline to use ordinary means to prolong life. And so, even a terminally ill patient must be fed and given water, must eat and drink--to the extent that this is reasonably possible.

Examples may help. A child is born with serious defects: a malformed heart, let us say. This child is also a Mongoloid. To save the baby's life at all, there is need of an immediate and quite serious, delicate operation to repair the heart; chances for survival are at best questionable. Are the parents obligated to have the surgery performed? No, they are not. (Again, we have to remind ourselves that our question is what they are *obligated* to do, not what they might wish to do.) For such surgery is clearly an extraordinary means to preserve life; it would not be obligatory even in the case of an otherwise normal child. Ordinary care is, of course, required: the child must be fed, etc. But extraordinary surgical intervention is not mandatory.

Another example: my aged parent can survive only if I move him or her into a quite expensive specialist hospital, where a certain type of therapy is available which cannot be given elsewhere. The cost of care in this hospital, however, is such that, if I do make use of it, my own family will be seriously deprived. Must I do so? No. I may wish to, of course. But that is not the question.

Again: a cancer patient will surely die if he or she does not undergo an extensive course of painful radiation therapy. There is no absolute guarantee of the therapy's success, of course; but it has been used with good results on other patients. Must this patient undergo it? No.

C. Some common risks to health

So, I am obligated to use ordinary means to preserve my health, and to take ordinary means to avoid risks to it. In American culture, however, risks to health seem fairly widespread. Let us now consider some of them. We might speak, for instance, about the use of narcotics, of alcohol, and of tobacco.

1) Narcotics
a) Chemical substances in general

First, let it be recognized that alcohol is a drug, a chemical substance. So is the nicotine in tobacco. We separate our consideration of these only because the circumstances that surround their use differ in our culture, and that fact introduces some corresponding differences in the ethical obligations that result in their regard.

To look first at the question of the use of narcotics, then. In general, the Principle of Double Effect governs the morality of introducing any chemical substances into the body. It is good to remember that all chemical substances, when so introduced, have at least one effect and, according to most medical authorities, one or more side effects as well. This is true of such common chemical substances as aspirin; it is *a fortiori* true of such things as LSD and the like. In applying the double-effect principle, two areas will need special attention: the nature of the evil effect, and the presence or absence of a sufficient reason.

In the case of some chemical substances, we know fairly well what their principal effects are, and their side effects as well. We know that the major effect of aspirin, for example, is to act as a pain killer. We also know that, in some cases, it can be a stomach irritant, that it can have an effect on the blood's ability to clot, etc. So also in the case of many prescription and over-the-counter drugs: we know what their chief effect is, and we have a fairly good idea of the side effects that their use can cause; long experience in pharmacology has taught us this. And so, the risks involved in their use can be estimated with reasonable accuracy, and consequently the presence or absence of a sufficient reason for their use can be judged somewhat easily. In the case of some newer, experimental drugs, our knowledge is much slighter. We may have some experience with their primary effect; we also may have little or no knowledge of what else they may do to us. Consequently, the risk they pose is correspondingly greater. Notice, however, that this is a statement, not about these drugs themselves, but rather about the state of our knowledge in their regard.

When chemical substances such as these are taken under the supervision of someone who specializes in a knowledge of their effects and side-effects (e.g., a physician), the risk involved in their use can normally be judged to be acceptable. However, when they are taken without such supervision, that risk grows exponentially--and with it, the gravity of the sufficient reason required to justify their use. (In ethics, as well as in medicine, the old saying is true: he who is his own doctor has a fool for a patient.)

With that as background, let us consider the use of certain chemical substances--"drugs," in the common sense of that term--in two quite disparate areas: as medical treatment, and for recreational purposes. What we say will, of course, apply to all chemical substances. But the ethical question, at least in our culture, focuses upon certain specific chemical substances; no one is particularly concerned about the morality of the use of, say, digitalis!

b) Medical use of drugs

In the medical use of drugs, the prudent supervision that is provided normally sees to it that there is no special ethical problem. There is a risk, of course; there is in the use of any chemical substance. But the guidance of the doctor is usually sufficient to minimize that risk, at least to an ethically acceptable level. Much the same thing can be said of the use of over-the-counter remedies whose effects have become well known over time. The only problem area that suggests itself would be the use of experimental drugs whose side effects are still pretty much unknown. A doctor would not be justified in prescribing such drugs (nor would a patient be justified in accepting them) if other, better-known drugs can do virtually the same job; that would simply be a case of using a human patient as a guinea pig, and that is impermissible. On the other hand, when there is question of a grave illness where no other available remedy is at hand, the use of an experimental drug as a sort of "last-ditch" measure could be justified.

c) Recreational use of drugs

The medical use of such substances does not ordinarily present much of an ethical problem. Or, if it does, that problem is relatively easily solved. A much thornier issue, however, is the non-medical use of drugs, i.e., their recreational use. Here is meant the casual use of substances such as marijuana, or of something much stronger (e.g., heroin, LSD, and the like). What are we to make of the use of such things, from a moral standpoint?

A distinction has to be made first. Some drugs have such well known (and disastrous) immediate effects that it is hard to see any sort of recreational reason that would justify their use. For example, heroin has been found to be viciously addictive (instances are on record where a single use of it has induced addiction); the evil consequences of its use would seem to be so severe as to preclude any recreational benefit as being a sufficient reason for its use. The same thing is true of such things as LSD, "Angel Dust" (PCP), and the like; the risk of "fried brains" is much too proximate, too certain, and too extraordinary for these to find moral acceptance merely on the basis of any recreational grounds.

Other drugs have less severe immediate consequences--things like marijuana, "uppers" and "downers," and the like. In the case of drugs like these, normal principles would apply: if the risk they involve is within acceptable limits (technically, if that risk is remote, ordinary, and merely possible), then the justifying reason need not be a particularly grave one--recreation would suffice. *However:* the problem lies precisely in establishing that the risk is, indeed, such. For we simply do not know enough about the long-term effects of many drugs to state with confidence that they do not in fact present a grave risk. Some recent studies in the area of genetics, for example, indicate the real possibility of chromosome damage traceable to the use of marijuana. If this should indeed prove to be the case, it would take a very serious reason to justify the use of a drug like this, particularly when one contemplates the possibility of a future generation of chromosome-damaged offspring of marijuana-using parents. At the very least, in the face of such a possibility, it becomes very difficult to see how mere recreation could suffice as a sufficient reason for use.

More specifically (to use a type of reasoning with which we are already familiar), as long as there are serious scientific questions about the long-term effects of substances like these, one who uses them for recreational purposes finds himself or herself in the position of saying, "This may be harmful (to me or to any offspring that I may ever have) and it may not; I shall use it anyway." The morality of that speaks for itself, for, at the very least, it involves the ready acceptance of the possibility of injury to some other person (a potential offspring) merely for the sake of transitory recreation. Of course, it also involves the ready acceptance of the possibility of serious harm to oneself.

2) Alcohol

Now, let us turn to the morality of the use of alcohol. To do this sensibly, we first need to do away with the facile parallel that we frequently find in the popular press between, let us say, the use of marijuana and the use of alcohol. The two are, indeed, alike in that each is a drug. But the parallel ends there. For, when we considered the morality of using things like marijuana, the reason that gave us pause was that our knowledge of its long-term (and short-term, for that matter) effects is deficient. That, again, is a statement about our knowledge, not about the particular chemical substance itself; and it is a statement that will change as the sophistication of our knowledge increases. For the present, however, the basic objection against the recreational use of marijuana and its ilk is that we do not know enough about them to enable us to make a truly reasonable judgment about the acceptability of the risk that their use presents. At some time in the future, we doubtless will. But we do not right now. And that means that we are, for now, left unable to decide whether or not a sufficient reason can be found in simple recreational use.

That is not the case with alcohol. We know a great deal about its short- and long-term effects. And so we are able to make a much more accurate judgment about the morality of its use—using, again, the same moral principles that we would have liked to use in the case of marijuana (etc.) but were unable to do so.

205

Is the use of alcohol moral or immoral? The question is too broad. If posed in that fashion, its only adequate answer is: sometimes yes, sometimes no. For a great deal depends upon the physical, chemical make-up of the person who is drinking it. For example, there are people who for one reason or other are incapable of tolerating the presence of alcohol in their systems: imbibing it, either in the short range or at least in the long range, involves becoming dependent upon it. At present, we do not know why this is the case; we merely know that it is. Alcoholism, as a pathology, is only in the infancy of its being understood. But we do know that for someone who is--for whatever reason--an alcoholic, alcohol is sheer poison and must be avoided, if that person is to live anything like a human life. Objectively speaking, the use of alcohol by such a person is immoral, for it involves the surrender of one's rational nature to dependency upon a chemical substance.

(Here we must note something carefully. Nothing is here said or implied about the subjective morality of an alcoholic's taking a drink. That can involve all sorts of factors [habit, fear, pain, etc.] that would have to be judged in each individual case. The author of these pages is well aware that alcoholism is an illness, not a moral fault. All that is being said here is that it is wrong, objectively speaking, for an alcoholic to drink--something which, if the objective and the subjective orders are sufficiently distinguished from each other, ought to be unobjectionable enough.)

Leaving aside the special case of the alcoholic, however, we can ask about the morality of an ordinary person's use of alcohol. In some instances, we are merely talking about the appropriate use of some creature to bring about a given effect: a certain relaxation, conviviality, etc.; there are no evil effects to be considered, or at least none of any significance. In such an instance, the operative moral principle is the general, over-arching one: does this action advance the gaining of one's final end, in some way? If so, it may be used. In other cases, particularly when there is question of heavy drinking, there can be a situation of double effect: conviviality, relaxation, etc., are indeed provided, but, for example, so is a raging headache the following morning (in the case of some individuals, even without question of overindulgence). Or, on a long-term basis, at least some organic damage (liver, etc.) can be sustained. There can be all sorts of shading to this, depending on individual situations. But, as a general principle, the normal rules of the double effect provide an adequate guide to the morality of the situation (or its immorality, as the case may be.)

3) Smoking

Another question, also normally brought up in parallelism to the use of marijuana and suchlike substances, is the use of tobacco. What are we to say about the morality of this? For, certainly, scientific reports abound that link smoking to all sorts of evils: lung cancer, heart diseast, emphysema, etc., etc. It would seem on the basis of this that smoking clearly involves an unacceptable risk to health, and thus is immoral.

Yet we need to be a little bit cautious here. For it is not the business of ethics to assert obligations that do not clearly exist. Neither is it the business of ethics to counsel prudence or to be exhortatory. Our business is to state clearly what the objective morality of a given action is, and leave the making of sermons to others. And the long and short of the situation is, the morality of smoking is not clear. For when we look at the medical reports, we notice that the sort of evidence that they provide is statistical. A given percentage of smokers, for instance, develop lung cancer. Smoking is a factor in the case histories of such-and-so percentage of patients with heart disease, and the like. What we do not have, thus far at any rate, is a definite causal link between smoking and the evils we know so well. After all, there are a fair number of people who smoke, but who do not develop lung cancer and the like (and there are a fair number of people who do not smoke, but who do develop such pathologies). This fact is of some ethical significance, for it limits the sorts of things that ethics can say on the matter. Suppose that an individual person is trying to make a moral judgment on his or her smoking, and suppose, say, it is statistically true that 65% of the smokers in his or her class develop a certain type of pathology. Nevertheless, one thing is still lacking that would enable a clear judgment to be made: does the particular individual belong to the 65% who will develop the pathology? Or to the 35% who will not?

This is somewhat different from the case wherein there is an unknown (but probable) risk involving 100% of the users. For in smoking, some users of a substance are at considerable and serious risk; others are at no risk at all. And the smoker's gamble, so to speak, is that he or she will be among the latter class rather than the former. If in fact a particular smoker is part of the group that will develop the pathology, then it would take a very serious reason indeed to justify his or her smoking.

If he or she is not, then there is not even question of a double effect, but rather merely of the over-arching principle governing the use of creatures in general. The problem, of course, is that there is no way of knowing which of the two groups any given smoker belongs to. The gamble itself, then, is the nub, and against that the seriousness of the sufficient reason must be judged. If there is adequate reason why the smoker should run such a risk, then well and good; his or her action can be justified morally by the Principle of Double Effect; life, after all, is filled with risks, and the decision whether or not to run a given one must be made. If there is not adequate reason, then there is no justification for running the risk of being a member of the susceptible group. And each individual must make the particular judgment as to the presence or absence of that sufficient reason.

Here again, we must remind ourselves that we are not speaking of what is advisable, in a given situation. Rather, we are speaking of what is obligatory. If we were in the business of merely giving advice, then the matter of smoking would be much more easily handled, and could be done in briefest fashion: *don't*. But, at least given present evidence, we have to stop short of apodictically saying, one *must* not.

So much, then, for the general obligation to care for health, including our consideration of some of the more prominent risks to health. Some special cases remain to be treated, however, for, while they are akin to what we have seen in some ways, they nevertheless present some special problems that warrant consideration.

d. The question of mutilation
1) In general

The first of these is mutilation. By this is meant some act by which a part of the body is permanently injured or destroyed. The question of the morality of this comes up because, since the body is a necessary tool for the accomplishment of one's final end, we might wonder whether there are circumstances under which a part of it can be sacrificed. For the body is a totality: it was given to us, as a whole, as part of our natures; and the obvious intention was that it *all* be used for acquiring our final end. What right have we to sacrifice some given part of it?

To answer this, we might first observe a universal characteristic of the activity of living beings. Any living

208

being (human or sub-human) engages in what is called "immanent action," i.e., an action whose (ordinarily beneficial) effects are aimed, not at the good of individual parts of the being in question, but at the good of the whole. Instances of immanent action are growth, nourishment, generation, organization, irritability, and adaptation. In growth, for example, living beings take in food, assimilate it, and by means of one part of the organism's assimilating matter the entire organism increases in size and develops itself until it arrives at its proper dimensions. In nourishment, living things, which use up energy and discard waste, replenish what they lose, and they heal themselves when injured, throughout their whole body--this by assimilation of food, chiefly by one part of the body. In generation, living things bring into existence a new individual of their own species. Through organization, living beings are composite beings, each of the parts of which have a definite structure and a definite function, all related to the good of the whole organism. In irritability, living things display a seemingly disproportionate response to a stimulus, which response is aimed at the good of the entire being. Finally, in adaptation, a living being adjusts to adverse elements in its own environment. Now, in each and every one of these immanent activities, the action in question, though carried on by part of the being, is none the less aimed at the good of the entire being rather than merely at the good of the acting part.

Living beings also, of course, exercise that sort of activity known technically as transient action: an activity which does not (at least necessarily) result in the perfecting of the acting being, but rather of some being outside the agent. An example would be my action of moving a book across my desk. The action does not result in *my* being any better or any different. It results in the book's being different, i.e., in having a new set of geographical co-ordinates. Transient action is not our principal concern here, so we will spend no further time on it, apart from noting that it is an activity which living beings (along with non-living ones) can exercise. Our real point is the contrasting one: there is also a distinctive kind of action, immanent action, which only living beings exercise.

In immanent action, then, the action distinctive of living beings: the activity is aimed at the good of the entire organism, not merely at the good of the part of the organism exercising the activity. For example: it is, indeed, the stomach that is primarily involved in nutrition. But this activity is exercised, not for the good of the stomach primarily, but rather for the good of the entire organism of which that stomach is a part. In irritability, a response is displayed to a stimulus by, say, an arm. But that response (in the case of the arm's being removed from the hot stove) is not primarily for the good of the arm; it is for the good of the entire organism of which the arm is a part. Indeed, immanent activity can sometimes be carried on, not at all for the good of the part exercising it, but rather only for the good of the whole: when the white cells of the blood carry on their anti-bacterial warfare, this is quite often not for their own good (because they perish in the proccess), but rather solely for the good of the organism as a whole.

So: living beings do have a distinctive, characteristic activity in the physical order. That action is not aimed chiefly at the good of the part performing it, and may sometimes even be to the detriment of that part. Is there a correlative to this sort of thing in the moral order? The answer is yes, and that correlative is called the Principle of Totality. According to this principle, a part (of the body) is not an end in itself, but rather is for the whole, i.e.,for the well-being of the entire organism. In other words, the parts of the whole are subordinated to the well-being of the whole itself, and can be, if necessary, sacrificed for the welfare of that whole. If the good of the whole requires it, a particular part can be sacrificed--as is the case with a gangrenous leg, an inflamed appendix, etc.

What justifies this principle? We recall our earlier statement that the entire body was given us as a means of achieving our final end. Ordinarily speaking, that does mean that the body as a whole is to be used for that purpose. But what happens when one part of the body goes out of whack, and threatens to destroy the entire body? Obviously, the purpose for which the body was given remains, and must be achieved (for the achievement of our final goal is an absolute end). It would, if course, be better if the entire body could be used for that end. But if this is impossible, and if one part of the body threatens the purpose of the whole, then, in order to achieve that absolute purpose, the offending part may (and sometimes must) be sacrificed. And thus the justification of the Principle of Totality.

We should note that this is a case wherein a good is, in fact, accomplished precisely in and through an evil: the health of the body is achieved precisely by the evil of a loss of a (diseased) member. True enough; but this is a physical evil, not a moral one. The principle remains true that one may not do a moral evil so that good may come of it. All that is said here is that the same principle does not necessarily apply to a physical evil.

For the most part, however, mutilation tends to be largely a theoretical question, rather than one which presents itself as having great moral urgency. If, say, the amputation of an arm or a leg, or the surgical excision of an appendix, etc., is medically necessary, we may regret this; but it is not ordinarily something which causes us moral scruples. It is good to know that such surgical procedures are indeed justified, when medically necessary; but the issue is not a burning one.

2) Sterilization and similar procedures

But there are cases wherein the moral issue has a somewhat more pointed impact. There is the question of surgical sterilization of the male. Tubal ligation of the female would be another example. For, ordinarily, these are not medically required procedures, done, say, in order to correct some physical malady. If they were, then they would fit into the same situation as amputation, excision of an appendix, and the like. More often, however, they turn out to be elective procedures: a deliberate mutilation of the human body for reasons that are extrinsic to the body, i.e., for purposes of birth control. This gives the matter quite another coloration. For, obviously, we are no longer speaking of something justifiable in terms of the Principle of Totality: it is not simply a matter of the health of the entire organism's requiring the sacrifice of a part of that organism. Rather, in these cases, there is question of some other good, real or apparent, demanding such a sacrifice. What are we to make of this, morally?

We will consider the whole question of birth control later on in this book. At the moment, let us simply confine our thoughts to this question: is mutilation of the body acceptable for any purpose other than one justified by the Principle of Totality? Which is to say, can one morally permit mutilation for some purpose external to the body itself?

In principle, the answer to this has to be yes, although we will need to qualify that somewhat carefully. If some external good is such that it must be achieved as a necessary means to achieving our final end, and if the sole way to achieve it is by the sacrifice of some part of our body, then that sacrifice is justified. If it were the case, for example (and the example is admittedly bizarre, since such absolutely demanded goods are rare), that only by means of allowing my hand to be cut off could I avert something like blasphemy (in a cultural situation, say, wherein the possession of both hands were symbolically tantamount to blasphemy), then such a thing would be both permissible and necessary. After all, there are higher and more

211

necessary goods than bodily integrity--though they are not many in number.

All this, however, does not in and of itself justify contraceptive sterilization and the like. For we should notice that such a mutilation is morally acceptable only when bodily integrity comes into conflict with an incompatible higher good, a good which must be achieved and can be so only through the sacrifice of bodily integrity. Whether or not contraception constitutes such a good is quite another question, and one that we will consider at a later point in this book. For now, we merely observe that mutilation can, in principle, be justified in ways other than the Principle of Totality. But the reasons for such a justification must be grave ones indeed.

SUMMARY OF CHAPTER TEN

The second question involved in our relationship to ourselves is that of health.

A. General Principles: We are obligated to take ordinary care for our health (proper food, exercise, etc.) to the precise degree that our health is necessary for us to use the means required in order to achieve our final goal; the specifics of this vary with each individual, though the fact of the obligation is common to all. We are not bound to employ extraordinary means in caring for our health (for no one can rationally be bound to do the [morally] impossible), although ordinary means are required. "Ordinary means" refers to those things which a normally prudent person, viewing all the circumstances, would reasonably judge to be required in a given case. "Extraordinary means" is a relative term, and depends on the particular circumstances of each individual; determination of it is a matter of prudential judgment in each case. Neither are we required to use extraordinary means to preserve life itself, even though one foresees that death will certainly or probably result from their non-use or discontinuance. Risks to life (and to health) are normally judged by the Principle of Double Effect, with special attention to the presence/absence of sufficient reason; in making this judgment, the classification of risks or dangers as ordinary/extraordinary, possible/probable/certain, and remote/proximate is useful, though these categories too are relative to the individual. Just as there is no obligation to use extraordinary means to preserve life or health, so there is no obligation to continue their use if that has been begun.

B. Several common risks to health can be cited. (a) The morality of the use of chemical substances (narcotics) is judged by the Double Effect Principle, with special attention to the risk that any individual such substance poses, and to the presence or absence of a sufficient reason to run such risks. If drugs are taken under competent supervision, or if their effects are sufficiently familiar through long and common usage, there is ordinarily no moral problem; however, any use of a human as an experimental guinea-pig is morally unacceptable. Recreational use of drugs can be divided into two categories: (i) the merely recreational use of certain drugs cannot be morally acceptable; the risks they pose are too great. (ii) Certain other drugs seem to have less drastic effects; if we could be sure that the risks they pose were within acceptable limits, their recreational use could be morally allowable--but at present we cannot be sure of this and hence mere recreational use of such substances is very questionable from a moral standpoint (although the passage of time may alter this one way or the other). (b) For an alcoholic, the use of alcohol is, objectively, morally wrong, since the risk is too great. Apart from this special case, however, normal Double Effect rules govern the use of alcohol. (c) The morality of smoking is unclear, for its evil effects may or may not be verified in a given individual case, and the risk that must be judged here concerns whether a given individual is or is not susceptible to those effects.

C. The question of mutilation is also a health question. Mutilation is an act whereby some part of the body is permanently injured or destroyed. Its moral justification is found in the Principle of Totality, according to which (on the analogy of immanent action in living beings) a part of the body is not an end in itself but rather exists for the whole, i.e., the well-being of the entire organism. If a part threatens the whole, then it may be sacrificed to ensure the good of the whole. Physical mutilation can also be justified when bodily integrity conflicts with an external, incompatible good, one which is absolutely required and which can be obtained only through mutilation; however, such cases are rare.

11. THE FAMILY SOCIETY

III. The Practical Part of Ethics
  C. Our relationships to others
    1. Society in general
      a. What a society is
      b. Types of societies,
         and requisites for each
    2. The family as a society
      a. What a family is
      b. The family as a natural society
        1) Generation and its purpose
        2) Requirements of the offspring
      c. Marriage
        1) Characteristics of all marriages
        2) Characteristics of some marriages
      d. Divorce
      e. Sexual activity
        1) Finality
        2) Sexual activity within marriage;
          the question of birth control
        3) Sexual activity outside of marriage
          a) Pre-marital and extra-marital
            heterosexual activity
          b) Homosexual activity.

C. Our relationships to others

We have seen some of the ethical consequences of the fact that we have certain relationships with ourselves, or with parts of ourselves. There are other such consequences, but perhaps what we have seen will do for a sample. Now we need to look at some of what follows from the fact that human beings also have relationships with other things around them, both human and sub-human; and this will occupy us for the next few chapters. The first topic we will examine is that immediate relationship that a human being normally has with the people nearest and dearest to him or her, the family.

1. Society in general

A family, however, is a society. And so perhaps it will pay us first to examine what a society is. In that way, we can better appreciate the particular sort of society that a family is; we will also be in a better position to appreciate other societies to which humans belong, particularly the state.

a. What a society is

What, then, is a society? Simply as a matter of observation, we note that human beings do in fact co-operate with one another in achieving common aims. Moreover, humans tend to congregate together, to live together. Is this merely a matter of happenstance, or of convenience? Or is there something deeper back of it?

Etymologically, "society" derives from the Latin word *societas,* and ultimately from *socius,* companion, associate. And a society (to start with a definition that is both descriptive and traditional) is an enduring union of a number of persons bound to co-operative activity for a common end. It is a number of persons: at a minimum, two; otherwise, co-operation is not possible (one cannot, after all, co-operate with oneself). But while the minimum is two, the maximum may run into the millions, for there is no immediately evident maximum number beyond which co-operation, and hence a society, is not possible. Moreover, we are speaking of an enduring union, something that lasts for some considerable period of time, depending on the purpose of the society. It need not last forever, but it does have to extend for whatever length of time is required for the mutual co-operation to take place. The humans are, moreover, bound together: by some sort of bond, whether this be a pledge, a promise, a contract, or some sort of law. Mere voluntary, ad-hoc co-operation (the sort of thing one might find in the case of a pick-up softball game) does not constitute a society; there is need for some sort of commitment, some sort of allegiance to the society that exacts a certain personal cost.

Next, in order to direct the society to its common end, there has to be some sort of authority, which selects the means to the common end and obligates the members of the society to use those means. The need for this is obvious enough; without it, we are left to the free-will agreement of all the members of the society regarding the means to be used for the end, and no one who has any experience in working with a considerable number of humans in a common enterprise has any illusions as to how well *that* works. We will return to the notion of authority in a society a little later; for now, let us simply note that it is a necessary feature of one. Finally, one last comment: since a society is a moral union, one bound together in terms of a consciously sought end, only humans can form a society, since a union of wills is presupposed. Herds are not societies, except in a metaphorical sense of the term; there can be such a thing as a "society" of, say, insects (bees, and the like) only in a poetical use of language.

b. Types of societies,
and requisites for each

Again, then: a society is an enduring union of a number of persons bound to co-operative activity for a common end. But even within that definition, there is room for quite a bit of variety; there can be quite different kinds of societies, even in the strict sense of the term. One can divide these in a number of ways. But perhaps a useful division would be into associations which one may join or not join, as he or she pleases, and societies which one has to join: optional and mandatory societies, in other words. An example of the first type of society would be a club, a fraternity or sorority, a volunteer neighborhood organization, and the like: groups which I can either join or not join, with little or no impact on human nature as such--I remain very much a human, irrespective of whether I do or do not belong to, say, the Rotary Club. Societies of this type we might call "conventional societies." But there are other types of associations, membership in which is not so optional, societies which seem to require membership as a necessary offshoot of human nature. The family would be one such, the state another. We will see these in some detail later in this chapter; for the moment, we need notice merely that they are societies, and not "conventional" ones. Let us rather call them "natural" societies, since they seem very closely linked to human nature itself.

This last fact gives us pause, since it seems to say that there is something about human nature that requires association with other humans. Is this, indeed, true? Yes, it is. There is something about human nature that requires us to band together in order to achieve a common end--a variety of common ends, indeed, and at the very least, our final end. We have a need, stemming from our very nature, to belong to certain societies.

For example: during the first few years of their lives, at least, human beings absolutely require the presence of others if they are to survive and develop into mature adults. A child requires the presence of his or her parents (or some human surrogate for them, in extraordinary cases) for quite a number of years in order to supply his or her basic needs--without which

217

that child cannot live. There are few things on the face of the earth quite as helpless as a newborn human infant, or, for that matter, a human baby for several years after its birth. If left on its own, it would not survive; it lacks the sort of instinctive behavior that the young of other species possess, whereby survival is possible independently, even at a quite tender age. Without someone to care for it, the human infant dies. Moreover, even as an adult, a human being is--with very rare exceptions--unable to supply all of his or her own needs for a decent human life and, indeed, for survival itself. It is only through the co-operation of others that a truly human life (and bare biological life itself) is realistically possible. This is not something that requires much proof. Let each of us simply try to imagine what would happen if, completely and totally on our own, we had to supply all of the many things that we need simply to exist, let alone to live anything like a decently human life.

Moreover, human life and development involve a good deal more than sheer physical, biological life. They also involve, as a basic (and perhaps the most important) part, an intellectual life. But intellectual development (and moral development)--the most distinctively human of all our traits--require constant communication with other human beings. Without that, either we do not develop intellectually and morally, or, at best, we do so in truncated fashion. This constant interplay of human ideas, however, is possible only in some sort of societal structure.

Moreover, humans have the ability to communicate their thoughts to others of their species: to speak. This would be a faculty of very questionable usefulness, were humans intended to live all by themselves, independently of a societal structure. What would be its point?

Finally, we can observe that, while some solitude is good for human beings (and sometimes even necessary for their well-being), too much of it can be devastating--even to the point of unhinging our reason, as certain psychological experiments in solitary confinement, sensory deprivation, and the like, have amply demonstrated. Factually, humans do shun solitude and seek companionship.

We could summarize much of what has been said as follows: something that is necessary for the full development of the human being, in both the physical and the intellectual arenas, is required by human nature. But society is, precisely, so required. Thus society is required by human nature; in other words, humans are, by their nature, social beings.

However, we have to be careful not to make this statement say too much. For one thing, while it is true that human nature requires the presence of *a* society, nothing is thereby said about the *type* of that society. We will see later that human nature requires the presence of more than one society--but here too, nothing is automatically said about the kind or type of such societies, apart from certain fairly broad parameters. Moreover, the argument that has been given is intended to apply to human beings in general, allowing for the occasional exceptional case. Most people do require the presence of others in order to survive and to develop as humans; but this does not negate the occasional possibility of the hermit in the desert, the occasional gentleman perched atop a flagpole somewhere for a period of years, and the like. (What is going on in such cases is this: some extraordinary means is being taken--by God, or by the individual himself or herself--to accomplish those goals which most of us need society to achieve. Well and good; but our concern here is with the *ordinary* means needed to reach our final end, rather than with the occasional extraordinary exceptions thereto.)

So, human beings are by nature social beings. But, as we have seen, societies (even natural societies) can differ rather widely. We need but look at history for confirmation of this: even leaving aside the forms of a family society that anthropology asserts may have existed over the years, we know from political history that many sorts of civil societies have existed and apparently served their purpose reasonably well: monarchies, tyrannies, democracies, oligarchies, and so on and on. Are there, however, any common elements that a society--any society--has to have in order to function?

Certainly one such element is authority. We have mentioned this before, but it will pay us to examine it in a little more detail at this point in our study. Again, the purpose of a society is the achievement of some common end. But unless there is some sort of mechanism available for compelling the pursuit of that end--choosing a particular means, and making sure that that means is used--the result will be anarchy, which is to say, a non-society. Often there are numerous ways available for reaching a given goal, and a decision has to be made by someone as to which means will in fact be used. Co-operation is not possible in such a case without some type of direction or leadership, particularly in the case of a larger society. Moreover, in any given society, there are people who will not know what means will and will not reach the proposed common goal; and so, once again, direction--with some clout--is necessary if that goal is to be attained. For that matter, even if everyone should chance to know the required means, whether they would therefore be willing to use those means is quite another question. And thus, again, the need for authority. In brief, authority is one common element that is necessary for every society, of whatever variety; without it, that society cannot fulfill its function of achieving a common goal. Indeed, without authority, a society cannot even exist.

We can ask about the source of authority within a society. Granted that it has to be had. Where does it come from? In the case of a conventional society (the Lions Club, the Denver Broncos), the source of the authority is the members themselves. If people freely band together to form a society of this sort--a club, an association--they obviously may do so on whatever terms they wish and agree to. However, since authority is necessary for any kind of society, even a conventional one, people are bound to obey that authority once they join the society (or else are bound to leave the society). A given Bronco does not have to join the club. But if he does, then he has to do what the manager, the coach, etc., tell him--or else he has to get out.

In a natural society, however, the situation is quite different. People do not join natural societies freely; they do so because of natural law. Consequently, obedience to the authority of that society is also a matter of natural law. Ultimately, of course, the source of a natural society's authority is the author of the nature in question. However: again, we have to be careful not to make this say too much, lest we seem to be defending the divine right of kings, or some similar historical oddity. The author of human nature wills *some* sort of family, *some* sort of state (the two natural societies)--but not necessarily any particular kind. The determination of what kind of family or state we live in depends in significant measure on circumstances of age, culture, and time--though the family (as will be seen shortly) is somewhat more determined in its type than is the state.

For the remainder of this chapter, we will be concerned with the first of the two types of natural society, i.e., the family--along with a number of topics that are closely allied to the family. We will consider the state in the next chapter.

2. The family as a society

To turn, then, to considering the family. We might start by observing that there is probably no topic in ethics (or in moral theology, for that matter) where one encounters such a wide disparity of views as in questions regarding the family: when the discussion turns to such items as divorce, birth control, sex, and the like, it seems that everyone has his or her own favorite theories.

In all honesty, however, it also has to be said that this is also the area where one encounters the greatest amount of muddleheadedness. A great deal of "wish being father to the thought" takes place here, and a whole lot of simple desires and preferences masquerade as reasoned thought. It is particularly in this area that one needs to remember that ethics is not a popularity contest: one does not judge morality on the basis of some sort of poll about what people think. Neither is it the case that one person's views are necessarily as good as anyone else's. There are certain conclusions to which we can reason, and the fact that these conclusions may not happen to be popular says little about those conclusions' validity.

And while we are in the business of saying harsh things: it has been noted before that no one ever said that the living of a morally good life would necessarily be an easy, carefree thing. If anything, the value of the final end suggests the likelihood that it is probably won only by means of a struggle. And it is in the area of the family where--in contemporary America, anyway--that struggle makes itself most sharply felt.

a. What a family is

So much for cautions and preliminaries. What is a family? The sense in which we are using the word is simple enough: a husband, a wife, and their children. There is, of course, a wider sense of the word that is sometimes found, embracing aunts, uncles, cousins, grandparents, and so forth. That is a perfectly legitimate use of the word, but it is not the sense which is used here. We might note in passing that "family," in this wider sense of the term, is very likely not a natural society, whereas "family" in the narrow sense is.

b. The family as a natural society

That last statement, however, needs some proof. Is the family a natural society, in the sense in which we have defined that term? Let us see.

221

1) Generation and its purpose

A universal characteristic of human beings is the possession of the generative faculty and the urge to make use of it. Not everyone follows this urge, obviously; there are, after all, such things as celibate people. But everyone has it. Now, we might ask about the purpose of this generative faculty in human beings. The answer is a little complex. Individual people, of course, may use their sex powers for all sorts of reasons: pleasure, the expression of love, and so on and on. But this is what we have already learned to call the "goal of the worker." The "goal of the work" in the use of the sex powers, on the other hand, is procreation, i.e., the continuation of the human race. That is to say: if the act of sexual intercourse, in and of itself, achieves anything, that is what it will achieve. One could take an obvious parallel from the act of eating. When I am eating a good steak, I may be doing so for all sorts of reasons: pleasure, hunger, social relationships with friends, etc. Very likely, my expressed purpose is *not* the repair and replacement of worn-out cells in my body. However, that repair and replacement is what the act, in and of itself, will achieve. And it will do so (or at least aim at doing so) independently of whether or not any of the reasons I have in mind are in fact achieved. The steak may not taste good, and so I may not achieve my goal of pleasure; the effort to repair and replace my bodily cells will still be made. I may have an argument with the person with whom I am dining, and so the social relationship I had in mind may be disrupted or made impossible; the repair and replacement effort still goes on. While, therefore, in performing the act I may have all sorts of purposes--which may or may not be achieved--the act itself has a fixed and set purpose, which, as long as that act is successfully performed (as long as I *do* eat the steak), will in fact be achieved, if anything is achieved.

The purpose of the generative faculty in humans--the "goal of the work," in the terminology we have been using--is generation, the continuation of the human race. The "goal of the worker," i.e., my purpose in placing the generative act, may be generation; it may be all sorts of other things as well.

We might take a moment to consider something here. For it has been challenged, particularly in recent years, whether generation can truly be said to be the purpose of the sex act, or at least its exclusive purpose. It is said, for example, that the expression of mutual love is also a purpose of that act, and a purpose of no less rank than generation. But it is difficult to see how this could be true. Surely, the expression of love can be a "goal of the worker"; in normal instances of human intercourse, it is indeed such a goal. But it cannot equally be said to be a goal of the work. For if that were the case, it would need to be such a goal whenever the act is placed. And there are instances--rape being the most brutal and vivid--where this simply is not the case: whatever else is being expressed in rape, it is not mutual love. If something is to be a "goal of the work," it must be a goal (not, incidentally, one that is necessarily achieved, but a goal for all that) in any and all instances wherein that work is performed.

All this has been prefatory, but necessary. We could sum up what has been said by noting that the purpose of the use of the generative faculty--the goal of the work--is generation, the continuation of the human race; the goal of the worker (my purpose in performing the act) may be generation, but it may also be a variety of other things.

2) Requirements of the offspring

Now: we have already noted that the newborn child--the result of generation, the effect toward which generation is of its very nature aimed--is unique among animals for the duration and extent of its helplessness: it requires long years of care, by both parents (ordinarily) to provide for its needs. Moreover, while some of its needs could be provided for in a number of ways (e.g., the need for clothing, shelter, food), certain needs can be provided only by the parents. Most obvious among these is the need for love. The child is, precisely, the living expression of the mutual love of the parents, and only they can provide it with the degree and kind of love that it needs for its proper development, particularly in the psychological sphere. The need, incidentally, is for *both* parents: each contributes something unique to the development of the child. It is of course possible to have the exceptional case wherein a single parent can do an adequate or even an outstanding job on raising a child. But even this generally requires the use of surrogate parents or role models--an attempt to approximate the normal state of having both parents present.

If, then, the sex act is naturally (i.e., by our very natures) ordered to the continuation of the human race through generation, and if the child--the product of that sex act and, in any given instance, that very continuation of the human race--naturally requires the presence of both parents throughout a lengthy period of development and rearing, then it follows that

223

the family is an institution required for the appropriate continuation of the race: is, in other words, a natural society (as opposed to a conventional one).

c. Marriage

The family, then, is a natural society. That is all we have attempted to see thus far. But let us turn our attention to that human institution that seems to be at the root of the family--marriage--and see what we can conclude about it. Using, once again, only natural reason, can we decide whether marriage is, say, a sheerly conventional institution, something to be entered into and exited from as casually as one might join (and subsequently leave) the Lions Club? Or is it something deeper, more rooted in our natures?

Again, the aim here is a modest one. We are limited to what human reason can tell us. There are other sources of knowledge which go beyond this: for instance, religious considerations, such as the status of marriage as a sacrament, can add considerably to what sheer human reasoning can achieve. But these are outside our scope.

1) Characteristics of all marriages

In contrast to the urge to procreate, the urge to mate is not one which can be said to be shared by every human being. A large number of humans do have this urge, true; but a significantly large number do not--there are, after all, such things as bachelors and spinsters, and that by choice. And so we can reasonably conclude that marriage is a matter of choice, rather than one of strict natural urge. That choice, however, is not a totally unconditioned one. We cannot set up whatever sort of marriage arrangement happens to appeal to us in particular circumstances. For marriage involves several relationships of which we must take account: a relationship to offspring, a relationship to a spouse, and a relationship to the civil society in which we live. Each of these dictates something about the sort of thing that marriage must be.

From the needs of offspring, certain things about the institution of marriage become clear. Marriage will need to be stable, lasting for a significant period of time--long enough, anyway, for the child(ren) to be adequately reared. Thus marriage, as a choice, requires the choice of the parents to remain together for a lengthy period. Next, from the fact that marriage exists within a civil society, it follows that the partners' choice to remain together must be a publicly expressed one. For civil society has the need (and therefore the right) to know the status of its members, and in particular to know who is responsible for the care and rearing of its junior members (the children). That public expression, however, can take whatever form will effectively make itself known. Thus, there can be such things as common-law marriages, formal marriages before a justice of the peace, or before a religious authority—whatever form a given civil society can recognize as informing it adequately of the status of the persons involved.

Finally, from the fact that marriage involves a relationship with a spouse, other things become clear. For obligations in justice arise between two spouses sheerly from the fact that each has devoted a significant part of his or her life to the other during the period of rearing the children—and therefore has *not* devoted that part of his or her life to something else: such as making independent provisions for old age, for physical or emotional support in later life, and so forth. These mutual obligations in justice argue at least to the equity of the continuation of the marriage beyond the child-rearing years. However, these obligations (like most other obligations in justice) could be met in other ways; the continued marriage might be the method of choice, but it is not a unique means. And so, one can argue to the appropriateness of a life-long marriage on this basis; but one cannot argue to its strict necessity.

2) Characteristics of some marriages

If the choice to enter marriage is based on love, other characteristics of a marriage can come clear. For all love, by its nature, is unitive: it seeks to join the lover and the beloved. It is, quite literally, the attempt to bring two independent beings together into one, to the extent that this is possible. This unitive character will be present in any sort of love: the love of two equals, the love of parents for their children, the love of children for parents, etc. All love, moreover, is capable of degrees. And so we can talk of "how much" we love someone. Furthermore, love is a temporal thing: it has a beginning, and it can have an end—people can fall out of love, just as much as they can fall in love. All love, finally, is something that is actively chosen and deliberately fostered, not something that just "happens"; left unattended, it can wither and fail.

225

Conjugal love, however, adds another characteristic to all this, a characteristic of exclusivity. By the fact that I choose to unite myself in marriage with this person, I thereby also choose not to unite myself with someone else. As long as this sort of love is operative, the marriage will be a faithful one, and it will be lasting--for conjugal love is unreserved, either in aspect or in time: it is a constant striving for the most perfect kind of unity that is possible between a husband and a wife. Conversely, if there are any holdings-back on this, i.e., deliberate decisions that one or other partner will refrain from joining some aspect of himself or herself to his or her mate, then there is no question of conjugal love, whatever else may be taking place. Now, the sex act is the most perfect expression of this sort of love, of "twoness seeking to be oneness": by the union of the husband's sperm and the wife's ovum, a single new being is brought into existence, which new being is, precisely, the living expression of the parents' desire for union with each other. (That, incidentally, is also why the sex act, taken out of a context of love, seems to be such a strangely perverted thing, for it has been robbed of its essential meaning.) At all events: *if* a marriage is based on conjugal love--and as long as it is so based--one can argue to its characteristics as unreserved, faithful, and lasting.

Marriage, of course, can also be based on other things: convenience, political considerations, and shotguns, to name only a few. For marriage is a choice, and I can make a valid choice for a wide variety of reasons. In such cases, one of two things happens: either the husband and wife come to love each other over the years, or they don't. If they don't, then one simply cannot make the sorts of statements about their marriage that one can make about a marriage that is founded on love.

It is possible, then, to say some things about marriage absolutely: things required by the relationships that marriage has to offspring, to a spouse, and to civil society. It is also possible to say some things conditionally, i.e., if a given marriage is founded on conjugal love. In the light of all this, however, what are we to make of the all-too-common phenomenon of divorce? If marriage is indeed what we have said it is, then what of its break-up? Is it morally good, morally evil, or morally indifferent? The question is easy to pose, and difficult to answer.

d. Divorce

A satisfactory way of looking at this question is through the Principle of Double Effect, with special attention to the fourth step, i.e., the presence or absence of sufficient reason. For divorce involves a great number of evil effects: deprivation of the children's proper conditions of upbringing and injustice to one or both spouses come to mind as immediate possibilities. But the effects of divorce are not limited merely to the married couple (and their children) in question; divorce also has evil consequences for society as a whole. If divorce becomes common in a society, then the family structure of that society is threatened, and therefore so is that society itself, since the family is the cornerstone of a civilized society. It would take an extremely serious reason for a divorce to be morally justified, then, since a proportionality between good effect and evil effect would be difficult to achieve. This is not to say that there could not be such a reason; but it is intended to suggest that that reason would be uncommon (and it is also intended to suggest that most of the reasons commonly alleged for divorce in contemporary American society are inadequate for providing moral justification).

e. Sexual activity

The comment was made earlier that the use of the sex act is an excellent symbol of love, or a striving for the achievement of unity between two individuals. That leads us to the whole area of the use of our reproductive powers: what norms of conduct can we reason to in this area, using, again, only the unaided reason (i.e., independently of revelation and other sources)?

1) Finality

We need first to review a few things we already know, for they are necessary for our purposes here. First, there is no such thing as a random, purposeless act, i.e., one which we place but have no notion of what it is going to achieve. Every act, without exception--even a non-imputable act--has a "goal of the work," which can be known and which can be expected to recur whenever the act is performed. (It will recur, however, *as a goal*, not as something that is inevitably achieved; after all, there can be such things as unsuccessful acts.) Imputable acts add something to this. They also have a "goal of the worker," i.e., the motive that a person has in performing a given act. This can differ from act to act, and can differ even as regards one and the same act at different times: I may, for example, take a walk on Tuesday in order to get some exercise; on Wednesday, I may perform the same act (take the identical walk) for the

227

purpose of getting groceries, and so on. Moreover, the "goal of the worker" can be multiple: I may have all sorts of purposes in mind when I take my walk.

The "goal of the work" and the "goal of the worker" may be one and the same: my motive in eating this particular health food, say, may be to develop large muscles—which is precisely what the act itself is aimed at. Or, the two goals may differ: I may eat a large steak in order to enjoy its taste (and not, explicitly, for the purpose of repairing and replacing worn-out cells). However, the two goals may not be antithetical to each other without rendering the performance of that act irrational. The reason is obvious. If I perform an action in order to achieve some purpose, but the action is such that, in and of itself, it achieves not that purpose but some other one, I act irrationally. If my goal is to get exercise, and the means which I choose to this goal is to take a nap, I obviously have antithetical goals, and am not acting rationally. Or, if my goal is to lose 25 pounds, and the actions I take toward this end consist in eating large pieces of rich chocolate cake, again, I am obviously acting at cross purposes to my professed goals. For I am both willing a goal (my "goal of the worker" here) and not willing it (in that I am performing an act which will not achieve my goal). I am acting contradictorily, and that is to act irrationally.

To generalize: to place some act wherein the "goal of the work" and the "goal of the worker" are antithetical is to act irrationally, for it is both to will a goal and not will that goal at the same time. But deliberately to act irrationally is to act immorally: again, the proximate objective norm of morality is acting in accord with our natures, i.e., rationally.

All this we have already seen. But its application to human sexual activity is the real point of our recalling it to mind here.

As we have seen, the "goal of the work" of the human sex act is clear enough: it is generation. We know that this purpose will not always be achieved; this means nothing more than that the sex act, like most other human activities, can be unsuccessful. But if anything *is* achieved by the act itself, generation is what will be achieved. The sex act, in and of itself, never results in the production of, say, greater intelligence, or improved physical stamina, or anything of the sort; it results in one thing and one thing only: human offspring.

In saying that the "goal of the work" of the sex act is generation, however, we should notice carefully that we mean a good deal more than simply conception. We mean all that conception implies: the gestation, birth, and rearing of offspring. For the sex act is the cause of all these other things (gestation, birth, rearing); and, as we have seen, the cause of a cause, as cause, is thereby the cause of the caused.

The "goal of the worker" in human sexual activity may, of course, be the same as the "goal of the work": people do occasionally have intercourse for the precise purpose of having children. Or, the "goal of the worker" may be quite different: the expression of love, the satisfaction of physical craving, etc. There is no moral problem in the two goals' diverging—except that, as in the case of every imputable act, the "goal of the worker" may not be antithetical to the "goal of the work" without thereby rendering the act irrational and hence immoral.

Everything we have said so far applies to human sexual activity in general. Now, however, we need to divide our consideration a bit, and consider first the question of sexual activity within marriage, and then sexual activity outside of marriage. The reason is obvious. Within marriage, generation—in its full sense—is clearly feasible. Outside of marriage, however, the possibility of generation is quite another matter.

2) Sexual activity within marriage; the question of birth control

To look first, then, at sexual activity within marriage. Much that ought to be said on this topic has already been covered in our discussion of the family a few pages ago, and so—apart from the vexed question of birth control—we can be fairly brief here. For generally speaking, only a few moral questions arise about the use of sex within marriage. One may wonder, in given cases, about *how* the sex act is performed: one partner may be unreasonably demanding and inconsiderate of another, and so on; but these are not really questions about the use of sex as such. Nor is there often a significant moral question about the non-use of sex within marriage, although questions of justice can enter in here: there is question of a true right, on the part of each spouse, to the sex act; and this fact has to be judged according to the general norms regarding rights which we shall see a little later on. In general, however, we can say that, within marriage, any reasonable use of sexual activity is morally acceptable—though the term "reasonable" will turn out to involve some limitations, as we shall see immediately.

The question of birth control, however, is an area where there are significant (and hotly debated) moral questions. And so we need to spend a little time on this area.

First, there is the matter of natural birth control, which takes the forms of abstinence, the rhythm method, natural family planning, and the like. There is relatively little moral problem in this, as such. In the case of abstinence: if I do not wish the consequences of an act, and choose to avoid them by not placing the act in the first place, then this is reasonable enough. Assuming that both spouses agree to abstinence--i.e., assuming that we are not dealing with a consideration of justice--then abstinence is certainly moral enough. Similarly when there is question of placing the sex act at a time when both parties know it will not, in fact, be successful (as in rhythm, natural planning, and the like): the goal of the work remains the same, even though it is known in advance that that goal will not be achieved. There are many times when imputable acts, of a quite differing variety, will be unsuccessful, and the sex act is simply one of many of which this is true. I may still go ahead and place these acts, even with this foreknowledge. For the "goal of the worker" is not antithetical to the "goal of the work" (even though it may be and usually is quite different from it), and thus the act does not have the contradictory and hence irrational character to it that would make it morally objectionable.

Artificial birth control, however, is quite another matter. By "artificial" is here meant the use of pills, condoms, diaphragms, and the like. In using such means, I am placing an act that has a definite goal of the work, and consequently, simply by placing the act, I am willing that generation take place. Simultaneously, I am taking means to see that generation cannot take place. But this is both to will and not to will something simultaneously. And that is contradictory and hence irrational--and consequently immoral.

Students perennially have difficulty in seeing the moral difference between natural and artificial birth control. And so, even at the risk of some repetition, perhaps a comparison of the moral factors at work will help. (a) In natural birth control, (i) I place an act (generation), and I thereby will that act's goal; (ii) however, I know that in fact that goal will not be achieved. (b) In artificial birth control, on the other hand, (i) I place an act (generation), and I thereby will that act's goal; (ii) I also take active means to frustrate the achievement of that goal, and I thereby also (and simultaneously) will the non-fulfillment of that goal; (iii) I know that the goal will in fact not be achieved.

Schematically:

In natural birth control:	*In artificial birth control:*
1. I will X	*1. I will X*
2. I know that X will not happen.	*2. I simultaneously will non-X*
	3. I know that X will not happen.

It is the presence of the contradictory will act in artificial birth control that causes the moral problem.

> *(In both cases, I probably would prefer that X do not happen--else why practice birth control [of whatever variety] in the first place? But in natural birth control, I am willing to accept X if it does happen; I take no positive action--and hence place no will act--to the contrary. That is not the case in artificial birth control, wherein a contradictory will act is in fact made.*
>
> *Then too, it may be helpful to remember that to want [or not want] something is not the same as to will it [or actively not-will it]. I want a lot of things that I don't will: I want to have a fabulous vacation in Rio, but I don't will it, since it is obviously out of my financial grasp. Similarly, I will a lot of things that I don't want--such as going to class on a day when I would far rather be somewhere else.)*

Several comments need to be made on the position that has been taken here. First, to say that this line of reasoning is unpopular is to lay claim to the understatement of the year. That is recognized and accepted. But ethics, as has been said, is not a popularity contest. Our question is not whether our reasoning is popular; our question is whether that reasoning is sound.

Next: much of the current hue and cry over the question of artificial birth control has its roots in the various (real or imagined) goods that can be achieved by its use. Thus, questions of overpopulation in certain countries arise; so do questions of an individual mother's health, family economic circumstances, and so forth. The achievement of these goods (or the eradication of these evils, as appropriate) is a worthy goal. But let us be honest. There is a great deal of confusion in the whole discussion because a worthwhile motive is not distinguished from an unacceptable means. There may be excellent reasons why, in a given case, a particular couple ought not have more children, or why a group of people in a given country ought not do so; and their right to make a reasoned decision in that regard is not in

231

question here. Surely, no one would want to hold that a particular married couple, or married people in general, ought to have the greatest number of children that they possibly can. But the conclusion that follows from this is not that artificial means may therefore be employed which vitiate the sex act of its essential purpose (again, evil may not be done so that good will come of it). The conclusion that does follow is that the good effects of birth control ought indeed to be sought--but through moral means.

Unquestionably, the sex drive is one of the strongest urges that are part of human nature. But its strength, the enjoyment that comes with its use, and all the other goods that using it can cause (the fostering of mutual love, etc.), neither singly nor collectively justify irresponsibility or irrationality in its use, any more than such characteristics would justify them in any other free act that humans perform. And neither, by the way, is the sex act a sole means toward the achievement of the various goods, even within marriage, which it does in fact foster. If, because of individual circumstances, a husband and wife cannot accept the consequences of generation, well and good; there are other means that can be used to foster the expression of their mutual love.

3) Sexual activity outside of marriage

We should turn now to the question of the use of sex outside of marriage. We might ask, first, about pre-marital or extra-marital sex between a man and a woman. Then we might give some thought to the whole question of homosexuality, a phenomenon whose popularity in our day justifies explicit treatment of the subject even though the principles on which its morality has to be judged are reasonably familiar to us by this time.

a) Pre-marital and extra-marital heterosexual activity

In heterosexual, pre-marital or extra-marital sexual intercourse, the moral reasoning required is parallel to what has gone before. Even if such intercourse is open to conception (i.e., even if positive means to prevent conception are not taken), it is nevertheless not open to generation with all that that implies (conception, birth, rearing of offspring). By the very nature of the case, it cannot be. And so, people engaging in such intercourse are both willing generation (in its wide sense) by the very fact that they perform the sex act, and not willing it, since they are incapable of doing so (i.e., they are in no position to take on, say, the rearing of children; if they were, why are they not married?). Again, this is contradictory, and therefore irrational and hence immoral. It might, indeed, be exciting, pleasant, fun. But that is not the issue.

b) Homosexual activity

Much the same sort of reasoning is applicable in regard to the morality of homosexual activity. By way of preface to this topic, however, we should note that, in the brief discussion that follows, we are presuming the quite real distinction between homosexual orientation and homosexual behavior. The former does not involve any question of choice and so, not being imputable, is not an ethical matter at all. The latter, however, does and is.

In homosexual activity, an act with a given purpose ("goal of the work") is being performed, but performed in such a manner as to render the achievement of that purpose completely impossible. Once again, this is simply both to will a goal (by performing an act that has that goal) and simultaneously not to will that goal (by performing the act in a manner that renders the attainment of that goal absolutely impossible). Once more: contradictory, hence irrational, hence immoral.

(All this, let it be frankly admitted, makes a very complex question sound deceptively simple. The entire area of sexual morality is one that has been endlessly studied in our day, in all of its ramifications. Yet the paragraphs that have preceded this one might seem to take no account of the nuances that all this study has introduced. In one limited sense, that is true. This is, after all, a book on fundamental ethics, not one specifically on sexual morality; and there are certain limitations of space involved. Still, the writer of these pages probably has a better grasp than most of the literature on this whole subject, and is well aware of the disagreements and arguments that populate that literature.

A sample: a homosexually inclined male remarks—quite accurately—that he did not choose his own sexual orientation. He therefore should not be deprived of the use of sex because of something not of his own making.

233

One can emphathize with the real anguish that such a situation causes. But it no more follows that homosexual acts ought to be morally acceptable for such an individual than it does that someone deprived of legs ought to be able to walk. About all that does follow is that, in the short run at least, there is much injustice in the world--the remedy for which does not consist in immorality, but rather in the acceptance of reality and in working for justice in those areas where it can be achieved.

No. The morality of homosexual activity is not a particularly complicated question. The matter tends to resolve itself simply into the question of whether a person [even one who may have been wronged, in one way or other] may or may not perform evil in order that good may come of it, whether one may or may not act irrationally because of individual pressures of the moment. One can, indeed, do so. The question, of course, is whether one may do so. And unless we wish to go to the extreme length of saying that human nature is not essentially rational, and therefore that humans need not act rationally, then we are left with some stark and unconsoling [and certainly--to some--uncomfortable] conclusions in the area of sexual ethics. That may be regrettable. But it is also factual.

A final comment should be made on the topic of "gay rights," which is so widely bandied about today. As was the case in the abortion debate, much of this is a remarkable muddle of many things.

If the term "gay rights" means the right, from a moral point of view, to engage in homosexual sex, i.e., a declaration that such activities are morally acceptable as some sort of "alternate lifestyle," then it simply has to be said that something which is objectively wrong cannot be rendered right just by people's wanting it to be. If on the other hand the term means the fact that homosexual people have certain rights, unconnected with their sexuality, which tend to be trampled on because of that sexuality, and that this shouldn't be done: well and good, it shouldn't be. People have rights as people, not as heterosexual or homosexual. Thus, employment should not be denied to homosexuals simply on that basis, unless their sexuality presents a clear and present danger to other people--which would need to be clearly shown rather than merely assumed. Discrimination in housing, services, etc., is inappropriate--not because the people are homosexuals, but because they are people. Such problems should indeed be equitably resolved--but not on the basis of sexuality.

SUMMARY OF CHAPTER ELEVEN

Society in General: A society is an enduring [over an extended period of time] union of a number of persons [at least two] bound to co-operative activity [by some sort of bond] for a common end. For a society to operate effectively, authority is necessary; otherwise the requisite co-operative activity is impossible and anarchy results. As a moral union, a society is something of which only humans are capable. A conventional society is one which I may or may not join, as I please; a necessary society is one which by nature I must join. Humans are by nature social beings: during their very early years, they depend on others for survival and development; in later years, they depend on others to provide other, equally requisite, needs (physical, intellectual, and moral) if they are to lead a truly human life. Moreover, humans have the natural ability to communicate (useless outside a society) and suffer when exposed to excessive isolation. However, though their nature requires a society, humans have no special need of any particular type of society, apart from certain broad parameters. The source of authority in a conventional society is the members themselves; in a natural society, natural law.

The Family as a Natural Society: A family (husband, wife, and children) is a natural society. For the purpose of the human generative faculty (the "goal of the work") is generation. (The "goal of the worker" may be generation; it may be other things as well.) And while some of the needs of the offspring--the product of generation--can be provided for in a variety of ways (e.g., such things as food, clothing, shelter), other needs (particularly that for love) can be adequately provided for only within a family structure. The necessary foundation for family life is marriage, for only within this can the several relationships in question (to offspring, to spouse, to civil society) be adequately handled. Marriage, as a contract, can be validly based on a number of things; if it is based on love, it will be unitive, and if based on conjugal love, it will be exclusive, unreserved, and lasting. Divorce can be shown to involve great evils, but it cannot be shown to be intrinsically wrong.

Sexuality: Again, the "goal of the work" in the use of the human reproductive powers is generation (i.e., conception plus everything that that implies), for this is what the sex act in itself will achieve if it achieves anything; the "goal of the worker" may also be generation or it may be something different from that (expression of love, satisfaction of desire, etc.)--but it may not be antithetical to the "goal of the work" without thereby becoming irrational and hence immoral: in such a case, one ends up both willing an end (by performing an act that has that end) and simultaneously not willing it (by intending some goal that is incompatible with the first one), and that is contradictory and therefore irrational. Relatively few moral problems arise concerning the use of sex within marriage (for generation is here clearly possible); among those that do, artificial birth control presents itself as involving contradictory will acts and therefore as immoral, though the same problem does not attend such "birth control" measures as rhythm and natural family planning, since the contradictory will act is absent. Heterosexual sex outside of marriage, even if open to conception, is not (and cannot be) open to generation in the full sense; this, again, is both to will something (by placing an act that has that something as its "goal of the work") and not to will it (by being incapable of doing so), and consequently such activity is immoral. The same reasoning governs the morality of homosexual sex: a goal is willed (by placing an act that involves that goal), and simultaneously is not willed (since the act is placed in such a way as to render that goal impossible in principle).

235

12. CIVIL SOCIETY

III. The Practical Part of Ethics
   C. Our relationship to others
      3. The state as a society
         a. General considerations about the state
            1) A preliminary question: rights and duties
               a) Rights
                  (1) Meaning of a "right"
                  (2) Basis of rights
                  (3) Elements of a right
                  (4) Source of rights
                  (5) Right and might
                     (a) Types of rights
                     (b) Justice and its types
                     (c) Enforcement of rights
                b) Duties
                  (1) Meaning of a "duty"
                  (2) Types of duties
                  (3) Conflicts between rights and duties
                  (4) Excusation from duties
             2) The state, or "civil society"
               a) What it is, and why it is needed
               b) Possibility of different kinds of states
               c) The individual and the state
                  (1) Rights of the individual
                  (2) Rights of the state
            3) The relationship of charity among citizens
               a) Basis for the relationship
               b) Obligations the relationship imposes
               c) Limitations on these obligations

a. General considerations about the state

We have seen the first of the two natural societies to which humans must belong, the family. Now we turn our attention to the other: the state, or "civil society." In this chapter, we will look at some fairly broad concepts concerning the state, reserving more particular topics and applications for the following chapter or two.

1) A preliminary question: rights and duties

A preliminary question needs to be examined right at the

outset, and that is the whole matter of rights and duties. For we will need to speak a good bit about a human's rights, and his or her duties, in regard to the state; and we need to know exactly what we mean by those terms.

a) Rights
(1) Meaning of a "right"

What, then, is a "right"? First, we should notice that the word "right" is being used here as it would be used in the sentence, "I have a *right* to be here," as opposed to something like, "It is right that we should come." The latter use of the term may mean nothing more than "it is fitting," "it is appropriate." In our use of the word, we mean something considerably stronger than that.

We can get some insight into what the term "right" means by examining the difference between "might" (physical power) and "right" (moral power). Both are instances of power, i.e., the ability to achieve an end or goal. But physical power (whether this be my own personal muscles, nerves, etc., or these plus various tools that I might use, or indeed an army that I might command) always accomplishes its purpose by sheer physical force. Moral power, on the other hand, achieves its end by an appeal to someone else's will by way of that person's intellect: it points out that I claim something as mine, and that the other person must respect that claim if he or she is to attain his or her own last end. A *right,* then, in this sense, can be defined as the moral power to do, hold, or exact something.

It is perfectly possible for me to have moral power, without having the physical power to back it up. It is also possible for me to have physical power, without any moral power on which to exercise it. Physical power is a neutral sort of thing in itself, from an ethical point of view; it gets its goodness or badness from why I use it, i.e., whether I use it to enforce a legitimate moral power or to transgress such a power.

A semantic observation might be in order. We sometimes transfer the term "right" to whatever it is that we say we have a right to. And so I might say that life, liberty, and the pursuit of happiness are rights that I have. All right; what is really being said, of course, is that these are *things to which* I have a right.

(2) Basis of rights

That is what a right is. What grounds it? Why do I have a right, of whatever kind? That leads us to the connection between obligation and right. As we know, one cannot be bound to do the impossible; if I have the moral duty to do something, then I must also have the means, the power, to do it. To be obligated to do something, and simultaneously to be completely unable to do it, is an irrational state of affairs; it is contradictory. And thus, the real foundation for a right is an obligation that I have. Now, obligation is founded on, imposed by, law, whether natural or positive law. And so one can say that right is founded on law. Depending, then, on the particular focus that we wish to adopt, we can say that right is founded on obligation, or that right is founded on law (since obligation is founded on law), or that right is founded on the obligation that I have to achieve my final end (since all law is ultimately founded on that obligation).

(3) Elements of a right

What makes up a right? Four things, really--or rather, the set of relationships that exists among those four things. There is, first of all, (a) a subject, or the person who has the right in question; (b) a term, or the person(s) bound to respect or fulfill that right; (c) a matter, or what the person has the right *to*; and finally (d) a title, or the reason why the person has this right. To illustrate: suppose that I inherit $5000 from my grandfather. In saying that I have a right to this money, I am saying that there exists a relationship between a subject (me), a term (the executor of my grandfather's estate, or the state itself--whoever has the responsibility under the law of making sure that I get the $5000), a matter ($5000), and a title (Grandfather's will, along with the state law that governs inheritances and enables Grandfather to leave the money to me in the first place). Or: in saying that you have a right to life, you are saying that there exists a relationship between a subject (you), a term (people who have the obligation to sustain your life, as long as that is necessary--your parents; people who have the obligation not to take it away from you later on), a matter (life), and a title (the obligation you have to achieve your last end, which can only be achieved by living rationally--a necessary precondition for which is that one be allowed to go on living!).

These are the four elements of a right. But some comments should perhaps be made on each of them, for misunderstandings in this area are fairly common.

First, as regards the subject of a right. Only a person can be the subject of a right; a non-person cannot. The reason for this is that only a person can incur a moral obligation; and obligation, as we have seen, is the basis for a right. Thus, animals, trees, etc., do not have rights. We sometimes find ourselves speaking as if they had (e.g., that poor starving puppy has a right to a decent home, to be fed, etc.; those baby seals in Alaska [or wherever] have a right to life; the whales in the Pacific have a right to existence; and so on). But this is poetry, or perhaps analogy. These creatures will achieve their last end no matter what. They have no obligations, and consequently they have no rights. This, of course, is not to say that I can treat non-persons in whatever way I want. Animals may not have rights, but I certainly have duties--one of which is to use creatures on the sub-human level in a rational way. And generally speaking, when we speak of an animal's having a right to something, what we really mean is that it is not right--i.e., it is not fitting, it is not proper--that they be deprived of whatever that something is. True; but the reason it is not fitting or proper is not that the animal has a strict right to whatever is in question. It is rather that we have an obligation to act in a certain way in the animal's regard.

However, in saying that only persons have rights, we need to be aware that "person" can refer either to an individual person (a single human being) or to a moral person (a group of human beings acting in concert: a corporation, a society, or something of the sort). Ordinary language, with all of its emotional overtones, can deceive us; but the fact of the matter is, General Motors can have rights, and the animals in the zoo cannot.

For the same reason, the term of a right must also be a person. For a right imposes a moral obligation, and only a person can be the subject of such an obligation. This, again, can be either an individual or a moral person. General Motors can owe me something; my pet dog or cat cannot.

The matter of a right, on the other hand, can never be a person. I can never have the right *to* some other person, in the sense of claiming total ownership or possession of him or her. The reason for this is that all persons equally have the obligation to attain their last end, and consequently one person cannot be subordinated to the interests of another person, i.e., cannot be used as a mere means in that person's achievement of his or her last end. However, we need to distinguish something carefully here. There is a difference between a person and his or her

240

knowledge, work, and so forth. I can, therefore, hire someone for pay, and have a strict right to his or her work. I can hire a computer genius, and have a strict right to the fruits of his or her intellectual powers. The reason for this, again, is that a person's work (or intellectual capability) is not identified with his or her personhood.

This is usually the place where the question of slavery comes up for consideration. Slavery presents the risk of moral evil in many ways (chiefly in that it presents the potential for multiple abuse); but one cannot say that, as an institution, it is intrinsically evil. To establish that, it would be necessary to assert the claimed right to own a slave's entire person—which is an impossibility, since a slave's intellect and will always remain under his or her control and simply cannot be anyone else's property. It is possible for certain forms of slavery to be moral, albeit distasteful; a life sentence in a penitentiary is a form of slavery, after all. And the sort of indentured service by which the ancestors of many Americans arrived in this country was certainly moral enough, even though in some cases perhaps harsh. On the other hand, it should also be said that the sort of slavery of blacks that was common in this country in past centuries was morally evil, both because of how it was practiced in some instances, and because of the injustice involved in the original deprivation of the slaves' liberty when they were captured and deported from their homelands in the first place.

Finally, on the question of a right's title. This establishes a connection between this particular subject and this particular matter. For instance, I have the right to own property in general, for that is necessary if I am to live a human life. But what is to specify *which* property? That is the function of the title. By means of, say, this amount of money handed over, I acquire a title to this particular piece of real estate, and therefore someone else does not have the right to its ownership (since I have). There are various kinds of titles; perhaps a useful enough distinction is between congenital titles (those that come with the mere fact of having been born a human being) and acquired titles (those depending on some contingent historical fact such as purchase, inheritance, and the like).

(4) Source of rights

So, we have seen what a right is, something of what grounds it, and what makes it up. Before going much further, we might return briefly to the subject of the source of rights, for there

241

are some historical items in this area that are of some interest. Let us recall first the relationship between law, obligation, and right. Since there is a law, I have an obligation; hence I must also have what is needed to fulfill that obligation, and this means rights. Now, in all this, nothing has been said thus far about the different kinds of law or the different kinds of rights. The relationship that we have sketched holds true for any kind of law or any kind of obligation. Consequently, there can be rights based on natural law, and there can be rights based on positive law. For example, there can be a right based sheerly on positive law (a determinative one, of course, not a declarative one): I have the right to drive through an intersection that is governed by a green traffic light. There can also be rights based on both natural law and positive law (as in the case of a declarative civil law): I have the right not to be murdered while walking down the street. Or there can be rights based on natural law alone, in cases where there is no pertinent civil law: I have a right to my own sanity.

Now, all this depends on an acceptance of the entire notion of natural law, and of its relationship to civil law, which we have seen earlier. Historically, however, and for a wide variety of reasons, individual thinkers have rejected the concept of natural law. In an attempt to find some other ground for rights, various theories have been proposed. One of the more popular has been the idea that the state grants all rights. Over the centuries, this is a notion that has been popular with dictators and tyrants of one stripe or other, for it gives an enormous amount of power to individual governments: what the state gives, after all, the state can also take away. The problem that this theory runs into, however, is this: if the state has the right to exist, one can legitimately ask where it got that right. If, as the theory would insist, all rights come from the state, then the ludicrous conclusion has to follow that the state existed before it existed, so as to be able to give itself the right to exist. No matter what theory one wishes to adopt, then, it seems absolutely necessary to say that there has to be some source of rights apart from and independent of the state. (Another interesting consequence of the "all rights come from the state" theory: one state could have no rights against another state, for, after all, a state can rule--and consequently "give rights to"--only its own citizens.)

(5) Right and might

Next, we can ask about the relationship between right and might: can a right legitimately be backed up with might, i.e., may a moral power be enforced by a physical power? The answer to this is, sometimes yes, sometimes no. For there are differing types of rights.

(a) Types of rights

Some rights, by their nature, are such that they can be backed up with force. Thus, property rights, the right to a good name: all these can be enforced. These are termed "coactive" rights. But other rights are simply not of that sort. For example, a father has the (earned) right to the respect and love of his child. But this isn't the sort of thing that can be backed up with physical force. This sort of right is a "non-coactive" one; and the difference between it and a coactive right lies simply in the nature of the right in question. Some things to which we may have a right just aren't such that they can be coerced. Other rights, normally coactive, may not be so in particular circumstances: I have the right not to be mugged, but in particular circumstances I may not be able to enforce that right, and there may not be anyone else around who can enforce it for me.

Another useful distinction of types of rights is between alienable and inalienable ones. The distinction is a fairly obvious one, but perhaps it should be stated somewhere. Inalienable rights are those which, because of their very nature, cannot be renounced by their possessor: they are required for obtaining one's last end, and so, since that end cannot be renounced, neither can the right in question. The right to sanity would be an example of such a right. An alienable right, on the other hand, can be renounced by its possessor: I have the right to marriage, but I can forego it, since its exercise is not necessary to my last end.

The terms "alienable" and "inalienable" are familiar to us through a study of U.S. history. Unfortunately, when the Declaration of Independence speaks of "life, liberty, and the pursuit of happiness" as being inalienable rights, it uses the term somewhat loosely. These certainly are natural rights, i.e., ones grounded in natural law; but they are not inalienable: I can give them up, in particular circumstances, if there is question of obtaining an incompatible good which is of a higher order and which is more necessary for me in terms of achieving my final goal.

Some rights, then, can be enforced by physical power. Some

243

cannot, simply because of the sorts of things they are. In the case of those that can, however: who may enforce them? And under what circumstances?

(b) Justice and its types

We need a preliminary distinction before we can handle that question. That distinction concerns justice and its various types. In general, justice is that virtue by which we give to each one that which is his or her own. But that definition needs to be looked at closely, for people differ fairly widely in the status they have within a given society.

For example, there can be a justice relationship between two (or more) equal people: between man and man, woman and man, woman and woman, two equal states, two equal countries. If we are considering "justice" in such a case, we are speaking of what is termed "commutative justice." Or, we can be talking about the sort of justice relationship that exists between a community (taken as a whole) and its members, i.e., that relationship which requires a fair distribution of both benefits and burdens among the members of a given society. This is not a relationship of justice among equals, but rather one between a superior (of whatever sort) and his, her, or its inferiors; and the traditional term for this is "distributive justice." Finally, there can be a justice relationship between the individual members of a community and that community considered as a whole, through which each individual is required to contribute his or her share to the common good. The usual name for this is "legal justice," i.e., the justice that inferiors owe superiors. In brief, there are three types of justice relationship: equal to equal, superior to inferior, inferior to superior: quite different relationships, although analogous. And when we speak of "justice," we have to be clear as to which type of it we mean.

(c) Enforcement of rights

In the matter of enforcement of rights, now: when there is question of a right that I have in commutative justice, the enforcement of that right is the business of the judicial system of the state, ordinarily speaking. And so, if I have a complaint against one of my fellow citizens, the ordinary way to resolve it would be through a lawsuit, assuming that gentler methods are not successful. For if every person arrogated to himself or herself, on every occasion, the task of taking care of such things on his or her own, the result would be chaos: murder in the streets, vendettas, and so on. However, on the supposition--rare, but possible--that the ordinary mechanisms of the state cannot or will not handle such matters, it is allowable for the individual to enforce his or her right personally, for otherwise that right becomes meaningless.

When there is question of a right that I have in distributive justice, i.e., when the state or community owes me something in justice and refuses to honor that obligation, then the matter gets much trickier. Ordinarily an individual is limited in such cases to appeal, petition, arousing public opinion, etc.; to do much more would be to use private force against the state, i.e., to engage in rebellion--something which, given the amount of evil it brings with it, is ordinarily not justified unless there is question of a state which is genuinely tyrannical. Here, the same norms apply as we have previously seen in the case of an unjust law.

Finally, if we are speaking of a right in legal justice, the ordinary means of enforcement is the state itself--of which the Internal Revenue Service, in contemporary America, is perhaps the best known example!

b) Duties

Now let us look at the reverse side of rights. We know that rights are not always absolute things; there are many rights that are somewhat limited, either by their very nature or by the fact that they conflict with others' rights. (As has been quite correctly said: my right to swing my fist in the air stops at the point where your nose begins!) After all, there are many human beings, all of whom have the same final end and the same obligation to attain that end; and they all have rights. Inevitably, given how human affairs proceed, there will be conflict among those rights.

Moreover, the correlative of right is duty. Not only is it correct to say that I have a right because I have a duty, but it is also accurate to say that, if I have a right, *you* have a duty in regard to that right. That is to say: if I have a right, you have the duty to allow me to do, to have, or to require whatever it is that I have a right to. Rights and duties, then, are correlative in a double sense: (i) I have rights, which stem from the fact that I have a duty to attain my last end. (ii) But since I have rights, you (or whoever is affected in a given case) also

245

have duties--the duty to allow me whatever my rights entitle me to. Of course, this works the other way as well: you have rights because you have duties, and therefore I have duties in your regard as well.

(1) Meaning of a "duty"

The notion of duty will repay some study. In general, a duty is the moral obligation to do or not to do something. (Notice the similarity between this definition and that of a right, i.e., the moral power to do, have, or exact something. Again, a right is merely the obverse side of a duty, and vice-versa.)

(2) Types of duties

There can be different types of duties. An affirmative duty, for example, is one which stems from an affirmative law and requires the performance of some positive act: e.g., pay your taxes, honor your father and mother, etc. A negative duty, on the other hand, stems from a prohibitive law, and requires the omission or avoidance of some act: e.g., do not steal. The distinction is more than a merely verbal one. For the two types of duties impose quite different obligations. A negative duty is constantly in force: for example, I may never steal--the prohibition is constantly in force. A positive duty, on the other hand, obliges only at stated times: pay your taxes--but not every day of the year (rather, only on April 15). There are some further differences between the two types that we shall see shortly, when we look at the question of excusation.

(3) Conflicts between rights and duties

To return, now, to the subject of the clash of rights. If it is true that I have both rights and duties, and the same can be said for you, then, given human nature, it will not be long before there is a conflict between my right and your right, my duty and your duty. What happens, in general, when there is a conflict of rights and/or duties?

In general, it can be said that right is limited by duty, and duty in turn by right. I may exercise a right up to the point where my duty to someone else supersedes my right. And, a duty which I have to someone else binds me, up to the point where a right that I have supersedes that duty. So, for example, I have the right to enjoy my stereo set--up to the point where your right to peace and quiet (and consequently my duty to let you have that peace and quiet) supersedes that right. I have the duty to allow you the freedom to be yourself--up to the point where *my* right to be *myself* is infringed.

Like most general principles, however, this one can get somewhat problematic when it has to be reduced to individual cases. We can say that, when your rights and my rights come into conflict, or when your duty and my rights do so, etc., the stronger right or duty prevails, i.e., the one that is the most clear, the most sure. Obviously, my right to life would prevail over your right to listen to your stereo set, should these two rights ever come into conflict; your duty to attain your final end would prevail over, say, my duty to observe a given traffic law, should there ever be a conflict between the two. But it takes little imagination to realize that there are many cases when the answer is by no means as cut and dried as all that. There are lots of instances where only a prudential judgment is available as to which is the stronger right or the stronger duty. There are some norms available which can help, but they do not obviate the necessity of making such a prudential judgment or the possibility that, even with the best will in the world, the judgment could be in error.

Of these norms, some are derived from the subject of a particular right. The rights of a higher-ranking being supersede those of a lower one, for example: God before humans. Or, the right of someone having a closer relationship to me prevails: given limited resources, I take care of family and relatives before strangers. Other norms can be derived from a right's term: the greater common good will prevail in a conflict with the more private one: the right of the human race generally to, say, world peace takes precedence over my individual right to comfort, ease, and leisure, and so my duty to world peace would supersede my right to leisure. Similarly, a wider social good prevails over a more narrow one: the good of the state comes before the good of the city.

Still other norms can come from a right's matter: a more important matter will prevail over a lesser one--the right to life prevails over the right to property, for example. You have a right to your belongings; but if (by hypothesis) the sole way that I can preserve my life is by appropriating some of your property, then my right to life prevails. Similarly, the urgency of a right's matter can be a factor: I do have the right to sit in my living room and read a book; but if your house is on fire and you are not there, your right to having the fire department called prevails over my right to leisure.

Finally, norms can be derived from a right's title: a higher law prevails over a lower one, as, for example, when a right I have by natural law comes into conflict with a duty imposed by a positive law. The early Christians' right to follow their conscience prevailed over their civil duty to offer sacrifice to pagan gods, for example. (Admittedly, this can be a difficult area to judge, in a concrete case; but that fact does not alter the principle.) Or, a clearer title prevails over a less clear one: my ownership of a piece of property by purchase prevails over your right that is based on an ancient and dubious land grant.

Once more, these are merely norms, based principally on a common-sense estimate of what rational behavior requires; and they require that a prudential judgment be made. Such a judgment will not, obviously, afford metaphysical certainty. One ends up making a moral judgment as to what is the best thing to do, and then acting accordingly--all the while knowing that one *might* be wrong.

(4) Excusation from duties

So much for conflicts between rights and duties, or rights and rights, or duties and duties. One further preliminary question could be posed in this whole area, however, and that concerns the excusation from performing a duty. Under what circumstances am I *not* obligated to perform some duty that I have? We have already seen some instances where we are excused from performing a duty, in accord with the Principle of Double Effect. But it is now time to formalize this a bit more. In general, any excusation from duty will take the form of either a practical impossibility or a disproportionate hardship. But both of these have to be understood rather carefully, for there are differing kinds of duties, some of which admit of excusation and some of which do not. Moreover, there are differing bases for duties; and, again, some of these admit of excusation and some do not.

First of all, a hardship that arises from the very nature of the duty does not, in and of itself, excuse from that duty. For example, a soldier in battle is not excused from his duty of remaining at his post simply because it is dangerous for him to remain there. Battles are by their very nature dangerous.

Next, we need to recall the distinction between an affirmative duty and a negative one, which we saw a few pages ago. In brief, a negative duty obliges us *not* to do something, and its binding force is constant; an affirmative duty obliges us to do something, and it binds only at a particular time.

Of negative duties, now: some of these arise from natural law, and some from positive law. The excusation that a negative duty can have depends on which sort of law grounds that duty. A negative duty arising from natural law admits of no excuse. And so we are always bound to observe the strictures against murder, blasphemy, suicide, and so on, no matter what sort of hardship be involved in their observance.

A negative duty that arises from a human law, by contrast, needs a further distinction. If the law is merely a declarative one, then the same lack of excusation pertains as would be the case with natural law--a declarative law, as we remember, merely states something that is already contained in natural law. And so we are merely speaking of natural law, but as known from some other source. A negative duty that arises from a determinative law, however, is another matter. For this is not a simple declaration of natural law, but rather is a specification of a particular means leading to an end required by natural law. It is quite possible to have an excusation from the use of a given means, while at the same time not being excused from the requirement of attaining the end that is intended--for other means could be used to achieve that end. A determinative law, for example, might specify that a stop sign never be run. But this is merely a means to achieving the end of public safety. In special circumstances, other means could be substituted to achieve that goal. And so, even though this is a negative law, its obligation could be subject to excusation on the grounds of excessive hardship or practical impossibility.

Similarly, a positive duty, arising from either natural law or human law, admits of excusation. Natural law requires me to honor my parents, and to take care of them in their old age. But what if I am a penniless paraplegic? An affirmative positive law might require that I have a valid driver's license if I am to operate a car. But what if I am the only one available to drive an emergency case to the hospital?

In summary, then: (i) The very fact that a duty I have is difficult does not, in and of itself, excuse me from that duty; (ii) a negative duty arising from the natural law admits of no excuse, nor does a negative duty arising from a human declarative law; (iii) a negative duty arising from a human determinative law does admit of excusation, and so does a positive duty, arising from either natural or human law.

2) The state, or "civil society"

All this, though necessary and important, has been preliminary to the main question of this chapter, which is: what is the state? For that is the second of the two natural societies to which humans belong.

a) What it is, and why it is needed

For practical purposes, a state can be defined as that civil society which possesses sufficient means to ensure that the families that make it up can achieve their final end. For although a family is a natural society, it is not a perfect one, i.e., one that possesses all the means necessary to achieve its end. In other words, while the family is required, it is not sufficient. Suppose that a family were living on a desert isle somewhere. Suppose further, for the sake of argument, that the family members possessed adequate food, clothing, housing, and the like, to ensure survival--quite a supposition, but perhaps possible in a limiting case. Just by the nature of the case, however, there would be some things that they would not and could not have. Perhaps the most basic of these would be education, both intellectual and moral. It is true that there would be some sort of "education," based on knowledge already possessed by older members of the family; but there would be no growth in education, no way to check family lore for error, and so forth. Lacking research, and the ability to exchange and challenge other views (and, indeed, to have their own views challenged), the members of the family would find their "education" a pretty inbred sort of thing. And that would be a clear obstacle to the living of a human, rational life.

Other things would be lacking as well: art, music, and, in general, all those things which make human life specifically human. That is important, for human, rational life cannot be equated with mere physical survival. Rational life really means growth to each individual's maximum potential. We can state this the other way around, too: deliberately to ignore or frustrate a potential which one has is an irrational act, unless there is some compelling reason for doing so. That, of course, is simply another way of saying that the possession of items needed for a fully human life is, ordinarily speaking, something demanded by natural law.

Or, put in familiar terms, the state is a natural society. It is such because the family, itself a natural society, requires the state, and does so absolutely, i.e., requires it in order to achieve its fundamental goal. If human nature requires X (the family), and if X itself requires Y (the state) in order effectively to achieve its end, then it is valid to say that human nature requires Y.

b) Possibility of different kinds of states

Again, though, we should notice something. Human nature requires the presence of some sort of state. It doesn't require any one particular variety. For there can be all sorts of different types of civil societies. After all, there can frequently be multiple means that can be used in order to fulfill the family's needs, thus enabling it to achieve its end. On the other hand, this is not to say that one type of state is as good as any other. It is true that there can be multiple effective means, but that does not say that one type of means cannot be better, more effective, than some other type. Any given state is good or bad to the exact degree that it does or does not achieve its end effectively, i.e., does or does not promote the living of a rational, human life by its members. Obviously, a state which makes available the possibility of a truly human life to a majority of its members is better than one which does so only for a limited number (while keeping the remainder in some sort of sub-human serfdom). None the less, given individual circumstances of time and place, it is conceivable that a dictatorship might be best in some instances, a democracy in others, and variants on one or other of these extremes in still others. The criterion is the effectiveness with which the civil society achieves its end, not the particular mechanism it uses to do so.

Americans, in particular, have to be a little careful on this point. In general, we tend to think that our way of doing things is the best way, and that other people's forms of government are good or bad to the degree that they do or do not approximate our democratic way of doing things. That really isn't necessarily so. It is perfectly conceivable that democracy might be completely inappropriate for certain states, even in our present world. A great deal depends on circumstances, upon the particular needs of the families that make up a given state.

251

Who decides, rightfully, on the type of state that ought to be used? The people, the families involved. They are the ones who have the obligation to achieve their final end, and thus they have the right to determine the means that will best achieve that end. This much, at least, is certain: no one has the right to impose on people a form of government that will be unconducive to their final end.

States can have varying degrees of complexity, as well. It is perfectly possible to have a very good, but quite simple, state--one that provides only a rather minimal amount of services to its citizens. That's fine, if that's all a particular group of people require in order to achieve their goal of living a rational life. Americans, again, tend to think that a state should provide all sorts of services for its citizens: education, welfare, health insurance, and so on. But there can be people who don't need all that. And there could well be instances of a state's providing services for its people which are in fact detrimental to the pursuit of that people's rationality.

c) The individual and the state

We have been speaking of the relationship of the family to the state. We might also wonder about the relationship of the individual to it. Specifically, what does an individual have a right to expect from civil society? And what does civil society have the right to expect from the individual?

(1) Rights of the individual

From the very nature of the state, an individual has the right to expect that the state will take some sort of effective means to enable him or her to live a rational life, to maximize the potential that he or she has. That statement, however, means exactly what it says: *some* sort of effective means--not any particular means that an individual might prefer. Moreover, the statement carefully says that the means must enable the individual to maximize his or her potential. It isn't the business of civil society actually to maximize that potential, but rather to enable the individual to do so. The means chosen might be disliked ("jobfare" as opposed to "welfare," for example); that is beside the point, as long as those means are effective. The individual might choose not to use the means made available. Well and good; but that is the individual's choice, and it is not necessarily the business of the state to come up with all sorts of alternative means in order to provide one that is acceptable to a particular individual.

(2) Rights of the state

On the other hand, the state has certain legitimate expectations of the individual as well. Briefly, it has the right to expect that he or she perform the duties that are necessary so that other members of the state can achieve their goal of rational living. For the state is by nature a co-operative enterprise: I derive certain quite necessary benefits from it, but so do other people. I have my rights within the state, but so do others--which means that I have duties. And so, to give a concrete illustration or two, I have the duty to support the state (by my taxes, or whatever means a particular state has chosen for that purpose). As long as the burden this imposes on me is a just one, then support of the state is a duty, binding in conscience. Similarly, such things as are termed "civic duties" come to mind: items like serving on a jury, and the like. These are genuine duties, not merely inconveniences to be avoided whenever possible.

The question is sometimes posed as to whether the individual exists for the state or the state for the individual. In one sense, this is to mis-pose the question. If one insists on those terms, then the state clearly exists for the family, primarily, and therefore for the individuals who make up that family. But the dichotomy that is thereby posed tends to obscure the fact that, from its very nature as a mandatorily co-operative enterprise, the state also imposes some very real duties upon its members: if I band together with others (as, by my nature, I must do), I do, indeed, expand my rights. But I also expand my duties correspondingly.

It is in that light that another question on the state can be asked, i.e., concerning the duty that I have to defend the state, even though that involves the risk of physical death. It may seem paradoxical that, in order to defend the possibility of living rationally, one has to risk not living at all. But it has to be remembered that the ultimate goal of human nature is not merely living rationally, but rather doing so as a means to the eventual possession of perfect happiness--something not had in this life. And so, while I could not have the duty (imposed by the state) of doing something that would make me miss that last end, I could very well have the duty--if the welfare of the state and of those who make it up demanded it--of doing something less than that,

253

even (if the matter were serious enough) of sacrificing my own life. For again, life—even human, rational life—is not the greatest single value in the world. There are things that surpass it: in this case, the duty (imposed, through our own nature and by living in the natural society that is the state) to provide for others the sort of setting in which *they* can live a rational life.

Another question, which we deferred in an earlier chapter, can now be addressed within the context of our discussion of the state. That is the matter of capital punishment.

The question is a hotly debated one, and one where emotions play perhaps too large a role in the positions one finds taken on it. There are really two questions involved. First, does the state have the right to exact the death penalty for serious crime? And second, if it does have that right, should it use it?

Justification of capital punishment, if there is to be such, would seem to have to come from one or both of two sources: the principles governing the rightful use of self-defense, and the aspects of sanction. Let us look at each of these in turn.

(a) If we recall that the state is a necessary means, absolutely required so that its citizens can live a rational life and thereby attain their final goal, it follows that the state has the right to protect its own existence. Moreover, it has the absolute duty to do so. If, then, there is question of a crime so serious that it threatens to undermine the very fabric of the state, then that state may (and must) take any moral means to defend itself. Does this include taking the life of a person guilty of such a crime? In principle, at least, the answer to this has to be yes. If it is acceptable for an individual person to take an aggressor's life in accord with the four principles of legitimate self-defense, then it is equally acceptable for the moral person that is the state to do the same, if there is no other way for it to defend itself.

But two "if" clauses emerge from this line of reasoning: *if* there is question of a crime that is of such gravity, and *if* the state has no other means of defending itself. Do murder and the other crimes traditionally punishable by death constitute such crimes? Certainly if left unpunished at all, they would do so; few states could survive the chaos that would result. But are these crimes that destructive to the state if their commission is punished by, say, imprisonment? It is difficult to see that they are; murders have been committed and murderers imprisoned for centuries, and most states seem to have survived reasonably well. Moreover, does the state have no alternative means of self-defense? That does not seem likely either, at least in ordinary circumstances in modern times. In a particular case, it might be conceivable that for extraordinary reasons a state would simply be unable to incarcerate those guilty of crimes such as these, and the only recourse would be their execution; such might be the case if there were a tremendous number of murderers in a small, poor state, or if war made incarceration impossible in a given state. Perhaps, too, the exorbitant cost of maintaining murderers sentenced to life imprisonment could be a factor, particularly when weighed against other fiscal obligations that a state has (e.g., to the maintenance and support of the poor); however, given the serious issue involved--the taking of a life, the unique means needed by its possessor to reach his or her final goal--that maintenance cost would have to be very high indeed.

Subject to the "if" clauses we noted, a state does, then, have the right to exact capital punishment. Should it use that right? Assuming that the conditional clauses are fulfilled, it not only should but must. If on the other hand those conditions are not fulfilled, then it would seem that the state not only should not but must not employ capital punishment--at least as far as the question of legitimate self-defense is concerned.

(b) A second perspective can be gotten from the aspects of sanction (vindicative, corrective, deterrent) that we saw earlier. Let us grant that capital punishment, like virtually any other sanction, will not fulfill all of these aspects: the injustice to the murdered person is not addressed by the sanction, for instance. And let us leave aside the argument as to whether capital punishment has deterrent value--not that the question is without value, but rather that its resolution is unclear enough right now that it would not be a helpful topic to us in our study. Now, in a macabre sense, capital punishment could, perhaps, be said to be corrective: certainly, this particular criminal will not commit the crime again! But let us leave that consideration aside, too. In the last analysis, however, the one aspect of sanction that capital punishment certainly does fulfill is the vindication of the objective order of justice, i.e., the redressing of the (violated) right that the citizens of a society collectively have not to be unjustly killed. However, the question that would need to be asked is this: granted that capital punishment does achieve this goal of sanction, could some lesser punishment also do so? If a lesser punishment can achieve the same goal, then, once again, one may not inflict needless harm on someone else, and therefore capital punishment would not be justified. If, however, in individual circumstances a lesser punishment will not achieve that goal of sanction, then capital punishment could be justified.

255

In brief: does the state have the right to inflict capital punishment for serious crimes? In certain circumstances (although not in all), yes. Should it make use of that right? In certain circumstances, it not only should but must. In others, it should not--at least, until its moral justification in a given case can be clearly demonstrated.

That, then, is what the state is. We have examined one large area that governs what a state is and how it operates, i.e., the whole area of rights and duties. And yet considerations like this, though obviously necessary and part of the total picture, tend to leave us somewhat cold. Surely, if the only relationships that I have with the others who have banded together with me in a state are those founded on justice, and if I truly observe all of the requirements of those relationships, my dealings with my fellow citizens will be correct. They will also be chilly and impersonal. Surely, there has to be more of a basis to living in society than this.

3) The relationship of charity among citizens

There is, indeed. Three facts suggest that, in addition to justice and rights, another area of relationship ought to govern our dealings with our fellow citizens. (i) We all have a common goal, and a common obligation to seek that goal. (ii) We do (and must, as essentially social beings) live together, and we are all intellectual beings. (iii) We all know (or at least can know) that we have that common goal. It follows from all this that we are all equals, at least in terms of the goal that we are seeking. Consequently, I must (if I am to act reasonably, anyway) regard my neighbor with the same level of esteem with which I regard myself, for we are all equals in the one thing that really makes much difference, in the long run: the goal that we seek. For, again, nature is by and large defined in terms of goal: there may be (and are) accidental differences between my neighbor and me, but in any comparison of him or her and me, the identities are far more important than the differences.

Now, we regard ourselves with a certain amount of affection, care, concern; we think well of ourselves (or we ought to); we look out for our own welfare; we seek to achieve that goal which will make for our own happiness. In brief, we love ourselves--or we should. But: if we are to regard our neighbor with the same degree of esteem which we exercise on ourselves, then we are to love our neighbor.

256

a) Basis for the relationship

The reasoning back of all this should be carefully noted. The basis for saying that we must love our neighbor is not one of duty. Ordinarily, my neighbor does not have a right to my love, since that would not normally be required for his achieving the ultimate goal, and since no other title to my love is evident. Rather, the basis for the obligation to love one's neighbor is a species of truthfulness, a realization of the identity in ultimate end and essential nature which he or she shares with me. The real basis, then, for this obligation is my obligation to live rationally, an obligation that includes recognizing my neighbor's commonality with me in end and nature and also includes esteeming him or her on that basis accordingly.

Charity, as we have discussed it so far, is not something that depends on how my neighbor treats me. He or she can be the worst sort of rogue, can be bent on destroying me, can do everything possible to injure me. The obligation to love him or her remains, for it is based, not on whether or not he or she is in fact *achieving* the ultimate end, but rather on the fact that he or she *has* that end and has the same obligation I have of seeking it. Paradoxically, I am not obliged to *like* my neighbor, with all the connotations of special esteem and regard that that word has in English. The obligation is to *love* him or her, to perform whatever services that love requires of me--something to which we must now turn.

b) Obligations that the relationship imposes

Are there obligations based on the charity which I must have toward my neighbor? There are, indeed. The obligation to regard and esteem my neighbor is one such, independently of individual differences which he or she may have from me. For example, one could argue (and people have) that racial prejudice is something contrary to justice. Whatever one would want to say on that point--and it is arguable--it is none the less clear that such a thing is forbidden by the obligation of charity--a true obligation, and one which, albeit with a different basis, binds no less stringently than does one in justice.

Similarly, charity can oblige me to come to the aid of my neighbor when he or she is in need. If I am wealthy, and my next-door neighbor is starving, my assisting him or her by providing food is not a matter of simple beneficence, something

257

which I either may or may not do, depending on how I feel. It is an obligation, and one which I ignore only at my own great peril.

c) Limitations on these obligations

However, that poses a question. For, obviously, there are always going to be people who, relative to me, are needy--just as, in all likelihood, there are going to be people relative to whom I myself am likely to be needy. This is the case as long as people have different amounts of the goods of the world--a condition likely to perdure for some time to come. And, perfectly obviously, I am not going to be able to assist every needy person in the world. What sorts of criteria are there that would spell out the obligations I have in charity to assist my neighbor in his or her need?

Three criteria, really, can do this. They can be put in the form of questions: (i) How great is my neighbor's need? (ii) What will it cost me (in time, effort, money, etc.) to assist him or her? (iii) How useful will my help be?

As regards (i): I have a greater obligation to assist my neighbor when his or her need is greater. When the need is slight, the obligation is slight (and the reason required for excusation from that obligation is correspondingly less, as we remember from the general rules governing excusation from duty). As for (ii): I am not obligated to incur a hardship greater than the one I am trying to save my neighbor from. I am obligated to love my neighbor as myself--but not more than myself. I may, of course, choose to incur such a hardship in assisting my neighbor. But the question under discussion here is what I am obligated to do. And finally, in regard to (iii): I might have an obligation in charity to assist a given poor individual or individuals; but I cannot be said to have the obligation to aid all poor people, since my resources would then be spread so thin that my help to them would be virtually useless--and no one is obligated to perform a totally useless act.

As is obvious, this whole area is another one where prudential judgment is required in any given case. For example, if I am very wealthy, I can say accurately that I have an obligation to help the poor, and that I must take *some* concrete steps to meet that obligation. But just what those steps will be, is a matter for the individual to judge in his or her own case. Ethics can reason to certain norms and conclusions, but there does come a point where individual conscience must regulate each concrete case. But it still should be remembered: the obligation to assist my neighbor in his or her need--whatever concrete means might be chosen to do this in any given case--is precisely that: an obligation, not an option.

SUMMARY OF CHAPTER TWELVE

(A) Preliminary considerations concern (i) rights, (ii) justice, and (iii) duties.

(i) A right is the moral power to do, hold, or exact something. A right is the reverse side of an obligation: if I have an obligation, I must have the requisite means to fulfill it; and those means are rights. Obligations are based on law, whether natural or positive; hence so are rights. In a right, one can distinguish a subject (the one having the right), a term (the one bound to honor that right), a matter (what one has a right to), and a title (the reason why one has a particular right). Only a human person (individual or moral) can be either the subject or the term of a right, since there is question of moral obligation; the matter of a right can never be a person as such; and a right's title can be either congenital or acquired. Some rights ("coactive") can be backed up with force, whereas others ("non-coactive") simply by their nature cannot. Some rights can be voluntarily surrendered (are "alienable"); others cannot (are "inalienable"), and that because of their very nature.

(ii) Justice, in general, is the virtue by which we give to each one that which is his/her own. "Commutative" justice is that existing between individuals; "distributive" justice, that between a society and an individual; "legal" justice, that between an individual and a society. The enforcement of a right held in commutative justice is ordinarily the prerogative of the state, though on certain occasions it may be enforced by the individual him/herself; enforcement of distributive justice is ordinarily limited to petition, protest, etc., since to do more would constitute rebellion; enforcement of a right based on legal justice is the business of the state itself.

(iii) Rights are frequently limited in their scope, either by their nature or because they conflict with others' rights. The term of a right will have corresponding duties, i.e., the moral obligation to do or not do something. A right is the reverse side of a duty, and vice-versa. Duties can be affirmative or negative; the former oblige only at stated times, the latter oblige at all times. In general, rights are limited by duties and duties by rights.

In the case of a conflict of rights (or of duties), some general norms (based on a right's subject, term, matter, and title) can be set down; but in individual cases a conflict of rights and/or duties must inevitably be settled by prudential judgment. Some duties--because of their type and basis--admit of excusation; some do not; the basis for excusation will ordinarily be disproportionate hardship or moral impossibility. A hardship arising from the very nature of a duty does not, ordinarily, admit of excusation; negative duties, arising from natural law or from a declarative positive law, do not admit of excusation; a negative duty arising from a determinative positive law can be subject to excusation, as can a positive duty, arising from either natural or positive law.

(B) A state is that civil society which possesses sufficient means to ensure that its constitutive families can reach their final end. It is a natural society because the family, itself a natural society (but an imperfect one) absolutely requires it. However, no one particular type of state is required by human nature, and any given state is good or bad to the extent that it does or does not promote the living of a rational, human life by its members. The choice of a state's type is the prerogative of its members. An individual living within a state has the right to expect that the state will take some sort of effective means to enable him/her to live a rational life, to maximize his/her potential; the state, on the other hand, has the right to expect individuals to perform such duties as are necessary so that other member individuals can live rationally as well, and in an extreme case, this can involve the duty of defending the state, even at the risk of the individual's life. Both on the norms for legitimate self-defense and because of the very nature of sanction, the state must in principle have the right (and even the duty) to exact capital punishment for crimes so serious that they threaten the fabric of society, though whether conditions actually exist in modern times that warrant using that right is ordinarily questionable.

In addition to justice relationships, humans also have a relationship of charity toward one another, based on our shared knowledge that we are all equals in terms of our common final end. This relationship involves regarding our neighbor with the same care and concern which we show to ourselves, i.e., involves our loving our neighbor. This is not a matter of a duty (based on justice), but rather on simple truthfulness. To be effective, this love for neighbor must be carried out in deeds. General norms regarding obligations arising from charity can be stated (based on the degree of our neighbor's need, our relative cost in providing assistance, and the usefulness of our assistance), but prudential judgment must be the final norm in any given case.

13. LIVING IN CIVIL SOCIETY

III. The Practical Part of Ethics
  C. Our relationship to others
    3. The state as a society
      b. Humans within a particular society
        1) Actions bearing chiefly on oneself: example, work
          a) How labor evolves
          b) Reasons for work
          c) Work as a right, a duty, and a dignity
          d) A worker's rights
          e) A worker's duties
          f) Enforcement of a worker's rights
        2) Actions bearing chiefly on one's family: example, education
          a) Meaning of the term
          b) Primary responsibility for education
          c) Role of the state and other individuals
          d) Moral education
          e) Higher education
        3) Actions bearing on people outside one's family
          a) First example: truthfulness and confidentiality
            (1) Truthfulness
              (a) What speech is
              (b) What lying is
              (c) Conventional speech and fiction
              (d) The morality of untruthfulness
            (2) Confidentiality
              (a) Basis of the right to secrecy
              (b) Types of secrets
              (c) Obligation to keep secrets
              (d) Means of keeping secrets
          b) Second example: contracts
            (1) What a contract is
            (2) Elements of a contract
            (3) Validity and liceity

We have spent some time examining what a state is, and we have seen a few general characteristics that every state will have. Now it will be useful to change the focus a little bit and try to see the actual, day-to-day interactions that humans have with a particular state. In other words, we have seen some general theory; now let us turn to some practical applications. And so, let us put ourselves in the position of John Smith, citizen.

b. Humans within a particular society

Now, Mr. Smith has multiple dealings with his fellow citizens. Some of these focus primarily on himself. Others are of chief interest to his family (including, of course, himself). And others involve just about everyone in the civil society--or at least are certainly not limited in their scope to Mr. Smith and his clan. These divisions of Smith's activities are obviously not perfect; there will inevitably be some overlapping. But, as a principle of organization for the present chapter, they are useful enough.

Citizen Smith also has some dealings with states other than his own; and these, too, we should look at in some way, however briefly. That will be the purpose of the chapter following this one.

1) Actions bearing chiefly on oneself: example, work

For now, though, let us concentrate on the three types of dealings that we mentioned. To illustrate the activities of Mr. Smith which are of greatest interest to himself, we will look at the notion of labor, or work. A sample of his dealings with his community that would have their chief impact on his own family could be gotten by examining the question of education. And two areas that would exemplify his communal dealings that impact a wider field than just himself and his family would be truthfulness (with its related field, confidentiality) and contracts.

a) How labor evolves

In a very primitive society--which may or may not ever have existed, in the real order--it is possible that a small number of humans could have arranged a system of mutual barter, so as to supply themselves and their families with what they needed. The farmer could have agreed to provide the blacksmith with food, in return for the blacksmith's keeping the farm horses well shod; the smith, in turn, would perform his particular services for the dairyman, in return for milk, eggs, and the like; the dairyman would provide his particular products to the medicine man, in return for medical treatment for himself and his family, and so on. Once things progress beyond a very primitive level, however, this quickly becomes unfeasible: it is simply too complicated. And so a common system of exchange is fastened upon: money, of one sort or other. A certain value is agreed upon for the farmer's food, for the blacksmith's art, for the dairyman's eggs, and for the medicine man's incantations; and some sort of symbol, frequently but not always precious in nature, is chosen to represent that value. The game thus changes from simply producing enough of a product to exchange directly for what one needs, to producing enough of a product to earn sufficient money to be able to purchase those needs--and, of course, to do so with some consistency, even when things aren't going very well with whatever product one happens to be producing. In other words, the point is now to accumulate enough money to take care of one's present needs and also one's future ones, at least to some extent.

Fine, but what of the individual who doesn't happen to be a farmer, a blacksmith, a dairyman, or a shaman? Some people are simply none of these things, nor anything comparable. How do they get into the money-making business?

The answer, of course, is that the farm gets too big for one man to handle, or even one family. The blacksmith shop has far too much work for the one blacksmith. The dairyman has more eggs than he can deliver in a 24-hour span. And the medicine man also has too much to do. And so a bargain is struck. The non-farmer agrees to assist the farmer, in return for a given sum of money. The blacksmith acquires a helper, or more than one--again, in return for a set sum of money. Similarly the dairyman and the medicine man. And so we get the system of businesses: owners and workers.

b) Reasons for work

Obviously, all this is vastly simplified, nearly to the point of being a caricature. But there are advantages to simplicity. One chief advantage is that the answer to an important question becomes clear: why work? Obviously, one works--either as an employer or as an employee--to obtain the things that are necessary for life. In a complicated society--or at least in *our* complicated society--there is no other way in which the average individual can obtain these things. Could there be some other system? Probably, in some other universe somewhere; at least the concept of some other way of doing things is not inherently contradictory. However, at least as things go in our civilization (and have gone for about as long as recorded history has anything to say about the matter), work is a necessity of human life. In and of itself, it is not a unique means. But for most people, given the world in which we live, it comes very close to that status. At least, it is the only viable means that the vast majority of us have in our circumstances.

c) Work as a right, a duty, and a dignity

That, however, says something about work immediately. If work is a practical necessity for us to live humanly, then it is something which we have to have in order to achieve our last end. Working is, therefore, a human right. Or, to put matters more exactly, for every human being for whom work is the only available means to living rationally, there exists a right to work. (There are, after all, certain fortunate souls whose accumulated wealth is such that work is not the only available means to obtaining what they need. Such people, however, do not constitute the majority of the human race, to put matters mildly.) One can turn all this around, too. For the average individual, work is a duty as well as a right. For it is the only available means to achieving his or her last end--the achievement of which is, indeed, a duty. However, it is worth noting immediately that the right to work--and the duty to work--extend only to work in general, in virtually all cases. I do not automatically have the right to any particular job, or even to any particular type of job. I don't necessarily have the right to work that I like, or even to work that I am good at. I have the right to such work as will allow me to live a human life--period.

The language of rights and duties, however, does not do full justice to the matter. For, as we have noted, work is the means through which we attain our last end. If that is the case, then the dignity and excellence which attach themselves to the possession of that last end are also shared in by the means to that end. Put briefly, work is a human right, and it is a human duty; but it is also a human dignity and a human excellence. It is not something to be shunned, to be done grudgingly and only under duress. In principle, it is something to glory in, to take pride in--not indeed primarily for its own sake, but for the sake of the end to which it is the means.

d) A worker's rights

If all this is true, then something follows about the conditions under which humans ought to work. For if work, as a means to one's last end, is a uniquely human sort of thing, it follows that the work itself should be befitting to humans. Obviously, there are all kinds of work, and the conditions under which work takes place vary tremendously according to the type of work in question. And so it is impossible to make any sort of general statement as to what work conditions should be. But it is quite possible to make a general statement or two about what those conditions should *not* be. Any work situation that is sub-human is obviously out of order and is moreover immoral, for it forces humans to exist in a sub-human way. If an employer contracts with a fellow human being for his or her work, that employer has the obligation to provide decently human conditions for the employee. Nor will it do for such an employer to say, "Well, if someone is not satisfied with the conditions I offer, even if they are sub-human, he or she does not have to work for me." While an employee may or may not have to work for such an employer, the point here is that it is immoral on the part of the employer to attempt to contract for work in such circumstances, quite independently of whether anyone accepts the contract or not. For if it is immoral to do something, it is immoral to attempt to do it.

Exactly what constitutes conditions suitable to humans is obviously something that varies considerably with circumstances of time and place, and something which has to be determined in particular situations by prudential judgment. But the principle itself--that an employer may not treat humans as sub-humans--is valid for any time and place.

The term "working conditions" is deliberately broad. It is intended to include such things as physical location and conditions, working hours, and salary, among other things. All these are part of the contract that the employer makes with the worker, and all of them are included in the principle requiring human conditions for human workers. One aspect of this, though, does deserve special mention, for its prominence if for no other reason; and that is the question of salary.

Is there such a thing as a minimum salary that an employer must pay, under threat of moral sanction? Yes, there is. The so-called "minimum wage"--whatever its specifics in a given culture--is that amount of money which an employee must have if he or she is to lead a decently human life. If an employer pays less than that wage, then he or she is treating humans as sub-humans, is using human beings as mere instruments in the achievement of his or her final end--something that we have already seen is outside the pale of morality. Deciding just what constitutes a minimum wage is a complicated exercise in economics, in any given country and age; and determining it specifically for any particular time and place is not our business. It *is* our business, though, to say that there does exist such a thing as a minimum wage, the payment of which is a moral requirement for an employer. For the employee has a right to work, a right to earn what he or she needs for a human, rational life; and if that employee is in the full-time employ of a given employer, the duty which is the reverse side of the employee's right falls squarely on that employer.

While we make no attempt to get into the economics of determining a minimum wage, we should point out that the term means more than just what the employee alone requires for the living of a human life. It also embraces what that employee's dependents (family, etc.) require. For the employee's duty of support (and therefore his or her right to the means of that support) does not stop with the employee; he or she also has duties (and hence rights) in regard to others who depend on him or her. Furthermore, by a "human life" is meant a good deal more than mere subsistence or survival. It means the sort of life that is worthy of a human being: the sort of setting (adequate food, housing, rest and relaxation, etc.) that is befitting a rational being, that allows that rational being the reasonable opportunity to develop his or her potential.

In the practical order, a developed society generally has some sort of mechanism for setting a minimum wage, although the degree and means of enforcement of this may differ widely from country to country. The only point that is made here is that an employee does have a right to a certain minimum wage, and the employer has an obligation in conscience to pay it--both of these because of the nature of work as an ordinarily required means for the achievement of the final end of humankind.

e) A worker's duties

If the employer has clear obligations based on the nature of human work, however, the employee also has. Once again, the reverse side of right is duty. And if it is true that I have a right to work, and that I have a right to a certain set of working conditions, it is also true that I have the duty to perform the work for which I am being paid, and to perform it in a fashion worthy of a rational being: conscientiously and well. That, after all, is what I am being paid for; no employer hires a worker with the deliberate intention that that worker shall perform sloppily, shall turn out inferior products, etc. If I am paid to do a job well, then I am obligated to do that job well--the obligation being one in strict justice. My agreement to work for my employer is two things. It is the title I have to my right to this particular job (for, as we have seen, while human nature gives me the right to work in general, it does not give me the right to any particular job as opposed to any other one; the agreement does that). It is also a contract. In short, the agreement gives me rights. It also gives me duties.

But there is more to it than that. If, as has been claimed, working is a dignity of a human being, then it would be strange indeed if the fulfillment of that dignity could be achieved by work that is half-hearted and slipshod. To put it mildly, something seems amiss with the fundamental reasonableness of any proposition that would allow that to be possible or permissible.

f) Enforcement of a worker's rights

Only the very naive would assume that, since employers have duties and employees have rights (and, conversely, since employers have rights and employees have duties), all is therefore going to be well on the labor front. And so at least a brief word needs to be said about the mechanism available to either side for the enforcement of their respective rights. The employer, of course, has available the immediate tool of firing the employee if that employee does not live up to the terms of his or her contract. Not a great deal needs to be said about this here; like any other tool, it is one that can be used justly or unjustly, morally or immorally, in accord with general rules that we have already seen. The employee, on the other hand, has the important tool of unionization, with all that that implies: collective bargaining, the sanction of strikes, etc. This could be the topic for many pages or chapters, and we do not propose to examine it fully here. The sole points that should perhaps be made for our purposes are that unions are legitimate, and they can very well be a matter of right. They are legitimate, for if it is permissible for a person to seek a just wage alone, it is equally permissible to do so in concert with others. If the goal is morally good, then whether it is sought by one or by many is a matter of moral indifference. Unions can be a matter of right: for in some circumstances, at least, an employee's right to a just wage, adequate working conditions, etc., can be secured in no other way. Without the right to organize, the right to human working conditions becomes (or can become) meaningless. On the other hand, the fact that someone has a right does not necessarily mean that that right has to be exercised: union membership could hardly be seen as a duty, unless the sole means to acquiring a just wage lay in membership therein--a condition not likely to be verified in our present culture in the United States, at any rate. Moreover, the employee's tool of unionization, strikes, etc., is also something that can be used morally or immorally, justly or unjustly--exactly as was the case with the employer's tool of dismissal.

2) Actions bearing chiefly on one's family: example, education

So much, then, for John Smith's civil activities that bear mostly on himself. There is next the question of his family, and the effects his civil acts have on them. An illustration of this can be found in the whole area of education.

a) Meaning of the term

First, the term "education": as used here, it means that amount of intellectual and moral training which a person needs in order to live effectively within a given society. As stated, that is not very precise; neither is it intended to be. For the level of education required to meet that criterion will vary in any given culture. The ability to read and write is not necessary, even today, for a member of a tribal culture in Central Africa to operate very effectively within his or her civil society; the same could not be said for someone trying to live and work in Chicago or New York City. Again, it used to be the case that completing even grade school was not necessary in the United States in order to live a quite human life; that would not be the case in the computer age in which we live. Similarly, it is not necessary for a coal miner in Pennsylvania to have the same knowledge of business ethics which the president of the company needs, if both of them are to lead moral, rational lives.

b) Primary responsibility for education

Our particular focus here is not on John Smith's own education, except indirectly. Rather, we are interested in the question of his children's education. In particular, we ask who has the basic responsibility for the education of those children: Smith? The state? Both? Neither?

A little reflection makes it clear that it is the parents who have the basic duty (and therefore the basic right) to see to the education of their children. For education is a necessary part of generation--taking this term in the wide sense in which we have been using it. As a result of the act of human intercourse, there comes into being an individual with a definite final end, for the attainment of which certain things are necessary, education being one of them. On the sheerly human level (i.e., leaving aside for the moment the role of the Creator), it is the parents who are responsible for the existence of that individual--the entire individual, i.e., the individual *with his or her final goal*. It is therefore the parents who are responsible for that goal's ability to be fulfilled. To say otherwise is to claim that the parents both are and are not the causes of their child's final end or goal: they are its causes, in that they bring it into being; and they are simultaneously not its causes, since they do not bring a goal into being but rather something other than a goal, something whose fulfillment is, as far as they are concerned, a matter of indifference. (As we have seen, a goal whose fulfillment is not a matter of concern is not a goal at all.)

c) Role of the state and other individuals

If, then, the parents have the primary responsibility and right to see to their children's education, it follows that they may see to that responsibility in any way they wish, provided that the way chosen be effective. In a relatively simple society, in which the degree of education required for human living is not high, it could be possible for the parents to provide everything necessary themselves, with or without the aid of others in the society in which they live. In a more complex society, it may well be the case that the parents will need help in carrying out this duty, and they may seek that help from whatever useful source they choose. That source may be the civil society itself; it may be something else. But we should carefully note: the duty remains with the parents; anyone or anything apart from them is merely a means, which they may or may not elect to use in carrying out their duty.

Commonly, in highly developed societies, the state does provide a system of education for this purpose. It is, of course, to the state's advantage to do so; it clearly has a vested interest (and a rightful one) in possessing an educated citizenry. Indeed, we can say that the state has a right to educated citizens--at least to the level required for intelligent participation in the state. However, such state-provided education is not a unique means to a necessary goal: educated citizens can be provided for the state in a variety of ways. And thus no state could validly claim the exclusive right to provide the educational system for its citizens. The primary right over choosing the means to education in any particular case will always remain with the parents, for it is they who have the primary duty in this matter. If they fail in the performance of this duty, the state does have the right to step in and force them to see to its fulfillment; the state, again, does have the right to educated citizenry. But even then, the state could not legitimately force parents to use one particular means of education rather than some other one; it could only make sure that the parents used *some* effective means toward educating their children adequately.

It is in the light of all this that the question of private schools, church-related schools, and the like, must be seen. If a group of parents choose to establish a private school for their children, and if that school proves itself capable of adequately educating the children entrusted to it, well and good. The duty of the parents is satisfied, and the right of the state to educated citizens is satisfied. Private education, then, is simply an alternate means which parents may choose to use; and no state could justly outlaw it. Obviously, the state can legitimately require certain standards of it--this, again, in terms of the state's clear right to have citizens who have achieved certain educational standards. But the point to notice is that private education has as much right to exist as does public education: both are tools which parents may elect to use.

(The state's right to set standards forestalls an abuse. Do parents have the right to send their children to private schools in which something inimical to the state [e.g., racism, or--in an extreme case--revolution] is fostered? No, or at least not necessarily. The state has the right to set standards of education, based on its own needs--which may well exclude racism and such things. Thus state standards may well dictate that private schools not foster these things. The state may not legitimately outlaw private schools whose viewpoint is merely different from that of the state. But it may outlaw the teaching and fostering of things that are inimical to itself. Thus, the parents' right to choose the individual style they wish for their children can come into direct conflict with the state's right to exist; should that happen, the situation would have to be resolved in terms of the general doctrine of conflict of rights that we have already seen.)

However, it does not follow from all of this that the state has the obligation to support private education, any more than it follows that the state has the obligation to provide alternate means in many other areas of human life where an individual person or group of persons might find those alternate means more suited to their taste. It might be wise for the state to do so, on other grounds (e.g., the possibility that the state's own system of education can benefit from healthy competition with some other system). But it cannot be said that state support of private education is obligatory.

d) Moral education

Two further comments in the area of education need to be made. The first of these concerns moral education in general. It is sometimes said (generally with an exaggerated sense of fair play and respect for the individual) that parents ought not try to impose their system of values on their children, but should rather wait until those children are capable of choosing their own system of morality. One can only shake one's head in wonder at something like this. We certainly would not wait until our children made their own decision as to whether or not they wished to learn the multiplication tables, or the alphabet, or English grammar. Why the fundamental principles of morality should be any different is not at all clear. Whether our children do or do not *follow* those principles of morality is, of course, their business. But that they should *know* them would seem to be the parents' business, the neglect of which can only be seen as a dereliction of duty on the part of those parents.

e) Higher education

Finally, there is the question of education beyond the level required for adequate functioning within a society. In the case of a United States citizen, this means college or university education. Are parents obligated to provide this for their children? No--precisely because it is beyond what is minimally necessary for the living of a human life in our society. Parents may wish to provide their children with that advantage, and may have the means to do so; fine, and all that is being said here is that there is no *obligation* to do so. But the other side of this is true, too: no one has the strict right to higher education. It can be said that certain members of an advanced society must have had that education, since the needs of the state may well require it. But no given individual, simply because he or she exists as a

271

human being, therefore enjoys that right. Education beyond that required for human living is a privilege rather than a right, however desirable it may be (and unquestionably is). And thus to say (as some have said) that everyone has the right to go to college is at best rhetoric and at worst sheer nonsense. Not everyone has the capability for higher learning, in the first place; and of those who do, no one has the automatic right to it.

3) Actions bearing on people outside one's family

To turn, now, to the third major area of this chapter, i.e., Citizen Smith's dealings in his civil society that affect a wider group than just himself or his family (though, of course, these may also affect Mr. Smith and clan as well). Naturally, there are many such dealings. But as a sample, we could look at the whole area of truthfulness (with its allied area of confidentiality) as a first illustration of how our general principles might find application.

a) First example: truthfulness and confidentiality
(1) Truthfulness

Truthfulness, in general, can be defined as "speech in accord with one's mind," and lying as "speech contrary to one's mind." But the term "speech" in this context will need to be carefully understood.

(a) What speech is

In general, the word "speech," as we are using it here, refers to any sign that I use to communicate my thought or my judgment. And so words can be speech; so can looks, gestures, shrugs, etc. Speech, in other words, need not be vocal. But this "sign," whatever it is, must be intended to convey a meaning. An involuntary look, sign, gesture, groan, etc., is not speech. Since there is question of conveying a meaning, there must be some other person to whom that meaning is intended to be conveyed. One does not "speak" to a dog, in the proper sense of the term; neither does one "speak" to oneself. For that matter, one can't rightly be said to "speak" to eavesdroppers, either; even though words carrying a meaning may be in question, the intention to communicate that meaning to the eavesdropper is lacking, and so we are not talking of speech in such a case.

(b) What lying is

In truthful speech, this intentionally conveyed meaning expresses my own judgment about the matter at hand, which judgment I believe to be true. In untruthful speech (lying), on the other hand, the intentionally conveyed meaning does not do so. There is, then, a difference between an error and a lie. When I speak in error, I am expressing my own judgment and I believe that judgment to be true; unfortunately, I'm wrong. When I lie, I am not expressing my own judgment about what I believe to be true. I am expressing quite another judgment—one which I believe to be false—but which I am conveying to another person as if I believed it to be true. There is also a difference between lying and mere deception. Things like feints, disguises, aliases, and the like, are deceptions; but they are not lies, since there is no communication ("speech," as defined above) involved in them. Deceptions, generally speaking, are morally neutral in themselves: they derive their morality from the motive and circumstances from and in which they are done. Most games, for example, involve deception, and these are perfectly permissible from a moral point of view (i.e., considering their motive and circumstances). Military deceptions are a similar case in point: these are deceptions, and no communication is intended—if a military enemy is foolish enough to read a meaning into such a strategem and thereby be deceived, that is his problem. Similarly, if an opponent in a football game reads a meaning into a quarterback's fake and is thereby drawn off side, that is his own fault; he has inferred a communication where none is implied.

(c) Conventional speech and fiction

This is also a good place to note the role of convention in speech. There are certain expressions in our language which, taken literally, mean one thing, but which everyone understands (or should understand) to mean something quite different. Thus, a secretary says that her boss is not in (when as a matter of fact he is sitting in his office with the door closed): this is simply a conventional way of saying, "He doesn't want to see you." In the same category are things like "What a nice dress!" (when as a matter of fact we think the thing is a monstrosity); "What a pretty baby!" (when in fact we wonder how the mother ever managed to spirit that kid away from the ape cage in the zoo);

and the like. These are merely conventional put-offs, arbitrary "nice things to say" in certain circumstances. Only the very naive would interpret them as being meant literally. The sole meaning that they do convey is that we hope to maintain the social niceties, even in circumstances where that may not be all that easy. Other familiar expressions are "Fine," in response to a question as to how we are--whether we feel fine or not, we understand that the questioner is not really interested in the state of our health, or at least does not want a detailed account of it here and now; "I hope that you have a nice day," which really means nothing more than "Good-bye"; and so on and on. (We can get some interesting insight into the conventional nature of expressions like these by noting our reaction when they *are* taken literally: when, for example, in response to a "How are you?" question, someone tells us exactly, and in wearisome detail, just how they happen to be feeling at the moment. We are surprised; that is not what we expected, for that is not what our question really meant.)

A related area is that of story-telling, fiction, imagery, figures of speech, and the like. Here, we either are not expressing our judgment about the truth or falsity of something, but rather are simply entertaining our listeners (and that fact is understood--or can reasonably be expected to be understood--by those listeners), or else we are speaking conventionally, in a way that everyone understands should not be taken literally. Thus, no one expects that a novel be a recitation of something that actually happened; and when I say, "He is a pig," no one thereby ought to be led to believe that he possesses four feet, a large snout, and an inordinate liking for either swill or mud.

(d) The morality of untruthfulness

The morality of untruthfulness is one that has, over the years, occupied many . pages in ethics books. One common historical argument is that lying is immoral because it is a misuse of the natural faculty of speech. The problem with this argument, however, is that it is at least difficult to specify just what this "faculty" is: there is no human faculty (i.e., human power) that is solely concerned with "speech," in the sense in which it has been defined. Humans have a power whereby they can make sounds; but speech is not identified with merely this. Moreover, "speech," as defined, can be the operation of more than one human power (again, gestures, nods, etc., can constitute "speech"). Thus, it seems better not to make very much of this particular argument.

A much more forceful argument for the immorality of lying comes from the consequences that would ensue if lying were morally acceptable. Since humans are by nature social animals, and since society is built on mutual trust and requires constant communication among its members, it is clear that, were lying morally allowable, the level of trust required for society would be rendered impossible. Thus, the argument is: human nature requires society; society requires both communication and mutual confidence in the veracity of that communication; communication and mutual confidence require truthfulness; therefore human nature requires truthfulness. Or, schematically, A requires B, B requires C and D, C and D require E, therefore A requires E. And, of course, if human nature requires truthfulness, then the converse is that untruthfulness is contrary to human nature, i.e., is immoral.

This is normally the place where all manner of horror stories are brought forth, usually designed to point to the lack of proportion between a small lie and a huge evil which telling that lie would avert. Suppose, for example, that by telling one small lie I could avert an atomic holocaust; would I not be justified in doing so? Or: suppose a robber, holding me at gunpoint, demands to know the combination to the safe; must I tell him? Or could I not be justified in saying that I don't know (even though I do)? And so on. Each person doubtless has his or her own version of these old chestnuts. They are generally more seeming problems than real ones. In any such case, I have to ask myself whether I am dealing with real speech, in the first place, or whether I might well be dealing with a mere conventional use of words, or a fiction, or something of the sort. Thus, I can legitimately say to the robber, "I don't know the combination." Even if in fact I do know it, what the robber could reasonably be expected to understand by my words, in those circumstances, is, "I don't want to tell you." So also in the case of the enemy spy who tells his captors all about who sent him, what he is doing there, etc.: he can reasonably expect that those captors interpret whatever he says as being a fantasy, not intended to have any relation to the truth. If it truly is the case that a real lie is in question, then the general moral principle holds: I may not legitimately do evil that good may come of it, no matter how great the good (even the good of averting an atomic holocaust). But we need to be very sure that we are, indeed, dealing with a real lie. In most of the horror-story cases, we are not.

(2) Confidentiality

An area closely allied to truthfulness is the matter of

confidentiality, or the keeping of a secret. Put generally, a secret is a truth that one has a duty to conceal. Now, it is indeed true that we must speak truthfully--if we speak. But there are occasions on which we must not speak, on which we must not use real speech. There are, then, occasions on which we must conceal the truth, in one way or other. This, however, means exactly what it says: conceal the truth, not lie.

(a) Basis of the right to secrecy

The basis of the right to secrets is this. Besides being members of a society, human beings are also individuals; in addition to public and social relationships, men and women have private and personal dealings of their own, which are not the business of society (since society has no need to know them in order to fulfill its goal). Just as humans have the right to things necessary to constitute them as members of a state, so also do they have the right to the things necessary to constitute them as individuals. This means that they have the right to certain things which are quite private, things not to be shared with their fellow humans in the society in which they live. Moreover, even within society, one of the purposes of speech and communication is to sollicit help from one's fellow human beings, to ask for their advice--without the danger of making private things public. Unless it be permissible somehow to control how far knowledge will spread, one major function of speech and communication is lost.

Moreover, just as an individual person has the right to secrets because he or she is an individual as well as a member of a society, so also does a moral person (again, a group of persons united for some common purpose): a moral person, too, is an individual as well as a member of the larger society.

(b) Types of secrets

By their nature, secrets are of two types. A *natural* secret is one dealing with matter which is private of its very nature. Thus, matters pertaining to one's private life, to one's family, etc., are natural secrets. Matters of sexuality, or family ancestry, and so forth, are examples of this. A moral person, too, can have natural secrets, whether this be a business firm, or even an entire country, considered as a moral individual rather than as a member of the wider world community. An *entrusted* secret, on the other hand, is one which a person makes an explicit promise to keep secret. The obligation to keep secrets of this type arises from the implied contract because of which the secret is shared: the information is given precisely on the condition that it not be revealed to others, a condition to which the recipient of the information agrees and binds himself or herself. It is possible that some secrets could be of both kinds (natural and entrusted), whereas others may be one or the other; the categories are not mutually exclusive.

(c) Obligation to keep secrets

What obligation do I have to keep secrets, whether natural or entrusted? In general, the answer to that question is merely a particular application of something that we have already seen, i.e., the conflict of rights: my right to have a secret kept confidential can come into conflict with the difficulties you have in trying to keep it secret. First, the obligation to keep something secret ceases if the matter of the secret becomes otherwise known. This is obvious enough. Next, the obligation also ceases if the consent of the owner can reasonably be presumed for its revelation, in accord with the rules for excusation from duty that we have already seen. No one, for instance, can reasonably be expected to keep a somewhat ordinary secret at the expense of his or her own life. In general, if my right to do something which involves the revealing of the secret is stronger than your right to have the secret kept, then I may reveal it.

However, two comments need to be made on this general principle. (i) A more serious reason is needed to release one from the obligation to keep an entrusted secret than would be required in the case of a natural secret. The reason for this is the contractual nature of the entrusted secret. It is possible for one to promise not to reveal a secret even under severe hardship; if one does this, then that promise must be kept. (ii) A matter not strictly proper to ethics, but of interest anyhow, is the question of the entrusted secrecy of the Confessional. That secret is absolute--it is, in fact, perhaps the only case of the totally absolute secret that can be cited. Something revealed in the secrecy of Confession may never, for any reason or in any circumstances, be revealed to anyone, unless the penitent gives explicit permission for this. It makes no difference how severe the hardship may be that is involved in keeping it (even death itself). There are no exceptions to this; the contractual duty a priest has to safeguard such a secret remains under all conditions--period.

(d) Means of keeping secrets

Under certain circumstances, then, I can have the obligation to keep something secret. What means can legitimately be used to do this?

The most obvious way is simply to keep silence, to refuse to answer a question about the secret matter. However, there are times when this will not work; sometimes, "silence means consent," i.e., one can actually reveal a secret by refusing to speak of it. In such cases, gifted individuals can resort to evasion, i.e., giving the questioner an answer, not to the question which he or she asks, but to some quite different question. Some people (politicians, for example) are quite adept at this; most of us, however, are not.

Another way of safeguarding a secret is mental reservation. In broad terms, a mental reservation is the limiting of the obvious sense of words to some particular meaning intended by the speaker. However, we have to distinguish between what is usually called a strict mental reservation and a broad one. A strict mental reservation is one wherein the particular meaning the speaker intends cannot be known by the hearer; no clue is given to the intended meaning. An example of this would be: "I didn't steal your car," when the intended meaning is, "I didn't steal your car on Sunday" (the theft having occurred on Monday). A strict mental reservation is simply a fancy name for a lie; its use is morally impermissible.

A broad mental reservation, on the other hand, is one wherein the limited meaning *could* reasonably be known (whether or not it is actually so known). A clue to the intended meaning is given, whether by how the answer is phrased, or by gesture, or by tone of voice, or even by the circumstances in which the broad mental reservation is uttered. Thus, a psychiatrist, questioned about a patient by a nosy person, might say, "I don't know"; he means—and, given the psychiatrist's professional standing, the nosy questioner should know that he means—"I don't know, by means of any knowledge that I can share with you." A broad mental reservation, used for sufficient reason, is a quite permissible means of safeguarding a secret. The phrase "used for a sufficient reason," however, is significant. One could not use broad mental reservation randomly, for no particular reason, without running into the same problems that the legitimacy of lying would generate: the level of trust necessary for communication (and hence for society itself) would quickly evaporate. There is question of using a potentially dangerous device here; there needs to be adequate reason for making use of it.

A subspecies of broad mental reservation is equivocation: the use of an expression that has a double meaning. If both meanings are legitimate in a particular language, and if the hearer could reasonably be expected to know about both (even if one is less commonly used or less obvious than the other), then, for sufficient reason, equivocation can be used. Thus, "This is my child" could mean, "This is my natural child"; it could also mean, "This is my adopted child." If the hearer incautiously presumes that one meaning is intended rather than the other, then that is the hearer's problem rather than the speaker's.

b) Second example: contracts

That, then, is one area of dealings which Citizen Smith has with his fellow humans in society. There are numerous others. One area of interest, though, is the means whereby a person acquires what he or she needs from fellow-citizens. For we have seen that one chief reason why humans band together into a civil society is so that one human can supply what another lacks (and vice-versa), with the result that both--or however many there happen to be in the process--can live a human life. Suppose, then, a particular person needs something, say, a house. Assuming that he or she is not a skilled builder, how to go about acquiring the house? One way, of course, would be to receive it as a gift from some kindly soul, perhaps a relative. Another would be to have a friend make it, simply on the basis of friendship. The most common way, however (since wealthy relatives and friends of that degree of benevolence are in relatively short supply), is to find someone who knows how to build a house, and make an agreement with that person--a *quid-pro-quo* sort of thing: if you build me my house, then I will give you such-and-so amount of money, or something similar. Since this is probably the most common way in which humans set about satisfying their needs, it will repay us to give some consideration to a transaction like this. And so we turn to the question of contracts.

(1) What a contract is

A contract, in its most broad sense, is a mutual agreement between responsible human beings whereby a transfer of rights is

279

effected. In the case of the builder and me, I agree to transfer the right of ownership over a particular sum of money to the builder, in return for the latter's performing a certain specified service for me (building my house).

(2) Elements of a contract

Now, we can distinguish several elements in all that is going on here. There are, first, the persons making the contract. Then there is the subject matter of the contract--what the contract is all about. And finally there is the manner in which the agreement is made. Some comments about each of these may be useful.

First, the parties agreeing to a contract. Since a contract involves the mutual conferral of rights, it follows that in any valid contract, those rights will have to be in the possession of those who plan to confer them on their partner. In the case of my getting the house built, I must either have the specified sum of money, or else have reasonable hope of being able to lay my hands on it when it is needed. If I am a complete pauper, with no financial resources whatever and no hope of getting any, I am simply not capable of entering into a contract with someone to build a house for me. Similarly the other party in a contract: if the builder does not in fact know how to build houses, or does not have effective control over people who do have that knowledge and who can do the job for him, then neither can he enter into the building contract in question. Moreover, since a contract is a voluntary mutual conferral of rights, it is an imputable act; consequently only one capable of placing an imputable act can enter into a contract. If I am drugged, or drunk, or otherwise incapable of placing a human act, I cannot make a contract with the builder, and any such "contract" which might seem to get made in such circumstances is invalid. If I happen to be a six-year-old child, I am incapable of making such a contract, as presumably lacking the use of reason necessary for doing so.

People can be incapable of making a contract for one of two reasons. Either they are, in fact, mentally incapable of understanding the terms of the contract at the time, and consequently cannot voluntarily enter into it, or else, in certain circumstances, a positive law of the state intervenes which declares them thus incapable. A sixteen-year-old might well be able to understand the implications of a contract, but he or she cannot enter into one since state laws (in the case of most states, anyhow) prohibit his or her doing so. The state, with its over-all concern for the common good, does have the right to declare certain categories of individuals incapable of taking on contractual obligations, even when otherwise they might be able to do so.

Then there is the subject matter. This can be a wide variety of things: goods, services, etc. Whatever it may be, however, it will have to have several characteristics. First, it must be something possible. I cannot give someone else the right to something, when that something is clearly outside the bounds of possibility. Next, it must be something that I am free to bind myself to, i.e., something whose disposition is not already prohibited by some prior obligation. I cannot promise (to take a somewhat bizarre example) to give someone else my wife, in the sense that she would become *his* wife, as part of a contract; my prior obligation to my wife (to love and cherish her as my own) stands in the way of this. Neither can the matter of a contract be something evil, something immoral; I have the prior obligation not to do evil, and thus am not free to contract to do so.

Finally, there is the manner in which the agreement is made. Specifically, the agreement must be a matter of mutual free consent, in which each knows what is involved and freely binds himself or herself thereto. One party must freely offer the terms of the contract, and the other freely accept them. Prior to that acceptance, either party is free to walk away from the contract; but once the acceptance has been made, then the contract binds and may not be broken except, again, by mutual consent (which is, in effect, another contract cancelling the first one). Obviously, fraud on the part of either party, or at least substantial fraud, voids the contract, for it deprives the other contracting party of the knowledge necessary for free consent. Again, since there is question of external actions, there must be some sort of externally manifested agreement; an assumed or implied consent is ordinarily insufficient to make a contract. The state, too, may legitimately require certain external forms to be observed before a contract can be considered valid; should it do so, then the validity of the contract depends on the observance of these external forms. Thus for example, it may be required that certain contracts be notarized for validity; in that case, without the notary's signature and seal there is no contract, even if all the other necessary elements are present.

Since there is question of the mutual giving of rights, a contractual agreement is one that binds in justice (usually, commutative justice). Ordinarily speaking, it must be fulfilled--though what has been said earlier about the excusation from the performance of duty applies here as well. If, in good faith, I contract for a house, and later on, because of unforeseen financial reverses, lose all my money, I am not morally bound by my contract (though, for other reasons, I may continue to be civilly bound), for no one can be bound to do the impossible.

(3) Validity and liceity

Two other characteristics of a contract are of interest to us; these are validity and liceity. A valid contract is one that is a true contract, one in which the mutual transfer of rights does in fact take place. A licit contract, on the other hand, is one in which I have the moral power to transfer the right in question: it is truly mine, and I may dispose of it as I wish. Simply by the laws of combinations and permutations, we can see that a given contract could be:

(1) Valid and licit: I have a particular right, and it is morally permissible for me to transfer it if I wish. The same is true of the other contracting party. The transfer of rights does in fact take place.

(2) Valid but illicit: it is morally wrong for me to transfer a particular right, although I have the physical power to do so; and I do in fact transfer it.

(3) Invalid but licit: I do not have a particular right, though I think that I do and I believe it morally permissible for me to transfer it; in fact, I do not transfer it.

(4) Invalid and illicit: I do not have a particular right, though I think that I do; I further believe that it is morally impermissible for me to transfer it, but I nevertheless attempt to do so. The transfer does not take place.

To illustrate: (1) If I have rightful possession of the necessary funds, the builder has the necessary skill, and we contract for the building of a house, then we have a valid and licit contract. (2) If I am using funds that I am not free to dispose of (e.g., those needed for observing prior obligations, such as the maintenance of my family), but which I do possess and do physically transfer to the builder, the contract is valid but illicit. (3) If I actually do not have (and cannot get) the funds, but I mistakenly believe that I do have them, and I go ahead with my agreement with the builder, the contract is invalid but licit. (4) If I actually do not have (and cannot get) the funds, but mistakenly believe that I do have them, but also am aware that those funds are committed to prior obligations, and if I nevertheless go ahead with my agreement with the builder, the contract is invalid and illicit.

If a contract is invalid, it simply is no contract, despite appearances; no right is transferred, and no obligation results. If a contract is illicit but valid, the transfer of rights does take place, with resulting obligations; in addition, the one guilty of the illiceity, being guilty of an injustice, is bound to make good the injustice to whoever has been wronged. And if a contract is both invalid and illicit, there is no contract, and the guilty party is obligated to make good the injustice to whoever has suffered it.

SUMMARY OF CHAPTER THIRTEEN

Living in a state involves actions dealing with (i) oneself, (ii) one's family, and (iii) others outside one's family.

(i) An instance of actions dealing primarily with oneself is the question of work. Labor, in general, at least conceptually evolves from a primitive barter system to a more complicated arrangement wherein a medium of exchange is used, initially for goods and later on for work. As factually the sole practical means whereby things necessary for life can be attained, work is a necessity of human life and is, for most people, practically a unique means to living. For most people, therefore, work is a human right and a human duty. The right (and the duty) to work, however, extend only to work in general, rather than to any specific job that one might prefer, excel at, etc. Work is, furthermore, a human dignity and a human excellence. Since work is a uniquely human sort of thing, it should be befitting to humans in its nature and in its conditions; a work situation may not morally be sub-human. There exists a right to a certain minimum wage (variable according to circumstances of time and place), i.e., that amount of money which is necessary for a worker to provide a decently human life for himself and those who depend on him; nor is this limited to mere subsistence or survival, but rather it extends to the level of living worthy of a human being. The right to work, however, carries with it the duty to work conscientiously and well, not merely as a metter of justice but as something required by work's status as a human dignity and excellence. Both employer and employee may legitimately enforce their respective rights, provided that this is done in a moral way. For the employee, unionization and collective bargaining are legitimate and can very well be matters of right (though not necessarily of duty).

(ii) An example of actions bearing on one's family is education, or that amount of intellectual and moral training that a person needs in order to live effectively within a given society. This varies according to circumstances of time, place, and culture. Parents have the primary responsibility for education, since this is a part of generation: the parents have caused the child--with its particular nature and therefore with its final goal--to exist, and thus are responsible for the fulfillment of that goal until such time as the child can assume responsibility for it. Parents may satisfy this obligation in whatever effective way they wish; if help is needed to accomplish this, it may legitimately be sought from whatever source the parents wish. While the state has a legitimate interest in education (it has the right to educated citizens, at least to a certain degree), state-sponsored education is not a unique means to the formation of citizens, and therefore the state has no exclusive right to determine what education will be. If parents fail in their duty, the state may step in (for it does have a legitimate interest), but the basic right is still with the parents; the state can legitimately ensure only that parents use some effective means, not any particular one, toward fulfilling their obligations. Private education is a means which parents may legitimately use; no state may legitimately outlaw it, since it--as also public education--is simply a means that parents may utilize. The state does have the right to set standards of education, based on its own needs, and it has the right to outlaw the sorts of "education" that would be inimical to itself (though not those whose viewpoint is merely different from its own). The state, however, has no obligation to support private education, since it has no obligation to provide alternate means to those which it normally offers for the effective achievement of its ends. Moral education, too, is the primary responsibility of the parents, as also their duty. To provide higher (college or university) education cannot be said to be the duty of either parents or state if such education is beyond what is minimally required for the living of a human life. While a state may require that some of its citizens have higher education, no one individual can be said to have a strict right to this; for any given individual, higher education is a privilege rather than a right.

(iii) Two examples of actions bearing on people outside one's family are truthfulness/confidentiality and contracts.

(a) Truthfulness is defined as "speech in accord with one's mind" and lying as "speech contrary to one's mind"; "speech" here means any sign (word, gesture, look, shrug, etc.) that I use to communicate my thought or my judgment. Speech must be the intentional communication of meaning; thus it can take place only with another human. A lie differs from an error in that in an error I communicate a judgment which I believe to be true (but which is in fact not so); in a lie, I communicate a judgment as if it were true, whereas I know that it is not. Similarly, a lie differs from a deception, since the latter does not involve speech, i.e., an intended communication. Conventional speech (an expression which, taken literally, has one meaning, but which by common convention has a quite different one) is not a lie; neither are such things as story-telling, fiction, figures of speech, etc. The morality of lying is judged from the consequences that would ensue if it were morally acceptable: society would be rendered impossible, since it requires communication and the latter requires confidence that the communication is trustworthy.

Confidentiality, or the keeping of a secret, deals with a truth that one has a duty to conceal. There exists a right to secrecy, in general, because humans are individuals as well as members of a society; they have private and personal dealings of their own which society has no need (and therefore no right) to know in order to fulfill its goal. A moral person, too, has the right to secrecy. A natural secret is one dealing with a matter that is private by its very nature; an entrusted secret, one which a person makes an explicit promise to keep secret. The obligation to keep secrets ceases (in accord with the principles governing the conflict of rights and duties) when the secret becomes otherwise known, or when the permission of the owner of the secret can be reasonably presumed. A more serious reason is needed to release one from an entrusted secret than from a natural one because of the contractual nature of the secret. The secrecy of the Confessional is absolute, and admits of no exceptions. Means of keeping secrets are: silence (when this is feasible), evasion (answering not what a questioner asks but some other question instead--which some gifted individuals can do), or mental reservation. This latter is a limiting of the obvious sense of words to some particular meaning intended by the speaker. In a strict mental reservation, there is no way that the hearer can reasonably know of the restricted meaning; a strict mental reservation is simply a lie. In a broad mental reservation, that restricted meaning could reasonably be known (even if in fact it isn't); a broad mental reservation can, for sufficient reason, be used to safeguard a secret. Equivocation, or the use of an expression which has a double meaning, can legitimately be used if both meanings could reasonably be known by the hearer.

(b) A contract is a mutual agreement between responsible human beings whereby a voluntary transfer of rights is effected. As regards the persons in a contract: the rights to be transferred must actually be possessed in the first

284

place, and their transfer must take place by means of an imputable act; someone incapable of understanding the terms of a contract, or someone prohibited by civil law from undertaking a contract, cannot enter into one. The subject matter of a contract must be something possible, something I am free to bind myself to, and something at least morally indifferent. The manner: a contract must be a matter of mutual free consent (and hence fraud invalidates a contract, since adequate knowledge is lacking to the consent); ordinarily, there must be some external sign of the contract, since there is question of external actions. Certain other formalities may be required for validity by civil law. A contract binds in (usually commutative) justice, though excusation is possible in certain instances. A valid contract is one that is a true contract, one in which the transfer of rights does take place; a licit contract, one in which I truly have the moral power (the right) to transfer the rights in question. Thus, a contract can be valid and licit, valid but illicit, invalid but licit, or invalid and illicit. An invalid contract is no contract at all; an illicit one imposes on the guilty party the obligation to make good the injustice involved.

14. LOOKING TO OTHER CIVIL SOCIETIES

III. The Practical Part of Ethics
    C. Our relationship with others
        3. The state as a society
            c. Humans amid societies
                1) Environment
                    a) Meaning of the term
                    b) Human influence on environment
                    c) Morality of environmental issues
                        (1) Unique human relationship
                              to environment
                        (2) Types of environmental questions
                            (a) Individuals
                            (b) Collectively
                2) International justice
                    a) The problem
                    b) Seeming helplessness
                    c) Obligations
                        (1) Knowledge
                        (2) Doing something about it
                            (a) Individual differences
                            (b) Voting
                  d) An international society
                      (1) Desirability in theory and in practice
                      (2) The United Nations
                3) War
                  a) What a war is
                  b) Kinds of wars
                  c) Morality of wars in general
                      (1) The "why" and "how" of war
                      (2) The "just war" theory
                      (3) Actual morality of a given war
                d) Nuclear war
                    (1) Dimensions of wars in general
                    (2) Special characteristics of nuclear war
                    (3) Morality of a nuclear war
                        (a) Limited war
                        (b) Total war
                    (4) Morality of possessing nuclear weapons.

c. Humans amid societies

We have seen some practical applications of general principles that touch any human being living in a particular society. And yet there is a certain arbitrary quality to being a citizen of any given state: the fact that someone lives in one society rather than another is more a question of accident of birth than anything else. And the question arises: even apart from the particular society in which a person actually lives, are there obligations which that person has toward *any* society, whether he or she is an actual member of it or not? In other words, does the individual have any obligations toward countries other than his or her own? Do I, as an American, have any obligations to the people that live in Africa, or Iran, or Australia?

There are several areas where this becomes a real question. We will consider three of them. The first is the thorny question of the environment. Then, there is international justice. Finally, there is the matter of war.

1) Environment
a) Meaning of the term

First, then, the environment. The term is used in a deliberately broad sense here, referring to the general physical surroundings in which we live. It refers to the air we breathe, the cities or towns we live in, the earth we walk on, and so forth. Ours is a shared environment, one that in at least some respects we have in common with all of the people of our own nation, and all of the people of the entire world as well. For example, our weather is something that affects us as individuals; it also affects our entire nation, and it at least can affect everyone on the globe. If we do something to affect the weather (cloud seeding, for example), we are not the only ones affected--for good or ill. Our environment is shared in another sense too: future generations will need to make use of it just as we ourselves do, and any permanent changes we make in it will have impact on those who come after us.

b) Human influence on environment

It would be emphasizing the obvious to say that humans can influence the environment. We do it every day. Sad to say, our influence on the environment has not always been particularly beneficent. We have polluted our air, fouled our streams, poisoned parts of our earth. Not that we have done so deliberately or of set purpose; in most cases, it has been through carelessness, whether culpable or otherwise. But we have managed to do it, for whatever reason. Of course, we are also capable of exerting a benevolent influence on the environment: we can and sometimes do re-forest our timberlands, clean up our lakes and streams, etc. However, we also do harm to things that are not as easily repaired. We use up (at an alarming rate) the natural resources of our lands--oil, for example, which cannot easily be replaced: dinosaurs and other fossils are just not all that easy to come by. We experiment with things that are said to have an effect on the ozone layer of our planet, something that is incapable of repair, as far as we know.

c) Morality of environmental issues

We do things to our environment, in other words, which can be repaired. We also do things that cannot. Is there any question of morality in all this?

(1) Unique human relationship to environment

A deeper question underlies this. What is the relationship between humans and their environment, and what responsibility do they have for it? For, if we look closely at the matter, we see some opposing trends of reasoning. On the one hand, it seems that everything on the face of the earth is for the sake of humans, in order to help them achieve their last end. This follows from the fact that, apart from humans, everything on the face of the earth is going to achieve its last end, no matter what; there is simply no way that the finality of sub-human things can be subverted. Human beings, however, are another matter entirely. They either will or will not achieve their last end, depending in large measure on how they use other things in the world surrounding them. Of all the beings on earth, they alone can lose their final end. Since the achievement or non-achievement of that last end depends on their use of other things, it follows that humans have a right to that use. On the other hand, it is equally true to say that *all* humans have the same last end, to be achieved in the same way. Thus, the use of all other things on the earth is a common right--common to every human now living, but also common to every human that will eventually come into being in the future. We can, rightfully, use the things of the earth. But we cannot necessarily use them in such a way as to deprive other humans--present or future--of their use.

The adverb "necessarily," in that last sentence, is used deliberately. For some things, of their very nature, are destroyed by being used. Other things are quite durable, and will withstand a good deal of use and even abuse. Finally, yet other things are fragile by nature: they can be used, and if they are treated carefully they will continue to exist and offer use to future generations; on the other hand, if treated roughly, they are destroyed. Of each of these three types of things, humans have need.

(2) Types of environmental issues

Let us look first at the morality of an individual person's use of his or her environment. Later on, we will examine the situation where humans use their environment collectively.

(a) Individuals

If, in the nature of the case, something is consumed simply by being used, well and good; if one has the right to use it, then one has the right to what that use implies, i.e., to consume it, to destroy it. If others also need it, and if it can be replaced, then there is some obligation to do so, of course; a right to use (and to consume) does not automatically contravene someone else's right to use, when there is question of something common. On the other extreme, if something can hardily withstand abuse as well as use, then there is no particular moral problem in our using it. But if something is capable of being preserved through careful use and of being destroyed by careless use, and if that something is required by more than one person for the achievement of the final end, then the obligation exists to use it in such a way that it is not destroyed. Alternatively, the obligation exists to restore it after its destruction.

Some examples may help to make all this clearer. If our physical surroundings are such that, if used, they will necessarily be destroyed, fair enough; as has been said, if their use is necessary, then their destruction also is. An example would be animals that are grown for food. If food of a particular kind is to be had, then certain animals will have to be destroyed. On the other hand, since other humans also have a need for food, there is some obligation to see to the birth and rearing of other animals (or to see to the production of some other source of food) which can serve the purposes of those other humans; the obligation, obviously, can be satisfied in a number of ways, direct and indirect. On the other end of the spectrum we have things that can withstand use and abuse alike. Air must be breathed to sustain life; but, though there is an intermediate process of chemical change involved, there are sufficient plants, trees, etc., which take in carbon monoxide and release oxygen that the air we breathe can be considered hardy enough, as far as simple human respiratory use is concerned. Little if any moral problem is involved here.

Many other things, however, fall into that intermediate area, wherein if we use them carefully, they will satisfy our needs, without at the same time being destroyed in the process. If we use them carelessly, they will still satisfy our needs, but they will be destroyed. An obvious example once more involves the air around us, but this time in a different sort of use: if, for instance, I am a factory owner, I can, if I wish, simply let pollutants roar out the top of my smokestack. I can also go to the considerable expense of installing filters, and thus cut the pollutants to an acceptable level. Or, if I own a chemical plant, I can simply dump my toxic wastes in some out-of-the-way place. I can also spend a fair amount of money and dispose of them safely. Morally, I am bound to go the more difficult route, because breatheable air and an inhabitable earth are common possessions, not things that are exclusively mine to do with as I wish.

The examples in the previous paragraph, however, are a little too easy. Suppose my factory pollutes the air, but not in such a way as to make it unbreatheable--it merely makes it less pleasant for others than it otherwise might be. Or, the waste from my chemical plant makes the surrounding area less beautiful and salubrious than it otherwise might be, but it is still habitable: what are my obligations then? In such a situation, I have a conflict of rights: my right to make a legitimate profit comes into conflict with others' rights to completely pure air, to beautiful and healthful countryside. The ordinary rules that govern such conflicts are operative. Quite often, we will find ourselves in the area of prudential judgment; and it is likely that the ultimate decision-maker will end up being civil law.

This sort of situation can extend beyond the boundaries of any one country, of course. What if the atmospheric pollution generated by individuals in one country infringes on the right of those of another country to enjoy a clean and pure atmosphere (as happened, for example, in the case of the acid rain that Canadians experienced as a result of Americans' industrial efforts south of the Canadian border)? Again, we have at least a conflict

291

of rights situation, probably capable of being settled only by civil law or its equivalent--in this case, international treaties. One cannot automatically assume that one side or the other is in the right in such cases; individual judgments have to be made, taking into account the particular circumstances of each situation.

As is clear enough, an individual's moral duties in the matter of environment are not terribly complicated--in theory. The problem, of course, comes when we try to reduce them to practice. If we are thinking about only acts over which we have complete dominion, there is no major problem: clearly, we should treat our environment with some care, conscious of the fact that it is a common possession rather than something to which we have a sole right. Thus, for example, littering the countryside is impermissible (unless there is a sufficient and compelling reason for it), for others have a right to a decent-looking physical surrounding in which to live. The matter is, as we have noted, one of rights and duties, governed by the same rules on those mutually related items that we have already seen. But it is worth stressing that matters such as these are in the domain of commutative or legal justice; they are not merely items that pertain to some sort of civic benevolence or public-spiritedness. That is to say, they carry true moral obligation with them.

(b) Collectively

The area that causes real problems, however, is the one where our dominion over the environment (and our pollution thereof) is something that we share with others, and usually with many others. My automobile, for instance, may not cause a great deal of pollution; but when it is joined by thousands of others, the result is smog. My gold mine may do negligible damage to the beauty of a mountain countryside; but what happens when there are a lot of such mines? The result is devastation.

And worse. What happens when an entire nation, perhaps through its defense effort, pollutes the environment in a serious and perhaps irreparable way? Or when a state (or country), in pursuit of nuclear sources of electricity, also produces large quantities of radioactive material, which will be around to cause trouble for thousands of years? Worse yet: what happens when (or, more accurately, if) the collective pollution of a country or group of countries irreparably damages the ozone layer? Examples could be multiplied, but the point is clear enough: when humans are collectively responsible for environmental damage, what responsibility does the individual have to repair that damage?

The obligation in such a case is clear: repair the damage. Also clear is the identity of the individuals who have that obligation: everyone who caused it. But at that point clarity vanishes. For quite often, not everyone who is responsible for damage is willing to repair it; and, on the other hand, it seems a bit much to say that only those who are willing to do so have the obligation to make good the damage that has been caused. They are, indeed, responsible for their share of the damage; but they are not responsible for it all. And yet, if the damage is to be repaired, all the responsible parties must make it good; even though a given individual is willing to satisfy the claims of justice, he or she alone simply cannot do so.

In such a case, we have to fall back on principles that we already know. No one can be obligated to do the impossible; thus, no individual member of a society is obligated to repair the damage which that society has caused, since to do so would be far beyond his or her means. On the other hand, if I have a justice obligation, and am unable to meet it completely, it does not ordinarily follow that I am therefore excused from the entire obligation. Rather, I am required to make good that part of the obligation which is within my power. In the case of environmental damage caused by an entire group (a state, a nation), then, I am obligated to do whatever I reasonably can: to take such measures as are realistically in my power to halt the damage and to see that no further damage is done. These measures, of course, will depend on the individual circumstances in which I find myself; and their concrete form will be determined by a prudential judgment. For example, active participation in environmental groups may or may not be possible (or--for that matter--desirable, since many such groups are more noted for their enthusiasm than for their effectiveness). Or, political lobbying may or may not be possible for me. But whatever realistic contribution I can make to the correction of a communal injustice of which I am a part, I must make--even though that contribution may not, in the long run, prove terribly effective. Otherwise, I simply abandon a very real responsibility I have to my fellow humans--and to the future of the race.

2) International justice

In seriously considering the question of his or her personal responsibility for the human environment, a person often feels a real sense of helplessness. The questions and problems are so large and so complicated that the temptation simply to shrug them off as being insuperable is very great indeed. And if this is true as regards the environment, it is more so in regard to other matters.

a) The problem

For example: we know from the radio and TV that there are millions, indeed tens of millions, of persons who suffer from hunger and a lack of the basic necessities of life. That same radio and TV will bring us news of thousands upon thousands of persons who are suffering injustice or persecution in their homelands. Tales of assassination squads in South America are commonplace. Terrorism raises its ugly head increasingly throughout the world. There are reports--which there seems to be no realistic reason to doubt--of what are euphemistically called "human rights violations" in many areas: in less laundered terms, there are murders, torture, and heaven knows what else going on in our world. In our own country of the United States, there are instances of racial repression and discrimination--which, though no one thinks that they should be ignored, are almost "small potatoes" when compared with some of the other things going on elsewhere on the globe. Entire nations live in slavery. Intellectual and moral freedom is something that is a precious commodity indeed in a large percentage of the population of the earth.

b) Seeming helplessness

Our reaction to all this is likely to be: yes, these are evils, and serious evils. But what in the world can I do about them? More to the point, what am I, as an individual, *obligated* to do about them? I have precious little control over juntas in South or Central America, Kremlin leaders who enslave millions, and Iranian terrorists who have the peculiar idea that the surest way to heaven is to blow up people and institutions of an opposing ideology. Given the size and complexity of these problems, the temptation is strong merely to shrug one's shoulders, and leave the solutions--if any--to others.

c) Obligations

To do so, however, is to abdicate one's humanity. We have noted earlier that there is more to living in a society than merely justice relationships; there are also the very real obligations of charity. And that applies to the wider society of humankind in general every bit as much as it does to any particular society we could name.

Or, to put matters bluntly, it *is* the concern of every human being that others are starving, are enslaved, are deprived of basic freedoms and needs. It is everyone's concern that there exist such things as exploitation, selfish interest leading to the oppression of men and women, murder, torture, and all the rest of it. For the human beings who are on the receiving end of all this unholy activity share with each and every one of us a common goal, and are therefore deserving of our fraternal love. If truthfulness is to have any meaning, they must have that love--and, presumably, have it in some sort of efficacious way. For fraternal charity is not mere pious sentiment; it is something that has to be shown in deeds as well as in words and thoughts; otherwise--whatever else it may be--it is not charity at all.

Noble sentiments, all these. And no one, in all likelihood, would quibble with them--provided they are left peacefully and safely in the theoretical order. But how in the world is one to reduce them to anything like effective practice?

Once again, an ethical obligation cannot extend beyond the ranges of possibility. We must do only that which we can do. But the whole question is, what can we do?

Perhaps a great deal more than we might think. As earlier stated, simply to abandon these problems is to abdicate one's humanity. Granted that these are immense problems, far beyond the capability of any individual person to solve. None the less, they are human problems, and must be solved by human means.

(1) Knowledge

The first obligation that would seem to be possible and realistic is that of knowledge. If I have an obligation in charity to assist my neighbor in his or her troubles, then I certainly have an obligation to know about those problems, in whatever depth and scope I can. That is to say, I have the obligation to study such problem areas, to whatever extent I have the means and the ability to understand them. Again, this is not something that might be nice to do, diverting to do. It is something that is obligatory on me, as a responsible human being who has the duty in charity to care for my neighbor. Nor is this an obligation that I can leave for others to fulfill; I have the obligation as well as they. Nor is it enough for me to become aware of my neighbor's problems. I also must do what I can to learn the causes and probable solutions to those problems, to whatever extent I reasonably can.

All this is merely saying that, as far as my neighbor's needs are concerned, I have the obligation to be informed. A caution is needed here. I may not reasonably just abandon this to the experts. If experience has taught us anything, it is that such experts are not necessarily likely to be useful, dispassionate guides. If anything, they are likely to be quite the opposite, or at least can be so. I have the obligation to form my own conclusions on these matters, for they concern duties which I have. For each individual, the method to be used in forming those conclusions will differ, obviously: for some, reasoned belief will be the best that can be achieved; for others, first-hand knowledge; and for the vast majority of us, somewhere in between. But for none of us is lethargy and indifference a morally acceptable alternative.

Knowledge, of course, is a reasonably safe, harmless thing that generally does not cost us very much. And so, even when the obligation to be aware of our neighbor's situation impinges on our consciousness, it is a duty that is scarcely impossible, or even necessarily difficult. At this stage of the game, doing what we are obligated to do is still relatively easy.

(2) Doing something about it
(a) Individual differences

The scope of the obligation, however, extends further than that. For, armed with such knowledge of our neighbor's problems as we have (by whatever means) acquired, we must then do something about them. At this point, it becomes difficult to speak in general terms. For each person's ability to act on his or her knowledge will differ. There are those who are in a position to take effective action, once they have learned what, in charity, must be done. They have one set of obligations. Then there are those, on the opposite extreme, who are in no position to take any sort of action--and these, let it be said candidly, are very, very few in number. Most of us end up in the middle, at various places depending on our own circumstances. Some of us, to give a concrete example, find ourselves holding stock in a corporation which we know to be fostering oppression somewhere in the world. The duty becomes rather clear in such cases: to do whatever is possible to ensure that this oppression ceases.

(b) Voting

Certainly, the vast majority of us find ourselves able to vote for national officials, if nothing else--which officials will set the policy that the country will follow in matters pertaining to problems like these. From a moral point of view, that a responsible person would fail to vote in such elections is incomprehensible. Less intelligible still, morally, is how (as is in fact the case) a significant part of the electorate can fail to go to the polls. Whatever be a given individual's personal judgment as to the nature and cause of the world's evils, the fact remains that the greatest single instrument that we have for influencing the course of world affairs is the officials that we elect. It is commonly said that the right to vote is a privilege. In the light of the duty that we owe in charity to our fellow human beings, the right to vote is a good deal more than that. It is a duty, and a very serious one.

d) An international society
(1) Desirability in theory and in practice

It is commonly said that the world's problems--our neighbors' problems, to avoid the comfortable abstraction--cannot be solved on a national or regional basis, and that therefore there is need (indeed, a moral requirement) for some sort of world state, a sort of super-nation that would embrace the whole human family. Certainly, if such a thing could be effectively brought about, it would solve many of the problems that bother us. But that is a very large "if." For the moment, it can only be considered an open question whether such an arrangement would be either feasible or desirable; all too often, in the rush of extolling the good things that such a universal society could accomplish, we give insufficient thought to the evils that it could also bring in its train. Humans have thus far not been notoriously successful in establishing and humanely running smaller states, and it is not at all clear that they yet have the ability to do so on a much larger and more comprehensive scale. The concept of a world state that is at the same time a totalitarian one is, to put matters softly, at least a daunting one. If a universal state could be established, and could be guaranteed as being reasonably abuse-free, then certainly it would be desirable in terms of solving world problems. However, it is unlikely that the "if" clause can be assured at any foreseeable time in the future of the human race.

(2) The United Nations

In this connection, a word or two about the United Nations might not be out of place. This organization, begun in the latter half of the 1940's, aimed at being at least the start of the sort of world state that we have discussed. Its mission has been to be at least a sounding board where world problems could be discussed and, hopefully, solved. Its success in its mission has been at best marginal to minimal. World problems are indeed discussed there; and this is a benefit. Solutions to a few of the world's problems, at least, have originated there. And, on balance, it can perhaps be said that it is better to have had the U.N. than not to have had it--though there are thoughtful people who will say that it is not much better. Its shortcomings, indeed, do seem to have outweighed its merits by a considerable margin, and one wishing to point out its failures will not be lacking in ammunition. Yet, whatever be its faltering history (and even more doubtful prognosis), it does represent an attempt on the part of humankind to address its collective ills on something wider than a merely national basis. That attempt, certainly (whether in its present incarnation of the U.N. or some other) is deserving of the support of thoughtful humans who, while realizing the magnitude of the problems which fraternal charity demands that they somehow make their own, nevertheless also realize their own individual insufficiency and helplessness.

3) War

The next area of dealings between a citizen and some other state is a melancholy one, but one which needs to be examined for all that. This is the matter of war. It is an area that has to be examined with some care, for it is one in which emotions (dislike, revulsion at the very idea, etc.) can cloud the judgment. No one likes (or at least should like) the idea of war; it is a terrible thing, perhaps the worst thing that humans have come up with in their long and checkered history. But that fact does not dispense us from the moral need to have clear ideas about it.

a) What war is

First of all, the word "war" is used somewhat loosely in contemporary society; and so it will pay us to define exactly what we mean by it. As used here, then, the word means a hostile act (or series of acts), carried out by authority of the state itself (in the person of the highest officials of the state), against some other state, involving the use of some degree of force, with the intent of imposing the state's will on the enemy. More briefly, war is the state-sanctioned use of violence against some other state in order to subjugate it, in one way or other.

We should notice immediately that there are numerous common uses of the word "war" which do not fit this definition--and which, therefore, are not being talked about here. There is, for instance, the metaphorical term "war of nerves"; since no actual violence is involved, such a "war" is not a real war except by dint of metaphor. Another example: the "cold war" between Russia (and its allies) and the countries of the western hemisphere. Again, this is a war only in a figurative sense of the term. So also, a "war" carried on against terrorism, or a "war" against drug traffic, etc., are not truly wars. Even a "civil war" is not, properly speaking, a war, ordinarily (but is, rather, a rebellion).

b) Kinds of wars

There are different kinds of wars, even within the narrow sense of the term. A defensive war, for example, is one waged with the purpose of repelling some aggression against a state. An offensive war, on the other hand, is waged in order to inflict an aggression on some other state. Notice that the term "aggression" is, in itself, a neutral one; there can be good reasons for engaging in aggression, and the term itself merely means, etymologically, a "moving against." The terms "defensive" and "offensive" should be kept quite separate from the terms "just" and "unjust" when there is question of war. In principle at any rate, it is possible to have a war that is defensive and just, defensive and unjust, offensive and just, offensive and unjust. The term "just war" means simply one that is waged for a sufficient reason and in a moral way, whereas the word "unjust war" is reserved for one that is carried on either for an insufficient reason or in a manner which violates justice--or both.

c) Morality of war in general

Let us first consider the whole question of the morality of war in general. Then we will look at the special case of the morality

299

of modern war, particularly nuclear war.

(1) The "why" and "how" of war

In days gone by, war was a reasonably simple thing, at least conceptually. An entire state, of whatever size, threw virtually all its resources into defeating some other state. In such cases, we can ask two pertinent questions: why was it done, and how was it done?

In asking the "why" question, we first have to realize that war is a very serious evil, perhaps the most serious evil of which we have experience. But: it is a *physical* evil, not necessarily a moral one. It causes damage; but it is not, by that fact alone, impermissible or immoral. Lots of things cause damage and are justifiable, as we know from the Principle of Double Effect. The simple fact of war's being destructive does not, in and of itself, rule it out as being morally acceptable.

The fact that war does cause physical damage, however, and sometimes immense physical damage (to property, to lives) suggests that the reasons for its being permissible (the "why") are going to have to be quite serious ones indeed. The fourth condition of the Double Effect Principle alerts us to this: a strongly sufficient reason will be required in order to permit the evils that war inevitably brings in its train. However, once given those reasons, the morality of war is no different from that of the legitimate use of self-defense. War is, in fact, merely a form--the most drastic form, to be sure--of self-defense that the moral person that is the state can engage in. Immediately we know something about the legitimacy of war, since we already know something about the legitimacy of self-defense: if something less than war can be used to solve the problem in question, then it must be used and war in turn cannot be morally justified. This is merely an extension of the principle that we have already learned: force may be used against an unjust attack only to the extent (and to the degree) that it is required to repel that attack.

None the less, historically there have been situations in which the alternatives presented a given state have been stark and clear: either wage war, or else submit to an enemy. Nothing less than a war will suffice: every lesser alternative (negotiations, intercessions of third parties, etc., etc.) has been tried and has failed, and now only one alternative remains apart from simple surrender. In such cases, a state has to be mindful of the basic reason for which it exists, i.e., to provide its citizens the sort of surroundings in which they can live a human life. If a potential enemy will--at least very likely--not allow a state's citizens to do so, but will rather plunder, rob, and kill them, then the state is faced with the necessity of using a unique means to achieving its own goal. Put briefly, it must go to war, or else it will be untrue to its own nature as a state.

Then there is the question of "how" a war is waged. We have already seen that an individual, having the right to use force to repel an attacker, may nonetheless be guilty of moral wrongdoing if he or she either uses excessive force, or else uses force in an unacceptable way. The same is true with the state, when it is in the position of having to use force to maintain itself. It is possible for a state to use too much force in war, or to use it in an immoral manner. An example of the latter would be a state's decision simply to kill all the inhabitants of another state against which it was waging war--whether or not those inhabitants were part of the war effort against it. Even a right may be wrongly exercised, either by an individual or by a state.

(2) The "just war" theory

Since war is such a tremendous evil, it is not surprising that a good deal of thought has been given to its morality (or lack of it). Perhaps the most famous effort in this direction has been the "just war theory," a doctrine that was developed over the course of many centuries, beginning perhaps with St. Augustine in the fifth century, given its classic formulation by St. Thomas Aquinas in the thirteenth, and developed and commented on by numerous individuals since then. We can perhaps most easily look at St. Thomas's formulation of the doctrine *(Summa Theologiae,* II-II, q. 40) for a typically clear expression of it. He states that three things are required for a just war: it must be waged under the aegis of the supreme power within a state (its government--a thing already hinted at in the definition of war with which we began this section); there must be a just cause (i.e., the defense or vindication of a strict right); and the persons waging the war must have a rightful intention (e.g., securing peace, righting a wrong, promoting the common good--but not simply exacting revenge, seeking merely to inflict harm, and the like). To this classic formulation, one other thing can be added from general moral theory: the means of war must be used justly (e.g., force must be used against the right objects: military personnel and not civilians, ammunition dumps and not orphanages).

(3) Actual morality of a given war

It is probably only in the conceptual order that such a thing as a perfectly just war has ever existed. In the real world, people often operate with mixed motives--while there may be the rightful intention of vindicating a nation's right to something, there also may be present the intent of acquiring further territory by means of the war; while perhaps the majority of an army's soldiers use force justly, there will be occasional Mi Lai incidents and other atrocities. A real war, as opposed to an idea of war, can be called just only in a relative sense of the term: it is preponderantly more just than it is unjust.

d) Nuclear war

All of this classic theory on the nature and morality of war, however, became at least somewhat dated when the atomic bomb was dropped on Hiroshima and Nagasaki in 1945. The coming of atomic weapons in that year, and the development of them in the years since that time, have raised a new and quite unparalleled set of questions about warfare. And so we need to spend some time on an explicit consideration of nuclear war.

(1) Dimensions of wars in general

Of course, wars have varied in their scope and complexity all throughout history. There have been wars restricted simply to two tribes in some given area. There have been wars fought between two (and only two) nations. Other wars have involved several nations, with alliances and choosing of sides. It seems to have been reserved for our own century to witness the grim spectacle of truly global wars, i.e., wars in which the preponderance of the major nations on the earth were involved. Even these were not total; there were neutral nations even during the Second World War. Moreover, wars have always varied in the amount of physical damage that they have caused. A tribal war may have resulted in little more than the burning of a small group of towns or hamlets--serious damage, certainly, to the inhabitants thereof, but not terribly significant when compared to the destruction of entire cities that occurred from 1939-45. None the less, prior to 1945 humans were at least mercifully limited in the amount of destruction that they could wreak: weapons had only so much power, and there were limits on the number of weapons that could be used to do that damage.

(2) Special characteristics of nuclear war

Now, however, a nation which possesses nuclear weapons has the means to do untold damage, far greater than ever before in history. It is not exaggerating matters in the least to say that, for the first time in history, humans now have the means to obliterate themselves totally, and to render the earth an uninhabitable wasteland.

It is precisely this factor that makes a contemporary discussion of war different from any that might have been held prior to Hiroshima. The possibility of physical damage from war is now virtually unlimited.

That damage, should it ever occur, is unique in quite another sense too. For it involves the future as well as the present, and does so in a way that may well be irreparable. Radiation poisoning of the atmosphere, genetic mutations in humans and other living beings (if there are any left): all these--or at least their possibility--are part and parcel of the increased ability of doing damage that the era of nuclear weapons has brought with it.

(3) Morality of a nuclear war

Unfortunately, however, the level of rhetoric about nuclear weapons seems to have developed at about the same rate that the weapons themselves have. And so we are told, as some sort of nuclear gospel, that nuclear weapons are immoral in themselves, that war is no longer permissible for any reason, that even the possession of these weapons is illicit, and so on and on. Some or all of this may be true; some or all of it may be false. None of it is self-evident. And so there is need to examine closely the morality of the use of nuclear weapons.

The first distinction that has to be made is between that which is immoral and that which is repugnant. The mere fact that we do not like something (and perhaps quite justly so) does not thereby render it immoral. Neither does the fact that something has terrible destructive potential and we are afraid of it. If the use of something is properly to be called immoral, it will have to have the same characteristics which other immoral acts have and which

303

we have already seen: it must be contrary to human nature, fundamentally irrational. And it must be shown to be so.

Basically, the same criteria for judging the morality of a nuclear war apply as for a non-nuclear one. If there is to be such a thing as a just nuclear war, it will have to be one waged between two or more states, one waged for a just cause, waged with a correct intention, and waged in a just manner. The nature of war has not changed, simply because humans have discovered new and more horrible ways of waging it. In a nutshell, the only real difference that has to be taken into account concerns the fourth of the classic criteria, the requirement that it be waged in a just manner. And the precise question to be asked is this: given the immense evils that nuclear weapons can cause, can the fourth step of the Double Effect Principle ever be verified? Can there ever be sufficient reason for using such weapons, i.e., a proportionality between the evil that will be done and the good that might be achieved by their use? If so, then a nuclear war could be waged in a just manner. If not, then nuclear war must be judged to be immoral.

Let us distinguish four cases: (i) a limited nuclear war (one fought for specific objectives, contained within certain limits), and one wherein the goods to be achieved are of the physical order: territory, possessions of one sort or other; (ii) a limited nuclear war, but one fought for spiritual goods: freedom, the right to live in peace and without the threat of imminent aggression; (iii) a total nuclear war (one in which each nation who possessed these weapons threw everything it had into the fray), and one wherein the goods are of the physical order; and (iv) a total war, where the stakes are of the spiritual order.

(Let us note something first. Is a limited nuclear war even a possibility? For would not the losing side, if it had the capability, escalate the war to whatever degree was necessary in order to win? The answer to that question is two-fold: (a) there is a difference between whether something could happen and whether it would happen; and (b) the decision to escalate a limited war to an unlimited one is a separate imputable act, with its own morality; at least for purposes of consideration, there is no need to assume that such an escalation would have to take place, whatever the degree of likelihood that it might. At all events, a limited nuclear war is a possibility, even if an unlikely one; and therefore its morality can be considered and judged.)

(a) Limited war

(i) In the first of our four cases, the damage that would be done in any given limited nuclear war could be estimated with a fair degree of accuracy, and thus one could reasonably make a judgment about whether a sufficient reason for the use of this amount of force is present or not. No general rule can be given, since the circumstances of each case would differ and would have to be taken into account individually. But, in principle, such a limited nuclear war could be permissible, if the good to be achieved is high enough--a matter of prudential judgment, but clearly something within the range of possibility.

(ii) If a limited nuclear war fought for material goods is permissible in principle, then *a fortiori* so is one fought for spiritual goods, if, again, these are of sufficient importance.

(b) Total war

(iii) An all-out nuclear holocaust would very likely do just what everyone is afraid that it would do: wipe out the human race, either immediately or else as a result of radiation sickness and atmospheric pollution; and certainly, large parts of the earth would be rendered uninhabitable--almost a moot point, paradoxically, since there probably would be no one around to inhabit it anyway. At all events, it is extremely difficult to imagine any single material good or any aggregate of goods that would counterbalance the inflicting of such an evil; and thus, such a war could only be termed morally evil. No sufficient reason for tolerating it can be imagined.

(iv) The very sticky question, however, is the one concerning an all-out war in which the stakes are spiritual ones. If my choice is either to use nuclear weapons in this way, or else to be enslaved, to have all my freedoms taken away (along with those of my countrymen), and the like: this is very much harder. In the preceding case, the measure was a quantitative one: a certain amount of good and evil on one side, a certain amount on the other; which side has the greater amount of good or evil? In this case, however, our question is not quantitative but rather qualitative. On the one side, there is the evil of total physical destruction, including that of life itself. On the other, there lurks the evil of loss of freedom, enslavement, and so on. Of these, which is to be preferred?

(To be sure, the "loss of freedom" question can be a matter of degree: the threat of total enslavement is one thing, whereas partial [or temporary] loss of freedom is another. And this factor too would have to be weighed in the moral equation. The discussion which follows assumes total enslavement, as a limiting case. Partial enslavement might well alter the conclusion; but the outlines of the argument would follow the same general direction in any event.)

From a theoretical point of view, the question is probably unanswerable, at least by means of natural reason alone. At the very least, attempting to answer it is an instructive exercise in intellectual humility.

Suppose that we say that a war like this is morally allowable. That can only be because the good to be achieved outweighs the evil to be incurred. We already know what that evil is. The only good that can outweigh a massive physical evil like this is a good of a higher order. Now, we know that human life is not the greatest single value in the world, and that this is true whether we are speaking of an individual life or that of the entire race. There are higher values, perhaps the most obvious of which, in this discussion, is freedom. Thus, if the morality of an all-out nuclear war is to be demonstrated, it can only be because the preservation and vindication of human freedom--the prevention of universal enslavement--outweighs even the good of the possession of life.

That line of reasoning, however, involves some serious difficulties. Freedom's victory, in such a case, would be a Pyrrhic one indeed. What would freedom mean, if there is no one left to be free? In familiar terms, freedom would be both a goal (the sufficient reason for whose attainment immense physical evil is tolerated) and not a goal--for something which is a goal for no one (there being no one left to use it) is not a goal at all. That, of course, is a contradiction.

Suppose, on the other hand, that we say that such a war is not morally allowable. It is granted that one's realistic choices seem to be an unfree life or no life at all--a "lesser of two evils" situation, perhaps, but the best that one can do under the circumstances. None the less, no realizeable goal (and hence no real goal or good) can be said to outweigh the immense physical evil involved, and consequently the fourth step of the Double Effect Principle can never in principle be verified. Thus, all-out nuclear war, even for spiritual goods, is immoral.

But there is a problem with this, too. For in this view, we end up saying that whatever nation has the greater physical might will--*and must be allowed to*--prevail. But this comes remarkably close to saying, not merely that we *may*, morally, accept being treated unjustly (something that we have seen before), but that we are morally *obligated* to do so. That would mean that it is unjust to resist injustice, that we have a moral duty actively to acquiesce in evil. It would also mean that we both have a right to self-defense (as we have seen before), and simultaneously that we do not have a right to self-defense (since we are morally obligated to acquiesce to a physically superior force). That looks suspiciously like a contradiction.

What all this means, of course, is that natural reason alone does not seem to be capable of answering the question of the morality of an all-out nuclear war fought for spiritual values. Admittedly, this is not a very sayisfying position. Each of us, of course, may have his or her own preferences in the matter. But that is subjective. It is in the objective order that we are faced with an insoluble problem. It is cold comfort, but perhaps the comment should be made that there are a fair number of areas in our lives wherein we are unable to determine the correct answer to something and, if action be necessary none the less, we must rely simply on prudential judgment. This is merely one more such. As we have seen, prudential judgments can be correct or they can be erroneous. If nothing else, the nuclear debate ought to lead us to a greater level of tolerance for a viewpoint opposite to our own, for there is at least the possibility that it might be just as good as--or perhaps better than--our own.

Two further comments on nuclear war ought to be made. First, the conclusion that the previous paragraphs reached is deliberately phrased: the morality of such a nuclear war is one that does not seem capable of being definitively decided by the unaided human reason, at least at present. It can be judged, from a prudential standpoint. But such a judgment carries no assurance of accuracy·, for it involves a large measure of individual preferences, and these are not capable of being rationally analyzed and determined. All this, however, is not to say that the question could not be decided, by given individuals, on other grounds (i.e., on knowledge gained from other sources, probably authoritative ones). And so what we have said thus far should not be read as necessarily disagreeing with individuals or groups who claim access to such authoritative knowledge and thus claim the ability to answer the question. There are such groups, ranging from the far-out to the normally staid United States Catholic Bishops' Conference. We disagree with the conclusions of none of these; we merely say that, in order to reach the conclusions they do, they have to have access to some source of knowledge other than the unaided human reason. Such sources are quite conceivable, in principle; however, they are not the proper concern of ethics.

(4) Morality of possessing nuclear weapons

Secondly, a comment on the question of possessing nuclear weapons (as opposed to using them). It is sometimes said that even the possession of these powerful tools of destruction is immoral. Moreover, it is also claimed that the weapons themselves are intrinsically immoral, evil. What should we say about this?

The latter point first. No *thing* is either moral or immoral. Things, as such, are morally neutral. The only time the question of morality arises is when there is the case of a human being's using that particular thing. That use can be moral or immoral, good or evil. But the thing itself is neither moral nor immoral. Nor can one say that nuclear weapons are intrinsically evil in themselves. No creature is intrinsically evil. On the contrary, as an existing being, it is in itself a good. It partakes of being, and therefore it partakes of all the transcendent qualities that are found wherever being is found: unity, truth, goodness. Again: moral good and evil are proper qualifications of actions, not of things.

Then there is the question of the act of possessing nuclear weapons. In and of itself, their possession is legitimate enough. If their use can be moral (and, as we have seen, there can be moral--albeit distasteful--uses for them, e.g., a limited war), then their possession is moral. Their possession could become immoral, however, if the only way they could be acquired was through injustice: depriving others of something that is rightfully theirs, as would happen, for instance, if a government spent virtually all of its resources on acquiring such weapons, while depriving its citizens of things that they have the right in distributive justice to expect from the state. The possession of nuclear weapons could also become evil for another reason, i.e., if the mere fact of their possession were to give rise to the possibility (and likelihood) of their indiscriminate use. However, possession would become immoral in this latter case only on the supposition that no adequate means of controlling their use were available--a condition not easily verified in a modern state.

To say--as some do--that weapons as dangerous as these should not even be possessed is frankly unrealistic. They *are* possessed, and that state of affairs is not likely to change in the foreseeable future. It is also unproveable, again as far as the unaided human reason is concerned--which, as has been said, does not obviate the possibility of its being proveable by some sort of higher knowledge. In the latter case, however, it is at least reasonable to expect that proponents of such a view would explicitly identify their sources.

SUMMARY OF CHAPTER FOURTEEN

Three questions serve as an example of the area of relationships among societies.

(A) Environment (the general physical surroundings in which we live) is something that we share with others who live on earth, and also with those who will come after us. We are capable of using or misusing it. While it is true that a human must use the things that surround him or her in order to attain the final end (and thus each has a right to that use), it is also true that every human being must do so, and hence environment is not simply a personal prerogative. In our individual use of the environment, some things are destroyed by being used; other things can withstand both use and abuse; still others can withstand use, but not abuse. Of the first of these, one may legitimately use (and therefore destroy) them, though the common need for them dictates that they be replaced in some way if possible; of the third, the obligation exists to use them in such a way that they are not destroyed, or else to replace them if they are. In many cases, use of one's environment will involved a conflict of rights, to be settled according to the principles governing such conflicts. In the case of collective use (and abuse) of environment: one is obligated to repair damage to a common possession (the environment), but only to the extent that this is reasonably possible in a given case: i.e., the obligation exists to repair damage to the extent that this is within the individual's capacity--something that will vary with each individual's circumstances.

(B) Problems in international justice (hunger, oppression, etc.) are the legitimate concern and moral duty of every human being. Though ethical obligations arising from these problems cannot extend beyond what each person can reasonably do, the duty of personal awareness is incumbent upon all; and each is bound (in charity) to take such further measures as his or her individual circumstances make possible. If an international society, a sort of world-state, could be set up in such a way as to be virtually abuse-free, it might serve as an effective vehicle for solving global problems; the possibility of its being thus established is, however, open to serious question. The U.N. represents one attempt at problem-solving on a more than regional or national basis, though its success leaves a good bit to be desired.

(C) A war is a hostile act (or series of acts) carried out by authority of the state itself, in the person of the state's highest officials, against some other state, involving the use of force, with the intent of imposing the state's will upon the enemy. A "just war," whether offensive or defensive, is one waged for a sufficient reason and in a moral way. A sufficiently strong reason is required (by the 4th step of the Double Effect) to justify the evils that war brings with it; apart from that, war is simply an instance of justifiable self-defense on the part of the moral person that is the state, and is subject to the conditions justifying self-defense. If all else fails, war can be a state's duty. The "Just War Theory" states that (i) war must be waged under the aegis of a state's supreme power; (ii) for a just cause; (iii) with a rightful intention; (iv) in a just manner. In actual practice, a perfectly just war is non-existent, and a "just" war is one that is preponderantly more just than unjust. Nuclear war presents special moral problems because of its potential for unprecedented, and virtually unlimited, damage, both in the present and for future generations. The question is again one of sufficient reason: in a (conceptually possible, at least) limited war fought for physical goods, in principle a nuclear war could be justified in a given case; a fortiori, the same is true for a limited war fought for spiritual values. A total nuclear war fought for physical goods could not be justified, since no physical goods would outweigh the damage that would be caused. The question of the morality of a total nuclear war fought for spiritual values does not seem to be answerable by natural reason, since it seems to involve either a contradiction on the positive side (freedom would be rescued, but there would be no one around to enjoy it--in which case what would freedom mean?), or the unacceptable consequence that one is morally obliged to acquiesce positively in evil, and that there simultaneously is and is not a right to self-defense. A prudential judgment can be made on the subject, but there is no guarantee of accuracy. The possession of nuclear weapons is, in itself, moral, since there can be a moral use for them and since only actions, not things, are properly qualified as moral or immoral; their possession could be immoral if the sole way they could be possessed was by injustice, or if their possession guaranteed their indiscriminate use (an unlikely consequence).

15. HUMANS AND GOD

III. The Practical Part of Ethics
  D. Our relationship to God
    1. What we can know about God
      a. How we know anything about God
      b. What we know about God in himself
        1) Indivisibility
        2) Possession of whatever
           perfections creatures have
        3) Goodness
        4) Ubiquity
        5) Unchangeableness
        6) Eternality
        7) Possession of knowledge
        8) Life
        9) Love
        10) Freedom
        11) Personality and uniqueness
      c. What we can know about God's actions
         toward us
        1) Creation
        2) Providence and governance
    2. Obligations that all this entails
      a. Knowledge, gratitude, acknowledgement
      b. The moral life.

D. Our relationship to God

We now turn to the final area we have to consider. We have looked at some of the relationships that we have to ourselves, and the obligations that follow upon them; and we spent some time examining the relationships we have with others (humans and non-humans) with which we share the earth. There remains the relationship that we have to God. Is there such a relationship? If so, what is it, and what obligations does it entail? And, how are we supposed to know about it--and them?

Again a reminder of what we mean by the word "God": we are talking only of the first uncaused cause, whose existence we discovered in Chapter 6. We are not speaking on religious grounds at all. There may, indeed, be relationships to God (and consequent obligations) that are known through religion; but they are not the business of ethics. Because of ethics' method, we are limited to what we can discover by the unaided human reason; and in our discussion, we will respect that limitation.

311

1. What we can know about God

The first thing to do is to take stock of what we know. We have seen in Chapter 6 that there exists a first uncaused cause. And we know that that cause is pure act. Thus far, that is all we have seen, at least in any detail. That is not a large store of knowledge, and so perhaps the first order of business will be to discover what else we can know about God. There, too, a distinction can be helpful: there are some things we can know about God, considered just in himself; and there are things we can know about his activity toward us. Once we have gathered together everything that we can know about God, then we can explore what obligations we might have in his regard.

(Throughout this book, some care has been taken to avoid the exclusive use of masculine pronouns when referring to human beings in general. Stylistically, this can be done, though it is occasionally awkward. However, when we speak of God, we will see that neither the masculine nor the feminine pronoun is particularly appropriate; a distinction of sexes is something that is found only on the level of creatures [humans and sub-humans]. On the other hand, it seems a bit much to refer to God as "it"--for this implies a lack of personality which we are not warranted in affirming. Now, while one can, with difficulty, juggle two pronouns as the subject or object of a sentence, to attempt to do so with three is to enter into the absurd. Thus, out of a sense of desperation if nothing else, we will refer to God in these pages as "he"--rather than he/she/it. Apologies are hereby proffered to those to whom this is offensive; unfortunately, human language, like humans themselves, is a necessarily fallible thing.)

a. How we know anything about God

What, then, can we know of God? Right at the start, another question has to be handled first. *How* do we know anything about God? For our knowledge of him is somewhat different from our knowledge of other things.

When I know, say, a baseball, how do I do it? I pick it up, hold it in my hand, feel its hardness, its leathery surface, note the stitching, guess its weight, etc. I may also ask someone what is inside it (or, if I am the adventurous type, I may just undo the stitching and see for myself). I observe what it is used for--what it can do and what it cannot do, and so forth. I can, if I wish, research the history of baseballs, and learn yet more about them.

Obviously, however, I do not come to know God in this way. It does not follow from that fact that I cannot come to know him at all; rather, it merely follows that the method of direct experience will not work in his case. On the other hand: I know about a lot of other things through methods other than direct experience, too. For example, I know that there are millions and millions of stars. How do I know this? Certainly, I have never seen them, or at least all of them. I know this because others, who have access to the appropriate scientific equipment and information, tell me that they exist; and I have no particular reason to doubt them. I know a great number of things in this way--through human faith.

Then again: I personally have never seen Moscow. How, then, do I know that there is such a place? One way, as we have just seen, is to accept the word of those who have been there. Another way is to turn on the short-wave radio and tune in Radio Moscow. Here, I am coming to know about something's existence simply by witnessing its actions.

But I can know more than simply existence in this way. Suppose I am walking down the street one day, and in the middle of Main Street I see a large blue cube, which is glowing brilliantly. And suppose that I have never seen anything like it. But I know at least two things about it. I know that it exists (by my direct perceptual experience of it). I also know that, whatever in the world it is, it is at least such that it is able to give off a radiant brilliance. That, of course, doesn't tell me a single thing about what the cube is in and of itself. After all, if the only thing I knew about a human being were that he or she can make sounds, I wouldn't know anything at all about what a human being is in itself; I'd merely have experience of something that it can do, and I could conclude that, whatever it is, it is at least such that it can emit sound waves. As we shall see, our knowledge of God will work along much the same lines.

Of what we shall call "causal knowledge" (Radio Moscow, the blue cube), at least two things are true. (i) In some cases, I do in fact get to know something about the nature of the cause in question. For example, by knowing a son, I can know something about his father--even though I have never met the father--and I can, furthermore, know something about that father's nature. I can know that the father is a human being, for one thing. I can know (with reasonable certainty, anyway) something about his

313

racial status, and perhaps even something about his physical attributes. That is to say, I can know something about his essential nature, and even something about his accidental characteristics. The reason for this is that I know that, barring miracles, only a human being can generate another human being. And so, given the fact that only such-and-so cause can produce a certain effect, then, if I am given the effect, I automatically know something about the nature of the cause. (ii) But there are other instances where this is not true. Suppose that any one of five different kinds of things can produce some particular effect. Then, given that effect, I know only that the cause has to be one of the five--I don't know which one. I am then limited to saying merely that the cause has to be such that it can produce this particular effect; I have no notion of what else it could cause, or what it might be in itself.

Our knowledge of God belongs in this latter category. For all of our knowledge of him is causal knowledge. And there are all sorts of effects that he has caused, some of them differing vastly in their essential natures: rocks, zebras, humans. All I know here is that God must be such as to be able to produce these effects. But what else he can do, and what he is in himself, I simply do not know.

In a sense, this is not surprising, and for two reasons. (i) Any cause, of which I have direct perceptual experience, always works by activity, and that activity is not identified with that cause's nature. A man makes a tool, say, by carving it. The activity of carving is not the same as human nature; humans can do a great deal more than just carve wood. Or, a dog generates puppies. But the activity of generating puppies is not identical with being a dog; otherwise, the dog would have to be generating ceaselessly--which, fortunately for the SPCA, is not true. In general, every cause of which we have knowledge is distinguished by this fact: its causal activity is not identical with its nature. To put it another way: to act in some given way is not the same as to exist; "to exist" is a much broader term.

In the case of God, however, we have quite another situation. For, as we have already seen (and will see further), there can be no distinctions in God, no differences between activity and essence. If there could be, then the one (essence) would stand to the other (activity) in the relationship of potency to act; and we have already seen that there is no potency in God.

(ii) Secondly, when we reflect on human experience, we realize that there has to be some sort of proportion between a knowing power and the object which is known. If the object surpasses the knowing power, then knowledge cannot take place. For instance, if a light is too bright for the human eye, then seeing does not take place (rather, physical damage does); if a sound is too loud, hearing does not occur (damage to the ear does). I do not hear a tone that is voiced at 350 decibels. I might hear a noise (among the last things that I ever do hear), but I do not hear that tone. The object that is to be known has to be proportioned to the power that is to know it. Now, our intellects are finite; of this, little proof needs to be given: the number of things we can learn is limited, by the amount of time available for us to learn if by nothing else. But God, as pure act, is infinite. And so it follows that, since there is no proportion between the finite and the infinite, not only *do* we not know God as he is in himself--a fact of which we are aware by experience--but we *should not expect to*. In and of himself, he is not proportioned to our intellects; he is unknowable by us, directly. (Or, to run all this the other way: if we could know what God is in himself, then, as an object of our intellect, he would have to be proportioned to that intellect, i.e., finite. But a finite God would just not qualify as being pure act.)

It is usually said that we know God only by analogy, in and through our knowledge of creatures. For general erudition, if for no other reason, we should perhaps spend a little time on the notion of analogy, so as to understand why our knowledge of God is termed analogical. The idea of analogy is not terribly complicated. Suppose, in the first place, I have two items, a book and a rug, each of which is brown. (To simplify the discussion, let us grant that they are the same shade of brown.) Now, the word "brown," when applied to both the book and the rug, means exactly the same thing. It means that both items emit light waves of a certain specified frequency, which waves, when reacting on our sense organs (our eyes), produce the sensation that we call "brown." It is true that the book is brown, and it is true that the rug is brown. *And* it is true that they are both brown in exactly the same sense. "Brown," in this usage, is said to be an "univocal term": it means the same thing in both cases.

Now let us take the word "pen." If I say that something is a pen, I might mean that it is something I can use to write with. I might also mean that it is a place I can use to house pigs. Here, the meaning of the two words is completely different and unrelated; it is only by an accident of language that I use the same word to mean two quite disparate things. "Pen," in such a case, would be an "equivocal term." Another example might be the word "fire," when, in the one case, I mean to ignite something ("Fire up the engine!"), and in another to discharge an employee. The same letters and the same pronunciation, but

315

totally different meanings.

However, I can also have the situation where a word, in two or more different uses, means partially the same thing and partially something else. The standard example, which will do for our purposes, is "healthy." I can say that you are healthy, that this food is healthy, and that your complexion is healthy. In one sense, I am talking about the same thing in each case: a certain state of well-being in a human. But in the first case, I mean that the item in question possesses that state of well-being; in the second, that it causes that state; in the third, that it manifests that state. A word like this, wherein the meaning in different uses is partially the same and partially different, is said to be an "analogical," or "analogous," word.

Now, when we speak of God, we are said to be using analogy. Why? Suppose we take the expression, "God acts." Our knowledge of what "to act" means, of course, comes from our observation of humans and other creatures acting; and, as we have seen, activity is always distinct from essence on that level. In God, activity is not distinct from essence. And thus, the term means partially the same thing when we speak of a creature and of God acting: in both cases, we mean that an agent is producing some sort of effect. But it is also partially different: in one case (creatures), an agent is producing an effect by an activity that is distinct from its essence; in the other (God), the agent is producing an effect by an action which is identical with its essence. And in general, whenever we say that God is something, or is doing something, we are always speaking this way: for the source of our knowledge is always creatures, and we predicate our statements on how they do things. How God exists, and how he acts, are always quite different from how a creature does so, simply because of the constant presence of potency and act in the creature and the total lack of potency in God. Put briefly, when we say that a creature acts, and when we say that God acts: *what* happens is the same in both cases (i.e., an effect is produced); *how* it happens is different in each case (by activity distinct from essence, by activity identical with essence). And so we have only analogy, or analogical knowledge, as our sole means of knowing God.

That is probably enough on the question of *how* we know anything about God. Perhaps we could summarize it this way: we have no direct perceptual experience of God; we know him only through causal knowledge. However, we do not know him through the sort of causal knowledge that would give us knowledge of what he is in himself. Furthermore, our knowledge is also limited in that it is only analogical knowledge. Knowledge by analogy is

316

true knowledge, but it is also limited knowledge.

b. What we know about God in himself

Turning, now to *what* we can know about God, and first of all to what we can know about him in himself (i.e., without reference to his actions toward us): a number of things about God follow from just two items--the principle of efficient causality, and the fact that God is pure act (and consequently that there is no potency to be found in him). It can be shown, for example, (1) that God is undivided, (2) that he in some manner possesses whatever perfections that creatures have, and (3) that he is good. It can also be shown that he is (4) everywhere, and that he is (5) unchangeable and (6) eternal. It will also be true that (7) he possesses knowledge. God can be shown to be (8) living, (9) loving, and (10) free. Finally, God can be shown to be (11) a person, and (12) unique. We will spend a little time on each of these characteristics, both to see why it is true to say that God possesses them, and also to see in what sense he possesses them.

1) Indivisibility

(1) First, God is undivided, without parts of any kind. We have already seen this, in passing. But let us include it explicitly and perhaps more fully here. Obviously, we are not speaking of material parts (arms, legs, etc.); we have already seen that matter implies potency, and there is none of that in God. Rather, we mean that there is no division of *any* kind to be found in God: there is no division between his intellect and his essence, between his will and his essence, between his activity and his essence, between his existence and his essence. For God, to act is precisely the same thing as to exist; to know is the same as to exist; to will is the same as to exist; and to exist is the same as to exist as God. To call all this difficult to imagine is to belabor the obvious; but it has to be the case. In the first place, whenever a being has parts of any sort, those parts have to stand to one another in the relationship of potency to act (at least, they must do so if the being is to be one being and not many); and that is impossible in the case of God. Then too, whenever there is question of parts, one can always ask what puts them together, i.e., what is the cause of their being united. That, however, would be to ask what is the cause of God--who, as ultimate cause of all beings, himself has no cause.

317

2) Possession of whatever perfections creatures have

(2) Next, God somehow possesses all the qualities ("perfections," technically) that creatures have. That he does so is obvious: he caused them in creatures, and therefore is such as to be able to cause them--which is merely another way of saying that he has the perfection in question (for no one--not even God--gives someone else something that he doesn't have). The adverb "somehow" is important here, though. For it would hardly do to say, without qualification, that God has color, for example. Only material bodies have colors, and God has no material body. Some perfections (size, shape, color, etc.) by their very nature imply the presence of potency; others (wisdom, knowledge, etc.) do not. Perfections that do imply potency are said to be found in God "virtually"--which means that he is able to cause them. While God does not properly have the perfection of color, he does have some higher perfection which enables him to cause the lower one. An analogy may help here. Suppose someone asks me whether I have a $5 bill. I don't--but I do have a $50 bill. Strictly speaking, I do not have the five-dollar bill. What I've got is something considerably higher, something that can do everything a $5 bill can and a good deal more. So also with God, in the case of perfections which of their nature imply the presence of potency. Other perfections, which do not imply potency, can be said to be found in God properly; thus it is perfectly correct to say that God is wise, is alive, etc. There is, though, always this difference between the perfections found in God and those found in creatures: God's perfections are possessed as identical with his essence; again, there is no division in God. Human perfections are distinct from essence; to be wise is not the same as to be human (otherwise all humans would be wise, which is evidently not true). And so on.

3) Goodness

(3) When we say that something is good, we ordinarily mean that it is desirable: it has a certain perfection to it, it has everything that it ought to have. Thus, a car is good if it is what a car is supposed to be: a smoothly running, efficient means of transportation. A house is good if it is all it should be: a comfortable, adequate means of shelter. Now, God must possess every perfection that exists, for otherwise there would be some perfection of which he is not the cause; and this cannot be the case. For the proof for the existence of the uncaused cause,

though it uses a particular perfection as a starting point (my own acquisition or a substantial or accidental form, for example), also works equally well for *all* changes, the acquisition or loss of any form or perfection of any type. Thus, no perfection can be cited that escapes God's causality, and therefore there can be no perfection which he does not have. Moreover, presumably God would be in potency to acquiring whatever perfection he did not have; and that, also, is not possible. Now, anything that contains all perfections certainly meets the criterion for being desirable, and hence for being good.

(Here is where we usually encounter the standard objection: if God is good, how can he either cause or at least allow evil? Entire books have been written on this question, and neither space nor our present purpose allows our looking at the question very deeply. But two comments can be made. (i) God does not cause evil. Evil is the lack of some good that ought to exist; it is something that does not exist, and ought to. But it makes no sense to inquire about the cause of non-being; only beings have causes. The fact that we tend to reify evil, to think of it as something positive, something actually existing, does not change its actual status as a non-being. Of course, while evil may be a non-being, a lack of being, evil people and evil actions are certainly real enough. But locating the responsible cause of evil in that situation is much easier: the people who perform evil actions are the cause; God isn't. (ii) Why God allows evil is, ultimately, a mystery, in the strict sense of that word: something that we do not and cannot know. That isn't very satisfying, to be sure; but it can be shown to be true. To understand why God does [or does not do] something, we would either have to be told about it by him [which hasn't happened very often in any sense in which ethics would be interested], or else would have to understand him perfectly, thus rendering an explanation from him unnecessary. The latter, however, is not possible. If we understood God perfectly, then [since there has to be a proportion between a knowing power and the known object, as we have seen] either we would be God or God would be human or sub-human. Since we are not infinite and God is not finite, the sort of knowledge required to understand the "why" of evil is simply not available to us, unless God makes it so--which, apparently for reasons of his own, he has not seen fit to do.)

4) Ubiquity

(4) In saying that God is ubiquitous, or everywhere, we have

to remember that we are using that term in a somewhat loose sense. For the "where" question always implies bodies. Only corporeal things properly occupy space. To see this, we need only ask ourselves something like, "Where is an idea?" or "Where is beauty?" Strictly speaking, the proper answer to these questions is, "Nowhere," meaning it literally: no-*where*. An idea is an immaterial item, the product of the immaterial power of the intellect. We commonly say that we have an idea in our heads, but this is not strictly true. An idea occupies no space. "Beauty," as such, cannot be localized. We can point to a beautiful sunset, or to a beautiful picture, and say, "There is beauty." But, again, that is not strictly true. What we are pointing to is *a* beautiful *thing,* not beauty itself. The only way that it makes sense to speak of the location of an immaterial thing is to understand the term as referring to where that immaterial thing's *activity* is taking place. That, sometimes, can be localized (though not always). I might say that my ideas are located in the words on this page; but what I really mean is that the result of my ideas' activity is located there. For my ideas caused the physical words, which are indeed located on the written page. But my words, not my ideas, are what are literally located there.

With that in mind, we can see how it is true that God is everywhere. For God is the cause, by his activity, of the being and activity of every creature, in whatever place. And wherever his activity is, there also is God--in, again, a loose sense of "there."

5) Unchangeableness
6) Eternality

(5-6) God's being unchangeable and eternal follows directly from the fact of his being pure act without potency. For change, as we have seen, is the transition from potency to act--which means that there has to have been potency present in the first place, and this is not possible in the case of God. God's being eternal follows from his unchangeability, although the word "eternal" needs to be understood carefully. It refers to something which has neither a beginning nor an end. If God had a beginning, he would have undergone a change, from non-being to being; on the other hand, if he had an end, again there would be a change, this time from being to non-being. Neither of these possibilities is reconcileable with his being pure act. (Incidentally, we might note too that God is not properly said to be in time either, any more than he is properly said to be in a place. Time is the measure of duration and of change, and God does not change.) The notion that a being could exist neither in time nor in place is a difficult one for us to get our minds around, and understandably so: all the items of our direct experience *are* in time and place, and we have no precedent for anything that might exist otherwise. Well and good, but this is a statement about the limitation of our experience and our knowledge, not about the possibility of something's having existence in a manner to which we are not accustomed.

7) Possession of knowledge

(7) Does God possess knowledge? Obviously; he causes it in us, and therefore must possess it somehow. Again, however, the "somehow" is significant. For God possesses knowledge in a way that is consonant with his being--which is merely a fancy way of saying that the knowledge God has is perfect knowledge (since, as we have seen, he possesses all possible perfections). It is also true to say that, since there is no composition in God, no difference between his knowledge and his essence, God *is* knowledge, or, as it is usually stated, he is "subsistent knowledge."

What does God know? Everything possible, everything that can be known. It is contradictory to say that there is something which God has yet to learn, for, once again, being able to learn would imply the possibility of a change in his essence. Neither could there ever have been a time when God did not know everything, for the same reason (not to mention the baffling fact that, as we have seen, God is not in time in the first place). One might raise a verbal objection: fine, God knows everything that he can, since he cannot learn; and he has always known everything that he can. But could there be something which he could not know--something to which he simply is not in potency to know? Such a thing, at least, would not run up against the objection of placing potency in God. However, apart from the obvious reply that God would not in that case possess every possible perfection, this would also mean that there is something that God does not cause, which as we have seen is not possible. But even the idea itself is contradictory. For if the item in question were intelligible, it could be known; that is what "intelligible" means. If it could be understood, it could be understood by God. If, on the other hand, it were unintelligible, then God could indeed not know it. But neither could it exist, since there would be no cause to know it and bring it into existence in the first place. And out of all this the interesting corollary emerges: in itself, every being is intelligible (although it may or may not be intelligible *to us).* That fact perhaps sheds a little more light on why evil is so difficult to comprehend--for it is non-being, thus carrying with it no guarantee of intelligibility.

8) Life

(8) The same sort of argument we used before can be used to prove that God possesses life: he caused it in others, therefore he has to have it himself. Again, we have to remember that he possesses life in a way that is proper to his own essence--that is to say, there is no distinction between God's essence and his life. He is, to use the technical term once more, subsistent life.

A point worth noticing, though, is that "life," as a perfection, is somewhat different from a perfection such as "wisdom." We can separate being human from being wise; they are not identical, as we have seen. But even in human beings, it is only conceptually that we can separate "life" from "existence": if a human is to exist *as a human,* then he or she must be alive. Life is an essential part of being a human; a non-living "human" is simply not a human, whatever else it may be. The same is true of all living things. For them, no realistic distinction can be drawn between existence and life: when a living thing--any living thing--dies, it goes out of existence as the type of being that it was, although some non-living residue may continue to exist. A dead tree is not a tree any more, though a certain amount of wood remains. Since life, as a perfection, is properly found in God, the same characteristic will be true of God's life: it is inseparable from his existence. However, God is subsistent life, whereas other living beings are not.

9) Love

(9) In showing that God is a loving being, we first have to demonstrate that he possesses a will. That is not difficult; will is something that God causes in us, and so he also must possess it. The perfection of willing is not one that of its own nature implies the presence of potency, and so it is one that can be said to exist properly in God (i.e., we are saying that God possesses a will, not some higher perfection that could do whatever a will can do and more besides); and, as is always the case, God possesses that will in a manner that is proper to his nature: his will is

identical with essence; he is subsistent will as well as subsistent life and subsistent intelligence.

Proving that God has a will, however, is not quite the same as proving that he is a loving God. For there are other will acts apart from love: desire, for example, or hope. When we are said to love someone or something, what does that mean? In general, it means that we wish good to someone or something else: we esteem him, her, or it highly, and we wish the object of our love to enjoy the best possible set of circumstances. However, we can do this for at least two reasons: either because we ourselves hope to derive some profit from our act of love, or else in a sort of disinterested (not, however, *un*interested) fashion: we simply wish a person or thing "all the best" just for his, her, or its own sake, and because we happen to think a lot of that person or thing. For instance, I might love my Porsche because of the sense of power and influence its possession gives me--and I wouldn't love it if it didn't provide me with those benefits. On the other hand, a husband loves his wife, not *because of* any good that the wife can do him (even though he does, in fact, benefit from such good), but rather simply for her own sake--and he would love her even if she could do him no good whatever (as, for instance, in the case of a husband's love for a wife who has been a helpless invalid for many years).

Now, we have already seen that God possesses all perfections. One consequence of this--unflattering for the human ego, perhaps, but none the less true because of that--is that God doesn't need us. His own state of perfection, and his enjoyment of happiness (the possession of the perfect good--himself) are quite complete, and have no need for the existence of human beings in order to be everything that they ought to be. And yet, God does in fact create creatures, giving them existence and, in some cases, life. To humans, God gives a particular kind of nature with a special goal, as we have seen. This can only be because of love on his part. He is subsistent will, but the only will act that makes any sense on his part is love. Possessing all perfection, he could not be said to hope for anything, or to desire anything. Moreover, even love makes sense, when predicated of God, only if we are speaking of the sort of love that is not interested in gain on the lover's part, but rather only in the good of the beloved. Put briefly, since God doesn't need us, then if he does create us, it can only be because of love, and a love that looks solely to our own good.

(10) Freedom

(10) Given what we have already seen, it takes little effort to

323

prove that God is free. For we know that the will, by its nature, necessarily chooses a perfect good perfectly known; apart from that, it is free. Thus, while God could not but will himself (in the sense of taking pleasure in his own perfection, loving himself, and so on), toward anything less than complete perfection his will is free, just as ours is. Will is one of those perfections that are found properly in God, albeit according to his own nature; and thus it is fair to say that, granting the difference in being between God and us, none the less will is will, and what is true of the one is true of the other when we are speaking of the perfection as such.

These, then, are some of the things that we can know about God, simply from the causal principle and from the fact that God is pure act. Two other things follow from what we have just seen, however. In the first place, it has to be true that there is only one God. Secondly, it has to be true that God is a person.

11) Personality

(11) The latter point first, since it is simpler. A person, in the ordinary sense of the term, is a being possessed of intellect and will, a distinct individual with a particular nature. From all that we have seen, it is obvious that this is true of God.

12) Uniqueness

(12) But why couldn't there be more than one God? Isn't it possible to have two (or more) individuals who are pure act, one of whom, say, causes a certain class of beings, another causes another class, and so on?

In a word, no. We have already seen that one of the consequences of God's being pure act is that he possesses all perfections, and in perfect degree. Were there more than one God, the interesting consequence would immediately present itself that both (or however many) Gods were all-powerful--and therefore had power over each other, i.e., were both all-powerful (as God) and yet subordinate to each other (as being subject to the other God's all-powerfulness). That, needless to say, won't work (as no contradiction will). And so, it turns out that God, as pure act and as possessing all perfections in highest degree, is unique. There is only one.

c. What we can know about God's actions toward us

What we have seen thus far are items that we can know about God, considered largely in himself, and without much reference to his activity toward us, except in an incidental sense. But there are two other areas wherein we can know something about God, and these are areas that bear on us directly. These are the areas of creation and providence/governance.

1) Creation

The question of creation will not delay us very long. We simply want to know what it means, and what it doesn't mean. Creation is quite different from change, even substantial change. For in change, there is always something which remains at both ends of the change. In accidental change, for instance, substance remains the same, though it acquires some different accidental modification. In substantial change, at least prime matter (the ability to receive different substantial forms at different times) remains the same at both ends of the change. In creation, however, we are speaking of the coming-to-be of some creature, when there was absolutely nothing--either substance or prime matter--before. Creation is therefore the making of something out of absolutely nothing: at one moment, nothing existed; at another moment, something is in existence. In trying to visualize this, we have to be careful not to make "nothing" into something real. It is just what it says it is, i.e., a total lack of being, the absence of being.

When we say, then, that in creation God produces the world, we have to be careful not to think that the "world" had some one form before God took it in hand, and then became the world as we know it after God was finished. Rather, what is going on is this: there was absolutely nothing before God began his work of creation; afterwards, there was the world.

As an aside, we should note that to say that the world was made by creation doesn't contradict modern theories of how the world came to be. Suppose that one wants to say that, prior to the formation of our world, there were simply gasses or inert matter of one sort or other; and our world was formed from these. It may have been so, and it may not; in neither case is it terribly important for our purposes. For the question always recurs: where did the gasses or inert matter come from? If one

325

wishes to adopt a theory like this, well and good; all that happens is that the question of creation shifts from the creation of the world as such to the creation of whatever it was (gasses, inert matter, whatever was involved in the "Big Bang" theory--if one wants to adopt that theory--, etc.), that the world was formed from. What is being said is that, at some point, there existed nothing; after that, the world (whether in its present form or in the form of gasses, inert matter, or whatever) did exist. And the moment that separated the non-existence of these things from their existence is what we call the moment of creation. For, causally, there had to be some point in time (really, some point which constituted the beginning of time) when the uncaused cause exercised his unique original creative action. This we know. Whether the result was the created world as we know it, or some much more primitive form of matter out of which the world would later be formed, is a matter of little consequence. What is important is that that moment had to exist; otherwise, we are saying that there always existed some finite being that was not dependent upon a cause--and this we have seen to be impossible.

A further thought on creation: is creation simply an act that took place long ago, at the beginning of time, or is it something that happens even in our own day? The latter. For, while the world as such--in whatever form--was created long ago, items still come into existence each single day which require direct creation by God if they are to exist at all. These are human substantial forms, or human souls. Given the fact (established, as we have seen, by an analysis of its activities) that the human soul is essentially immaterial in nature (or "spiritual," as it is commonly called), we can legitimately ask what its adequate cause is. Now, the adequate cause of something has to be at least of the same metaphysical order as its effect; otherwise we are faced with the situation of a cause's giving something which it does not have. Human parents, however, contribute only the physical part of their offspring to the generation process: sperm and ovum. They do not, in fact, contribute the immaterial part. Where, then, does the soul of the child come from? There can be only one answer, i.e., that that soul is created, and by a spiritual, immaterial being. But there is only one spiritual being capable of creation, and that is God.

2) Providence and governance

God, then, created the world, whether in its present form or in some more primitive one. Having done so, what does he then do with it? That leads us into the consideration of what is called in the classical authors "providence" and "governance."

By "providence" is meant the fact that God knows the final end or goal for which any creature is intended. By "governance" we mean that God provides the appropriate means whereby that end can be achieved.

Again, not a great deal of time need be spent here. We have already seen that, in assigning a particular type of nature, the author of that nature automatically assigns a certain type of goal or end. Since God is an intellectual being, it follows readily that he knows what that end is. Moreover, he must will that that end be achieved; otherwise, it is not an end, whatever else it may be. But if God wills the achievement of that end, then he also wills whatever means are necessary for that. Consequently, God exercises both providence and governance over his creatures.

One thing should be noticed, though. God does not simply create human beings and then, as it were, "turn them loose." If we think back to the proof for the existence of God, we remember that its conclusion is this: back of each and every change in the world stands the ultimate causality of God. We should not think of this "back of" in some sort of temporal sense, referring somehow to the past. Whenever any change occurs, whenever any action takes place (for action is always a change), God's causality is operative at the same moment that that change or action happens. Moreover, even the simple process of continuing to live is an activity, and as such always involves the ultimate causality of God at the same time as that activity is going on. What this means in less formal terms is that God not only created the world, at some time in the past, but also continues to sustain each of his creatures in being, at each and every moment of its existence. Were God to withhold his causality from any activity of any creature, that activity would not take place; and if the activity in question happened to be the activity of simply existing, that creature would cease to exist. This is perhaps the deepest meaning and significance of the divine governance of the world.

2. Obligations that all this entails

Now, in all of the paragraphs of this chapter thus far, we have been trying to see what the unaided human mind can know about God. It is only fair to say that, though we have touched upon the major things that can be known, we have nevertheless done exactly and only that: touched upon them. Any one of the things that we have seen could be expanded into a full chapter all by itself, and perhaps a good deal more than that. Our purpose, however, has not been to investigate all of these areas in some detail, but rather merely to see whether and in what sense they are things that we can know about God by natural reason. We have simply been trying to get a general idea of the subject, and that in preparation for asking the question to which we must now turn: granted that we can know certain things about God, what difference does this make in the moral life? In other words, what obligations follow for us, in the light of the things that we can know about God? Our purpose, after all, is ethics, not the Philosophy of God.

We can perhaps focus the question this way: we are autonomous, free individual human beings. What right has anyone—God included—to foist a code of ethics on us, a set of rules which we must observe? Even granting that the rules are derived from human nature, why should we obey them?

Another (and perhaps more classic) way of phrasing the question is this: granted that a human is rational. Why does it therefore follow that he or she should act rationally? Suppose that I wish to act irrationally—should I not be free to do so? Put briefly, from an "is" statement (a man or a woman is rational), how is it shown that an "ought" statement (a man or a woman ought to act rationally) follows?

One answer to this might be found in an "if-then" sort of proposition, based on God considered as last end. If you wish to attain your last end, then you will act rationally—and otherwise you won't attain it. That is certainly true. Yet there is something unsatisfactory about it. It seems to be imposing an external necessity on humans, almost a threat. There is, perhaps, nothing wrong with that. But is there not also some deeper reason why humans should act rationally?

There is. It is based on the consideration of God, not as last end, but as creator, as the one who assigns our nature its final end. Implied in this is a human's status as a created and dependent being, one who does not set his or her own final end. That I should be bound to achieve a goal which I did not set is not something foreign to me, something alien to my free human nature. Rather, it is simply a matter of fundamental truth. I do not create myself, and I do not give myself either my nature or the goal which is intrinsic to it; that is done by another. And so my being subject to the will of another is not something imposed on me from without, but rather is something which is intrinsic to my very being: though free, indeed, I am an essentially dependent being, for my ultimate goal not only *is* but necessarily *has to be* set by another. It is, therefore, part and parcel of my nature that I am subject to the governance of a being outside myself. Consequently, when I act irrationally, I am not merely rejecting a goal set for me by another; I am rejecting an essential element of my own nature. Subordination --obedience, if you like--is built into what I am. I may dislike the idea; I may try to reject it. But it is there, and my dislike or rejection makes little difference to that fact. The "ought" turns out not to be something unrelated to the "is" and underivable from it; it turns out to be part and parcel of it. Perhaps it is true that one cannot linguistically derive an "ought" statement from an "is" one; it is also irrelevant from a moral point of view. There is no need for such a derivation, for the very good reason that the "ought" is an intrinsic part of the "is," when we are speaking of human nature. We have noted before that actions follow upon and manifest nature. Given the fact that our nature is, in all truth, a dependent one, it becomes perfectly understandable why our actions are--and ought to be--dependent ones.

a. Knowledge, gratitude, acknowledgement

And so we are at last in a position to see what sorts of obligations a human being has in terms of his or her relationship to God. We will merely mention the more obvious obligations. There is, for example, that of knowledge, i.e., a diligent search to discover whatever we can about this God who has made us and who governs us. Clearly, if this being plays the sort of role in our moral life (as final end, as creator assigning our nature) that we have suggested, we would be derelict in our moral duty indeed if we did not come to know everything about that being which we could. There is, next, the obligation of gratitude. There is that of acknowledgement, both private and--since we are social beings--public. All this is clear enough, and needs little proof.

b. The moral life

The major obligation that stems from our relationship to God, however, is much broader in scope. Essentially, it is the fundamental obligation to live a moral life, to live rationally. For if God is who and what we have argued him to be (our last end, indeed, but more importantly for our present purposes, our

329

creator and the one who gives our nature its final goal), and if humans are what we have seen them to be (beings who are essentially dependent both for their coming into existence and for their continuing to exist, beings who are essentially subordinate in that their final end not only is but must be assigned by another, beings from whom truthfulness itself demands acknowledgement of their dependent status), then the obligation to live rationally, to live morally, is a direct consequence of the relationship between God and humans. And so this relationship is not simply one of three co-ordinate ones (the others being relationships to ourselves and relationships to others in the world around us). It is, rather, the foundational relationship that grounds and governs the entire moral life.

SUMMARY OF CHAPTER FIFTEEN

In speaking of "God" and our relationships to him, we are referring solely to the uncaused cause of all being, discoverable by natural reason. We have no direct, perceptual knowledge of God; rather, we are limited to causal knowledge, and specifically that sort of causal knowledge that does not give us knowledge of what God is in himself. The limitation is not surprising; there must be a proportion between knower and known, and God is infinite whereas we are finite. Our knowledge of God is analogical knowledge: it always takes its rise in creatures, who are different from God at least in that there is always a distinction between their activity and their essence, whereas this is not true in God.

A. Our Knowledge of God: Knowledge of God can bear on what he is in himself, or how he acts toward us:

(i) What he is in himself: God must be: (a) undivided, i.e., without parts of any kind, for in any composed being, its parts stand to one another in a relationship of potency to act, and there is no potency in God; (b) in possession of whatever perfections creatures have (since he caused them); that possession is "proper" in the case of those perfections which do not of themselves imply potency, "virtual" in the case of those which do; (c) good, insofar as, being the cause of all perfections, he therefore possesses them all and hence is eminently desirable; (d) ubiquitous, in that he is the cause of both the being and the activity of anything that exists; (e) unchangeable and eternal, since the opposite of these would imply the presence of potency (change being the transition from potency to act); (f) intelligent (since he causes knowledge), and that in supreme degree (for otherwise there would be something that he would be in potency to learn); (g) living (as the cause of life in others); (h) loving, since there can be no other explanation for his act of creation than disinterested love; (i) free (in regard to anything other than himself); (j) a person, as possessing intellect and will; and (k) unique, in that the notion of pure act implies that there can be only one such being (it would be impossible, for instance, to have 2 all-powerful beings). All of the perfections which God possesses properly are identical with his essence: there is no distinction between his being and his wisdom, his goodness, etc.

(ii) How he acts toward us: unlike change, creation is the making of something out of complete nothingness, i.e., out of non-being. The causal principle requires that God must have created the world, whether basically in its present form or else in some more primitive form from which the present world developed. Creation is also an on-going activity, at least as regards the production of human substantial forms or souls, for only·God could be the adequate cause of the human soul. Providence refers to the fact that God knows the final end or goal which any given creature has; governance, to the fact that God provides the appropriate means whereby that end or goal can be achieved. God's exercise of causality is an on-going, everyday sort of thing, since as contingent creatures we could exercise no activity at all without God as necessary cause also acting whenever we do.

B. Obligations Stemming from Our Knowledge of God: The fact that, as humans, we are subject to a final goal which we did not set for ourselves, is part and parcel of the fact that we are essentially dependent beings. The consideration of God as Creator (and therefore as the one who sets our nature and our goal) is the fundamental ground of the entire moral life: the obligation to live rationally (and therefore morally) is the direct consequence of the dependency relationship between God and humans.

INDEX

-A-

Abortion, 178-79; meaning of, 179; inapplicability of Double Effect to, 179; arguments favoring, 179-81; critique of arguments favoring, 181-86; morality of, 186-88, legalization of, 188-89.

Accident(s), nature of, 103; as principles of being, 107; relationship to substance, 108-10.

Accidental series of causes, 113-14.

Act, and relationship to end or goal, 85-86.

Act, nature of, 110-11.

Act and potency, meaning of, 110-11; larger sense, 111.

Action, as part of imputable act, 31-33.

Act of Existence, see Esse.

Agent, nature of, 78-79.

Alcohol, 202; morality of use, 205-07.

Analogy, 315-16.

Apprehension, 15.

Arbitrary sanction, see Sanction.

Attributability, 34-35.

Authoritarianism, 72-74.

-B-

Birth control, 230-32; natural, 230; artificial, 230-31; morality of, 230-32.

-C-

Capital punishment, 254-56.

Certitude, 126-27; metaphysical, 126; physical, 126; moral, 126; degree needed in moral judgments, 126-27.

Change, analysis of, 101-11; substantial and accidental, 102-03; implies composition, 103.

Charity, 256-59; relationship of among citizens, 256-59; basis for, 257; obligations imposed by, 257-58; limitations on obligations of, 258-59.

Chemical substances, 202; morality of use of, 202-08.

Circumstances, as part of imputable act, 31-33.

Civil society, see State.

Commanded act(s), 16.

Conclusion, 15.

Confidentiality, 275-79.

Conjugal love, 226.

Conscience, 123-32; nature, 123-24; how expressed, 124; correct and incorrect, 125; antecedent and consequent, 125; scrupulous and lax, 125; certain and doubtful, 125-26; norms governing operation of certain, 127-29; norms governing doubtful, 129-32.

Conscience, binding in, 156-58.

Consent, to means in general, 15; to particular means, 16.

Consequences of imputable

acts, 51-69.

Contingence, 27.

Contingent being, 113.

Contracts, nature of, 279-80; elements of, 280-82.

Conventional speech, 273-74.

Co-operation in evil, 65-68; formal and material: meaning of, 66-67; morality of, 67-68.

Creation, 325-26.

-D-

Declarative law, see **Law.**

Deliberation, 15.

Determinative law, see **Law.**

Divorce, 226-27.

Double effect, principle of, statement, 50-52; basis for, 50; meaning and scope of, 53-55; examples of use of, 55-61; questions prior to, 55-56; justifying risks to health and life, 199-200, 202-08; in scandal, 67-68.

Doubt, means of solving: direct, 129-30; indirect, 130-32.

Drugs, 202-05; medical use, 203-04; recreational use, 204-05.

Duty, 245-50; nature of, 245-46; relationship to right, 245-46; affirmative and negative, 246; conflicting with rights, 246-48; excusation from, 248-50; a worker's, 266-67.

-E-

Education, meaning of the term, 268; primary responsibility for, 268; state and other individuals in relation to, 269; moral, 271; higher, 271-72.

Efficient causality, principle of, meaning, 111-12; proof of, 112.

Emotion, very strong, as factor in choice, 40-41; antecedent, 40-41; consequent, 40-42.

End, see **Goal.**

Enjoyment, 16.

Environment, as influencing choice, 46-48; meaning of, 288; human influence on, 288-89; morality of issues concerning, 289-93; unique human relationship to, 289-90; types of issues concerning, 290-93; individuals and, 290-92; humans collectively and, 292-93.

Esse, nature of, 105-06; as principle of being, 107; relationship to essence, 108-10.

Essence, nature of, 105-06; as principle of being, 107; relationship to esse, 108-10.

Essential series of causes, nature, 113-14; use in proof for existence of God, 114.

Eternality, of God, 320-21.

Ethics, definition of, 5-8.

Euthanasia, 177-78; meaning of, 177; morality of, 177-78.

Evil act, meaning of, 71–88; how reconciled with God's goodness, 319.

Extraordinary means, nature of, 197; relative to individuals, 197–99; no obligation to use, 197, 201–02; discontinuing once started, 201.

Extrinsic theories of morality, 72–78; problems with, 77–78.

–F–

Family, meaning, 221; as natural society, 221–24.

Fear, intellectual, as factor in choice, 42–43.

Fiction, 274.

Final causality, principle of, 78–85; proof for, 80–82; specific application to ethics, 83–85.

Force, as factor in choice, 43–44.

Freedom, nature, 27; and law, 146; of will, 27–30; possession of by God, 323–24.

–G–

Gay rights, 234.

Generation, 222–23.

Goal, meaning of, 26; every agent acts for, 78; ultimate and proximate, 79; of work and of worker, 79; intrinsic relationship of to act, 85–86; in generation, 222–23.

God, as ultimate objective norm of morality, 96–118; nature of ultimate norm, 97–100; philosophical argument for existence of, 100–18; significance of existence of for ethics, 117–18; our knowledge of, 312–27; unknowable in himself, 314–15; knowable qualities, 317–27.

Good act, meaning of, 71–88.

Goodness, of God, 318–19.

Goods equivalent to life, 192–93.

Governance, 326–27.

–H–

Habit, as factor in choice, 44–46; deliberately acquired, 44; indeliberately acquired, 44–45; unconscious, 45.

Happiness, as ultimate subjective norm of morality, 93–96; unlimited, 95–96.

Health, 195–208; ordinary care of, 195–97; extraordinary care of, 197; common risks to, 202–08.

Hedonism, 74–75.

Homosexuality, 233–34.

Human nature, completely considered, 132–37; as naturally social, 216, 217–19.

–I–

Ignorance, 37–39; invincible, 38–39; vincible, 39–40; affected, 39–40.

Illiceity, in contracts, 272–73.

Immanent action, 209–10.

Immateriality, 21–23.

Immortality, proof for, 166–68.

Imperium, 16.

Imputable acts, 11–13.

Incomplete being, see Principle of being.

Indivisibility of God, 317.

Intellect, nature of, 18–23.

Intention, 15; actual, 36; virtual, 36; habitual, 36–37; interpretative, 37.

Intrinsic theory of morality, 78–88.

"Is...ought" question, 328–33.

–J–

Judgment, 15.

Justice, nature of, 244; commutative, distributive, and legal, 244; international, 293–98.

Just war theory, 301.

–K–

Knowledge, possession of by God, 321.

–L–

Language, as distinctively human, 19–21.

Law, definition of, 144–45; characteristics of, 145–46; purpose of, 146; and freedom, 146; types, 147; eternal, 147–48; natural, 148–53: (nature,149–51; existence, 151; scope, 151–52; immutability, 152–53; as basis of rights, 241–42); positive, 154–60: (nature, 154; types, 154–55; declarative, 154; determinative, 155; need for, 155–56; binding force of, 156; popular acceptance of, 158; interpretation of, 159; unjust, 159–60; purely penal, 160–61).

"Lex dubia" principle, 131–32.

Life, possession of by God, 322.

Love, unitive in character, 225; possession of by God, 322–23.

Lying, nature of, 273; morality, 274–75.

–M–

Marriage, characteristics of all, 224–25; characteristics of some, 225–26.

Means, 26; pure, 26; unique, 26.

Merit, 35.

"Metaphysical parts," see Substance, Accident(s), Substantial Form, Prime Matter, Esse, Essence.

Method, in general, 6; in ethics, 6,8.

Moral life, as obligation based on foundational relationship, 329–30.

Moral theology and ethics, 8–9.

Motive, as part of imputable act, 31-33.

Murder, 176-77; meaning, 176; morality, 176-77.

Mutilation, nature, 208; morality, 208-212.

-N-

Narcotics, see Drugs.

Natural law, see Law.

Natural sanction, see Sanction.

Nature, 134.

Necessary being, 113.

Necessity, internal (metaphysical and physical), 26-27; external, 27.

Non-imputable acts, 11-13.

Norm of morality, meaning of, 91-92; subjective and objective, 92; ultimate and proximate, 92-93; four possible, 93.

Norms of morality, 91-140; ultimate, 91-118: (subjective, 93-96; objective, 96-100); proximate, 121-140: (subjective, 123-32; objective, 132-40).

Nuclear war, see War.

Nuclear arms, morality of possession of, 308-09.

-O-

Object, of knowledge, generic, 8; of ethics, 8; proper, 6; of ethics, 8.

Objective order, 86.

Ordinary means, 197; obligation to use, 197, 201.

"Oughtness," experiential fact of, 86-87.

-P-

Particulars, knowledge of, 18.

Penal law, see Law.

Personality, possession of by God, 324.

Philosophy, definition of, 2-4; branches of, 4-5; historical, divisions of, 5; systematic, divisions of, 5.

Pleasure-pain theories, 74-76.

Positive law, see Law.

Potency, nature of, 110-11.

Power, moral, 238; physical, 238.

Prime matter, nature of, 104, 106; as principle of being, 107; relationship to substantial form, 108-10.

Principles of being, 107; incapable of independent existence, 107; relationship to one another, 108-11.

Proper presence, of perfections in God, 318.

Providence, 326-27.

Proximate norms of morality, 121-40; need for, 122, 132-33; proximate subjective (conscience), 123-32; proximate objective (human nature, 132–37.

–Q–

–R–

Reason, right, 137.

Religion, and ethics, 8–9.

Right, meaning, 238; basis for, 239; elements of, 239–41; sources of, 241–42; and might, 242; coactive and non-coactive, 243; alienable and inalienable, 243; enforcement of, 244–45; relation of duty to, 245–46; conflict of duty and, 240–48; a worker's, 264–66; enforcement of a worker's, 267.

Right to die, 200–01.

Risk, ordinary and extraordinary, 199; possible, probable, or certain, 199; remote and proximate, 199; relative to individuals, 200; reasons justifying, 200.

–S–

Safer course, 130–31.

Sanction, meaning, 161; natural and arbitrary, 161–62; perfect and imperfect, 162; need for, 162; purposes, 162–63; how functions, 163; and natural law, 164–66; and positive law, 168; vindicative, corrective, and deterrent aspects of, 168–69.

Scandal, 61–65; knowingly caused and willed, 62–63; knowingly caused but not willed, 63–64; unknowingly caused, 64; morality of, 65.

Secrets, nature of, 276; basis of right to, 276; natural and entrusted, 276–77; obligation to keep, 277; of confessional, 277; means of keeping, 278–79.

Self-defense, 189–93; right to, 189–90; four conditions of, 190–92; duty of, 192; items included in, 192–93.

Sexual activity, finality of, 227–29; within marriage, 229; outside of marriage, 232–34; heterosexual, 232–33; homosexual, 233–34.

Slavery, 241.

Society, nature, 216; characteristics, 216–17; conventional and natural, 217; authority required in, 216, 219–20; source of authority in, 220; international, 297.

Speech, nature, 272–73.

Stages, in act of choice, 13–14.

State, nature of, 250; need for, 250–51; possibility of different kinds of, 251; right to determine type of, 252; degrees of complexity of, 252; and the individual, 252–53; rights of, 253–56.

Sterilization, nature, 211; morality, 211–12.

Subjective order, 86.

Substance, nature of, 103, 105–06; as principle of being, 107; relationship to accident(s), 108–10.

Substantial form, nature of, 104, 106; as principle of being, 107; relationship to prime matter, 108-10.

Suicide, meaning, 174; subjective morality of, 174-75; objective morality of, 175-76.

-T-

Teleological theory, see **Intrinsic theory of morality.**

Thales, achievement of, 1-3.

Tobacco, 202; morality of use of, 207-08.

Totality, principle of, 210; as justifying mutilation, 210-11.

Transient action, 209.

Truthfulness, 272-75.

-U-

Ubiquity, of God, 319-20.

Unchangeableness, of God, 320-24.

Uniqueness, of God, 324.

United Nations, 298.

Universals, knowledge of, 18.

Use, 16.

Utilitarianism, 75-76.

-V-

Validity, 282-83; in relation to contracts, 282-83.

Virtual presence, of perfections in God, 318.

Voluntariness, 34.

Voting, obligation of, 297.

-W-

War, 298-309; nature of, 298-99; kinds of, 299; morality of in general, 299-302; "why" and "how" of, 300-01; Just War Theory, 301; actual morality of a given, 302; dimensions of, in general, 302-03; nuclear, 302-09; special characteristics of nuclear, 303; morality of nuclear, 303-09.

Will, nature, 23-24; freedom of, 25-30.

Work, 262-68; how labor evolves, 262-63; reasons for, 263-64; as right, duty, and dignity, 264.

Worker, rights of, 264-66; duties of, 266-67.

-X-

-Y-

-Z-